THE ARBITRARINESS OF
THE DEATH PENALTY

The Arbitrariness of the Death Penalty

Barry Nakell and Kenneth A. Hardy

TEMPLE UNIVERSITY PRESS

PHILADELPHIA

Temple University Press, Philadelphia 19122
Copyright © 1987 by Temple University. All rights reserved
Published 1987
Printed in the United States of America

The paper used in this publication meets the minimum
requirements of American National Standard for Information
Sciences—Permanence of Paper for Printed Library Materials,
ANSI Z39.48-1984

Library of Congress Cataloging-in-Publication Data

Nakell, Barry.
    The arbitrariness of the death penalty.

    Includes index.
    1. Capital punishment—United States.
2. United States—Constitutional law.   3. Capital
punishment—North Carolina—Decision making.
4. Criminal statistics—North Carolina.   I. Hardy,
Kenneth A.   II. Title.
KF9227.C2N35   1987   345.756′0773   86-5931
ISBN 0-87722-443-9 (alk. paper)   347.5605773

For
Lynne, Jessica and Stacy,
Nancy and Travis

Contents

Figures and Tables

FIGURES

TABLES

Preface

In 1971, the U.S. Supreme Court upheld the constitutionality of procedures used by the states to decide whether to sentence a defendant convicted of a capital crime to the death penalty or to life imprisonment. One year later, the Court considered the way in which the capital punishment process operated in practice and held that the death penalty was being administered in too arbitrary a manner to survive constitutional scrutiny. The erratic imposition of the death penalty rendered it cruel and unusual as a punishment.

The states that provided capital punishment responded by developing procedures designed to control the exercise of jury discretion in the death or life decision. In 1976, the Supreme Court upheld the constitutionality of the new procedures. Reviewing them "on their face," without any evidence of how they were working in practice, the Court assumed that the new procedures would prove capable of protecting the process against arbitrariness.

To test that assumption, we undertook an empirical study of the relationship between the death penalty on the statute books and the death penalty in practice. We conducted our study on homicide cases that arose in North Carolina during the first year of that state's death penalty statute containing the new procedures. After collecting comprehensive information about the defendant, the victim, the circumstances of the offense (including the strength of the evidence for both sides), and the judicial processing of the cases, we subjected those data to statistical analysis. We find that although the legal standards were the most consistently significant factor in the outcomes at all stages of the capital punishment process,

considerable variation in the results cannot be explained by the legal standards alone and therefore represents arbitrariness. We identify some extralegal factors that had strong relationships with the outcomes at several
discretionary stages. Those extralegal factors are, in the pretrial stages, the
judicial district in which the case was processed and the race of the defendant; at the verdict stage, an extralegal factor is the race of the victim.
Obviously, the jury was an important discretionary decision maker for the
cases that went to trial. Nevertheless, the prosecutor exercised far greater
discretionary influence over the course of the process through control over
the charging and guilty plea negotiation decisions that determined whether
a case went to trial at all.

Our project requires an interdisciplinary collaboration. It draws on
law for the definition of the constitutional question for the empirical study,
on social science for the data collection and the statistical analysis, and on
law again for an evaluation of the constitutional significance of the results.
The project is a study of the death penalty in constitutional theory and in
numbers; it is not a study of the death penalty in particular cases. It is a
survey of the generality of cases designed to inform the factual premises
for a judgment whether the new death penalty procedures adequately
controlled the exercise of discretion or whether decisions in the death
penalty process were made in an arbitrary manner despite the new procedures. Thus it does not evaluate any particular case, but should be useful
for the resolution of the broad constitutional policy issue. Accordingly,
this report of the study does not contain any discussion or comparison
of the facts of individual cases.

This report may appear complex because it presents both legal doctrine (full of footnotes) and statistical analysis (teeming with tables). Nevertheless, we have tried to write it in a way that satisfies the demands of
experts in both fields and at the same time is understandable to readers
without specialized training in law or social science. In the process, we
probably included a few explanations that an expert might not need and a
few sections that a lay reader might struggle over. We hope that the book
will reward the patience of the one and the effort of the other.

Acknowledgments

We would like to express our deep appreciation to many people who provided us with invaluable assistance. Gary Koch consulted regularly in connection with the original project design and with the statistical analysis. John Humphrey and Angell Beza collaborated in the planning of the project. R. Page Hudson, Jr., the North Carolina medical examiner, encouraged us in the study and facilitated our use of the records of his office. David Wasserman collaborated in developing the strategy for scoring the strength of the evidence. Anthony Amsterdam gave advice on the data collection instrument. Elizabeth Fink and Frank Munger provided the administrative and support facilities of the Institute for Research in Social Science at the University of North Carolina.

The principal team for the collection and coding of the data consisted of Ron Boykin, Melissa H. Dowling, and Lisa Garafolo. An excellent cadre of students assisted them, including Warren L. Tadlock, John B. Meuser, John G. Britt, Jr., Janice Watson Davidson, Cathleen Plaut, Lisa M. Nieman, Edward A. Pone, Mark Nunalee, Ruth H. Goldsmith, Jerome Buting, Theresa G. Rhinehart, Laurie A. Miller, Robert M. Forman, Steven Sternberg, Marilyn Bair, Christopher J. Johnson, David E. Webb, and C. Nicholson Morrow.

The cooperation of many court clerks, police officers, prosecuting attorneys, and defense attorneys was critical to the success of this project. The Police Information Network of the North Carolina Department of Justice granted us access to its records of defendants' prior criminal histories.

Elliott Cramer advised us on the statistical analysis. Gary Koch,

David Baldus, Richard A. Rosen, Laughlin McDonald, John Humphrey, and Ron Boykin read drafts of the manuscript and recommended helpful revisions.

For painstaking and pleasant processing of innumerable drafts of the manuscript and working documents, we are heavily indebted to Paul Sherer, Bonita Summers, Sharon Brooks Laney, and Joyce Raby.

Funding for the study was provided by the National Science Foundation's Law and Social Science Program, Grant No. SES-7812178, and by the University of North Carolina. The findings, conclusions, opinions, and recommendations expressed in this publication are those of the authors and do not necessarily reflect the views of those who provided us funding, advice, or assistance.

The history of intellectual ferment surrounding all facets of capital punishment issues represents a remarkable advance of humanitarian values. We could not have spent as much time as we did with this subject without developing admiration for the scholars who have thought deeply about capital punishment; the activists who have spoken, written, and demonstrated eloquently on behalf of it; and the legislators, judges, and lawyers who have wrestled to resolve its challenges. Their contributions fill these pages.

THE ARBITRARINESS OF
THE DEATH PENALTY

CHAPTER I

The
Death Penalty Selection Process

An execution is not a common event in the United States. Yet capital punishment has sustained a level of controversy out of proportion to the infrequency of its occurrence. The public interest obviously reflects the moral dimension of the death penalty more than experience with its actual use. The principal issue in the public debate revolves around the ethics of the deliberate taking of life by the state, which involves the rationales of retribution and deterrence. That issue has been the subject of rigorous philosophical, religious, sociological, empirical, and ideological controversy. The relative infrequency of executions, however, compels us to undertake another inquiry as well, into the fairness of the selection process for the fateful few subject to capital punishment.

The death penalty has been a relatively rare phenomenon as long as reliable records of its incidence have been kept and probably since the beginning of the nineteenth century, when the introduction of the penitentiary system offered an alternative.[1] The federal government has maintained national records of civil executions since 1930. Between that year and 1967, when a moratorium on executions went into effect to permit the U.S. Supreme Court to resolve constitutional challenges to capital punishment, the average annual number of executions across the country for all crimes was 104.[2] The number never reached as high as 200 in any single year.[3] The heyday[4] of capital punishment was the 1930s when the average

1

annual number of executions was 167.[5] That number dropped to 128 in the next decade and to 71 in the 1950s.[6] The last year in which the number of executions exceeded 100 was 1951, with 105. Thereafter, the number dwindled steadily until, in the years before the moratorium on executions, there were only 21 executions in 1963, 15 in 1964, 1 in 1965, 1 in 1966, and 2 in 1967, in the entire country.[7] After the lifting of the moratorium in 1976, and through 1984—during a time when the annual average number of homicides exceeded 20,000[8]—there was a total of 32 executions: 1 in 1977, 2 in 1979, 1 in 1981, 2 in 1982, 5 in 1983, and 21 in 1984.[9]

The 5 states with the highest total number of executions between 1930 and 1967 were Georgia, New York, Texas, California, and North Carolina.[10] The annual averages for those states were, respectively, 10,[11] 9,[12] 8,[13] 8,[14] and 7.[15] Since the lifting of the moratorium, 11 states have held executions. Florida had the largest number, with a total in the eight years after 1976 of 10, followed by Louisiana with 6. Texas, in that eight-year period, had 4, Georgia 3, North Carolina and Virginia 2 each. All the other states—Mississippi, Alabama, Indiana, Nevada, and Utah—had only 1 execution each.[16]

If the death penalty is justified for some persons for some crimes, what persons and what crimes should qualify for that severe punishment? Any person may believe that he or she has a reasonably clear conception of the crimes or the criminals, if any, that merit the death penalty. Any person may conceive of an appropriate application of the penalty, if any, in terms of particularly worthy examples. No one individual can make the death or life decision in all cases, however, or, for that matter, not alone in any one case. It is necessary to achieve some common conception of the proper cases for the death penalty, to express that conception with sufficient precision that it will be understood by every decision maker summoned to participate in the judgment, and to formulate reliable processes to apply that conception to particular cases. That important task requires answers to at least five questions:

1. How should legislation define the offenses subject to the death penalty?
2. Will the death penalty be mandatory for all offenders convicted of those offenses, or, if not all offenders, how should legislation describe those who should suffer that penalty?
3. Who should decide whether a particular offense and offender satisfy the legislated standards?
4. What procedures should the decision maker use in reaching that judgment?
5. What assurances should we require that the decision is consistent with the legislated standards?

PART 1.

Offenses and Offenders

The death penalty was historically provided for a broad range of offenses. Early common law held seven felonies punishable by death: high treason,[17] homicide,[18] rape, burglary, arson, robbery, and theft of items worth twelvepence or more.[19] In 1769, however, Blackstone wrote: "It is a melancholy truth, that among the variety of actions which men are daily likely to commit, no less than a hundred and sixty have been declared by act of Parliament to be felonies without benefit of clergy; or, in other words, to be worthy of instant death."[20] Later estimates put the number at two hundred or more, many of them property crimes, such as forgery and shoplifting.[21] A large number of these crimes, however, were special instances of more general offenses that might fairly be consolidated for a modern count.[22]

The American colonies had a variety of death penalty policies. As in England, criminal homicides were punished by a mandatory death penalty.[23] In addition, the death penalty applied to about a dozen other crimes, typically including treason, piracy, arson, rape, robbery, kidnapping, burglary, train wrecking, and sodomy.[24] Rhode Island had the smallest number of capital crimes, with 10.[25] North Carolina probably maintained the largest number. The Revised Statutes passed by the North Carolina legislature at its session of 1836–1837 codified the death penalty as mandatory for the following offenses: murder; highway robbery; burglary; arson; dueling, if death results; castration; maiming; rape and statutory rape; the crime against nature (sodomy and bestiality); stealing or hiding a slave; taking a free Negro out of the state for sale into slavery; escape while under a capital charge; horse stealing; bigamy; and for a second conviction of forgery and inciting slaves to insurrection or circulating pamphlets that do so.[26] The codification ascribed the origin of one-quarter of those provisions to English statutes and the rest to state statutes enacted between 1754 and 1833. The next codification of the relevant statutes, enacted by the legislature in 1854, provided the death penalty for a principal or an accessory before the fact to essentially the same list of offenses.[27] The next codification was adopted by the legislature in 1872–1873. It provided the death penalty only for a principal or accessory to four crimes: "wilful murder of malice prepense," rape and statutory rape, arson and burglary.[28] North Carolina law continued to provide the death penalty for those four crimes until 1976.

The modern trend has been toward a reduction in the number of capital offenses and toward a restriction of the definition of those offenses that remain capital. In 1788 Ohio became the first state to limit the death penalty to the crime of murder; Pennsylvania followed suit in 1794.[29] Beginning with Michigan in 1847, several states abolished capital punishment. Many have restored it, and some of those have abolished it again. Now there are a dozen states (Alaska, Hawaii, Iowa, Kansas, Maine, Michigan, Minnesota, North Dakota, Oregon, Rhode Island, West Virginia, and Wisconsin), as well as the District of Columbia (and the federal government) that have no death penalty provisions. In the other states today, the death penalty is limited largely to aggravated forms of homicide.

Overwhelmingly, homicide has been the predominant offense for which capital sentences have been imposed in this country.[30] Homicide occurs in a variety of situations, however. It may be committed brutally in cold blood for the basest of motives. It may be committed intentionally or accidentally in the course of a robbery, a rape, or a burglary. It may be committed in emotional circumstances that overwhelm reason and judgment. In any case, whether the death of the victim, which is a necessary element of homicide, results from the offender's violent act may depend on a fortuitous circumstance, such as the accuracy of a blow or a bullet, the special vulnerability of the victim, or the success of a rescue effort. Although the act of killing may be the same in different cases, the extent of blameworthiness depends on all the circumstances. The moral culpability of the killer, and hence the propriety of the death penalty, may vary according to his or her mental state at the time. "American criminal law has long considered a defendant's intention—and therefore his moral guilt—to be critical to 'the degree of [his] criminal culpability.'"[31] As Aristotle wrote: "The worse of two acts of wrong done to others is that which is prompted by the worse disposition."[32] The indiscriminate imposition of capital punishment for the full range of homicides would be inconsistent with the principle that the severity of the penalty should reflect the seriousness of the offense. Sir James Fitzjames Stephen described the difficulty as follows in 1883:

> [T]here is no definite connection at all between the fact of death and the moral guilt or public danger of the act by which death is caused. The most deliberate, desperate and cruel attempt on life may not cause death, the most trifling assault may cause it. Death may be intentionally caused under circumstances of the greatest possible atrocity, or under circumstances which produce rather pity for the offender than horror at the offence; or, again under circumstances which indicate determined defiance of the law, but do not involve any special ill will to any particular person. This extreme variety in the circumstances under which, and the intentions with which death may be occasioned is the true cause of the great difficulty which has been found in giving satisfactory definitions of the different forms of homicide.[33]

To depict the difficulty, consider, for example, a young man pulling the trigger of a gun aimed at the head of a somewhat older man. The younger man might be judged as follows:

- Not guilty of homicide if he acted in self-defense, reasonably believing—whether true or not—that the older man was about to kill him and that he needed to use deadly force to protect himself.
- Not guilty of homicide if he was insane, believing that the older man was evil incarnate plotting wickedness for the world and that God had dispatched him with regular messages—hallucinatory—to prevent that event by destroying the satanic force.
- Guilty only of involuntary manslaughter if he was a weapons repairman to whom the older man had just given the gun for service and the younger man had discharged it carelessly, unaware that it was loaded.
- Guilty only of voluntary manslaughter if he acted in the heat of passion after the older man had angrily slugged him.
- Guilty of second degree murder if he was drunk and had drawn the gun simply to brandish it as an act of bravado and had pulled the trigger unintentionally.
- Guilty of first degree murder if the older man was his suffering father, in the terminal stage of a terrible cancer, who had begged the son to relieve his agony by killing him, even if the son acted reluctantly and with love for his father.
- Not guilty of homicide if he was a contract "hit man" who acted in cold blood and intended to kill the older man, but his victim was rushed to a hospital where skilled surgeons, using the latest medical technology and techniques, were able to save his life, though he would never be able to walk or talk again.

The development of homicide law has been a quest for definitions to distinguish those killings that should be punished with the death penalty from those that should receive a lesser punishment. In essence, that quest resulted, first, in the division of homicide into murder (capital) and manslaughter; then murder was divided into first degree murder (capital) and second degree murder, in a search for a standard to define an exclusive class of killings that should all qualify for the death penalty;[34] then, in an admission of the futility of finding a purely objective standard,[35] in the bestowal of undefined and unlimited discretion on the jury to grant mercy after a first degree murder conviction to exclude some first degree murderers from the capital penalty; and, most recently, in the imposition of a structure of standards and procedures on the exercise of that discretion.

The division into murder and manslaughter was a product of English history. The later developments were American innovations. The structure of homicide law that has evolved reflects the difficulty of the task.

The murder–manslaughter distinction developed over centuries in common-law England into the form that is familiar to American lawyers.[36] The difference between the two is that murder is defined as an unlawful killing committed with "malice aforethought" and manslaughter as an unlawful killing committed without "malice aforethought."[37] The apparent simplicity of that definition evaporates on consideration of the meaning of *malice aforethought*. The distinction was "worked out by slow degrees and in a cumbrous way by the labours of many generations of judges who have interpreted in reference to particular cases the expression 'malice aforethought.'"[38] That phrase became a term of art that does not mean either *malice* or *forethought* in the common sense of those words.[39] Nor can the distinction be ascribed to the difference between intentional and unintentional killings. There are intentional killings that constitute only manslaughter: intentional killings committed in the heat of passion on sudden and legally adequate provocation qualify as voluntary manslaughter. There are also unintentional killings that constitute murder: the common law called these "depraved heart" murders, but they can be described by the terms RECKLESS or GROSSLY NEGLIGENT.

Malice aforethought encompasses several states of mind, including (*a*) intent to cause the death of any person; (*b*) intent to cause serious bodily harm to any person; (*c*) knowledge that the act or omission that caused the death would probably cause death or serious bodily harm to any person, or was eminently dangerous to life; (*d*) intent to commit any felony;[40] (*e*) intent to oppose by force a law enforcement officer in making a lawful arrest or in keeping the peace.[41]

An exception to that list is that a killing committed in the heat of passion as a result of certain provocations (e.g., physical violence) is without malice aforethought and therefore constitutes only manslaughter. Manslaughter consists of all unlawful killings that are not murder, including, in addition to provoked passion killings, those committed with the following states of mind: (*a*) intent to cause bodily harm, but not serious harm, where the defendant is not committing a felony and the victim is not a law enforcement officer; and (*b*) gross negligence.[42]

Both murder and manslaughter were felonies at common law, and all felonies were punishable by death.[43] Why, then, two different crimes?

The division of homicide into murder and manslaughter was significant for the death penalty originally because it made a difference with regard to the power of pardon. The Crown's prerogative to issue pardons was the only source of flexibility in the criminal law, and pardons were easier to obtain for manslaughter than for murder. Indeed, pardons for "'murders done in await, assault or malice prepense [aforethought]' . . . were subjected to almost impossible conditions."[44] Later, in the mid-sixteenth through the mid-nineteenth centuries, the murder–manslaughter distinction became even more significant because it affected eligibility for the benefit of clergy.[45]

Benefit of clergy originated in the twelfth century when the Church won the right for its ordained clergy to be free from the jurisdiction, later (in 1576) only from the punishment, of the royal courts, and to be subject instead to ecclesiastical courts. There, trial was by the more favorable compurgation, or oath swearing, procedure, and there was no capital punishment.[46] The privilege was gradually extended so that, by the beginning of the eighteenth century, all persons could claim the benefit of clergy for a first offense if the offense was "clergyable."[47] That extension took place in increments. In 1350 the benefit of clergy was given to secular church clerks, such as doorkeepers, readers, exorcists, and subdeacons.[48] Because literacy was limited at that time, "every one that could read (a mark of great learning in those days of ignorance and her sister superstition) [was] . . . allowed the benefit of clerkship, though neither initiated in holy orders, nor trimmed with the clerical tonsure."[49] Thus, a defendant qualified as clergy by passing a reading test, usually by reading the first verse of Psalm 51: "Have mercy upon me, O God, according to thy lovingkindness: according unto the multitude of thy tender mercies blot out my transgressions." That verse therefore acquired the title of the "neck-verse."[50] By treating the reading test as perfunctory, the courts, where the dominant tendency was to restrict the scope of capital punishment,[51] extended the privilege to everyone who could read or who could memorize the verse,[52] except women (other than professed nuns) and men who were married for a second time or married to widows. Such "bigamus" men did not qualify until 1547, and women were not accorded the benefit of clergy until 1692.[53] In 1705, by a statute abolishing the requirement for reading, the privilege was made universally available.[54] Then true clergy in orders could be admitted to the privilege "as often as they offend" but others only once, although the claim would save the defendant from the gallows for all capital offenses committed until that time.[55]

Benefit of clergy consisted of being saved from hanging (and also from forfeiture of property and any rights of inheritance).[56] A person (except clergy or peers) who claimed it might be imprisoned for up to a year and transported to the colonies, which were in need of labor, for seven years.[57] To keep track of offenders who had received their quota of one claim of the benefit of clergy—in an era without computerized records or fingerprint identification—the defendant, if a commoner but not a lord of Parliament or peer of the realm, was also branded by being "burnt with a hot iron in the brawn of the left thumb."[58]

Until the sixteenth century most homicides, whether murder or manslaughter, like most felonies, were eligible for the benefit of clergy if the defendant qualified.[59] Between 1496 and 1671, several offenses were made non-clergyable.[60] By statutes in 1531 and 1547, murder was made a non-clergyable offense, except for clergy in orders, while manslaughter remained subject to the privilege.[61] The effect was to constitute murder a capital offense and manslaughter noncapital, at least for a first offense.

The benefit of clergy was, of course, important for the death penalty for all felonies, not just for homicide. It "reduced the administration of justice to a sort of farce. Till 1487 anyone who knew how to read might commit murder as often as he pleased . . . . That this should have been the law for several centuries seems hardly credible, but there is no doubt that it was. Even after 1487 a man who could read could commit murder once with no other punishment than that of having **M** branded on the brawn of his left thumb . . . ."[62] In its substitution of imprisonment and transportation for capital punishment, however, the system anticipated nineteenth-century penal reform.

Benefit of clergy was abolished between 1827 and 1841, but the law retained the distinctions it had created by excepting all clergyable offenses from the death penalty. England abolished the death penalty in 1965 on a trial basis[63] and in 1969 on a permanent basis.[64]

The American colonies adopted the English homicide law, including the murder–manslaughter distinction.[65] Most colonies also adopted benefit of clergy by judicial practice[66] and made it universally available. After the revolution, most of the states abolished the benefit of clergy, though it persisted in the Carolinas until the middle of the nineteenth century. The effect of abolishing the benefit of clergy was to make the formerly clergyable offense punishable by imprisonment.[67]

In 1790 Congress enacted a statute that provided: "The benefit of clergy shall not be used or allowed upon conviction of any crime for which the punishment is death."[68] That statute was repealed on March 4, 1909, apparently because the doctrine was obsolete.[69]

The next stage in the development of homicide law originated after Pennsylvania began the penitentiary movement with the Walnut Street prison block in the Philadelphia jail in 1790.[70] In 1794 Pennsylvania followed that progressive innovation by dividing murder into two degrees, reserving the death penalty only for first degree murder.[71] "[T]he primary objective was to limit the use of the death penalty."[72] Pennsylvania defined first degree murder as all "murder which shall be perpetrated by means of poison, lying in wait or any other kind of wilful, deliberate and premeditated killing or which shall be committed in the perpetration or attempt to perpetrate any arson, rape, robbery or burglary."[73] Second degree murder was defined simply as all other murder at common law.[74] Most states copied this reform.[75] The requirement of premeditation and deliberation was interpreted so narrowly, however, that almost any intention to kill satisfied it.[76] The result was to give the jury a considerable range of discretion in deciding whether the prosecution proved premeditation and deliberation and therefore to decide whether any killing was first degree murder (and therefore capital) or not.[77]

Unsatisfied because juries were often reluctant to convict of the capital offense, even in some first degree murder cases, where the consequence of conviction would be the death penalty,[78] Tennessee introduced the next stage in 1838.[79] It "adopted the method of forthrightly granting juries the discretion which they had been exercising in fact."[80] Once the jury found a defendant guilty of first degree murder, it proceeded—usually as part of the same deliberation and without any additional evidence—to decide the penalty, choosing between death and life without any guidance from the legislature or the court. The discretion was not controlled in any way. That was the system that predominated until the U.S. Supreme Court undertook to consider constitutional challenges to it.

In 1971 the Supreme Court reviewed the procedures used by the states to apply their death penalty statutes and gave those procedures its constitutional approval. The case was *McGautha v. California*,[81] and the vote was 6–3. The next year, in its 1972 landmark decision in *Furman v. Georgia*,[82] the Court surveyed those same procedures in practice, and this time held that their operation was unconstitutional. The vote was a tight 5–4. The five justices in the majority wrote five separate opinions presenting different rationales. The one concept common to all of them was that the death penalty was arbitrary. One justice analogized the death penalty selection process to "being struck by lightning."[83] Two agreed "that there is no meaningful basis for distinguishing the few cases in which it is imposed from the many in which it is not."[84] Two others contended that it was discriminatory.[85]

The *Furman* decision inspired the most recent general development in homicide law. The capital punishment states responded to *Furman* by promulgating standards to guide the jury in exercising its discretion to decide between death and life as the penalty and by instituting a new jury procedure, both measures in an effort to eliminate the arbitrariness in their death penalty selection systems. The new standards take a variety of forms. Essentially, they require the jury to find that a first degree murder case is also characterized by one of a fixed list of aggravating circumstances before a defendant can be sentenced to death. They also require the jury to consider mitigating circumstances and then to decide whether death is the proper punishment in the case.

The new capital punishment systems introduced a procedural reform into the selection process in addition to the new standards. That reform is a two-stage trial procedure, providing a trial first on the issue of guilt or innocence and then, if the verdict is guilty of capital murder, a separate trial on the issue of death or life. The advantage of this new procedure is that evidence relevant only to the penalty can be presented to the jury at the second trial without prejudicing its determination of guilt or innocence at the first. Another new procedure in most of the capital states is appellate review of the *sentence*—in addition to standard appellate review of the *conviction*—as a statewide stabilizer against disparity or discrimination in the decision for death.

In a group of five decisions in 1976, the Supreme Court assessed the new standards and procedures in much the same way as, in *McGautha v. California*, in 1971 it had evaluated the earlier procedures. Again the Court upheld the constitutionality of the system on its face, judging that the new standards and procedures appeared capable of correcting the arbitrariness that had caused the earlier systems to fall to constitutional condemnation. Those decisions naturally raise the question whether the death penalty in practice meets the expectations of the Court for the new standards and procedures, or whether the death penalty continues to be applied in an unconstitutional fashion. That question is the analogue for the new capital punishment system of *Furman* vis-à-vis *McGautha*: whether the death penalty in practice is as fair as the death penalty in the statute books; whether the law as written adequately controls the death penalty decision-making process; whether the death or life decisions made in the capital punishment process are in fact made in constitutionally sufficient compliance with the statutory standards.

PART 2.

Procedures and Discretion

The criminal justice process consists of a series of discretionary stages. The standards and procedures in the new statutes are expressly concerned with the stage involving discretion by the jury. Other stages are also of great importance to the decision-making process. In a death penalty case in a typical capital punishment state, the discretionary stages are the following (see Figure 1):

- The decision whether to arrest a defendant on a first degree murder charge
- The decision whether to present the first degree murder charge to a grand jury or to reduce or dismiss it
- The decision whether to indict the defendant for first degree murder
- The decision whether to bring the first degree murder indictment to trial or to reduce or dismiss the charge, with or without plea negotiations
- The decision whether to submit the first degree murder charge to the jury
- The decision whether to convict on the first degree murder charge

- The decision whether to impose a death sentence
- The decision whether to affirm the conviction and the death sentence
- The decision whether to execute the death sentence

The discretionary decisionmakers in the process include the following (see Figure 1):

- The police, who might (*a*) fail to identify the perpetrator; (*b*) fail to apprehend the perpetrator; (*c*) decide that the homicide was justifiable or excusable; or (*d*) decide to charge a degree of homicide less than capital (i.e., less than first degree murder)
- The prosecuting attorney, who, with or without negotiating with the defendant, might (*a*) decide not to seek an indictment because he or she believes that the evidence as to homicide or the evidence identifying the perpetrator is insufficient or that the homicide was justifiable or excusable; (*b*) decide to seek an indictment for a degree of homicide less than first degree murder; (*c*) decide after indictment to accept a guilty plea to a degree of homicide less than first degree murder or to some other crime (e.g., armed robbery) committed by the defendant; or (*d*) decide to pursue at trial only a charge less than first degree murder[86]
- The grand jury, which might (*a*) decide to return an indictment for a degree of homicide less than first degree murder; or (*b*) decline to indict for homicide
- The trial judge, who might make rulings on (*a*) the admissibility of evidence; or (*b*) what degrees of homicide, if any, the jury will be allowed to consider; and (*c*) whether to grant a new trial after a guilty verdict
- The jury at the trial, which might find the defendant (*a*) not guilty of homicide; or (*b*) not guilty of first degree murder but guilty of a lesser degree of homicide
- The jury at the sentencing stage, which might find (*a*) that no aggravating circumstance exists; or (*b*) that the mitigating circumstances outweigh any aggravating circumstances; or (*c*) that, based on the aggravating and mitigating circumstances, the sentence should be life imprisonment
- The state supreme court, which might reverse (*a*) the conviction; or (*b*) the death penalty only
- The governor, who might exercise the power of pardon or commutation

Discretion obviously plays a major role in the capital punishment process. "A public officer has discretion whenever the effective limits on his power leave him free to make a choice among possible courses of action or inaction."[87] Discretion may be left to a public officer either by

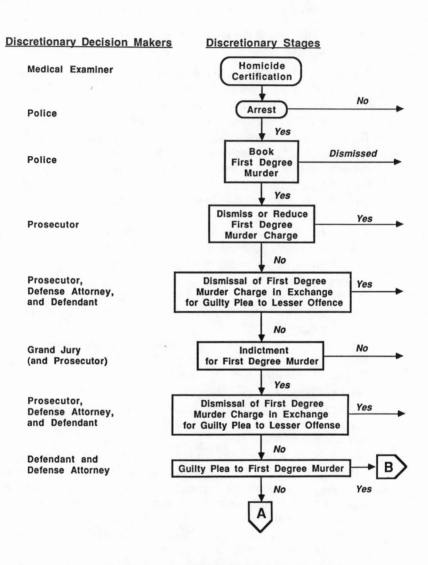

FIGURE 1
Major Discretionary Stages
in the Capital Punishment Process

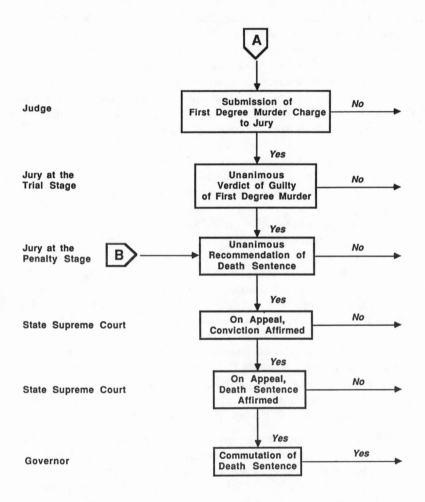

Judge	Submission of First Degree Murder Charge to Jury	*No* →
	↓ *Yes*	
Jury at the Trial Stage	Unanimous Verdict of Guilty of First Degree Murder	*No* →
	↓ *Yes*	
Jury at the Penalty Stage	Unanimous Recommendation of Death Sentence	*No* →
	↓ *Yes*	
State Supreme Court	On Appeal, Conviction Affirmed	*No* →
	↓ *Yes*	
State Supreme Court	On Appeal, Death Sentence Affirmed	*No* →
	↓ *Yes*	
Governor	Commutation of Death Sentence	*Yes* →

Note: The process may begin either at the arrest stage or at the indictment stage. The defendant may be arrested and then indicted, or indicted and then arrested.

deliberate decision of higher authority or by default in decision by higher authority. A public officer may also exercise discretion beyond what is authorized if there are no effective limits on the officer's power. The extent of discretion depends on the extent to which it is circumscribed by statutes, precedents, rules, principles, or other legal standards and by effective review in the context of the relationship the discretionary officer has with supervisory or coordinate authority.[88] Thus, as Dworkin observed, discretion is "a relative concept. It always makes sense to ask, 'Discretion under which standards?' or 'Discretion as to which authority?' "[89]

The concept of discretion describes a range of decisional autonomy. Unlike tyranny, however, discretion operates within a legal context that imposes limits on its range.[90] Discretion in the judicial process means sound discretion guided by law. Discretion is expected to be exercised within standards of rationality, fairness, and effectiveness.[91] Discretion should be exercised not on the basis of personal preference but on the basis of reasons grounded in legal principles.[92] Thus, the word "discretion" carries not only this meaning of *decisional autonomy* but also of *discernment* or *sound judgment*.[93]

The impact of discretion on the capital punishment process, like its impact on government generally, may be regarded on balance as favorable or unfavorable.[94] In either event, discretion seems to be unavoidable because of the difficulty of capturing in objective legal terms the judgment process evaluating a wide range of relevant considerations.[95] Those who support discretion believe that "although discretion can be exercised unjustly, *there can be no justice without discretion.*"[96] They observe that it "is necessary in criminal administration because of the immense variety of factual situations faced at each stage of the system and the complex interrelationship of the goals sought."[97] "The chief advantage of discretion can be summed up in one word: flexibility. Discretion enables the law to take into account the features of the individual case."[98] Aristotle for that reason called judicial discretion "Equity."[99] Plato taught that

> laws by definition are general rules; this is their essence and their weakness. Generalities falter before the complexities of life. They must usually concern themselves more with form than with substance. That is why, in Plato's view, law is far inferior to the wise discretion of a Philosopher-King, who could give each man his due — whereas law must be satisfied to prescribe what is due in abstract categories regardless of much that is unique in the men and events that they embrace.[100]

From this perspective, "any norm or rule, though it has its ideal, 'pure' formulation, also has its tolerable leeways."[101]

Conversely, Packer declared, "The basic trouble with discretion is simply that it is lawless, in the literal sense of that term."[102] Fuller contended that one of the requirements for "the internal morality of law [is] congruence between official action and the law."[103] The exercise of discretion is thus seen as a departure from the principle of legality or the rule of law, which has as its distinctive contribution "a progressive reduction of the arbitrary element in positive law and its administration."[104] Davis surmised that "nine-tenths of injustice in our legal system flows from discretion and perhaps only one-tenth from rules."[105] Packer explained, "If police or prosecutors find themselves free (or compelled) to pick and choose among known or knowable instances of criminal conduct, they are making a judgment which in a society based on law should be made only by those to whom the making of law is entrusted."[106]

The significance of discretion in the criminal process is that it may determine the difference between formal law and law in action. Thus, there may be four levels of "law": the first is law declared in statutes and appellate opinions; the second, law applied by trial courts; the third, law reflected in the "rules that arise in the course of applying the formal rules in private negotiated settlements,"[107] such as plea bargains; and the fourth, discretionary decisions made by officials without negotiations. "Two of the major insights of the sociology of law are that legal rights in contemporary society are most often determined by bureaucratic actors and that the results differ systematically from those predictable on the basis of formal law alone."[108] "The law is written by legislators, interpreted occasionally by appellate courts, but applied by countless individuals, each acting largely for himself. How it is applied outweighs in importance its enactment or its interpretation."[109]

The impact of discretion may take either of two forms: it may mean simply that the formal laws are not the real governing rules; public officials are governed by operating rules but they are informal rules that we can understand with a little more sophistication.[110] Or it may raise the more fundamental objection that "those who apply the rules actually govern in their discretion, using the rules as mere handles or shams."[111]

"Some people have argued that the only way to achieve the 'rule of law' is to eliminate all discretion setting down complete sets of detailed rules for government officials to follow. Others, most notably, Kenneth Davis, have argued that discretion cannot and should not be completely eliminated but can only be constrained—structured, channeled, checked."[112] Davis adopted three essential techniques for controlling the exercise of discretion: the first is to "confine" discretion by fixing its boundaries with clean lines, either by legislation, administrative rules, or, possibly, executive policy announcements; the second is to "structure" discretion by opening up to public scrutiny the processes by which it is exercised; the third is to "check" discretion by subjecting its exercise to review by a superior officer.[113] The new death penalty procedures utilize each of these approaches with regard to jury decision making. Discretion is confined by the standards promulgated to guide the jury in the exercise of its discretion to decide death or life as the penalty; discretion is structured by providing a separate trial on the issue of death or life so that evidence relevant to the decision-making process can be presented to the jury in adversary fashion; and discretion is checked by appellate review of the sentence.

PART 3.

Discrimination and Arbitrariness

The fairness issue focuses naturally on the operation of discretion in the process for meting out the death penalty among the qualified defendants whose cases satisfy the minimum standards for it. The issue of fairness may involve two different questions, one of discrimination and another of arbitrariness. The discrimination question is whether discretion permits the death penalty to be deliberately directed disproportionately against certain qualified defendants, not because of the nature of their crimes, but because they belong to a particular class or group, determined by such considerations as race, sex, nationality, religion, or wealth. The arbitrariness question is whether discretion permits the death penalty to be applied randomly, capriciously, irregularly, or disproportionately among the qualified defendants without any evident regard for the legal criteria designed to determine the selection. Discrimination requires a demonstration of the particular invidious factor that is influencing the decision. Arbitrariness has a different character. Arbitrariness may be established simply by a showing that the decisions are not controlled by the legal standards. Arbitrariness may result in sentences that are too lenient or too harsh or both.[114] There may be a host of factors that affect the decisions other than those authorized by law. If the decisions are not loyal to the legal standards, or if the decisions in some cases are disproportionate to the decisions in others, they may be arbitrary without regard to whether the influencing extralegal factors can be identified. As long as they are irrelevant to the legal standards, to the extent that they have an impact on the decision-making process, that process may be arbitrary. Arbitrariness may therefore be demonstrated by evidence that the decisions are not explained by the legal standards. That is enough. There need be no evidence identifying the extralegal factors that do affect the decision. Evidence that does pinpoint those factors might enhance the conclusion that the legal criteria are not determinative, but such evidence is not essential to the conclusion.[115]

Thus understood, discrimination is the antithesis of arbitrariness: discrimination is deliberate, while arbitrariness is random; discrimination follows a discriminating pattern, while arbitrariness need have no discernible determining principle; discrimination is systematic, while arbitrariness need not be structured at all. Given a pool of death penalty qualified defendants who are therefore within the category subject to discretionary selection, a discriminatory exercise of the power might, for example, deliberately choose the nonwhites at twice the rate of whites, or those in one section of the state at twice the rate of those in another; an arbitrary exercise of the power could make the choice without any predictable pattern.

In the characterization of a death penalty system, a discriminatory system would be one that makes its selections deliberately but according to impermissible criteria. An arbitrary system would simply be one that lacks adequate controls to assure that the selection conforms to the legal standards. From this system perspective, an arbitrary system may be not only one in which selection is totally random or capricious but also one in which there is simply inadequate protection against the selection being random or capricious. A system that cannot control against randomness or caprice may also be unable to control against discrimination. An arbitrary system, in this sense, may well harbor discriminatory as well as random selection standards. For this reason, discrimination and arbitrariness have tended to blend into a single critical concept in the context of death penalty discussion.

Either discrimination or arbitrariness in the death penalty system may be unsettling. Although discrimination may have more invidious overtones, if the legally established standards fairly represent the goals of a capital punishment system, even arbitrariness in its administration without any discriminatory characteristics must undermine confidence that the system is pursuing the objectives. Whatever rationale of retribution or deterrence capital punishment promotes[116] cannot be achieved by a system that is not tailored to accomplish it in practice. Random, capricious, disproportionate, or discriminatory executions cannot satisfy any legitimate purpose. Both retribution and deterrence require that the person executed be one who "deserved" that punishment.[117]

Respect for the legal system depends on a perception that it is equitably administered in accordance with legal principles. That popular condition for the validity of a capital punishment system has, of course, a foundation in the U.S. Constitution. Two relevant provisions of the Constitution are the equal protection clause[118] and the cruel and unusual punishment clause.[119] The Supreme Court has interpreted the equal protection clause to require, in order to establish a violation, either that the law is discriminatory in its terms[120] or that it is administered with an intent to discriminate.[121] If the law is facially neutral, therefore, the Court has held that proof that its administration has a discriminatory impact alone is not enough to invalidate it under the equal protection clause. Proof that the discriminatory impact was produced by an intent to discriminate on the part of the officials administering the law would be necessary in such a case. Moreover, it might be necessary to demonstrate that such discriminatory intent applied to a particular case.[122]

Although discriminatory attitudes or stereotypes may affect decision-making processes without conscious discrimination,[123] "[p]roving the motivation behind official action is often a problematic undertaking."[124] Even if prosecuting officials, judges, or jurors make discriminatory comments, evidence of such comments is difficult to obtain. Survey evidence is not likely to show intentional discrimination in a particular case.[125] Such information portrays the overall pattern of cases. It does not purport to prove where in the pattern a particular case fits. Its contribution is to identify circumstances operating on the generality of cases that are not apparent from an examination of any one case in isolation. It will not be useful to an understanding of any aspect of an individual case. For those reasons, the death penalty administration is not likely to be vulnerable to a discrimination theory based on the equal protection clause.

An arbitrariness theory, however, seems better suited accurately to describe the potential objection to the death penalty. On that constitutional basis, decisions at any stage that were not consistent with the statutory standards were arbitrary regardless of whether the responsible factors were the race or sex of the defendant, or of the victim, or the character of the judicial district where the offense occurred, or the policies or practices of the prosecutor for that district, or other factors that cannot be pinpointed. Evidence of discrimination in particular cases might contribute to a finding that a system is arbitrary, but such evidence is not essential to an arbitrariness standard. Survey data of the generality of relevant cases could inform the factual premises upon which the Court might judge whether the death penalty is being applied in an arbitrary manner.

Although an arbitrariness theory under the equal protection clause may be foreclosed by the need to establish discriminatory intent, arbitrariness was precisely the basis for *Furman*. That decision was based, not on the equal protection clause, but on the cruel and unusual punishment clause.[126] The cruel and unusual punishment clause tests the enforcement of the death penalty under a more rigorous standard than the equal protection clause employs for review of the administration of legislative policy generally. Because the death penalty is different from all other punishments in kind rather than degree, it is a special concern of the cruel and unusual punishment clause.

CHAPTER II

The Development of the Arbitrariness Standard for Capital Punishment

In the constitutional climate created by the Supreme Court during the Warren era, it was natural that questions about the validity of the death penalty should confront the courts. The constitutional consciousness concerning discrimination and procedural justice that the Court aroused in the nation alighted on the death penalty as a subject for scrutiny. It developed interest in the question whether the death penalty constituted cruel and unusual punishment in violation of the eighth and fourteenth amendments and also the question whether it was administered fairly under the due process clause of the fifth and fourteenth amendments.[1] Though independent, those questions were also intertwined: the unique severity of the death penalty heightened sensitivity to procedural flaws; and defendants attacking their capital sentences could not ignore the procedural issues in their cases. The Supreme Court reviewed the procedural issues before it was ready to confront the meaning of its constitutional criminal procedure reforms for the validity of the penalty of death itself. Underlying the procedural questions was an unspoken perception of an arbitrary and capricious pattern in the imposition of the death penalty. The Court undertook to review the procedural issues without adequate empirical data about such a pattern.

PART 1.

The Prelude to *Furman v. Georgia*

In 1968 the Court decided two cases dealing with the discretionary roles of the prosecutor and the jury in the processing of a capital case. In *United States v. Jackson*,[2] the Court held the death penalty provision of the federal kidnapping statute unconstitutional because the statute provided that it could be imposed only upon a jury recommendation, automatically relieving a defendant who waived the right to a jury trial or who entered a plea of guilty. The Court held that the procedure impermissibly burdened the exercise of the right to a jury trial with the risk of a death sentence. In *Witherspoon v. Illinois*,[3] the Court held that prospective jurors could not be excused simply because they were opposed to capital punishment.

Witherspoon arose because of the unusual discretionary role of the jury in deciding the penalty for a first degree murder conviction. At the time, the jury was given no instructions on the standards to apply in its decision, and no procedures were established to confine, structure, or check its exercise of discretion. When a perception of arbitrariness in the imposition of the death penalty developed, this jury discretion was often identified as the site of the discrimination. In an effort to remedy the problem, the American Law Institute proposed in its Model Penal Code in 1959 a system of guidelines for the jury to follow in making its life or death decision.[4]

In *McGautha v. California* in 1971, the U.S. Supreme Court held that permitting "the jury to impose the death penalty without any governing standards" did not violate the Constitution.[5] The Court did not specify any particular constitutional provision as the basis for its inquiry. Instead, it ruled broadly that it could not "say that committing to the untrammeled discretion of the jury the power to pronounce life or death in capital cases is offensive to *anything* in the Constitution."[6] The Court also held that the procedure by which the jury imposed a "death sentence in the same proceeding and verdict as determined the issue of guilt was constitutionally permissible."[7]

The rationale for the Court's decision was its conclusion that it is not possible "to identify before the fact those homicides for which the slayer should die."[8] As the Court explained:

> To identify before the fact those characteristics of criminal homicides and their perpetrators which call for the death penalty, and to express those characteristics in language which can be fairly understood and applied by the sentencing authority, appear to be tasks which are beyond present human ability.[9]

The Court considered the Model Penal Code proposal for jury guidelines and included the proposal as an appendix to its opinion. The Court decided, however, that the proposal confirmed its judgment of the impossibility of devising workable standards for jury death penalty decision making:

> It is apparent that such criteria do not purport to provide more than the most minimal control over the sentencing authority's exercise of discretion. They do not purport to give an exhaustive list of the relevant considerations or the way in which they may be affected by the presence or absence of other circumstances. They do not even undertake to exclude constitutionally impermissible considerations. And, of course, they provide no protection against the jury determination to decide on whimsy or caprice. In short, they do no more than suggest some subjects for the jury to consider during its deliberations, and they bear witness to the intractable nature of the problem of "standards" which the history of capital punishment has from the beginning reflected. Thus, they indeed caution against this Court's undertaking to establish such standards itself, or to pronounce at large that standards in this realm are constitutionally required.[10]

In *Godfrey v. Georgia*,[11] Justices Marshall and Brennan later agreed that the Court was correct in *McGautha*[12] that "[t]he task of eliminating arbitrariness in the infliction of capital punishment is proving to be one which our criminal justice system—and perhaps any criminal justice system—is unable to perform."[13] They dissented, however, together with Justice Douglas, in *McGautha*. Their dissenting opinion, authored by Justice Brennan, expressed the theory that later prevailed in the 1976 decisions to uphold the death penalty. In 1976, however, Justices Brennan and Marshall refused to subscribe to their *McGautha* theory.[14]

Justice Brennan's opinion for the dissenters in *McGautha* consisted of two parts. First, he argued that the standardless jury sentencing procedure constituted an "unguided, unbridled, unreviewable exercise of naked power" that violated due process[15] unless it was impossible to prevent.[16] He then argued "that the Court has provided no explanation for its conclusion that capital sentencing is inherently incapable of rational treatment."[17] The majority, he said, exaggerated the demand that the defendant was making for due process standards. The defendant was not asking, according to Justice Brennan, for "predetermined standards so precise as to be capable of purely mechanical application, entirely eliminating any vestiges of flexibility or discretion in their use."[18] Instead, Justice Brennan wrote, due process should tolerate discretion in this realm but only if it is "guided by reason and kept within bounds."[19] The state should at least have to legislate the penological policy—deterrence, retribution, isolation, or rehabilitation—that its capital punishment is to serve.[20] Beyond that, the state should also establish the appropriate criteria.[21] "[T]he precise amount of weight to be given to any one factor in any particular case," Justice

Brennan agreed, may be "incapable of determination beforehand. But that is no excuse for refusing to tell the decision maker whether he should consider a particular factor *at all.*"[22]

The primary constitutional interest that Justice Brennan sought to serve with the standards requirement was protection against arbitrariness.[23] Just one year later, in *Furman v. Georgia*,[24] Justices Brennan and Marshall disclosed that their concern about the death penalty was deeper than its arbitrary administration. Only in part because of their sense of the arbitrariness of the capital punishment system,[25] they agreed that the death penalty is an excessive and unnecessary punishment that violates the eighth amendment. Justices Stewart and White, however, who silently concurred in the majority opinion in *McGautha*, took up the focus on arbitrariness in casting deciding votes against the death penalty systems as then applied. As Chief Justice Burger later complained, in *Furman* "what had been approved under the Due Process Clause of the Fourteenth Amendment in *McGautha* became impermissible under the Eighth and Fourteenth Amendments."[26]

PART 2.

The *Furman* Rationales

The substance of the opinion for the Court in *Furman* consisted of a *per curiam* sentence: "The Court holds that the imposition and carrying out of the death penalty in these cases[27] constitutes cruel and unusual punishment in violation of the eighth and fourteenth amendments."[28] Five justices concurred in that holding. Each wrote a separate opinion expressing his views alone. Justices Brennan and Marshall decided that the death penalty was an unconstitutional form of punishment.[29] Justices Douglas, Stewart, and White confined their decisions to the death penalty as they perceived it was applied. The Court and the conventional wisdom have considered their opinions the law of *Furman* in some collective sense,[30] often focusing primarily on Justice Stewart's opinion.[31] The theme common to all five opinions for the majority justices was an arbitrariness rationale. Justice Stewart relied almost completely on that theory. Justice White relied on arbitrariness and on a related infrequency theory. Justice Brennan considered the arbitrariness rationale one of four principles by which he determined that the death penalty is unconstitutional. Justice Douglas concentrated on the discrimination component of arbitrariness. Justice Marshall considered the discrimination theory as one reason the death penalty was morally unacceptable in the sense that it " 'shocks the conscience and sense of justice of the people.' "[32]

Justice Stewart

Justice Stewart crafted his opinion to conform to the literal language of the eighth amendment, which prohibits "cruel and unusual punishments." The death penalties in the cases before the court were "cruel," he wrote, "in the sense that they excessively go beyond, not in degree but in kind, the punishments that the state legislatures have determined to be necessary."[33] He explained that the states had not made death the mandatory punishment for murder or rape, but had provided death or life imprisonment as alternative penalties for those offenses.[34] The death penalty was "unusual," Justice Stewart continued, "in the sense that the penalty of death is infrequently imposed for murder, and that its imposition for rape is extraordinarily rare."[35]

Justice Stewart then wrote: "But I do not rest my conclusion upon these two propositions alone."[36] Still invoking the constitutional language, he explained:

> These death sentences are cruel and unusual in the same way that being struck by lightning is cruel and unusual. For, of all the people convicted of rapes and murders in 1967 and 1968, many just as reprehensible as these, the petitioners are among a capriciously selected random handful upon whom the sentence of death has in fact been imposed . . . . I simply conclude that the eighth and fourteenth amendments cannot tolerate the infliction of a sentence of death under legal systems that permit this penalty to be so wantonly and so freakishly imposed.[37]

Justice Brennan

Justice Brennan agreed:

> When the punishment of death is inflicted in a trivial number of the cases in which it is legally available, the conclusion is virtually inescapable that it is being inflicted arbitrarily. Indeed, it smacks of little more than a lottery system. . . . When the rate of infliction is at this low level, it is highly implausible that only the worst criminals or the criminals who commit the worst crimes are selected for this punishment. No one has yet suggested a rational basis that could differentiate in those terms the few who die from the many who go to prison. Crimes and criminals simply do not admit of a distinction that can be drawn so finely as to explain, on that ground, the execution of such a tiny sample of those eligible. Certainly the laws that provide for this punishment do not attempt to draw that distinction; all cases to which the laws apply are necessarily "extreme.' . . . [O]ur procedures in death cases, rather than resulting in the selection of "extreme" cases for this punishment, actually sanction an arbitrary

selection. For this Court has held that juries may, as they do, make the decision whether to impose a death sentence wholly unguided by standards governing that decision. . . . In other words, our procedures are not constructed to guard against the totally capricious selection of criminals for the punishment of death.[38]

Justice Douglas

Justice Douglas based his vote on a conclusion that the discretion given judges and juries in imposing the death penalty rendered the procedures "pregnant with discrimination and discrimination is an ingredient not compatible with the idea of equal protection of the laws that is implicit in the ban on 'cruel and unusual' punishments."[39] Justice Douglas was concerned about possible arbitrariness in the administration of the death penalty[40] but was moved more by his perception that it was administered, not with complete arbitrariness, but with discrimination against "minorities whose numbers are few, who are outcasts of society, and who are unpopular."[41]

For evidence of such discrimination, Justice Douglas cited four sources: (*a*) the President's Commission on Law Enforcement and Administration of Justice, which concluded that there is evidence that the death penalty is imposed disproportionately against "the poor, the Negro, and the members of unpopular groups;"[42] (*b*) a study of capital cases in Texas from 1924–1968 that concluded that "most of those executed were poor, young, and ignorant;"[43] (*c*) a statement by former Warden Lewis Lawes of Sing Sing that, though the law is impartial and juries do not intentionally favor the rich, the death penalty in fact is reserved for the poor;[44] (*d*) a statement by former Attorney General Ramsey Clark that "it is the poor, the sick, the ignorant, the powerless and the hated who are executed."[45] Justice Douglas added this observation: "One searches our chronicles in vain for the execution of any member of the affluent strata of this society. The Leopolds and Loebs are given prison terms, not sentenced to death."[46]

Justice Marshall

Justice Marshall, in his separate opinion, wrote:

Studies indicate that while the higher rate of executions among Negroes is partially due to a higher rate of crime, there is evidence of racial discrimination. . . . There is also overwhelming evidence that the death penalty is employed against men and not women. . . . It also is evident that the burden of capital punishment falls upon the poor, the ignorant, and the under-privileged members of society.[47]

Chief Justice Burger, in dissent, responded: "[T]he sources cited contain no empirical findings to undermine the general premise that juries impose the death penalty in the most extreme cases."[48] He also pointed out that those sources relied on data from periods when official policies of racial discrimination systematically excluded blacks from jury service.[49]

Justice Stewart agreed that "racial discrimination has not been proved, and I put it to one side."[50] For him, the arbitrariness of the imposition of the death penalty was its fatal flaw. Justice Stewart, in turn, however, referred to no evidence of that arbitrariness.[51] Moreover, he discussed the arbitrariness of the death penalty in general. He did not refer specifically to its administration in either Georgia or Texas, the two states whose procedures were before the Court. Abstract arbitrariness convinced Justice Stewart to condemn the states' capital punishment systems generally, and to vote to void the death sentences in three cases from two particular states on that basis. Understandably, his opinion was interpreted to apply to the contemporary capital sentencing systems in all states.[52]

Justice White

Justice White joined the majority with a rationale that resembled Justice Stewart's. Based on his 10 years of exposure to cases for which death was the authorized penalty, Justice White concluded that "the death penalty is exacted with great infrequency even for the most atrocious crimes and that there is no meaningful basis for distinguishing the few cases in which it is imposed from the many cases in which it is not."[53] Justice White expressly rested that conclusion on federal and state criminal cases across the country, not confined to those in the two states whose death penalty decisions were before the Court.

One legal effect that Justice White derived from his observation was that the imposition of the death penalty was occurring in the absence of any clearly defined legislative policy. Instead of the legislature defining the standards for the death penalty, he said, juries and judges were doing so "in exercising the discretion so regularly conferred upon them."[54]

A second, and paramount, legal effect that Justice White identified from his observation was that "as the statutes before us are now administered, the penalty is so infrequently imposed that the threat of execution is too attenuated to be of substantial service to criminal justice."[55] Justice White reasoned that the death penalty would be constitutional if it served a social purpose, such as deterrence, or any other legitimate end of punishment.[56] If it did not, its imposition would violate the eighth amendment because it "would then be the pointless and needless extinction of life with only marginal contributions to any discernible social or public purposes."[57] Justice White decided that the death penalty had reached that point because "the odds are now very much against imposition and execution of the penalty with respect to any convicted murderer or rapist."[58]

Justices Douglas, Stewart, and White thus cast votes between the extremes of Justices Brennan and Marshall that the death penalty is always unconstitutional and of Chief Justice Rehnquist, former Chief Justice Burger, and Justices Blackmun and Powell that the death penalty is not unconstitutional as a punishment for murder or rape. They decided that the death penalty was unconstitutional as they perceived that it was then being applied. Justice Stewart held that its application was too arbitrary, Justice White that it was too arbitrary and too infrequent, and Justice Douglas that it was too discriminatory.[59] Justice Brennan agreed that it was too arbitrary and Justice Marshall that it was too discriminatory, although they made clear that they would not uphold capital punishment even in the absence of those circumstances.

PART 3.

The New Death Penalty Procedures

On the same day that it decided *Furman*, the Supreme Court held in one opinion[60] and in a series of *per curiam* orders vacating judgments imposing capital punishment that *Furman* invalidated the death penalty statutes in several states in addition to Texas and Georgia, without any discussion of the statutes or their operation.[61] All the capital punishment states perceived that *Furman* invalidated their death penalties even if they were not involved in those cases.[62] At the same time, they recognized that *Furman* gave them an opportunity to reform their capital sentencing procedures to overcome the constitutional objections expressed by the three moderate justices. They all identified the role of jury discretion as the pressure point[63] but diverged in their remedial efforts. Some endeavored to eliminate that discretion. North Carolina and Louisiana took this approach, and the Supreme Court later reviewed and rejected their statutes. Most, however, elected to guide the discretion, and the Supreme Court later approved that approach.

The North Carolina response was adopted first by judicial decision, then by statute. In *State v. Waddell*[64] in 1973, the North Carolina Supreme Court reviewed the history of the death penalty in the state and concluded that the legislature gave a higher priority to retention of that penalty, which it had provided for two centuries, than to the proviso that it added to the statute as late as 1949 to empower the jury in its discretion to reduce the penalty to life imprisonment. Although setting aside all death sentences imposed under that procedure,[65] the Court for future cases severed the proviso from the statute, leaving death as the mandatory penalty for the capital offenses then existing of first degree murder, rape, first degree burglary, and arson.[66] The next year, the North Carolina legislature amended its statutes to provide death as the only penalty for those offenses.[67]

The states that decided to retain the discretion but to try to control it employed a variety of procedures. Because the Supreme Court later upheld their efforts, Georgia, Florida, and Texas turned out to be prominent examples. Both Georgia and Florida introduced two innovations recommended by the American Law Institute in its Model Penal Code:[68] a separate evidentiary hearing on the issue of penalty if the trial on the issue of guilt results in a conviction of a capital offense; and a requirement that the penalty hearing establish one or more aggravating circumstances from a statutory list before a death sentence can be imposed.[69] Georgia also required consideration of mitigating circumstances.[70] Florida, which modeled its new procedures more closely on the American Law Institute's formulation,[71] included a statutory list of mitigating circumstances to guide the jury.[72] Both Georgia and Florida also devised one additional new safeguard, appellate review of the sentence,[73] a procedure rare in the states at the time.

Texas developed a different approach. It limited capital homicides to five specific categories of intentional murders. As the Supreme Court described the Texas procedure, this narrowing of capital murder to five carefully defined situations served much the same purpose as the list of statutory aggravating circumstances in the Georgia and Florida systems.[74] In addition, Texas provided a separate evidentiary hearing in the event that the jury convicted a defendant of one of the five capital categories. At that hearing, the jury was required to answer three additional questions about the responsibility of the defendant and the probability that the defendant would commit criminal acts of violence that would constitute a continuing threat to society.[75] Texas provided for expedited review of a death sentence but did not empower the appellate court to review the sentence itself.[76]

The states legislated the new procedures for their capital punishment systems without undertaking any reported study of their potential effectiveness.[77] The new procedures they selected do not, of course, exhaust the possible protections.[78] They do not, for example, impose any controls on the prosecutor's pretrial discretionary authority. They do not establish any statewide standards for the exercise of that discretion or subject it to any statewide review or other stabilizing process. At the guilt stage of the trial, except in a statutory scheme such as that in Texas, they do not clarify the distinction between first degree murder and second degree murder. At the penalty stage, many of the new guidelines are vague, some unnecessarily so. Finally, at the appellate stage, they do not all provide for statewide comparative proportionality review, and few of them provide for that review to be based on the pool of all homicide cases, including cases that do not result in a death penalty. Thus, there is substantial room for reasonable measures to improve the capital sentencing process even with the new procedures in place.

PART 4.

The 1976 Death Penalty Decisions

When the new statutes in Georgia, Florida, Texas, North Carolina, and Louisiana were barely three years old, and before any persons had been executed under them (or anywhere in the country since the moratorium before *Furman*), the Supreme Court decided to review the constitutionality of death sentences imposed under them for murder.[79] At the time, the Court had no empirical evidence of the administration of the new statutes in those or any other states, as it also had no new empirical studies of the administration of the pre-*Furman* death penalty statutes. Although the formal procedures had changed, there were then no new developments in regard to the frequency of the actual imposition of capital punishment—and certainly none with regard to its regularity or evenhandedness.

The Court had little choice but to review the statutes in that posture. There could hardly be any executions without Supreme Court approval of the new procedures. Although *Furman* had not outlawed the death penalty, it had engendered uncertainty about what kind of capital punishment system, if any, the Court might approve. Unless the Court permitted executions under the new statutes before it passed on their validity, it needed to decide the constitutional sufficiency of the new procedures before it could accumulate the kind of historical experience on which Justices Stewart, White, and Douglas had based their *Furman* opinions. The only middle course might have been to stay executions under the statutes and study the states' patterns of meting out sentences of death, although not their practices in carrying out such sentences. The Court apparently was not inclined, however, simply to establish another moratorium on executions. Accordingly, it chose to review the statutes on their face. Once it made that decision, the Court also expedited the cases to enable it to complete its consideration of them during its current term.[80]

Since *Furman*, the composition of the Court had changed in respect to one member: Justice Stevens had replaced Justice Douglas. Given the tenuous two plus three to four vote in *Furman*, this change had a potentially critical impact. That individual impact did not materialize.

The Court announced its decisions in all five cases, *Gregg v. Georgia*,[81] *Proffitt v. Florida*,[82] *Jurek v. Texas*,[83] *Woodson v. North Carolina*,[84] and *Roberts v. Louisiana*,[85] on July 2, 1976. In *Gregg*, *Proffitt*, and *Jurek*, the Court upheld the guided discretion systems. In *Woodson* and *Roberts*, the Court struck down the mandatory systems. The plurality based its decisions in *Gregg*, *Proffitt*, and *Jurek* on its conclusion that the new procedures *on their face* seemed to satisfy the concerns of *Furman*.[86] The plurality thus insisted that its decisions were consistent with *Furman*.

The alignment of the justices continued its two–three–four pattern from *Furman*. Two justices voted to strike down the death penalty statutes in all five states. Four justices voted to uphold all five capital sentencing systems.[87] The three swing justices this time voted in favor of the three guided discretion systems and against the two mandatory systems. Thus, seven justices voted to permit capital punishment to pass constitutional muster and to approve three statutory systems to carry it out.

Although the numerical alignment duplicated the *Furman* voting pattern, it represented one major shift. Justice White voted to uphold the death penalty procedures in all five states. Had the dissenting bloc in *Furman*[88] held in 1976, Justice White's vote would have given it a majority to approve the mandatory as well as the guided discretion capital sentencing systems. The bloc did not hold, however. Justice Powell left it to join Justices Stewart and Stevens in the plurality opinions in each of the five cases, and indeed authored their joint opinion in *Proffitt*. On that circumstance, the North Carolina and Louisiana mandatory systems fell to constitutional condemnation. Justice Stevens replaced Justice Douglas in the swing group. Whether Justice Douglas would have voted to uphold the guided discretion procedures, as Justice Stevens did, can only be a matter of conjecture. With Justices Stewart and White, as well as Powell, voting that way, however, Justice Douglas could have changed the count from seven-to-two to six-to-three but not the outcome. His departure from the Court, therefore, was not decisive.

The arbitrariness rationale in *Furman* was the product primarily of Justices Stewart and White, with the agreement of Justices Brennan and Marshall as well as Douglas. Justice Douglas left the Court before the 1976 decisions. Justice Stewart participated in those decisions, but he too has now left the Court. The Court has under consideration this term the first cases since its 1976 death penalty decisions that present questions directly related to the arbitrariness issue. Other capital cases that it has decided contribute to an understanding of its general death penalty doctrine. Will the arbitrariness position be able to muster a majority on the contemporary Court?

PART 5.

The Death Penalty is Different

The problem of controlling discretion is not unique to capital punishment; it is a characteristic of the criminal justice system in general. Any arbitrariness in sentencing, to the extent that it exists, is probably a product of processes common to capital and noncapital cases.[89] That arbitrariness may not be the unique feature; the severity of the penalty is. The over-arching question is whether that makes any difference.

Dissenting in *Furman*, Justice Powell refused to invalidate the death penalty because of what he described as its disproportionate use against "the relatively impoverished and underprivileged elements of society."[90] He reasoned: "The same discriminatory impact argument could be made with equal force and logic with respect to those sentenced to prison terms. The Due Process Clause admits of no distinction between the deprivation of 'life' and the deprivation of 'liberty.' If discriminatory impact renders capital punishment cruel and unusual, it likewise renders invalid most of the prescribed penalties for crimes of violence."[91]

On the same day that he wrote that dissent, however, Justice Powell joined the Court's opinion in *Morrissey v. Brewer*, in which the Court summarized: "Once it is determined that due process applies, the question remains what process is due. It has been said so often by this Court and others as not to require citation of authority that due process is flexible and calls for such procedural protections as the particular situation demands."[92] The requirements of due process may vary according to the seriousness of the offense or the authorized penalty. Based on that precise principle, *Furman's* answer to Justice Powell was the "death is different" doctrine: the proposition that the death penalty cannot constitutionally be administered in a manner that might be acceptable for sentences to prison, probation, and fines.[93] The death penalty requires the maximum measure of due process.

Seven of the nine justices currently on the Court, as well as former Chief Justice Burger and Justices Stewart and Douglas, have ascribed to the notion that the death penalty is unique for due process purposes. Although that proposition has informed the Court's judgments over a considerable period of time,[94] only since *Furman* has it been elevated to the status of a doctrine[95] that requires some extraordinary procedural precautions in the processing of capital cases. The Court has now clearly ruled that in regard to constitutional analysis, the death penalty "is a punishment different from all other sanctions in kind rather than degree."[96] "From the point of view of the defendant, it is different in both its severity and its finality. From the point of view of society the action of the sovereign in taking the life of its citizens also differs dramatically from any other legitimate state action."[97]

The Court reached that consensus in stages. Justices Brennan, Douglas, and Marshall first adopted it in dissent in their concurring and dissenting opinion in *Parker v. North Carolina* in 1970.[98] They repeated it in *McGautha v. California* in 1971 as a basis for requiring procedural protections in capital sentencing that would not be necessary in ordinary sentencing.[99] Justices Brennan, Stewart, and Marshall then incorporated the concept that the death penalty is different in their opinions in 1972 in *Fur-*

man v. Georgia. Justice Stewart expressed the concept in the formulation that has essentially become the prevailing doctrine:

> The penalty of death differs from all other forms of criminal punishment, not in degree but in kind. It is unique in its total irrevocability. It is unique in its rejection of rehabilitation of the convict as a basic purpose of criminal justice. And it is unique, finally, in its absolute renunciation of all that is embodied in our concept of humanity.[100]

Justice Brennan wrote at greater length in explaining why he considered that "[d]eath is a unique punishment in the United States."[101] His perspective differed from Justice Stewart's only in the legal effect he gave to his conclusion. For Justice Brennan, the unique severity of the death penalty justified a searching examination of the moral and practical rationales for its imposition.[102] He viewed the arbitrary infliction of a severe punishment as the violation of one of four principles that he considered essential to the eighth amendment analysis and, in combination with the violation of the other three, a basis for constitutionally outlawing the death penalty altogether. Justice Stewart concurred in that kind of analysis, but declined to base his opinion regarding the constitutionality of the death penalty on it "alone."[103] Instead, he held that the Constitution could not tolerate the arbitrary pattern that he perceived in the infliction of the death penalty, implying that perhaps it could in connection with other forms of punishment. Justice Brennan certainly agreed with that position.[104] Justice Stewart, however, considered the arbitrariness, not so much an inherent characteristic of the death penalty, but a correctible condition, as he clarified in later decisions.[105]

Justice Marshall, in his opinion in *Furman,* argued that the death penalty is more severe than life imprisonment.[106] He did not give that consideration a pervasive role in his constitutional doctrine, however, using it primarily to explain why the deterrence rationale did not justify the death penalty: "The question . . . is not simply whether capital punishment is a deterrent, but whether it is a better deterrent than life imprisonment."[107] In *Coleman v. Balkcom,*[108] Justice Marshall, joined by Justice Brennan, wrote that the unique irrevocability of the death penalty was just one reason for his view that the death penalty is unconstitutional.[109] Nevertheless, in *Caldwell v. Mississippi,*[110] writing for the Court, he invoked the doctrine in reversing a death sentence because the prosecutor had told the jury "not to view itself as determining whether the defendant would die, because a death sentence would be reviewed for correctness by the State Supreme Court."[111]

In the two 1976 death penalty decisions that Justice Stewart wrote, he repeated the point that "death as a punishment is unique in its severity and irrevocability," in *Gregg,*[112] and "that death is a punishment different from all other sanctions in kind rather than degree," in *Woodson*.[113] Justice Powell—who wrote the dissenting opinion that disagreed with that position in *Furman*[114]—and Justice Stevens—who was not yet on the Court when *Furman* was decided—joined in those opinions. The next year, in *Gardner v. Florida*, Justice Stevens, writing for the same three justices and taking account of the views of Justices Brennan and Marshall, observed that "five members of the Court have now expressly recognized that death is a different kind of punishment from any other which may be imposed in this country."[115] Justice Powell authored an opinion expressly accepting the doctrine in a noncapital case, *Solem v. Helm*.[116]

Former Chief Justice Burger joined that group in *Lockett v. Ohio*.[117] Writing the plurality opinion for himself and Justices Stewart, Powell, and Stevens, he said: *Woodson* "rested 'on the predicate that the penalty of death is qualitatively different' from any other sentence. We are satisfied that this qualitative difference between death and other penalties calls for a greater degree of reliability when the death sentence is imposed."[118]

In *Beck v. Alabama*,[119] Justice Blackmun (as well as Chief Justice Burger and Justices Stewart and Powell) joined in the opinion for the Court by Justice Stevens that, quoting from his opinion in *Gardner*, restated that "there is a significant constitutional difference between the death penalty and lesser punishments."[120] Then, in *Barefoot v. Estelle*,[121] Justice Blackmun wrote a dissenting opinion in which he expressly agreed that the death penalty is different for procedural issues: "[W]hen a person's life is at stake—no matter how heinous his offense—a requirement of greater reliability should prevail."[122]

Justice O'Connor joined the group shortly after she replaced Justice Stewart on the Court. Writing a separate concurring opinion in *Eddings v. Oklahoma*,[123] Justice O'Connor, citing Justice Stewart's opinion in *Woodson*, wrote: "Because sentences of death are 'qualitatively different' from prison sentences, this Court has gone to extraordinary measures to ensure that the prisoner sentenced to be executed is afforded process that will guarantee, as much as is humanly possible, that the sentence was not imposed out of whim, passion, prejudice or mistake."[124] Then, in an opinion for the Court in *California v. Ramos*, Justice O'Connor wrote: "The Court, as well as the separate opinions of a majority of the individual justices, has recognized that the qualitative difference of death from all other punishments requires a correspondingly greater degree of scrutiny of the capital sentencing determination."[125]

Justice White, although implicitly disavowing in *Gregg* the notion that the death penalty is different,[126] expressly accepted it in *Turner v. Murray*.[127] Justice Antonin Scalia joined the Court too recently to have had an opportunity to express a position on the doctrine. Chief Justice Rehnquist is the only member of the Court who has rejected it. He has contended that the differences between death as a penalty and other punishments are relevant only to the constitutional question of the proportionality of the penalty for a particular crime. The differences may motivate a legislature to enact more safeguards into the decision-making process for the death penalty than for other cases, he has agreed, but they are not in his view relevant to the question of the constitutional adequacy of the death penalty procedure. In his dissent in *Gardner*, Chief Justice Rehnquist wrote:

> [T]he use of particular sentencing procedures never previously held unfair under the Due Process Clause, in a case where the death sentence is imposed cannot convert that sentence into a cruel and unusual punishment. The . . . Eighth Amendment relates to the character of the punishment and not to the process by which it is imposed.[128]

Earlier, in his dissent in *Woodson*, Chief Justice Rehnquist explained his position more fully:

> [T]he respects in which death is "different" from other punishments which may be imposed upon convicted criminals do not seem to me to establish the proposition that the Constitution requires individualized sentencing.
>
> One of the principal reasons why death is different is because it is irreversible . . . . This . . . would undoubtedly support statutory provision for especially careful review of the fairness of the trial, the accuracy of the factfinding process, and the fairness of the sentencing procedure where the death penalty is imposed. But none of those aspects of the death sentence is at issue here.
>
> The second aspect of the death penalty which makes it "different" . . . is the fact that it . . . ends a human life. . . . This aspect of the difference may enter into the decision of whether or not it is a "cruel and unusual" penalty for a given offense. But since in this case the offense was first degree murder, that particular inquiry need go no further.[129]

The rest of the Court, however, has acknowledged the doctrine,[130] and its impact on capital trial and sentencing procedures and on appellate review of capital sentences has been profound.[131] Thus, the Court for a 16-year period forbad the states at the outset of the trial to exclude otherwise qualified persons as jurors because they are opposed to capital punishment unless they make "unmistakably clear (1) that they would *automatically* vote against the imposition of capital punishment without regard to any evidence that might be developed at the trial of the case before them, or (2) that their attitude toward the death penalty would prevent them from making an impartial decision as to the defendant's guilt."[132] The Court enforced this requirement so strictly that it held that the exclusion of even a single prospective juror in violation of that standard required reversal of a death sentence.[133] The Constitution would not ordinarily prohibit the states from denying jury service to a citizen who opposes or even has reservations about the law applicable to the case,[134] even if the prospective juror denies that his personal views "would prevent or substantially impair the performance of his duties as a juror in accordance with his instructions and his oath."[135] Recently, the Court relaxed the bias standard for capital jurors to "whether the juror's views 'would prevent or substantially impair the performance of his duties as a juror in accordance with his instructions and his oath.'"[136] The Court noted that the new standard does not require that a juror's bias be so strong as to counsel an "automatic" vote against the death penalty and that the bias no longer need be proved with unmistakable clarity.[137]

The Court has also required special precautions against racial prejudice in the jury selection process for capital cases. It has held that a capital defendant accused of an interracial killing is constitutionally entitled upon request to have prospective penalty phase jurors informed of the race of the victim and questioned on the issue of racial bias.[138] The Court recognized that the Constitution does not impose a similar requirement in a noncapital case in the absence of special circumstances injecting civil rights or racial issues into the case.[139] It reasoned that "[b]ecause of the range of discretion entrusted to a jury in a capital sentencing hearing, there is a unique opportunity for racial prejudice to operate but remain undetected"[140] and that the risk "is especially serious in light of the complete finality of the death sentence."[141]

In *Beck v. Alabama*,[142] the Court ruled that the trial court in a capital case must, at least if requested by the defendant, instruct the jury on a lesser-included noncapital offense supported by the evidence. It reserved the question of whether the same rule would apply in a noncapital case.[143] The Court, at the same time, has prohibited mandatory death sentences,[144] even for the murder of a police officer,[145] and required that the sentencing authority in a capital case "not be precluded from considering, as a *mitigating factor*, any aspect of a defendant's character or record and any of the circumstances of the offense that the defendant proffers as a basis for a sentence less than death."[146] It has not, however, restricted "the authority of a State or of the Congress to fix mandatory, minimum sentences for noncapital crimes."[147]

The Court has also decided that "if a state wishes to authorize capital punishment it has a constitutional responsibility to tailor and apply its law in a manner that avoids the arbitrary and capricious infliction of the death penalty."[148] The Court has approved as apparently capable of protecting against arbitrariness such special state procedures as sentencing guidelines for juries, separate trials for sentencing, and appellate review of sentences,[149] although it has not expressly required any of those procedures in any particular capital sentencing system.[150] The Court has required any sentencing guidelines to be adequate to "channel the sentencer's discretion by 'clear and objective standards' that provide 'specific and detailed guidance' and that 'make rationally reviewable the process for imposing a sentence of death,'" that is, that they not be vague.[151]

The Court has applied the privilege against compulsory self-incrimination,[152] including its *Miranda* component,[153] the double jeopardy clause[154] and the requirement of effective assistance of counsel,[155] to the sentencing phase of a capital case in a manner in which they would not apply to ordinary sentencing proceedings.[156] In doing so, the Court regarded capital sentencing proceedings as different in kind from ordinary sentencing. It reasoned that the sentencing stage of capital proceedings is sufficiently similar to the guilt stage of ordinary trials to necessitate parallel protections. Interestingly, the characteristics of the death penalty proceeding that the Court considered common to a trial were those that had essentially been deemed constitutionally compelled by the Court, again because the death penalty is different.

The Court also imposed a requirement for disclosure to the defense of information used for capital sentencing while acknowledging that the same requirement would not apply to sentencing in ordinary cases.[157] In addition, the Court has imposed controls on plea negotiation procedures for capital cases[158] that it has rejected for other cases.[159]

Special procedures are required, however, only where the Court judges that they make a meaningful contribution to the greater need for reliability in the death sentencing determination. The Court has accepted the proposition that "there can be 'no perfect procedure for deciding in which cases governmental authority should be used to impose death.'"[160] Thus, "not every imperfection in the deliberative process is sufficient, even in a capital case, to set aside a state court judgment."[161] For example, in *Strickland v. Washington,* [162] the Court held that the standard for establishing a claim for ineffective assistance of counsel is the same in a capital case as in any other criminal case.

In *Barefoot v. Estelle,*[163] the Court approved the use of psychiatric testimony[164] that the defendant would probably commit further acts of violence, despite evidence supported by the American Psychiatric Association that such predictions of future dangerousness are likely to be wrong two-thirds of the time. Responding to a dissent that invoked the "death is different" doctrine,[165] the Court held: "Although cases such as this involve the death penalty, we perceive no constitutional barrier to applying the ordinary rules of evidence governing the use of expert testimony."[166] In *Dobbert v. Florida,*[167] the Court applied to a capital case the same test for determining when pretrial publicity deprives a defendant of due process as it had adopted in a noncapital case. Another example is *Press-Enterprise Co. v. Superior Court,*[168] in which the Court was highly critical of a six-week jury *voir dire*. Even though the case involved an interracial rape and murder and the defendant was eventually sentenced to death, the Court said: "Properly conducted it is inconceivable that the [*voir dire*] process could extend over such a period."[169]

Similarly, in *Barclay v. Florida*,[170] the Court's plurality opinion upheld the use of the harmless error rule to sustain a death sentence based in part on an aggravating circumstance in violation of state, though not federal, law. The opinion emphasized, however, that its decision was "buttressed" by the state's proportionality review of death sentences on appeal,[171] thus salvaging some consideration for the special character of the case as capital.

The Court has also demonstrated the limits on the use of the "death is different" doctrine in settling the procedures for federal habeas corpus petitions from prisoners on death row. In *Woodward v. Hutchins*,[172] the Court vacated a stay of execution issued by a circuit judge on the ground that the defendant had failed to raise in an earlier federal habeas corpus petition the issue that formed the basis for the stay. In *Barefoot v. Estelle*, the Court said that "death penalty cases are no exception" to the general rule that direct appeal, not collateral attack, is the primary avenue for review of a conviction.[173] The Court did, however, recognize that the "death is different" doctrine has some limited vitality in this context. The standard habeas corpus rules provide that after a district court denies a petition, appellate review may be summary unless the district court or an appellate judge certifies that there is "probable cause" to appeal.[174] "In a capital case," the Court ruled, "the nature of the penalty is a proper consideration in determining whether to issue a certificate of probable cause . . . ."[175] The Court cautioned, however, that "the severity of the penalty does not in itself suffice to warrant the automatic issuing of a certificate."[176] If a certificate is issued, the court of appeals must hear the merits and should therefore grant a stay of execution.[177] But, the Court held, a court of appeals may use expedited procedures to dispose of the appeal. Now another respect in which the death penalty is different comes into play. "[U]nlike a term of years, a death sentence cannot begin to be carried out by the State while substantial legal issues remain outstanding."[178] Accordingly, a court of appeals may advance capital cases on its docket, may expedite the briefing and argument schedule, may hear argument on the merits at the same time as a motion for a stay and render a single opinion, and may even dismiss the appeal as frivolous after a hearing on the motion for a stay.[179] After the court of appeals acts, if the petitioner seeks review in the Supreme Court, he or she is not automatically entitled to a stay of execution.[180] The petitioner must show on the merits that there is a reasonable probability that he or she will succeed not only in getting certiorari granted but also in getting the Court to reverse the denial of habeas corpus, as well as making the rather obvious showing that he or she will suffer irreparable harm without a stay.[181] If the petitioner is unsuccessful and tries to start again with a new petition for federal habeas corpus, the standard rules for identical and successive petitions apply.[182]

These decisions signal that the concept of the death penalty as a qualitatively different exercise of state power does not necessarily mean that every aspect of the capital process relevant to the reliability of the ultimate judgment will command special procedural protections, nor even that every practical procedure that might enhance reliability will be constitutionally required. Limits on the extent of the "death is different" doctrine are natural developments if there is to be a death penalty. The decisions invoking them, however, attempted no discussion of a reasoned consideration of when the difference in the death penalty will be enough to tip the scales of justice in favor of a particular procedure and when it will not. Certainly, for example, a measure of validity attached to Justice Blackmun's point in *Barefoot*, though perhaps overstated, that "the specious testimony of a psychiatrist [on the question of future dangerousness], colored in the eyes of an impressionable jury by the inevitable untouchability of a medical specialist's words, equates with death itself."[183] Thus, *Barefoot* appeared to be an ideal case for a special rule. Yet the Court permitted the expert testimony, although not based on an examination of the defendant or special professional skills unavailable to a lay jury equally capable of predicting future violent conduct on the basis of a history of violent conduct. The decision not to invoke the "death is different" doctrine to screen expert testimony more carefully than in ordinary cases may be unexceptionable. The Court told us, however, only that the doctrine did not apply. It gave us no principled basis for distinguishing the procedures to which it would apply from the procedures to which it would not. There seems to be a point at which the Court will reject a procedure for death cases that it will tolerate for ordinary cases, but the Court has not identified that point.

PART 6.

Procedures versus Practice

The more relevant question for the present inquiry is whether the Court will utilize the "death is different" doctrine to evaluate the arbitrariness of the death penalty in practice as well as in the context of requiring more careful procedures. Has the settling of the positions of the justices in the 1976 death penalty decisions resulted in a policy of insisting on procedural protections in death penalty cases but no more? Chief Justice Burger may have suggested such an understanding in an ambiguous statement in his opinion for the Court in *Hopper v. Evans*.[184] The Court's eighth amendment decisions in the past decade, he wrote, were "concerned with insuring that sentencing discretion in capital cases is channeled so that arbitrary and capricious results are avoided."[185] The first part of the statement—"insuring that sentencing discretion in capital cases is channeled"—might mean that procedures that channel the capital sentencing discretion thereby satisfy the constitutional standard, without regard to how they work in practice. The later part of the statement—"so that arbitrary and capricious results are avoided"—might mean that the procedures must in fact achieve outcomes that are not arbitrary and capricious in order to satisfy the constitutional standard.

Ordinarily, a judicial decision about whether a decision-making process is arbitrary is based on a determination of whether the system lacks necessary procedures.[186] Therefore, the standard constitutional remedy for arbitrariness is simply the erection of procedural safeguards. Confidence in the efficacy of procedure as the instrument for the protection of liberty is a hallmark of our due process jurisprudence. Once the procedures are in place, the Court customarily assumes they will work and does not generally inspect their performance.

Furman was different. *McGautha* had already upheld the constitutionality of the absence of procedural safeguards in capital sentencing. *Furman* found arbitrariness in practice.[187] It held that because the death penalty is different, the traditional procedural remedies were not sufficient. Now that the Supreme Court in the 1976 decisions has upheld the new procedures on their face, as *McGautha* did for the former procedures, the "death is different" doctrine should require the Court to reexamine them in practice, as *Furman* did for the former procedures. As the Court recently noted in an equal protection context, "[t]he Constitution requires . . . that we look beyond the face of the statute" to evaluate the effect of "procedures implementing a neutral statute."[188]

A position that the procedures may be constitutionally adequate regardless of whether they achieve their purpose in connection with the actual results under them would be inconsistent with *Furman* and with the emphasis in the plurality opinions in the 1976 decisions that they were adjudicating the new procedures at that time only "on their face." The Court since 1976 has continued to make clear that a state must not only design its capital punishment law with proper procedures but also must "apply its law in a manner that avoids the arbitrary and capricious infliction of the death penalty."[189] The procedures must prove adequate to the task. Unsatisfied defendants may, of course, ask a court to revisit a remedy that appears deficient.

The Court has continued to evaluate some death penalty procedures in practice in the context of narrower issues than those presented in *Furman* and *Gregg*. For example, in *Baldwin v. Alabama*,[190] the Court reviewed the experience in Alabama under a capital sentencing procedure that appeared mandatory on its face. In *Woodson*, the Court had invalidated a mandatory death penalty for first degree murder because of concern that the jury might still arbitrarily nullify the mandatory death penalty by acquitting on the capital charge a defendant who is proved guilty, but who the jury, without any guidance, finds undeserving of the death penalty.[191] The Court in *Baldwin* nevertheless upheld the constitutionality of the Alabama procedure on the basis of its results in practice:

> The Alabama scheme, however, has not resulted in such arbitrariness. Juries deliberating under the 1975 statute did not act to nullify the mandatory "sentence" by refusing to convict in a significant number of cases; indeed, only 2 of the first 50 defendants tried for capital crimes during the time the 1975 Act was in effect were acquitted.[192]

A second example is *Godfrey v. Georgia*.[193] Although the Court reversed the death penalty in that case because it was based on an unconstitutionally vague aggravating circumstance, Justice Stewart's opinion for four justices also evaluated the facts. It concluded, in terms reminiscent of Justice White's description of arbitrariness in *Furman*: "There is no principled way to distinguish this case, in which the death penalty was imposed, from the many cases in which it was not."[194] Justice White dissented because he believed that the facts were more aggravated than the plurality had perceived them.

Nevertheless, Chief Justice Rehnquist and former Chief Justice Burger have regularly rejected the arbitrariness doctrine.[195] Justice Scalia has not yet had an opportunity to express an opinion on it. Justice Blackmun consistently resisted it until recently. In a dissenting opinion joined by Justices Brennan and Marshall, in *Cabana v. Bullock*,[196] Justice Blackmun wrote that the 1976 death penalty decisions "explicitly rested their approval of the capital-sentencing schemes before them on the *combination* of channeled factfinding by the sentencer and appellate review."[197] Whether that recent approval of strict procedural requirements in capital cases also suggests that Justice Blackmun would consider evidence about whether the procedures work can only be speculative. Justices Brennan and Marshall are reliable votes against any capital punishment system.

The positions of Justices Powell, Stevens, and White require further study.[198] That study necessarily begins with an analysis of Justice Stewart's position, although he is no longer on the Court.

Charting the Justices

Readers unfamiliar with the justices or their death penalty decisions may find this outline helpful in following the discussion of their opinions.

McGautha v. California (1971)

Voted that the pre-*Furman* death penalty procedures were constitutional:

Chief Justice Burger
Justices Harlan
        Black
        Stewart
        White
        Blackmun
Voted to require in death penalty cases a separate sentencing hearing and standards to guide the sentencing jury:
Justices Douglas
        Brennan
        Marshall

Furman v. Georgia (1972)
Voted that the administration of the death penalty was unconstitutionally arbitrary:

Justices Brennan	(arbitrariness as one of four principles violated by the death penalty)
Stewart	(arbitrariness)
Douglas	(discrimination and arbitrariness)
Marshall	(discrimination as a secondary reason for striking down the death penalty)
White	(arbitrariness and infrequency)

Voted that the administration of the death penalty was constitutional:
Chief Justice Burger
Justices Blackmun
        Powell
        Rehnquist

The 1976 Death Penalty Decisions
Voted to uphold death penalty statutes with the new procedures on the assumption that they would be capable of protecting against arbitrariness, but not to uphold mandatory death penalty statutes:
Justices Stewart
        Powell
        Stevens
Voted to uphold death penalty statutes with the new procedures and also mandatory death penalty statutes:
Chief Justice Burger
Justices White
        Rehnquist
        Blackmun
Voted to hold death penalty statutes with the new procedures and also mandatory death penalty statutes unconstitutional:
Justices Brennan
        Marshall

The Current Court
    Likely to follow the arbitrariness theory:
        Justices Brennan
                Marshall
                White
    Likely to reject the arbitrariness theory unless they can be persuaded that, because death is different,
        the presence of the new death penalty procedures should not preclude an arbitrariness challenge; and
        arbitrariness under the cruel and unusual punishment clause, as well as discrimination under the equal protection clause, should be a valid basis for a constitutional challenge to the death penalty:
        Justices Powell
                Stevens
    Uncertain:
        Justices Blackmun
                O'Connor
                Scalia
    Likely to reject an arbitrariness theory:
        Chief Justice Rehnquist

Justice Stewart

In the 1976 death penalty decisions, Justice Stewart, appropriately, authored the plurality opinion for himself and Justices Powell and Stevens in the lead cases, *Gregg v. Georgia* and *Woodson v. North Carolina.* Justice Powell wrote their opinion for himself in *Profitt v. Florida* and Justice Stevens in *Jurek v. Texas* and *Roberts v. Louisiana.* Their opinions confirmed *Furman*[199] and argued that their decisions were based on the three swing opinions in that case.

After stating the facts and describing the new Georgia law, Justice Stewart opened his opinion in *Gregg* by holding "that the punishment of death does not invariably violate the Constitution."[200] After explaining the rationale for that conclusion, Justice Stewart turned to the question of the validity of the new Georgia capital sentencing procedures. "On their face,"[201] he held, "these procedures seem to satisfy the concerns of *Furman.*"[202] He began his explanation of his approval of those procedures by indulging a revision of his *Furman* position. Citing his own and Justice White's opinions in *Furman,* Justice Stewart wrote in *Gregg:* "Because of the uniqueness of the death penalty, *Furman* held that it could not be imposed under sentencing procedures that created a substantial risk that it would be inflicted in an arbitrary and capricious manner."[203] But, in *Furman,* Justice Stewart did not criticize the death penalty procedures; he criticized the pattern of death penalty outcomes. Indeed, in *McGautha*, Justice Stewart had joined Justice Harlan's plurality opinion holding that "[i]n light of human history, experience, and the present limitations of human knowledge, we find it quite impossible to say that committing to the untrammeled discretion of the jury the power to pronounce life or death in capital cases is offensive to anything in the Constitution."[204] And, in *Furman*, Justice Stewart grounded his holding that the Constitution "cannot tolerate the infliction of a sentence of death under legal systems that permit this unique penalty to be so wantonly and so freakishly imposed,"[205] not on an abstract assessment of their procedural adequacy but on an observation that in fact "the penalty of death is infrequently imposed for murder, and that its imposition for rape is extraordinarily rare. . . . For, of all the people convicted of rapes and murders in 1967 and 1968, many just as reprehensible as these, the petitioners are among a capriciously selected random handful upon whom the sentence of death has in fact been imposed."[206]

Contradicting *McGautha*, as well as the practical assessment rationale of his *Furman* opinion, Justice Stewart wrote in *Gregg*: "*Furman* held only that, in order to minimize the risk that the death penalty would be imposed on a capriciously selected group of offenders, the decision to impose it had to be guided by standards so that the sentencing authority would focus on the particularized circumstances of the crime and the defendant."[207] Of course, nothing in *Furman*—and certainly nothing in Justice Stewart's opinion in *Furman*—said anything about such a standards requirement. Indeed, the Court had just a year earlier, in *McGautha*, with Justice Stewart's concurrence, rejected such a requirement. Justice Stewart cited Justice White's *Furman* opinion as well as his own in support of his *Gregg* revision. Justice White, however, expressly grounded his position in *Furman* on his "10 years of almost daily exposure to the facts and circumstances of hundreds and hundreds of federal and state criminal cases involving crimes for which death is the authorized penalty."[208] Indeed, in *Gregg*, Justice White wrote that the three plurality justices in *Furman* had performed "the task of deciding whether *in fact* the death penalty was being administered for any given class of crime in a discriminatory, standardless, or rare fashion."[209]

After thus deftly transforming his *Furman* rationale from a decision about the death penalty in practice to a decision about the facial adequacy of the procedures in the death penalty statutes, Justice Stewart approved the new Georgia statute on its face because of its separate penalty "proceeding at which the sentencing authority is apprised of the information relevant to the imposition of sentence and provided with standards to guide its use of the information."[210]

Evaluating, in *McGautha*, only five years earlier, similar procedures proposed by the American Law Institute, Justice Stewart joined Justice

Harlan's pronouncement that they were unlikely to be effective.[211] In *Gregg*, however, Justice Stewart noted that "[j]uries are invariably given careful instructions on the law and how to apply it before they are authorized to decide the merits of a lawsuit."[212] Now he decided that "[i]t would be virtually unthinkable to follow any other course in a legal system that has traditionally operated by following prior precedents and fixed rules of law. It is quite simply a hallmark of our legal system that juries be carefully and adequately guided in their deliberations."[213] Specifically citing Justice Brennan's dissent to his own position in *McGautha*, Justice Stewart continued:

> While such standards are by necessity somewhat general, they do provide guidance to the sentencing authority and thereby reduce the likelihood that it will impose a sentence that fairly can be called capricious or arbitrary. Where the sentencing authority is required to specify the factors it relied upon in reaching its decision, the further safeguard of meaningful appellate review is available to ensure that death sentences are not imposed capriciously or in a freakish manner.[214]

In his opinion for the plurality in *Woodson v. North Carolina*, Justice Stewart struck down North Carolina's mandatory death penalty statute because of three constitutional shortcomings.[215] The first was that a true mandatory death penalty would be cruel and unusual punishment.[216] The other two shortcomings are more relevant to the present inquiry. One was that statutes mandatory on their face have not in the past proved mandatory in practice because juries often simply refused to convict of the capital crime and thereby exercised "unguided and unchecked jury discretion."[217] The other was that the Constitution requires the death penalty determination to be made only after "particularized consideration of relevant aspects of the character and record of each convicted defendant" and the circumstances of the particular crime.[218] Thus, the Constitution requires discretion in the imposition of the death penalty to allow "consideration of compassionate or mitigating factors stemming from the diverse frailties of human kind."[219]

In *Furman*, Justice Stewart distinguished *McGautha* on the technical and unconvincing basis that the claims in that case invoked only the due process and equal protection clauses, whereas *Furman* was based on the cruel and unusual punishment clause.[220] The basis was technical because *McGautha* actually held that "we find it quite impossible to say that committing to the untrammeled discretion of the jury the power to pronounce life or death in capital cases is offensive to *anything* in the Constitution."[221] It was unconvincing because procedural protections are at least as appropriate to a due process as a cruel and unusual punishment analysis.[222] Not surprisingly, then, in *Furman* Chief Justice Burger[223] and Justice Powell[224] and, in *Woodson*, Justice Rehnquist[225] declared that the Court had over-ruled *McGautha*.

In *Gregg*, recognizing that his opinion was "in substantial tension" with *McGautha*,[226] Justice Stewart took cognizance of *McGautha's* suggestion "that standards to guide a capital jury's sentencing deliberations are impossible to formulate,"[227] but said that "the fact is that such standards have been developed."[228] He specifically referred to the Model Penal Code proposal as a successful example, without mentioning that it was the precise example that *McGautha* pronounced unworkable. Justice Stewart also wrote "that *McGautha's* assumption that it is not possible to devise standards to guide and regularize jury sentencing in capital cases has been undermined by subsequent experience."[229] He did not identify that "experience," unless it was simply the adoption by several states, under pressure from *Furman*, of some variation of the Model Penal Code proposal or some similar scheme.

The distinction between the adequacy on its face of a death penalty procedure and its performance in practice may not always be precisely honored. The experience with a statute may affect the assessment of its capacity to fulfill its purpose: consistency in its application may reflect favorably on its apparent adequacy; arbitrary administration may expose its inadequacy. Thus, in *Woodson*, Justice Stewart held that a mandatory death penalty on its face left too much room for arbitrariness, a conclusion he reached not on the mandatory language alone but on the basis of historical experience with mandatory statutes. In a later opinion, in *Godfrey v. Georgia*,[230] Justice Stewart continued to show a willingness to examine death penalty statutes in practice. In reversing a death sentence, he wrote: "There is no principled way to distinguish this case, in which the death penalty was imposed, from the many in which it was not."[231] Although he inserted that statement at the close of his opinion, Justice Stewart did not base his decision on it. He employed a rationale directed at the procedure rather than the arbitrary character of the result, finding unconstitutionally vague the aggravating circumstance that was the basis for the sentence. In deciding the procedural issue, however, he took account of the result it produced.[232] He did that, as he had in *Furman*, in an intuitive way, without referring to any comparable cases where the death penalty was not imposed.[233]

Tracing these decisions obviously follows a course of personal agonizing over a major ethical issue and over the extent of judicial responsibility for deciding it. Justice Stewart struggled with inconsistencies in his search for a satisfying resolution of a conscientious conflict.[234]

Justice Powell

Justice Powell's position must be regarded as somewhat enigmatic. He was a member of the dissenting bloc in *Furman*. When he joined the

1976 plurality, he did not explain his apparent change of heart. One explanation could be that he abandoned his *Furman* dissent in favor of the arbitrariness theory. That dissent rejected any different constitutional analysis for the death penalty than for a penalty of imprisonment, but Justice Powell later accepted the "death is different" doctrine. Another possible explanation is that he accepted *Furman* as stating the law and was abiding by it. The other possible explanation is that Justice Powell supports the constitutional imposition of strict procedural protections on the capital sentencing process, but would not likely condemn a capital punishment system wholesale for their absence. He did not approve of telling the states that their systems were unconstitutional, but does approve of telling the states that they need to include particular safeguards, more or less particularly described, in those systems.[235]

In *Stephens v. Kemp*,[236] Justice Powell wrote an opinion for four justices, dissenting from an order staying an execution, in which he seemed to say in dictum that the provision of the procedural guarantees forecloses any argument even of discrimination in the operation of the statute. In a footnote, he wrote:

> Surely, no contention can be made that the entire Georgia judicial system, at all levels, operates to discriminate in all cases. Arguments to this effect may have been directed to the types of statutes addressed in *Furman* . . . . As our subsequent cases make clear, such arguments cannot be taken seriously under statutes approved in *Gregg*.[237]

He added in the text:

> It should be apparent from the decisions of the Court since *Gregg* was decided that claims based merely on general statistics are likely to have little or no merit under statutes such as that in Georgia.[238]

These quotations are not without ambiguity. At least three interpretations are possible. Justice Powell might have meant that he had confidence in the new statutes to produce nonarbitrary results. Or he might have meant that, whether they did or not, general statistical evidence was not likely to be convincing on the question. The third interpretation is that he believed the constitutional responsibility of the states consisted of providing the fairest possible procedures, but that as long as they followed those procedures, their capital punishment systems would pass constitutional scrutiny: the Court would supervise the procedures but not the results.[239] That position seems congruent with the Brennan dissent in *McGautha*, a decision rendered shortly before Justice Powell joined the Court. The conundrum is that Justice Powell approved the majority position in *McGautha* in his dissenting opinion in *Furman*. Pointing out that Justice Stewart's theory in *Furman* "calls for a reconsideration of the 'standards' aspect of the Court's decision in *McGautha*,"[240] he wrote: "I see no reason to reassess the standards question considered so carefully in [*McGautha*] . . . last Term. Having so recently reaffirmed our historic dedication to entrusting the sentencing function to the jury's 'untrammeled discretion' . . . , it is difficult to see how the Court can now hold the entire process constitutionally defective under the Eighth Amendment."[241] Justice Powell must have reassessed his support for the *McGautha* resolution of the "standards question" and agreed also to stricter procedural scrutiny of death penalty decisions. The question is whether he would also agree to their outcome scrutiny. Although in the 1976 decisions Justice Powell embraced the "death is different" doctrine, he has never written anything expressly giving the difference significance for the level of constitutional tolerance of arbitrary impact of the different penalties.

Although Justice Powell formed the plurality with Justices Stewart and Stevens in the 1976 decisions, he has remained somewhat more permissive toward the death penalty than they. In *Coker v. Georgia*,[242] the Court, including Justices Stewart and Stevens, held that the death penalty is an unconstitutional punishment for rape. Justice Powell wrote a concurring and dissenting opinion in which he agreed with the result in the particular case but wrote that he would allow the death penalty for an aggravated rape such as one committed with excessive brutality.[243] Similarly in *Enmund v. Florida*,[244] when the Court—including Justice Stevens but with Justice Stewart now retired—held that the death penalty was an unconstitutionally disproportionate punishment for accomplice felony–murder,[245] Justice Powell joined Justice O'Connor's dissent. That dissent did recommend a remand for a new sentencing hearing on the ground that at the first hearing the sentencing judge, erroneously believing that the defendant actively participated in the killing, had not given adequate consideration to the minor nature of the defendant's role as a mitigating circumstance.[246]

After Justice Stewart retired, Justice Powell wrote an opinion for the Court, including Justice Stevens, in *Eddings v. Oklahoma*.[247] In it, he wrote that death penalty statutes must meet twin objectives: they must be "at once consistent and principled but also humane and sensible to the uniqueness of the individual."[248] He also joined a concurring opinion written by Justice Stevens in *Barclay v. Florida*.[249] That opinion agreed with a four-justice plurality that a capital sentencing judge's consideration of evidence that, although relevant to the character of the defendant or the circumstances of the crime, is not related to any statutory aggravating or mitigating circumstance, does not violate the Constitution. In the process, it stated:

> Since *Furman v. Georgia*, this Court's decisions have made clear that States may impose this ultimate sentence only if they follow pro-

cedures that are designed to assure reliability in sentencing determinations. . . . A constant theme of our cases . . . has been emphasis on
procedural protections that are intended to ensure that the death
penalty will be imposed in a consistent, rational manner. As stated in
Zant, we have stressed the necessity of "generally narrow[ing] the
class of persons eligible for the death penalty" and of assuring consistently applied appellate review.[250]

Justice Powell, however, disagreed with Justice Stevens in three cases
in addition to *Enmund*. In two of those cases, *Bullington v. Missouri*[251] and
California v. Ramos,[252] his positions did not demonstrate any dispute about
the arbitrariness theory. In *Bullington*, he wrote a dissenting opinion disagreeing that the double jeopardy clause applied to the capital sentencing
process. In *Ramos*, he formed part of the majority upholding an instruction
advising the jury that the governor could commute a sentence of life imprisonment without parole eligibility. Justice Stevens joined Justice Marshall's
dissent. In addition, in *Woodard v. Hutchins*,[253] in which the Court *per
curiam* vacated a stay of execution, Justice Powell wrote a concurring
opinion for four justices holding that the defendant's late filing of three
new claims constituted an abuse of the writ of habeas corpus. Justice
Stevens, however, joined Justice White's dissent objecting to that harsh
procedural judgment.

Those decisions demonstrate Justice Powell's commitment to the
procedural reforms required by the "death is different" doctrine. They do
not necessarily show that Justice Powell would invalidate a death penalty
system with those reforms if it still harbored arbitrariness.

Justice Powell has given some clues that the "death is different" doctrine might lead him to consider empirical evidence of arbitrariness or
discrimination in the death penalty process. One clue may be found in his
acceptance of the comparative proportionality principle. That principle
provides a perspective on arbitrariness in practice. It requires a meaningful distinction between cases that are treated differently for death penalty
purposes. In *Furman*, Justice Powell acknowledged the validity of the
principle of proportionality under the eighth amendment.[254] Although in
that case he may have recognized only that the death penalty might be an
unconstitutionally excessive punishment for a particular offense,[255] he later
clearly accepted comparative proportionality as well. In *Coker v. Georgia*,
he took the position that the death penalty might be disproportionate for
some rapes but not others.[256] And, in *Enmund v. Florida*, he joined Justice
O'Connor's dissent, which reasoned that proportionality turns on "considerations unique to each defendant's case . . . . It requires . . . that the
penalty imposed in a capital case be proportional to the harm caused and
the defendant's blameworthiness."[257]

Two noncapital cases provide further support. In the first case, *Stone*

v. Powell,[258] decided four days after the 1976 death penalty decisions, Justice Powell wrote that "the idea of proportionality . . . is essential to the concept of justice."[259] The other case is *Solem v. Helm*,[260] in which the Supreme Court held that a life sentence without possibility of parole violated the eighth amendment because it was significantly disproportionate to the defendant's crime. In applying the proportionality principle to a prison sentence, the Court acknowledged that it had greater force in the death penalty context:

> When we have applied the proportionality principle in capital cases, we have drawn no distinction with cases of imprisonment. . . . It is true that the "penalty of death differs from all other forms of punishment, not in degree but in kind." . . . As a result, "our decisions [in] capital cases are of limited assistance in deciding the constitutionality of the punishment" in a noncapital case . . . . We agree, therefore, that "[o]utside the context of capital punishment, successful challenges to the proportionality of particular sentences [will be] exceedingly rare." . . . This does not mean, however, that proportionality analysis is entirely inapplicable in non capital cases.[261]

Justice Powell wrote that opinion for the Court and thereby established a basis for repeating the *Furman* analysis in a capital context without placing the constitutionality of the entire criminal justice system at risk.[262] The death penalty is different for proportionality as well as procedural review.

Another clue may be found in Justice Powell's opinion for the Court in *Eddings v. Oklahoma*.[263] There he emphasized "the Court's insistence that capital punishment be imposed fairly, and with reasonable consistency, or not at all."[264] That language seems to embrace both the requirements for protective procedures ("that capital punishment be imposed fairly") and for outcomes free of arbitrariness ("and with reasonable consistency").

Justice Stevens

Justice Stevens joined Justices Stewart and Powell to form the prevailing plurality in the 1976 cases. During the time they served together on the Court, Justices Stevens and Stewart exhibited identical voting patterns in the death penalty cases the Court decided.[265] After Justice Stewart left the Court, Justice Stevens wrote a concurring opinion in *Pulley v. Harris*,[266] in which he independently explained his views in the terms of Justice Stewart's *Furman* and *Gregg* opinions.

Justice Stevens agreed in *Gregg* that the death penalty is not per se unconstitutional. Accordingly, he has voted to uphold death sentences in a number of cases.[267] At the same time, he has written in support of special procedures to safeguard the death sentencing decision against arbitrariness. In *Roberts v. Louisiana*, he wrote the opinion for the plurality that condemned the Louisiana mandatory death penalty because it provided "no safeguard against the arbitrary and capricious imposition of death sentences"[268] that could result from juries disregarding their oaths and choosing "a verdict for the lesser offense whenever they feel the death penalty is inappropriate."[269] He also wrote the opinions for the plurality in *Jurek v. Texas*[270] and *Gardner v. Florida*.[271]

In *Pulley v. Harris*, Justice Stevens wrote a separate concurring opinion to argue that "some form of meaningful appellate review is an essential safeguard against the arbitrary and capricious imposition of death sentences by individual juries and judges."[272] But, he agreed with the majority, that need not constitute comparative proportionality review.[273] In the process of reaching that conclusion, Justice Stevens explained his personal approval of Justice Stewart's *Gregg* position. He described that position as being based on a perception of two defects in the pre-*Furman* death sentencing statutes: too-broad capital categories and unfettered sentencing discretion. "Given these defects," he wrote, "arbitrariness and capriciousness in the imposition of the punishment were inevitable, and given the extreme nature of the punishment, constitutionally intolerable. The statutes we have approved in *Gregg*, *Proffitt* and *Jurek* were designed to eliminate each of these defects."[274] Whether Justice Stevens would condemn statutes with procedural safeguards against those two defects on the basis of evidence of actual arbitrariness in their administration in line with *Furman* cannot be considered certain.[275]

Justice O'Connor

Justice O'Connor joined the Court too late to take part in any decision bearing directly on the arbitrariness theory until now. Although decidedly supporting the death penalty in the capital cases on which she has sat, Justice O'Connor has also indicated that she supports the constitutional policy of requiring special procedures for capital cases.

In *Eddings v. Oklahoma*, Justice O'Connor wrote a concurring opinion "to address more fully why this case must be remanded in light of *Lockett v. Ohio* . . . , which requires the trial court to consider and weigh all of the mitigating evidence concerning the petitioner's family background and personal history."[276] Agreeing that the capital sentencer must be permitted to consider the youthfulness of the defendant as a mitigating factor, she explained her position as follows:

> [T]his Court has gone to extraordinary measures to ensure that the prisoner sentenced to be executed is afforded process that will guarantee, as much as is humanly possible, that the sentence was not imposed out of whim, passion, prejudice, or mistake. Surely, no less can be required when the defendant is a minor.[277]

Justice O'Connor has voted to reverse death sentences in two other cases. In *Arizona v. Rumsey*,[278] she wrote the opinion for the Court holding that the double jeopardy clause prohibited the imposition of a death sentence after a prison sentence was reversed on appeal because the sentencing judge misinterpreted an aggravating circumstance so that he erroneously believed that it did not apply. In *Caldwell v. Mississippi*,[279] she wrote a concurring opinion agreeing that the death penalty in that case should be reversed because the prosecutor told the jury that its decision would be reviewed for correctness by the state supreme court, but urged that accurate instructions to the jury regarding postsentencing procedures would be constitutional. Justice O'Connor has participated in 15 other death penalty cases, silently joining the majority in 13 of them.[280] In *California v. Ramos*,[281] she wrote the opinion for the Court upholding an instruction to a capital sentencing jury informing it accurately that the governor has power to commute a sentence of life imprisonment without parole to one that would include the possibility of parole. In *Enmund v. Florida*,[282] Justice O'Connor wrote a dissent that Justice Powell (as well as Chief Justice Burger and Justice Rehnquist) joined, arguing that the death penalty is not excessive for accomplice felony–murder. Justice O'Connor did urge that, because the trial judge erroneously believed that the defendant shot the victims, he did not give fair consideration to the minor nature of the defendant's participation as a mitigating factor and therefore the case should be remanded.

Justice O'Connor joined Justice Powell's dissent in *Stephens v. Kemp*.[283] Her signature on Justice Powell's ambiguous dictum in that opinion is too slender a basis for surmise about her position on the basic issue. It seems, however, to align her with Justice Powell in favor of enforcing exceptional procedural requirements in capital cases but uncertain to be persuaded to strike down any system as long as it does include such procedures, regardless of the pattern of the outcomes it produces.

Justice White

After casting a deciding vote against the death penalty in *Furman*, Justice White voted to uphold the death penalty in all five of the 1976 decisions, in the guided discretion as well as the mandatory systems, and —although since then he has voted in favor of the death penalty in some cases and against it in others depending on the nature of the challenge to the proceedings in the particular case—he has been responsible for a decisive vote in only one more capital case: *Enmund v. Florida*.[284] Indeed, in the 1976 decisions, Justice White not only replaced Justice Powell in the bloc supporting the death penalty but wrote an opinion in each of the five cases that Chief Justice Burger and Justice Rehnquist joined.[285]

In *Gregg*, Justice White stated the issue as "whether the death penalty may be carried out for murder under the Georgia legislative scheme consistent with the decision in *Furman*."[286] His five 1976 opinions explained why the new death penalty statutes gave him "reason to expect"[287] or "good reason to anticipate"[288] that they would avoid the infirmities identified by him and Justices Stewart and Douglas in *Furman*.[289] Clearly, he made his judgment on the promise of that result presented by the new statutes on their face: "I cannot accept the naked assertion that the effort is bound to fail."[290] He thus accepted his opinion, together with those of Justices Stewart and Douglas in *Furman*, as the governing law. Moreover, Chief Justice Burger and Justice Rehnquist, by joining Justice White's opinions, acquiesced in the *Furman* rationale.[291] Yet those three justices did not join in the plurality opinions written by Justices Stewart, Powell, and Stevens in the *Gregg, Proffitt*, and *Jurek* cases that employed the same rationale.

Justice White carefully embraced the arbitrariness theory of Justice Stewart and the discrimination theory of Justice Douglas in his opinions.[292] He concluded that "if the Georgia Supreme Court properly performs the task assigned to it under the Georgia statutes, death sentences imposed for discriminatory reasons or wantonly or freakishly for any given category of crimes will be set aside."[293] He also emphasized his own infrequency theory.[294] Thus he found the mandatory death penalty statutes in North Carolina and Louisiana easier to accept as constitutional than the guided discretion statutes,[295] although the mandatory statutes were the ones that Justices Stewart, Powell, and Stevens voted to strike down.[296] Justice White made clear that his judgment was based only on the information then available: "As I see it, we are now in no position to rule that the State's present law, having eliminated the overt discretionary power of juries, suffers from the same constitutional infirmities which led this Court to invalidate the Georgia death penalty statute in *Furman v. Georgia*."[297] Justice White simply had no experience under mandatory (or guided discretion) death penalty statutes to compare with his 10 years of exposure to the administration of standardless discretionary death penalty statutes on which to base a judgment about their operation in terms of frequency or fairness in achieving death penalties. He referred to no information about the number of death penalties meted out under the new mandatory statutes in Louisiana and North Carolina. The statutes had not, however, been in existence long enough for the absence of such information to be significant. Justice White's opinions in those cases made clear that he was willing to assume that their mandatory structure would yield a different pattern from what he had observed under the pre-*Furman* statutes.

Justice White did have numbers available about the death sentences imposed under the guided discretion system in Texas.[298] The experience there was still preliminary, and Justice White did not rely on the numbers to approve the statute. Instead, he assessed the statute there and in the other guided discretion states, Georgia and Florida, on their face.[299] Thus, he wrote:

The Georgia legislature has plainly made an effort to guide the jury in the exercise of its discretion, while at the same time permitting the jury to dispense mercy on the basis of factors too intangible to write into a statute, and I cannot accept the naked assertion that the effort is bound to fail. As the types of murders for which the death penalty may be imposed become more narrowly defined and are limited to those which are particularly serious or for which the death penalty is peculiarly appropriate as they are in Georgia by reason of the aggravating-circumstance requirement, it becomes reasonable to expect that juries—even given discretion not to impose the death penalty—will impose the death penalty in a substantial portion of the cases so defined.[300]

Justice White was also impressed that the Georgia Supreme Court had the responsibility to conduct a proportionality review of death sentences and to set aside such a sentence "whenever juries across the State impose it only rarely for the type of crime in question."[301] He noted favorably that

the Georgia Supreme Court concluded that the death penalty was so rarely imposed for the crime of robbery that it set aside the sentences on the robbery counts and effectively foreclosed that penalty from being imposed for that crime in the future under the legislative scheme now in existence. Similarly, the Georgia Supreme Court has determined that juries impose the death sentence too rarely with respect to certain classes of rape. . . . However, it concluded that juries "generally throughout the state" have imposed the death penalty for those who murder witnesses to armed robberies. . . . Consequently it affirmed the sentences in this case on the murder counts.[302]

Justice White thus made clear that in ruling on the constitutionality of this new statutory procedure, he was assuming that it would effectively assure that the death penalty was imposed with sufficient frequency to serve as a general deterrent for capital crime, and not "for discriminatory reasons or wantonly or freakishly for any given category of crime."[303] Accordingly, he seemed to leave open the possibility that experiential data of the kind that convinced him of the invalidity of the pre-*Furman* death penalty statutes might cause him to reevaluate his approval. Indeed, he noted that the guided discretion statutes leave juries considerable opportunity to exercise unbridled discretion.[304] He was willing, however, to permit the states to demonstrate that the new procedures, especially appellate review, could protect against juries abusing that opportunity.

In a sense, then, Justice White viewed the new death penalty statutes in much the same posture as he considered the pre-*Furman* statutes in *McGautha*. Justice White joined the majority opinion in *McGautha* and expressly reaffirmed that position in *Roberts v. Louisiana*.[305] *McGautha* treated the death penalty statutes on their face.[306] From that perspective, the Court judged that the unguided discretion procedure was as fair a system as could be designed. Only a year later, in *Furman*, Justice White consulted his 10 years of observation of death penalty cases to decide that the invocation of that penalty occurred too arbitrarily and too infrequently to serve any criminal justice purpose. Obviously, most of that experience had accumulated by the time of *McGautha*, but Justice White took no account of it in deciding the purely procedural issue in that case. He did in *Furman*, however, voting that the administration of the death penalty was unconstitutional—without directing any particular corrective procedure.

In the 1976 cases, Justice White reviewed new statutes that endeavored to provide protective procedures of two basic types, mandatory and guided discretion. He noted that these different procedures were promising in their potential to correct the deficiencies of the pre-*Furman* statutes. He had no experience that demonstrated the contrary and the parties did not present any data to that effect; indeed, they could not do so in view of the short time the statutes had been in effect. Accordingly, Justice White had no basis for rendering the kind of judgment that he pronounced in *Furman*. Only with time could he make the necessary observations of the death penalty practice of the kind that informed his vote in *Furman*.

Justice White further illuminated his position in his separate opinion in *Lockett v. Ohio*.[307] In *Lockett*, the plurality decision[308] held that "the Eighth and Fourteenth Amendments require that the sentencer, in all but the rarest kind of capital case, not be precluded from considering, *as a mitigating factor*, any aspect of a defendant's character or record and any of the circumstances of the offense that the defendant proffers as a basis for a sentence less than death."[309] The Court thus insisted that the death penalty decision be "individualized."[310] Because the Ohio capital sentencing statute at issue in *Lockett* "did not permit the sentencing judge to consider, as mitigating factors, [the defendant's] character, prior record, age, lack of specific intent to cause death, and her relatively minor part in the crime,"[311] the Court overturned the death sentence.

It fell to Justice White to complain: "The Court has now completed its about-face since *Furman*. . . . Today it is held . . . that the sentencer may constitutionally impose the death penalty only as an exercise of his unguided discretion after being presented with all circumstances which the defendant might believe to be conceivably relevant to the appropriateness of the penalty for the individual offender."[312] Accordingly, Justice White dissented from the plurality's rationale:

> I greatly fear that the effect of the Court's decision today will be to compel constitutionally a restoration of the state of affairs at the time *Furman* was decided, where the death penalty is imposed so er-

ratically and the threat of execution is so attenuated for even the most atrocious murders that "its imposition would then be the pointless and needless extinction of life with only marginal contributions to any discernible social or public purposes." . . . By requiring as a matter of constitutional law that sentencing authorities be permitted to consider and in their discretion to act upon any and all mitigating circumstances, the Court permits them to refuse to impose the death penalty no matter what the circumstances of the crime. This invites a return to the pre-*Furman* days when the death penalty was reserved for those very few for whom society has least consideration.[313]

Lockett, in the context of the 1976 decisions, certainly does challenge the meaning of *Furman*. *Furman* compelled the reform of all death penalty statutes, and the 1976 decisions approved those that added new procedures, primarily a separate sentencing hearing with guidelines to narrow the jury's discretion. Resurrecting the *McGautha* principle that it is not possible "to give an exhaustive list of the relevant considerations or the way in which they may be affected by the presence or absence of other circumstances,"[314] *Lockett* insisted that the states may not limit the category of mitigating circumstances. The Court found no constitutional inconsistency between this decision, enlarging as a constitutional imperative the range of discretionary factors, and *Furman*, condemning an excessively discretionary death penalty system.[315]

Lockett tested the limits of Justice White's tolerance for the new procedures, based on his assumption that the new procedures would control the jury discretion. With *Lockett*, Justice White was no longer content to confirm the new procedures on their face and await any possible indication that they could not perform as expected. Now he concluded that the new statutes had been infused with too much discretion, becoming too reminiscent of the pre-*Furman* statutes, so that he sounded an alarm without waiting for his experience under the new statutes to accumulate evidence of their operation. His alarm was for the prospect that juries would now be able to reduce the frequency of death sentences below the utilitarian level.

The puzzling aspect of this position is that the discretionary range that the Court required in *Lockett* was already a feature of the Georgia and Florida statutes that Justice White voted to approve in *Gregg*[316] and *Proffitt*.[317] Of course, Justice White voted in *Gregg* and *Proffitt* to permit statutes including that broad discretionary feature when it had been established by state law. In *Lockett*, by contrast, Justice White objected to its inclusion by means of a Supreme Court directive. His objection, however, that the effect of that feature would be to return the statute to the pre-*Furman* situation was an objection that the requirement imposed a procedure that would bring the statute under the *Furman* ban. Yet Justice

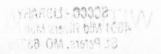

White upheld the Georgia and Florida statutes with the same feature. He was thus unwilling to defer to the *Lockett* majority's judgment that the increased discretion would not doom the statute to the erratic administration of the pre-*Furman* era, notwithstanding his acquiescence in the same judgment by state legislatures.

Justice White's dissent from the Court's expansion of the discretionary range in *Lockett* appears inconsistent with his dissent two years later in *Godfrey v. Georgia*,[318] where the Court endeavored to narrow the jury's permissible discretionary range. In *Godfrey*, a plurality of the Court[319] held unconstitutionally vague the aggravating circumstance in the Georgia statute that the murder "was outrageously or wantonly vile, horrible, or inhuman in that it involved torture, depravity of mind, or an aggravated battery to the victim," as it had been interpreted by the Georgia Supreme Court. The plurality observed that almost every murder could qualify under that standard. Indeed, the plurality characterized the facts of the crime in that case as not "reflecting a consciousness materially more 'depraved' than that of any person guilty of murder."[320]

Justice White took issue with that characterization.[321] More important, however, he argued that, especially in view of Georgia's appellate review of capital sentences, the aggravating factor was not too broad. That position seems to clash with his vigorous objection to a requirement broadening the guidelines in *Lockett*, where he argued that the effect would be to yield too much discretion to the jury.

The difference is that *Godfrey* involved leeway for an aggravating factor, while *Lockett* involved mitigating factors. Justice White disagreed with both the Court's insistence that the states "channel the sentencer's discretion by 'clear and objective standards' that provide 'specific and detailed guidance,'"[322] with regard to aggravating factors, in *Godfrey* and also the Court's insistence that the states not preclude consideration of "any aspect of a defendant's character or record or any of the circumstances of the offense," with regard to mitigating factors, in *Lockett*. For Justice White, those positions do not conflict, but serve his concern of assuring adequate numbers of death sentences. *Godfrey* reduced the number of convicted murderers who qualify for that penalty by insisting that the scope of the aggravating factor be restricted. *Lockett* increased the number of convicted murderers qualifying for capital punishment who might nevertheless escape it by insisting that the mitigating factors relating to the background of the murderer and the nature of the offense be unlimited. Both decisions, therefore, had the effect of reducing the number of likely death sentences, and Justice White objected for that reason. In his dissents in these cases, his concern with the number of death sentences stood out even more clearly than it had in his opinions in *Furman* and in the 1976 decisions.

Justice White's inclination to tolerate a more flexible range of discretion for aggravating circumstances also appeared in *Barclay v. Florida*,[323] *California v. Ramos*,[324] and *Wainwright v. Goode*,[325] all decided in 1983. In each of those cases, Justice White joined in the prevailing position. In *Barclay*, the trial judge considered the defendant's prior record as an aggravating circumstance, despite the fact that state law did not establish that as an aggravating circumstance. The Court upheld the death sentence. The plurality opinion, which Justice White joined, reasoned that the Constitution did not prohibit the state from including a defendant's prior record as an aggravating circumstance.[326] It then concluded that the state supreme court's conclusion that the consideration of this extralegal circumstance was a harmless state law error did not give rise to any federal constitutional concern. Similarly, in *Wainwright v. Goode*, the Court, including Justice White, declined to interfere with the same state supreme court's judgment that the trial judge's use (again in violation of state law) of future dangerousness as an aggravating factor in sentencing a defendant to death did not require reversal.

In *Ramos*, the trial judge instructed the capital sentencing jury, in accordance with state law, that the governor could commute a sentence of life imprisonment without possibility of parole to a sentence that included eligibility for parole. The Court interpreted that instruction "to inject into the sentencing calculus a consideration akin to the aggravating factor of future dangerousness,"[327] and upheld it because it just gave the jury accurate information.[328] The Court, including Justice White, held:

> [T]he fact that the jury is given no specific guidance on how the commutation factor is to figure into its determination presents no constitutional problem. . . . [T]he Constitutional prohibition on arbitrary and capricious sentencing is not violated by a capital sentencing scheme that permits the jury to exercise unbridled discretion in determining whether the death penalty should be imposed after it has found that the defendant is a member of the class made eligible for that penalty by statute.[329]

Justice White was satisfied in these three cases to permit the inclusion of discretionary factors influencing a decision in favor of the death penalty into the guidelines used by the sentencing jury or judge. This position is congruent with his opposition to a requirement narrowing the sentencing guidelines for the jury in *Godfrey*, for *Barclay*, *Ramos*, and *Goode* also involved aggravating factors.

Justice White has demonstrated that his interest in numbers is not met simply by having death sentences imposed; it includes seeing them carried out. He wrote the opinion for the Court in *Barefoot v. Estelle*,[330] in which the Court established procedures to expedite review of federal habeas corpus challenges to death sentences. It may seem strange, at first glance, that a justice who voted in 1972 to hold the death penalty unconstitutional also voted in 1983 to expedite the processing of capital cases. The explanation lies in the fact that Justice White's position in *Furman* was neutral with regard to capital punishment as such and reflected only frustration that it was invoked too arbitrarily and also too infrequently to serve as a deterrent. His position after the new statutory procedures were adopted reflects an effort to ensure that those new procedures be given a chance to produce a greater number of death sentences.

The emergence of concern for the number of death sentences as a focus of Justice White's evaluation of the cruel and unusual punishment issue has not distracted him from his commitment to ensuring fair procedures in the capital sentencing process. In *Godfrey, Barclay, Ramos,* and *Goode,* Justice White upheld the aggravating factors because they were likely to produce more death sentences, but he judged also that they would so do without injecting any unfairness into the decision-making process. Moreover, Justice White has joined the Court in several decisions setting aside death sentences arrived at by a constitutionally inadequate process.[331] For example, in *Green v. Georgia,*[332] Justice White supported the summary decision setting aside a death sentence because of the exclusion of a hearsay statement attributed to a co-defendant that he killed the kidnap victim after ordering the defendant to run an errand. The Court, including Justice White, relied on *Lockett* in explaining that the statement was highly relevant to the punishment phase of the trial because it related to the circumstances of the offense. Similarly, in *Estelle v. Smith,*[333] Justice White concurred in finding a violation of *Miranda*[334] and of the right to counsel in the use at the penalty hearing of the testimony of a psychiatrist appointed to examine the defendant only for competency. Justice White also wrote the opinion for the Court in *Adams v. Texas,* holding that *Witherspoon* continued to be good law because, despite the new procedures, the process of deciding life or death "is not an exact science, and the jurors . . . unavoidably exercise a range of judgment and discretion,"[335] although he later joined, in *Wainwright v. Witt,* in relaxing the *Witherspoon* standard.

Moreover, Justice White is not seeking numbers just for quantity but for a more qualitative concern with frequency. Chief Justice Burger, in *Furman,* interpreted Justice White's position as "more concerned with a regularized sentencing process than with the aggregate number of death sentences imposed for all crimes."[336] He has consistently emphasized concern about arbitrariness in conjunction with concern about infrequency. In *Furman,* Justice White complained not only about infrequency but also "that there is no meaningful basis for distinguishing the few cases in which [the death penalty] is imposed from the many in which it is not";[337] in *Proffitt,* he used the phrase "freakishly or rarely";[338] in *Jurek,* "so seldom and arbitrarily";[339] and in *Woodson,* so "seldom and arbitrarily" again.[340] Justice White has emphasized the infrequency prong of this combination, but not to the extent that it might be anticipated that he would not be constitutionally offended if the pattern of death penalty imposition were "often and arbitrary."[341] Aberrational use of the death penalty for cases that do not ordinarily attract it has received his condemnation. He wrote the plurality opinions in both *Coker v. Georgia*[342] and *Enmund v. Florida*.[343] In *Coker*, the Court held that "a sentence of death is grossly disproportionate and excessive punishment for the crime of rape."[344] In *Enmund*, the Court relied on *Coker* to hold the death penalty unconstitutional for the accomplice of a felony murderer where the accomplice did not intend or anticipate the killing. In both cases, Justice White's opinions expressed subjective judgments that rape and unintentional killings were not proper subjects for capital punishment and also canvassed the legislative judgments of other states and the sentencing decisions in other cases of the same kind that showed that the death penalty was only rarely reserved for these situations. Although those occasional cases would augment the overall death penalty numbers, they would not do so in a way that furthered the deterrence function. Justice White's concern for numbers is important only because of his view of the operation of deterrence. Thus, he wrote for the Court in *Enmund*:

> [H]owever often death occurs in the course of a felony such as robbery, the death penalty is rarely imposed on one only vicariously guilty of the murder, a fact which further attenuates its possible utility as an effective deterrence.[345]

Indeed, Justice White expressed an even more overarching view of the deterrence perspective: "We are quite unconvinced . . . that the threat that the death penalty will be imposed for murder will measurably deter one who does not kill and has no intention or purpose that life will be taken."[346] This language suggests that even if sentencing juries or judges regularly imposed death sentences for accomplices who did not intend murder, Justice White might not find that result consistent with the Constitution.

Justice White has never written whether he believes the death penalty deters capital crime. In *Roberts v. Louisiana*, he wrote that "the relative efficacy of capital punishment and life imprisonment to deter others from crime remains a matter about which reasonable men and reasonable legislators may easily differ."[347] In that light, he deferred to the legislative judgment. Although accepting in principle the justifications for the death penalty of retribution and specific deterrence,[348] he has steadfastly measured the validity of the use of that penalty and the processes for meting it out according to their impact on general deterrence. That explains his concern for quality of numbers—frequency—in death penalty decisions if that penalty is to meet his constitutional test. At the same time, Justice White has never waivered from his *Furman* concern about arbitrariness in the actual administration of the death penalty.

PART 7.

Appellate Proportionality Review

The procedures that primarily impressed the plurality in the 1976 decisions as holding out promise for controlling the exercise of discretion to avoid the pre-*Furman* arbitrariness were, first, a separate hearing to determine the sentence upon conviction of a capital offense,[349] and, second, guidelines for the sentencing decision consisting of aggravating and, in Florida, mitigating circumstances.[350] Justice Stewart explained in *Gregg* that the *Furman* concerns "are best met by a system that provides for a bifurcated proceeding at which the sentencing authority is apprised of the information relevant to the imposition of sentence and provided with standards to guide its use of the information."[351] The Georgia and Florida statutes contained such procedures in a more neatly fashioned package than the Texas statute, but the plurality judged the Texas scheme to be essentially equivalent to the other two.[352] Although satisfied with the potential of those procedures, the plurality emphasized: "We do not intend to suggest that only the above-described procedures would be permissible under *Furman* . . . ."[353]

Even with the new front-line safeguards the capital sentencing procedure retains considerable discretion.[354] The sentencing standards only "reduce the likelihood that [the jury] will impose a sentence that fairly can be called capricious or arbitrary."[355] Accordingly, "to assure that the death penalty will not be imposed on a capriciously selected group of convicted defendants,"[356] both Georgia and Florida provided for appellate review of capital sentences.[357] In Florida, the law "does not require the court to conduct any specific form of review."[358] The trial judge, however, "must justify the imposition of a death sentence with written findings,"[359] and the state supreme court in fact "reviews each death sentence to ensure that similar results are reached in similar cases."[360] In Georgia, the procedure is more precisely defined. The Georgia Supreme Court is required to "review every death sentence to determine whether it was imposed under the influence of passion, prejudice, or any other arbitrary factor, whether the evidence supports the findings of a statutory aggravating circumstance, and '[w]hether the sentence of death is excessive or disproportionate to the penalty imposed in similar cases, considering both the crime and the defendant.'"[361]

Ideally administered, this appellate review function could provide an effective check on the capital sentencing process.[362] The ideal would, however, constitute a massive task.[363] With automatic appeal of all capital sentences, the state supreme court would have a considerable quantum of information about cases in which the sentencing authority decided in favor of a capital sentence. The court would have only haphazard information about the cases in which the judge or jury declined to impose a capital sentence. Those cases would come before the appellate court only if the defendant decided to appeal and before the state supreme court only if the defendant—or the state—succeeded in obtaining a second level of appellate review. They would not be identified as capital cases, however, and the issues would not generally involve questions of capital punishment. Without some special effort, therefore, the state supreme court would not notice these cases in a capital punishment survey.

Moreover, a far broader group of cases would escape the attention of the state supreme court altogether. These are the cases in which the prosecutor declined to initiate or to pursue a capital charge, including those in which the defendant pleaded guilty to a noncapital offense. The absence of these cases from the state supreme court's survey might seriously skew its impression of the evenhandedness of the administration of the death penalty. For example, assume that in a state 100 defendants, 98 of them white and 2 of them nonwhite, were charged with driving the getaway car for an armed robbery felony—murder in which they knew that their accomplices intended to use deadly force if necessary to assure the success of their crimes. Assume further that the prosecutors permitted the white defendants to avoid the risk of the death penalty by pleading guilty to the underlying felony or to a noncapital homicide, but insisted that the nonwhite defendants stand trial for capital murder. Assume, finally, that the juries sentenced the two nonwhite defendants to death. The picture that this thoroughly hypothetical scenario would present to the state supreme court would be one of consistent imposition of the death penalty for felony murder for a getaway driver who anticipated a killing by his armed robbery accomplice. Essentially 100 percent of the cases visible to the court in that category resulted in death sentences. The other cases would change the picture considerably: in fact, only 2 percent of all the cases resulted in death sentences, and those only the ones with nonwhite defendants. To see the accurate picture, the state supreme court would need a composite of all the cases, not merely those that resulted in death sentences.

Meeting that ideal is unrealistic.[364] In *Gregg*, the Supreme Court noted that the Georgia Supreme Court points toward it.[365] That court does consider appealed cases in which a life sentence was imposed, and has discretion to consider nonappealed cases.[366] In addition, it has a staff to compile the relevant data.[367] Finally, that court is required to specify in its opinion the similar cases that it took into consideration.[368] In Florida, however, the state supreme court compares death penalty cases before it only with previous death penalty cases.[369] Interestingly, the Supreme Court observed that even with this limited appellate review, both state supreme courts had by that time reversed several death sentences on proportionality grounds[370]—thereby demonstrating a role for this appellate process even with the new sentencing stage procedures.

The plurality upheld the statutes in each of the three states without discussion of their appellate review provisions, then discussed those provisions as additional safeguards. In a similar vein, in *Roberts v. Louisiana*, the plurality opinion, explaining its rejection of the Louisiana "mandatory" death penalty scheme, noted: "As in North Carolina, there are no standards provided to guide the jury . . . , and there is no meaningful appellate review of the jury's decision."[371]

In *Gregg*, the plurality held:

> The provision for appellate review in the Georgia capital sentencing system serves as a check against the random or arbitrary imposition of the death penalty. In particular, the proportionality review substantially eliminates the possibility that a person will be sentenced to die by the action of an aberrant jury. If a time comes when juries generally do not impose the death sentence in a certain kind of murder case,[372] the appellate review procedures assure that no defendant convicted under such circumstances will suffer a sentence of death.[373]

In *Proffitt*, the Supreme Court approved the appellate proportionality review process in Florida as well, noting that, although not as elaborate as Georgia's and without

> a rigid objective test as its standard of review for all cases, it does not follow that the appellate review process is ineffective or arbitrary. In fact, it is apparent that the Florida court has undertaken responsibility to perform its function of death sentence review with a maximum of rationality and consistency. For example, it has several times compared the circumstances of a case under review with those of previous cases in which it has assessed the imposition of death sentences.[374]

The Texas statute that the Court reviewed in *Jurek* provided for appellate review without saying anything about review of the sentence. Nevertheless, upholding the statute because it contained procedures equivalent to the bifurcated sentencing hearing and sentencing guidelines, the Court added, without elaboration:

> By providing prompt judicial review of the jury's decision in a court with statewide jurisdiction, Texas has provided a means to promote the evenhanded, rational and consistent imposition of death sentences under law.[375]

The plurality thus regarded appellate review of a capital sentence as highly desirable but not necessary to the constitutionality of a state's death penalty process.[376] For the plurality, the purpose to be achieved by such review was to protect against comparatively disproportionate infliction of the death penalty.[377] To the extent that any risk of arbitrariness survives the new capital sentencing procedures, "it is minimized by [the] appellate review system . . . ."[378] This purpose could best be assured by a thorough review of all potentially capital cases. The plurality did not, by any means, insist that a death penalty statute measure up to that standard. It expressed regard for the Georgia scheme that strived in that direction, but it also upheld not only the Florida statute—where the Florida Supreme Court had taken a similar stride, although without an express statutory directive —but also the Texas statute, despite the absence of any special procedure with this objective and of any special practice by the state court to accomplish it. Appellate proportionality review helped secure the plurality's approval, but the plurality did not require it and certainly did not require it in any particular form.

Justice White's opinion in *Gregg* exuded more enthusiasm for appellate proportionality review. He introduced it as "[a]n important aspect of the new Georgia legislative scheme,"[379] and described its importance as follows:

> [T]he Georgia Legislature was not satisfied with a system which might, but also might not, turn out in practice to result in death sentences being imposed with reasonable consistency for certain serious murders. Instead, it gave the Georgia Supreme Court the power and the obligation to perform precisely the task which three Justices of this Court, whose opinions were necessary to the result, performed in *Furman*; namely, the task of deciding whether *in fact* the death penalty was being administered for any given class of crime in a discriminatory, standardless, or rare fashion.[380]

Justice White was satisfied that this review furnished the ultimate answer to his concern about infrequency,[381] as well as concerns about discrimination and arbitrariness. The Georgia Supreme Court "must do much more than determine whether the penalty was lawfully imposed,"[382] he noted. The statute required it to "set aside the death sentence whenever juries across the State impose it only rarely for the type of crime in question; but to require it to affirm death sentences whenever juries across the State generally impose it for the crime in question."[383]

In *Proffitt* and *Jurek*, however, Justice White wrote brief concurring opinions that omitted any discussion of appellate proportionality review. In both cases, he approved the statutes on the ground that, in Florida, "the sentencing judge is *required* to impose the death penalty on all first-degree murderers as to whom the statutory aggravating factors outweigh the mitigating factors,"[384] and, in Texas, "when a murder occurs in one of the five circumstances set out in the statute, the death penalty *must* be imposed if the jury also makes the certain additional findings against the defendant."[385] Thus interpreting those statutes to mandate the death penalty in the capital categories of cases, Justice White did not discuss any need for appellate review. Similarly, the mandatory death penalty statutes in North Carolina and Louisiana passed his scrutiny without any discussion of appellate review. Important, though not essential, for a system with express reservation of a discretionary responsibility, it did not even require discussion for a system that expressed the sentencing standard in mandatory terms.[386]

After the 1976 decisions, the Court encountered a series of cases that contained constitutional violations that it might have expected state appellate review to correct. The Court reversed the death sentences on the basis of the specific violations without expressing any disillusionment about its hopes for the appellate process in death penalty cases.

The first case in the series was *Gardner v. Florida*,[387] in which the Court reviewed a Florida death sentence that had survived that state's appellate review in a 5-to-2 *per curiam* opinion. The Court vacated the death sentence on the ground that the judge who imposed it had relied in part on information in a presentence report that had not been disclosed to the parties. The Court did not criticize the appellate review for failure to correct this error.[388] Justice Marshall, however, used the occasion to contend that the trial court's action and also the fact "that the Florida Supreme Court affirmed the sentence without discussing the omission and without concern that it did not even have the entire report before it . . . calls into question the very basis for this Court's approval of that system in *Proffitt*."[389] Justice Marshall argued that "the Florida Supreme Court engaged in precisely the 'cursory or rubber-stamp review' that the joint opinion in *Proffitt* trusted would not occur":[390] it did not discuss the undisclosed report issue, and it did not discuss the comparative proportionality of the death sentence in this case, although the two dissenting justices voted to overturn the sentence on both grounds. The Florida Supreme Court opinion, Justice Marshall pointed out, consisted of only a brief conclusory analysis; it did not make an independent determination whether death was the appropriate penalty and did not discuss any comparison with the facts in similar cases.[391] The rest of the Court, however, made no point of the appellate review process in the case, reversing on the ground of the sentencing judge's violation of due process.

In *Coker v. Georgia*,[392] the Court held the death penalty for rape unconstitutional. The rationale for that decision was that "a sentence of death is grossly disproportionate and excessive punishment for the crime of rape."[393] The court based that decision on three factors: (1) its own judgment[394]; (2) the general legislative rejection of the death penalty for rape among the other states[395]; and (3) the sentencing decisions of juries.[396] With regard to the behavior of juries, the Court looked only to sentences in Georgia because Georgia was the only state with a death penalty for rape generally. Considering all rape convictions actually reviewed by the Georgia Supreme Court since 1973, the Court found there had been a total of 63 with 6 death sentences, one of which had been set aside. Agreeing that 6 death penalties was "not a negligible number,"[397] the Court nevertheless found support for its conclusion from the fact that "in the vast majority of cases, at least 9 out of 10 juries have not imposed the death sentence."[398]

Justice White wrote the *Coker* opinion. Yet, in *Gregg*, he had noted that the Georgia Supreme Court conducted its proportionality review of death sentences for rape by dividing rape into classes and that it had set aside some death sentences because of its determination "that juries impose the death sentence too rarely with respect to certain classes of rape."[399] In its decision in *Coker*, however, the Georgia Supreme Court had said:

> We have compared the sentence in this case, considering both the crime and the defendant, with other similar cases and conclude the sentence of death is not excessive or disproportionate to the penalty imposed in those cases. Those similar cases we considered in reviewing the case are listed in the appendix.[400]

The appendix listed 10 cases in which Georgia juries had sentenced to death defendants convicted of rape. Seven of the cases arose before *Furman*, but the Supreme Court in *Gregg* approved the practice of considering such cases.[401] Three of the cases arose under the post-*Furman* Georgia statute. The Georgia Supreme Court affirmed 2 of those cases and reversed the third on its proportionality review. Justice White did not explain in *Coker* why he rejected the state court's judgment. Clearly, however, he did not treat the state's proportionality review as the final answer to the constitutional proportionality concerns.[402]

The next case in this series was *Godfrey v. Georgia*.[403] In *Godfrey*, the Court reversed the death sentence because it was based on an unconstitutionally vague aggravating circumstance. Justice Stewart's opinion for four justices also evaluated the facts of the case, a shotgun killing by the defendant of his wife and her mother, who were resisting his efforts at a marital reconciliation. It concluded, "There is no principled way to distinguish this case, in which the death penalty was imposed, from the many cases in which it was not."[404] Justice Stewart did not cite any comparable cases where the death penalty had not been imposed. The Georgia Supreme Court, in affirming the penalty, cited 15 cases that it said "support the affirmance of the death penalty in this case."[405] Dissenting, Justice White described the crime in very different terms from Justice Stewart[406] and concluded that a rational fact finder could have found that it involved torture, depravity of mind, or an aggravated battery to the victims.[407] Justice Stewart's opinion was not based on this evaluation, however, but on a legal conclusion that the aggravating circumstance was too vague. It therefore did not fault the proportionality review but the judicial interpretation of the aggravating circumstance.

Justice Marshall perceived this case as part of a pattern strongly suggesting "that appellate courts are incapable of guaranteeing the kind of objectivity and evenhandedness that the Court contemplated and hoped for in *Gregg*."[408] The Court was not convinced. It preferred to repair problems at the trial or sentencing stage[409] rather than reconsider its judgment of the new system simply because such problems continued to arise. Nevertheless, in two decisions, the Court continued to assign considerable credit to appellate proportionality review as an ultimate safeguard.

One case was *Zant v. Stephens*.[410] In that case, the jury sentenced the defendant to death for murder after finding three aggravating circumstances. One of those aggravating circumstances, the state supreme court later held in a separate case, was unconstitutionally vague. On defendant's appeal, however, the state supreme court held that the other two aggravating circumstances supported the sentence. The Supreme Court affirmed, satisfied with the procedure at sentencing but emphasizing also that the sentence had passed the state supreme court's comparative proportionality review. The Court said that the two aggravating circumstances "adequately differentiate this case in an objective, evenhanded, and substantively rational way from the many Georgia murder cases in which the death penalty may not be imposed,"[411] and added: "Moreover, the Georgia Supreme Court in this case reviewed the death sentence to determine whether it was arbitrary, excessive, or disproportionate,"[412] including a comparison of cases in which the death penalty was not imposed as well as cases in which it was.[413] The Court then emphasized:

> Our decision in this case depends in part on the existence of an important procedural safeguard, the mandatory appellate review of each death sentence to avoid arbitrariness and to assure proportionality. We accept that court's view that the subsequent invalidation of one of several statutory aggravating circumstances does not automatically require reversal of the death penalty, having been assured that a death sentence will be set aside if the invalidation of an aggravating circumstance makes the penalty arbitrary or capricious. . . . As we noted in *Gregg*, . . . we have also been assured that a death sentence will be vacated if it is excessive or substantially disproportionate to the penalties that have been imposed under similar circumstances.[414]

In *Barclay v. Florida*,[415] in the same term, the Court disposed of a similar problem in a Florida case in the same way. Again the Court emphasized: "In this case, as in *Zant*, our decision is buttressed by the Florida Supreme Court's practice of reviewing each death sentence to compare it with other Florida capital cases and to determine whether the punishment is too great."[416] In a concurring opinion, Justice Stevens, with Justice Powell, also attributed special reliance in affirming the sentence to the Florida Supreme Court's proportionality review.[417] In dissent, Justices Marshall and Brennan characterized that review as perfunctory.[418] The rest of the Court entertained no criticism of the Florida Supreme Court in the course of considering its review as an important factor in the decision.

In *Pulley v. Harris*,[419] the Court confirmed that appellate proportionality review is not a prerequisite of a constitutional capital sentencing structure. In *Pulley,* the Court upheld the California capital punishment system in the absence of such review because California adequately afforded at the sentencing stage the safeguard of a bifurcated proceeding at which the sentencing authority is given guidelines. In *Maggio v. Williams,*[420] moreover, the Court vacated a stay of execution for a Louisiana defendant who argued that Louisiana's appellate proportionality review was inadequate because it was conducted only on a districtwide rather than statewide basis, concluding that the issue did not even warrant its consideration. Both of these cases involved challenges to the lack of adequate appellate review that were presented in the abstract. The defendants in *Pulley* and *Maggio* did not identify independent weaknesses in the systems that imposed their death sentences of a nature that the Court in *Zant* and *Barclay* held could survive attack if the state provided appellate review as a backup safeguard.

The determination that a state supreme court need not perform a proportionality review does not undermine the *Furman* proposition that a death penalty system must not be arbitrary. As it did in the 1976 cases, the Supreme Court in *Pulley* upheld the statute before it "on its face."[421] The Court assumed that the sentencing procedures would produce proportional results without appellate policing of them. By focusing on the statute on its face rather than in practice, it expressly left open, again, the possibility of a capital defendant proving otherwise.[422]

PART 8.

Discrimination versus Arbitrariness

All the justices on the Supreme Court would agree that proof of discrimination on the basis of the race of the defendant or any other invidious factor would invalidate a death sentence under the equal protection clause.[423] Chief Justice Burger, dissenting in *Furman* with Justices Blackmun, Powell, and Rehnquist, "noted that any equal protection claim is totally distinct from the Eighth Amendment question."[424]

> If a statute that authorizes the discretionary imposition of a particular penalty for a particular crime is used primarily against defendants of a certain race, and if the pattern of use can be fairly explained only by reference to the race of the defendants, the Equal Protection Clause of the Fourteenth Amendment forbids continued enforcement of that statute in its existing form.[425]

An equal protection claim would succeed only upon a showing that the penalty was "used primarily against defendants of a certain race" because an equal protection analysis requires a showing of intentional discrimination.[426] Chief Justice Burger made clear that the standard of proof would be high: "While no statistical survey could be expected to bring forth absolute and irrefutable proof of a discriminatory pattern of imposition, a strong showing would have to be made, taking all relevant factors into account."[427]

Justice Powell has recently begun to suggest that proof of discrimination in the particular case might be not only adequate but also necessary to satisfy the arbitrariness standard. In *Stephens v. Kemp*,[428] his opinion dissenting from an order granting a stay of execution gave him an opportunity to outline the standard by which he might evaluate statistical evidence. The Court granted the stay pending the decision of a case before the Eleventh Circuit involving a claim based on statistical evidence "that the Georgia death penalty statute is being applied in an arbitrary and discriminatory manner."[429] The dissent was not grounded on the potential merits of that claim but on a conclusion that the defendant's failure to raise the claim in an earlier federal habeas corpus petition constituted an abuse of the writ. Justice Powell, nevertheless, wrote that "[i]t should be apparent from the decisions of this Court since *Gregg* was decided that claims based merely on general statistics are likely to have little or no merit under statutes such as that in Georgia."[430] He did not identify the cases he had in mind or otherwise explain that statement. He did append a footnote to his dissent in which he suggested at least two requirements that he would demand of statistical evidence: that it be particularized to the case before the Court and that it show intentional discrimination. He wrote that the studies he was familiar with were "merely general statistical surveys that are hardly *particularized* with respect to any alleged 'intentional' racial discrimination. Surely, no contention can be made that the entire Georgia judicial system, at all levels, operates to discriminate in all cases. Arguments to this effect may have been directed to the type of statutes addressed in *Furman* . . . . As our subsequent cases make clear, such arguments cannot be taken seriously under statutes approved in *Gregg*."[431] In *Wainwright v. Ford*,[432] Justice Powell wrote an opinion concurring in a decision declining to vacate a stay of execution. In the course of his opinion he observed: "[W]e have held in two prior cases that the statistical evidence relied upon by Ford to support his claim of discrimination was not sufficient to raise a substantial ground upon which relief might be granted."[433] The two cases he cited were *Wainwright v. Adams*[434] and *Sullivan v. Wainwright*.[435] *Adams* was a decision granting a motion to vacate a stay of execution. The Court wrote no opinion. Justice Marshall dissented in an opinion suggesting that the majority may have acted on procedural grounds. *Sullivan* was a *per curiam* opinion denying a stay of execution. The opinion held that the Court found "no basis for disagreeing in this case," with the decisions of the Florida Supreme Court and the Eleventh Circuit that the white defendant had not presented sufficient evidence to show that the Florida system is unconstitutionally discriminatory.[436]

Justice Powell seems therefore to have focused on the issue of discrimination, disregarding the issue of arbitrariness. The Fourth[437] and Eleventh[438] circuits appear to have followed that same direction. In *McCleskey v. Kemp,* an *en banc* majority of the Eleventh Circuit stated, "Since *Gregg,* we have consistently held that to state a claim of racial discrimination in the application of a constitutional capital statute, intent and motive must be alleged."[439] The Court explained: "Due process and cruel and unusual punishment cases do not normally focus on the intent of the governmental actor. But where racial discrimination is claimed not on the basis of procedural faults or flaws in the structure of the law, but on the basis of the decisions made within that process, then purpose, intent and motive are a natural component of the proof that discrimination actually occurred."[440] It then held "that proof of a disparate impact alone is insufficient to invalidate a capital sentencing system, unless that disparate impact is so great that it compels a conclusion that the system is unprincipled, irrational, arbitrary and capricious such that purposeful discrimination— i.e., race is intentionally being used as a factor in sentencing—can be presumed to permeate the system."[441]

Furman, however, was decided on an arbitrariness theory and not on an equal protection theory, or on any theory based on racial factor. Only Justice Douglas mentioned a discrimination rationale in *Furman,* and he discussed arbitrariness as a constitutional concern as well.[442] Justices Stewart and White rejected racial discrimination as the rationale for their position in *Furman.* Justice White was content to conclude that "there is no meaningful way for distinguishing the few cases in which [the death penalty] is imposed from the many cases in which it is not."[443] A showing that satisfied the intentional discrimination standard for equal protection would also satisfy the arbitrariness theory. Evidence of discrimination may demonstrate the arbitrariness of a system. To meet the arbitrariness standard, however, discrimination need not be shown.

The arbitrariness standard relates to the operation of a capital punishment system in general, without necessary regard to how it performs in any particular case. That was the basis for the Stewart, White, and Douglas opinions in *Furman.* They did not focus their evaluations of the death penalty on the particulars of the cases before them. Instead, they rendered judgments on the operation of capital punishment systems in general. That was also the basis for the Court's evaluation of the unconstitutionality of the death penalty in the other states that had cases before the Court at the time.[444] The defendants in all those cases realized relief from their death sentences without showing that any of them individually suffered intentional discrimination or that their death penalties were not justified under the law of their jurisdiction. They realized that relief because their death sentences were meted out by a system whose general operation did not measure up to constitutional standards, according to the three swing justices, regardless of the circumstances of their individual cases.

The 1976 decisions, then, were based on the premise that, with proper procedures, the arbitrariness in the capital sentencing process would largely disappear. After those decisions, the issue should be whether that premise is justified by experience with the new procedures. If experience does not undermine that premise, it would not be likely to establish a denial of equal protection either. If it does, assuming that the *Furman* standard continues in effect, there would be no need for the equal protection inquiry. Only if a majority of the Court would no longer enforce *Furman* would it be necessary to pursue the equal protection argument.[445] Concurring in *McCleskey*, Judge Vance made just this point:

> According to *Furman*, an eighth amendment inquiry centers on the general results of capital sentencing systems, and condemns those governed by such unpredictable factors as chance, caprice or whim. An equal protection inquiry is very different. It centers not on systemic irrationality but rather the independent evil of intentional, invidious discrimination against given individuals.
>
> I am conscious of the dicta in the various *Furman* opinions which note with disapproval the possibility that racial discrimination was a factor in the application of the death penalty under the Georgia and Texas statutes then in effect. To my mind, however, such dicta merely indicate the possibility that a system that permits the exercise of standardless discretion not only may be capricious, but may give play to discriminatory motives which violate equal protection standards as well. Whether a given set of facts make out an eighth amendment claim of systemic irrationality under *Furman* is, therefore, a question entirely independent of whether those facts establish deliberate discrimination violative of the equal protection clause.[446]

CHAPTER III

The Empirical Study

Supreme Court decisions on constitutional issues often require policy judgments that depend on information about social circumstances beyond the facts of a particular case. The Court has relied on a variety of sources for its understanding of the social and economic facts of life that underlie the issues that reach its attention. One source that is increasingly important is social science research.

PART 1.

Social Science Research and Supreme Court Methodology

Traditionally, the judicial method for developing the factual premises for policy decisions[1]—by contrast with the relevant historical facts for resolution of a particular case[2]—has been largely intuitive.[3] *Furman* is an example. The majority justices, drawing on their experience, decided that the death penalty was being administered too arbitrarily to survive constitutional analysis. They looked for the best information available, but did not find enough in the form of empirical research.[4] Without adequate scientific data to support their factual premises, they nevertheless had little hesitance to rely on them.[5] They invoked the classic judicial method out of the necessity of deciding the policy question presented.

The process of the development of precedent has produced the accumulated experience that constitutes the data on which the courts have generally relied.

> In their effort to give to the social sense of justice articulate expression in rules and in principles, the method of the lawfinding experts has always been experimental. The rules and principles of case law have never been treated as final truths, but as working hypotheses, continually retested in those great laboratories of the law, the courts of justice.[6]

The intuition on which the Supreme Court traditionally relies is shaped as well by the justices' experience of life, by their understanding of the prevailing canons of justice and morality, and by their study of history, philosophy, economics, and the social sciences.[7] The courts have also customarily consulted history, occasionally moral and political philosophy, and, increasingly, economics.[8] They have also used social science information for their general education about many areas out of which the cases before them arise without necessarily citing it in their opinions.[9] In that way, the teachings of social science have an informal influence on the Supreme Court's consideration of constitutional policy. The social sciences have recently begun to quantify phenomena that might be relevant to judicial policymaking, using modern experimental, observational, statistical, and survey techniques.[10] Direct consideration by the Court of particular pertinent studies also has a proper role.

The Supreme Court has begun to accord a measure of respect to the product of social science research in contributing to its policy premises. That Court, like others, is already accustomed to reviewing the use of statistical data in the determination of the factual issues relevant to the particular case before it, such as whether there was discrimination in the selection of a particular jury, in a particular employment decision, or in the drawing of particular political boundaries.[11] It would not be exceptional for the Court to utilize empirical studies to evaluate the constitutionality of the administration of the death penalty.

The standard method for making such evidence available to the Court, like evidence relevant only to the particular case, may be to present it through expert testimony at trial.[12] That is not the only possible procedure for presenting evidence relevant to general policy issues.[13] Not every case that reaches the Supreme Court begins with a vision of its ultimate national importance and with a commensurate investment of the resources necessary to develop a complete record of the relevant social science data. The customary method for reporting such research is publication in scholarly sources. In that way, the research can be subjected to scrutiny by

other investigators whose academic critiques, similarly published, can fulfill the role played by cross-examination in the trial process.[14] Since early in
this century, the Court has been receptive to generalized social science
research presented in the form of scholarly publications, even if they have
not endured the testing of the adversary process in the lower courts. The
Court has noticed them through its own research, or counsel have synthe-
sized their content in the briefs they file. The original "Brandeis brief"
persuasively presented to the Court, in support of the constitutionality of
state legislation, a variety of studies to the effect that long hours of labor
are dangerous for women, together with a collection of legislation enacted
by several states and foreign countries limiting the hours of labor that may
be required for women.[15] Today it is common for the Court to go outside
the record for relevant information of general import, although it does not
always acknowledge when it does so.[16]

One Supreme Court decision that gave considerable attention to
social science research was *In re: Gault*.[17] The case required the Court
to decide whether due process required certain procedures in juvenile delinquency proceedings. The Court first informed itself about the actual
operation of the juvenile courts by reading published studies of them.[18]
Finding that the "exalted ideal has failed of achievement,"[19] the Court
held that juveniles brought before such courts were entitled to notice of
the charges, the right to counsel, the privilege against compulsory self-
incrimination, and the right to confront the witnesses against them with
cross-examination. Without the outside information the Court would have
been ill equipped to make a realistic assessment of the juvenile court system it was called upon to evaluate from a constitutional perspective.

Another Supreme Court decision reflecting a strong influence of empirical data on a broad policy issue is *Ballew v. Georgia*,[20] dealing with the
issue of the constitutionally minimum jury size.[21] In *Williams v. Florida*,[22]
the Court had earlier upheld the use of a 6-person jury in a felony trial.
Writing the opinion for the Court in *Williams*, Justice White took account
of history,[23] the intent of the framers,[24] and precedent,[25] but, given the
perceived inconclusiveness of those guides, relied on the Court's institu-
tional determination of whether a 12-person requirement was essential to
the purposes of the jury trial.[26] In making that determination, the Court
used primarily its traditional judicial intuition.[27] Justice White's opinion
also canvassed with respect the available social science research and concluded that it did not controvert the intuitive assumption.[28] Just three years
later, in *Colegrove v. Battin*,[29] the Court also upheld the constitutionality of
a jury of 6 in civil cases. Again, the Court gave serious consideration to the
available social science studies and concluded that the evidence was conflicting.[30] The Court mentioned that "four very recent studies have provided convincing empirical evidence of the correctness of the *Williams*
conclusion."[31]

Williams and *Colegrove*, however, "generated a quantity of scholarly work on jury size."[32] That research was available to the Court in *Ballew v. Georgia*, in which it was asked to approve a jury of five persons. The plurality opinion of Justice Blackmun, joined by Justice Stevens and concurred in by Justices Brennan, Stewart, and Marshall, relied entirely on that empirical evidence in refusing to do so. Justice Blackmun's opinion carefully canvassed the studies[33] and held that the "assembled data raise substantial doubt about the reliability and appropriate representation of panels fewer than six."[34] Justice Powell, writing for himself, Chief Justice Burger, and Justice Rehnquist, expressed "reservations as to the wisdom—as well as the necessity—of Mr. Justice Blackmun's heavy reliance on numerology derived from statistical studies. Moreover, neither the validity nor the methodology employed by the studies cited was subjected to the traditional testing mechanisms of the adversary process."[35] Justice Blackmun responded, "We have considered them carefully because they provide the only basis, besides judicial hunch, for a decision about whether smaller and smaller juries will be able to fulfill the purpose and functions of the Sixth Amendment."[36]

In some opinions, the justices have alluded to such information without describing precisely the extent of its role on the Court's policy analysis. Often, social science findings are supportive, though not determinative, of Supreme Court decisions.[37] For example, in *United States v. Leon*,[38] the Court decided that the purposes of the exclusionary rule will be served only rarely in applying it where a law enforcement officer conducted a search in good faith reliance on a search warrant that was later held invalid. In two footnotes the Court summarized empirical studies of the effects of the exclusionary rule on the disposition of felony arrests[39] and the effectiveness of the warrant process in screening improper police conduct.[40] It is impossible to say that the studies had any real effect on the decision in that case, however. Similarly, in the landmark desegregation decision, *Brown v. Board of Education*, the Supreme Court devoted a footnote to the citation of several sociological and psychological studies in support of its textual statement upholding a finding that school segregation has a harmful effect on minority students.[41] Although that footnote generated considerable criticism, the language of the opinion[42] and historical evidence[43] indicate that the footnote references did not play a significant role in the decision.

The Court naturally welcomes empirical guidance in its policy formulation responsibility.[44] It can be useful in matters relating to the judicial process generally familiar to Supreme Court Justices, as the *Gault* and *Ballew* cases show, as it obviously is useful in matters less likely to be within the justices' personal experience. As Justice Cardozo said, the courts should "draw upon the whole range of human knowledge."[45] "The formulation of law and policy . . . obviously gains strength to the extent that information replaces guesswork or ignorance or hunch or intuition or general impressions."[46] As Justice Brandeis explained, "Knowledge is essential to understanding; and understanding should precede judging."[47] Justice Brennan has said that the increasing complexity of society and the increasing social aspects of law require that the law value "those disciplines that investigate and report on the functioning and nature of society."[48] At the same time, the Court must safeguard its judgmental prerogative in the exercise of its policy responsibility and therefore may regard social science research with some skepticism. Thus, in *Craig v. Boren*, the Court, speaking through Justice Brennan, observed that "proving broad sociological propositions by statistics is a dubious business; and one that inevitably is in tension with the normative philosophy that underlies the Equal Protection Clause."[49]

Unquestionably, the normative constitutional standards are for the Court to determine. Thus, the role of social science data is properly limited to situations in which the Court itself first formulates or invokes "propositions or norms conditioned upon knowledge within the competence of social sciences."[50] When the issue before the Court is one of broad policy, the data can inform the Court about the pertinent social and economic conditions. The Court must frame the question to which the empirical study is to respond; it then must interpret the results of that study and evaluate the weight that it deserves, if any, in the ultimate policy decision.

The Supreme Court must use legal doctrine to formulate the question for social science inquiry. In a footnote in *Craig v. Boren*, the Court demonstrated the importance of confining the use of social science data to legal issues for which it has relevance:

> Thus, if statistics were to govern the admissibility of state alcohol regulation without regard to the Equal Protection Clause as a limiting principle, it might follow that states could freely favor Jews and Italian Catholics at the expense of all other Americans, since available studies regularly demonstrate that the former two groups exhibit the lowest rates of problem drinking.[51]

The statistical information can only answer a question about whether there are differences in the tendencies toward problem drinking among certain groups. That footnote suggests that even if such differences do exist, they will not justify liquor laws that are more permissive to one religious group than another. If the answer to the question is not going to decide the issue, it is not because of any flaw in social science data; it is because the question was not a legally significant one.[52] If the Court wants to maintain a constitutional policy despite a convincing empirical challenge to its premises, there are probably other reasons that support the policy. The Court needs to consider expressing those premises, thereby formulating a more candid statement of the issue.

When the Court does ask a question that the social sciences can answer, the Court still must interpret that answer for the policy issue confronting it. *Craig v. Boren* also provides an example of the importance of this interpretation responsibility. In that case, the issue was the constitutionality of state legislation prohibiting the sale of 3.2 percent beer to males but not to females between the ages 18 and 21. The state presented evidence that 2 percent of males but only .18 percent of females in that age group were arrested for drunk driving. The state derived from these data an argument that males presented a substantially greater drunk driving problem than females, justifying special legislative concern. The Court, however, observed that the statistics showed that too few people of either sex in the age group were arrested for drunk driving to permit legislation to prohibit all persons of either sex in the group from drinking 3.2 percent beer. Looking at the two "glasses," one for males and one for females, the state saw one as partly filled and the other as primarily empty; the Court saw both as primarily empty.

The social sciences do not always have information that might be useful in a constitutional inquiry. Where their findings are incomplete or in conflict, of course, the Supreme Court may not rely on them. For example, in *Gregg v. Georgia* itself, the Supreme Court plurality, in holding that capital punishment for murder is not per se unconstitutional, reviewed the "[s]tatistical attempts to evaluate the worth of the death penalty as a deterrent to crimes by potential offenders."[53] None of that evidence had been presented in expert testimony. Instead, the Court considered it in the form of published scholarly works.[54] In the process, the Court considered the debate in the scientific community about the research and the assessments of its value. The Court then held:

> Although some of the studies suggest that the death penalty may not function as a significantly greater deterrent than lesser penalties, there is no convincing empirical evidence either supporting or refuting this view. We may nevertheless assume safely that there are murderers, such as those who act in passion, for whom the threat of death has little or no deterrent effect. But for many others, the death penalty undoubtedly is a significant deterrent. There are carefully contemplated murders, such as murder for hire, where the possible penalty of death may well enter into the cold calculus that precedes the decision to act. And there are some categories of murder, such as murder by a life prisoner, where other sanctions may not be adequate. . . .
>
> In sum, we cannot say that the judgment of the Georgia Legislature that capital punishment may be necessary in some cases is clearly wrong. Considerations of federalism, as well as respect for the ability of a legislature to evaluate, in terms of its particular State,

the moral consensus concerning the death penalty and its social utility as a sanction, require us to conclude, in the absence of more convincing evidence, that the infliction of death as a punishment for murder is not without justification . . . .[55]

When relevant and reliable social science information is available, the Court should certainly consider it to the extent that it is helpful. Constitutional decisions should strive to be realistic. Judicial intuition may be a satisfactory foundation for constitutional policy unless its conclusions are contradicted by empirical evidence that presents a more valid perspective on a pertinent social circumstance than the Court, left to its own resources, would have accessible. Social science research that addresses broad circumstances rather than particular cases, deals in probabilities rather than certainties, and is subject to replication and reassessment with advancing techniques[56] may, in appropriate cases, contribute to the Court's understanding of the social facts that provide context for its decisions. The Court must determine the constitutional question, assess the design of the research and the rigor of the methodology,[57] and exercise judgment about the value of the results. Where the research addresses a relevant issue and yields significant results according to professional standards, the Court should be as receptive to it for policy purposes as it is to similar data for establishing the facts specific to a particular case. As California's former Chief Justice Traynor recommended, "we should not disdain even the simplest sociological data that could prove useful to the law."[58]

PART 2.

The Constitutional Question for Empirical Study

In *Furman*, the Supreme Court decided that capital punishment is constitutional only if it is not in fact imposed in an "arbitrary" manner. In its 1976 death penalty decisions, the Court reaffirmed *Furman*. Those decisions upheld on their face capital punishment schemes in three states because they had new standards and procedures that appeared to the Court capable of protecting against arbitrary or haphazard application of the death penalty. Nevertheless, the plurality did not find that those standards and procedures would in fact protect against the "crazy-quilt" pattern perceived in *Furman*. Instead, it relied on an assumption that they appeared capable of doing so. It held that "*on their face* these procedures *seem* to satisfy the concerns of *Furman*." The plurality reached those decisions without any evidence contradicting the impressions of Justices Stewart, White, and Douglas in *Furman* about the actual operation of the death penalty in the past and without establishing any different contemporary experience. It had no relevant data about whether the procedures did in fact accomplish their intended result. Thus, the decisions left open the question whether they do.[59]

The emphasis that the decisions were based on an evaluation of the new procedures only on their face invited empirical analysis of the relationship between the statutory standards for the death penalty and its actual imposition. The new procedures were important to the plurality justices because of what they assumed those procedures would accomplish, not because they perceived the procedures to be an end in themselves. Accordingly, a study designed to investigate that assumption should determine whether in fact the new procedures have controlled the exercise of discretion in the capital decision-making process adequately to avoid the arbitrary pattern condemned in *Furman*. Its focus should be the effectiveness of the new procedures in confining the exercise of discretion to a range within the legal standards.

PART 3.

The Standards for the Empirical Study

The Comprehensive Character of the Study: Relevant Factors

Because the consequences of arbitrariness are simply results that are inconsistent with the legal standards, the beginning point for an empirical study should be information about the strength of the evidence in the cases that is relevant to the legal standards for guilt and for punishment. The arbitrariness inquiry is essentially a determination of the extent to which the evidence relevant to the legal standards correlates with the decisions made in the processing of defendants through the capital punishment system: that is, whether, taking into consideration all legally relevant factors, different sentencing outcomes can be meaningfully distinguished.

In the death penalty context, the evidence relating to guilt and the evidence of the aggravating and mitigating factors precisely reflect the legal standards. The range of discretionary choice should be no broader than the limits established by those standards. Any variation in the results from those that can be explained on the basis of the relevant evidence would establish arbitrariness in the system to the extent of the variation.

Information about the strength of the evidence on the issues relevant to guilt and to penalty would also be important to a discrimination inquiry.[60] Discretionary decisions that are reasonably made on the basis of an assessment of the probative strength of the evidence cannot be characterized as either arbitrary or discriminatory. Obviously, material differences in evidence would be a meaningful basis for distinguishing different sentencing outcomes.

Information about the strength of the evidence is difficult both to collect and to evaluate.[61] Care is required in the design and conduct of the study to assure that all relevant evidence is properly considered. For additional assurance that any variation is attributable to arbitrariness rather than a failure to include sufficiently accurate consideration of a relevant legal factor or combination of legal factors, a second phase should be added to the inquiry. This phase should consist of an effort to identify any extralegal factors that might have had an effect on the process. The study of these extralegal factors would not necessarily be for the purpose of ascertaining whether the process was characterized by discrimination on the basis of those factors. It might have that effect in a popular sense of the concept of discrimination but not satisfy the proof requirements for a constitutional claim of discrimination (a) that the decision makers acted with intent to discriminate; or (b) that any discrimination was directed at a particular case. Instead, the purpose of focusing on the extralegal factors is simply to subject any apparent variation from the legal standards to a second-stage test to determine whether the results can reliably be attributed to arbitrariness rather than methodological difficulties.

The study may appropriately focus on the experience of an individual death penalty jurisdiction. The three swing opinions in *Furman*, however, seemed to be based on the operation of the death penalty nationally. Those opinions did not concentrate on the particular states—and certainly not on the particular counties—involved in the cases before the Court. That is apparent from the opinions themselves and is confirmed by the action of the Court in reversing the discretionary death penalties in all cases before it at the time, regardless of the states that had imposed them or the systems that they had used to do so. The justices voted a lack of constitutional confidence in the way the capital sentencing decisions were being made. They could hardly have made their assessments on any basis more specific to the individual states, given the nature of the information available to them. The kind of experiential intuition that informed their judgment could not be catalogued by state.

In its later decisions in *Coker v. Georgia*[62] and *Enmund v. Florida*,[63] the Court, both times in opinions written by Justice White, again employed a national standard. In *Coker*, the Court said, "[W]e seek guidance in history and from the objective evidence of *the country's* present judgment concerning the acceptability of death as a penalty for rape of an adult woman."[64] To derive that objective evidence the Court looked to the statutes and the jury decisions in the several states.[65] Because the Court found that no state had a statute equivalent to Georgia's, it actually considered only Georgia jury decisions.[66] It considered that evidence in concluding that death is "a disproportionate penalty for the crime of raping an adult woman."[67] In *Enmund*, the Court, applying *Coker*, also looked to the death penalty statutes of all the capital punishment states for comparative purposes[68] and to the sentencing decisions of "American juries" nationwide.[69]

The issue in *Coker* and *Enmund* was whether the death penalty is a disproportionate penalty for a particular category of crime. That may arguably be different than the issue of whether an individual state applies its capital punishment system in a comparatively proportional manner among the homicide cases that come before its courts.[70] The national experience may be the appropriate consideration for the *Coker–Enmund* abstract proportionality question. The experience of each state, however, should be the focus of inquiry for an arbitrariness or comparative proportionality question. The state is the sovereign that is responsible for its own capital punishment system, but not that of any other state. Each state establishes and administers its system and imposes any death sentence within its jurisdiction. An arbitrary system in one state should not be saved because other states might regularly impose the death penalty in cases where the first does so only freakishly.[71] Moreover, the Constitution considers each state separately in its regulation of the police power: "nor shall any state deprive any person of life, liberty or property without due process of law."[72]

The individual state is a proper focus of inquiry for another reason. The basis for the plurality opinion in the 1976 cases, reiterated repeatedly in subsequent decisions as the theory of the Court, was that the new procedures appeared capable of protecting against the deficiencies identified in *Furman*. Empirical evidence simply tests that thesis. If it satisfactorily establishes that in any jurisdiction the arbitrary, infrequent, or discriminatory pre-*Furman* pattern has survived the new procedures, it challenges the assumption that the new procedures would effectively control the exercise of discretion responsible for that pattern.

A study conducted in any state should have significance for assessing the capital punishment system in any other state with similar procedures. The discretion of the decision makers in the study state, if inadequately controlled, might be influenced by different extralegal factors than that of the decision makers in another state. The focus of the study, however, is on the new procedures. If the study shows that the procedures cannot confine the exercise of discretion in the study state in accordance with the legal standards, there would no longer be any reason to assume that they would be capable of doing so in other states either.

The Contemporary Character of the Study

That, of course, assumes that the procedures in the two states are similar. The modern death penalty systems cannot be evaluated in the light of evidence of the operation of obsolete systems. *Furman* seems to mark an excellent dividing point for this purpose. The decade before the *Furman* decision saw substantial progressive development in American society and the American criminal justice system. The segregation in public life that the Supreme Court had begun to outlaw in its landmark *Brown v. Board of Education*[73] decision in 1954 began to surrender its influence on judicial processes. The Supreme Court interpreted the Constitution to guarantee every defendant in a serious criminal prosecution the right to counsel[74] and the right to a jury trial.[75] Moreover, the Court applied the Constitution to ensure that juries represented a fair cross-section of their communities,[76] without systematically excluding racial minorities[77] or women.[78] The Court also clarified that the Constitution requires the prosecution to bear the burden of persuasion beyond a reasonable doubt on all elements of the offense.[79] Finally, *Furman* closed the era of death penalty decisions made in the unguided discretion of juries.[80]

The death penalty systems enacted after *Furman* that measure up to the standards of the 1976 decisions are the proper subject of inquiry. If the question is whether they counteract the pre-*Furman* arbitrariness, it seems reasonable to study any of them during any time period they were in operation. Unless the time of the study preceded relevant reforms in the new procedures themselves or in any of the discretionary stages of the process, the results should be valid as a description of the operation of the system. Evidence that arbitrariness persists in any jurisdiction that employs the new procedural reforms would undermine the Supreme Court's assumption that they would protect against that situation.

The Longitudinal Quality of the Study

The subject of the study is the capital selection system within the judicial process. It should therefore include within its purview all the relevant cases that enter the process, that is, all cases in which an arrest is made subject to capital punishment processing.

The study cannot therefore simply calculate the percentage of nonwhites and the percentage of whites on death row. Nationwide in 1984, those percentages were 43 percent nonwhite and 57 percent white.[81] In North Carolina in September 1985 the death row population was 62 percent nonwhite (28 defendants) and 38 percent white (17 defendants). Consideration of such proportions alone has led many people too quickly to conclude that they demonstrate discrimination in the death penalty system.[82] Comparison of the racial ratio in the death row population with the racial ratio in the general population may be meaningful in terms of the political circumstances in the country. Nevertheless, it does not assign responsibility to the criminal justice system. The judicial selection process for capital punishment does not operate on the general population. Instead, that process operates only on persons arrested on a homicide charge. Whatever social circumstances or police policies and practices lie behind the occurrence of criminal conduct or the arrests of suspects for such conduct cannot directly be attributed to the judicial process. That process is accountable for the cases only after an arrest is made[83] and cannot be held responsible for any discrimination that skews the proportions of the population presented for processing. It can be credited only for what it does with the defendants when they are within its jurisdiction.

Similarly, the study cannot simply evaluate the cases of persons who had death sentences imposed on them to see whether they qualified for that penalty. The arbitrariness inquiry requires comparison of those cases with the cases of persons eligible for capital processing who did not receive death sentences. Accordingly, the study should include all homicide cases in which an arrest occurred. It might narrow the subject population to those arrested for homicides with characteristics qualifying them for the death penalty process: cases with evidence of first degree murder characteristics and at least one aggravating circumstance. It will be better informed, however, if it includes all homicide cases with an arrest because the judicial system may process them together through at least some stages. As long as the study carefully controls for the relevant capital characteristics, it is safer to begin with a pool of cases that is too broad rather than a pool that already excludes some pertinent cases.

For similar reasons, the study should follow the cases through all stages of the judicial process from the point of arrest. The new procedures are directed primarily at the sentencing decision to be made after a defendant has been convicted of a capital crime. Nevertheless, that decision is affected by discretionary decisions made at both earlier and later stages in the criminal justice process. The fairness of a decision made at any stage controlled by careful proceedings may be nullified by arbitrariness at other stages. Most homicide cases are disposed of short of trial. The decisions at the early stages determine the pool of cases available for the trial, sentencing, and later stages.[84] Any study that considers only the trial and later stages of the process would overlook the operation of the earlier stages. The cases that reach the study stage would have already been subjected to discretionary decisions that diverted other cases from further processing. They would reflect the earlier discretionary decisions, but those decisions would not be visible to a study beginning to look at the cases only after they had been made. Starting at the later stage, the study would miss any decisions occurring in the earlier stages and be unable to compare the cases that reached the study stage with those that did not. It would miss all stages in which the prosecutor is the principal discretionary officer. Thus, conclusions based only on those cases may mask the operation of the earlier processes. Remember the hypothetical case in Chapter II, Part 7 of the 100 felony–murder getaway-car drivers, 98 white and permitted to plead guilty to second degree murder, 2 nonwhite and required to stand trial for first degree murder where they were sentenced to death.[85]

Only a longitudinal approach following each case through each discretionary stage is able to evaluate the exercise of discretion throughout the process.[86]

In summary, the study should be sensitive to the constitutional dimensions of the arbitrariness issue it is evaluating. Its data should be contemporary, relevant, and comprehensive. It should evaluate, first, the relationship between the quality of evidence relevant to the legal standards and the discretionary decisions made. It should also evaluate the relationship between selected extralegal variables and the discretionary decisions. It should therefore include all serious homicide cases in which an arrest has been made and follow those cases through all stages of the judicial process.

PART 4.

Related Social Science Research

The subject of discrimination in the administration of the death penalty attracted considerable empirical research interest before *Furman*. The results of the studies of capital punishment systems in effect at that time may be summarized in three general conclusions: (*a*) in the South, where the majority of executions occurred, nonwhite defendants were more likely to receive death sentences than were white defendants; (*b*) outside the South, white defendants were more likely than nonwhite defendants to have death sentences imposed on them; (*c*) defendants convicted of killing white victims were more likely to receive death sentences than defendants convicted of killing nonwhite victims.[87]

Although these studies provide a helpful historical perspective, they are not useful for an evaluation of the current capital punishment process. They studied obsolete systems and were limited in terms of the legally relevant factors they took into consideration in the cases they examined. They did not control for the strength of the evidence, the seriousness of the cases, the prior criminal records of the defendants, or other characteristics that might legitimately have been relevant to the death penalty decision. Moreover, most were studies of the commutation or sentencing stage only.

Furman and the 1976 death penalty decisions inspired new studies. Some have evaluated aspects of the new systems against an arbitrariness standard. Most have tested the Supreme Court's assumption that the new standards and procedures would adequately control the exercise of discretion in the capital punishment process to avoid arbitrariness primarily by investigating whether racial or regional factors played a role in the decision process. The studies reported in published literature have been limited in the stages of the process they reviewed and the legally relevant factors they considered, but many have been more sophisticated than the pre-*Furman* studies in the range of variables they examined and the statistical techniques they employed. Although the post-*Furman* studies have not attempted to evaluate the strength of the evidence on the guilt or innocence issue for capital murder, they have endeavored to consider at least some aggravating factors. All have found arbitrariness in the capital punishment process by (*a*) demonstrating an irrational pattern of decision making; (*b*) showing that comparable cases resulted in unexplainably different sentences; or (*c*) identifying patterns in the death or life decisions correlated with such factors as the race of the victim or the region of the state in which the case was prosecuted.

The following is a capsule summary of most of the studies of the post-*Furman* systems.[88]

Execution Stage

Researcher: Streib.[89]

Data: The first 11 cases nationwide resulting in executions after the 1976 death penalty decisions.

Sources: The state supreme court opinions; newspapers and news magazines.

Analytic method: Subjective review.

Findings: The defendants in all 11 cases were male. Nine were white and 2 were black. Seven had long criminal records, but 4 had minimal criminal records with no previous involvement in violent crime. All but 1 defendant were executed for felony murders. Ten of the 11 victims in the cases were white; the eleventh was a black security guard.[90]

> That these eleven men were executed out of all those sentenced to die seems to contradict many of the basic premises of capital punishment theory and law. One premise is that the death sentence is appropriate for only the most heinous homicides. While all eleven of the executed men committed homicide, six of the homicides were fairly ordinary killings that occurred during armed robberies. They were not particularly brutal nor did they involve more than one victim. Only the child-murders by Judy and Gray, and the premeditated ambush by Smith, could be considered particularly heinous....
>
> Another premise of capital punishment is that it may deter some people from committing capital crimes. . . .
>
> Of these eleven executions, only the double homicides by Smith were carefully contemplated and planned over a period during which the deterrent effect of the death penalty could be expected to have been significant. None of the other crimes, except perhaps that of Sullivan, seemed to involve much "cold calculus" prior to the killings, but rather resulted from spur of the moment decisions.

A third premise is that capital punishment should not be freakishly imposed on a capriciously selected random handful of defendants who commit capital crimes. Comparative analysis of the eleven cases in which executions were carried out with the 3,000 other death sentences not resulting in executions or with the many thousands of similar crimes in which the death sentence was not imposed leads to only one conclusion: No particularly distinguishing factors can be identified which would place these eleven cases in a clearly unique category. Caprice may well have played a role in these executions and the rare and random pattern of their occurrence could lead one to conclude that the death penalty is being freakishly imposed and carried out.[91]

Appellate Stage

1. Researcher: Dix.[92]

Data: Decisions of the state supreme courts in Florida (66 cases), Georgia (81 cases), and Texas (69 cases).

The Florida Supreme Court affirmed the conviction and sentence in 33 of the cases; it reversed the conviction in 8 cases, reversed the sentence on procedural grounds in 10 cases, and reduced the sentence on the merits in 15 cases, 13 of which involved a judge's death sentence despite a jury recommendation of life imprisonment. The Georgia Supreme Court affirmed the conviction and sentencing in 61 of the cases; it reversed the conviction in 4 cases, reversed the death penalty on procedural grounds in 14 cases, and reduced the death penalty on the merits in 2 cases. The Texas Supreme Court affirmed the conviction and sentence in 46 cases, reversed the conviction in 14 cases, reversed the sentence on procedural grounds in 8 cases, and held the sentence invalid on the merits in 1 case.

Source: The state supreme court opinions.

Analytic method: Subjective review.

Findings: "[T]he appellate review process has not resulted in appellate opinions that provide an effective basis for the encouragement of proper and consistent sentencing practices."[93]

2. Researcher: Rosen.[94]

Data: Decisions of the state supreme courts in the 24 states that provide as one of the statutory aggravating circumstances some form of the "especially heinous" standard.

Source: The state supreme court opinions.

Analytic method: Subjective review.

Findings: Nine of the state supreme courts had not yet interpreted the standard adequately for evaluation; 4 had imposed limits on the standard. The other 11 state supreme courts had either imposed no meaningful restrictions on the standard or issued inconsistent decisions applying the standard. Rosen concluded that "the especially heinous aggravating circumstance, rather than channeling discretion, has broadened it; instead of limiting the opportunity for arbitrary, capricious, and discriminatory factors to enter the capital sentencing process, has expanded it; rather than providing a meaningful basis for distinguishing those few cases deserving the death penalty from those cases in which death is not imposed, has allowed death to be imposed at the complete discretion of the sentencer."[95]

In the process of studying the appellate decisions, Rosen had a view of the sentencing patterns applying the especially heinous standard. He found those patterns to be arbitrary, and it was that arbitrariness that the state supreme court decisions permitted to persist.

3. *Researchers*: Radelet and Vandiver.[96]

Data: The 145 reported Florida Supreme Court decisions in death penalty direct appeals between January 1, 1973, and December 31, 1981. The Florida Supreme Court affirmed the conviction and sentence in 75 of the cases (51.7 percent). Radelet and Vandiver compared those cases with the other 70, in which the court reversed the conviction in 22 (31.43 percent), remanded 18 for resentencing (25.71 percent), and reduced the sentence in 30 (42.86 percent).

Source: The state supreme court opinions are the only source reported.

Analytic method: Ordinary least squares regression analysis.

Findings: The jury's recommendation and the number of victims were strong predictors of whether the appellate decision was favorable to the defendant.[97] In addition, for cases with male victims, white defendants were more likely to have death sentences affirmed; for cases with female victims, black defendants were more likely to have the death penalty affirmed.[98]

4. *Researchers*: Baldus, Pulaski, and Woodworth.[99]

Data: The 68 death penalties affirmed by the Georgia Supreme Court between 1973 and 1979.[100]

Sources: Official records.

Analytic method: Ordinary least squares and logistic regression analysis.

Findings: The authors first looked at the sentencing stage of the cases. Using a method that compared the cases on the basis of "salient factors,"[101] they determined that relatively few of them "would qualify as presumptively evenhanded."[102] Nevertheless, the Georgia Supreme Court did not vacate any of the death sentences on the ground of comparative disproportionality.

The Georgia Supreme Court did reverse, on procedural grounds, more death sentences in the less aggravated than in the more aggravated cases, thus precluding the need for a comparative proportionality review in those cases.[103] Despite those procedural reversals, it "seems likely that the Georgia Supreme Court's appellate review process has left untouched a substantial number of cases which may be excessive."[104]

Sentencing Stage

1. Researchers: Baldus, Pulaski, and Woodworth.[105]

Data: Two sets of data from Georgia.

The first data set: Cases of defendants arrested for murder in Georgia between March 28, 1973, and June 30, 1978, who were later tried for murder and sentenced to death or life imprisonment or who pled guilty and were sentenced to death, and who either appealed to the Georgia Supreme Court or had a file in the Department of Offender Rehabilitation or Department of Pardons and Paroles. That included more than 600 defendants. Of that number, 184 had penalty trials; some had 2 or more penalty trials, for a total of 197 penalty trials. Those trials resulted in 113 death sentences for 110 defendants.

Sources: Official records in the Georgia Supreme Court, the Georgia Department of Offender Rehabilitation, the Georgia Department of Pardons and Paroles, and the Georgia Bureau of Vital Statistics; "when necessary we also sent questionnaires to defense counsel and prosecutors."[106]

Findings: Of the cases, 60 percent involved white victims and 40 percent black victims. However, 27 percent of the cases with white victims but only 6 percent of the cases with black victims resulted in death sentences.

The enlarged data set: Cases of defendants arrested for murder or voluntary manslaughter in Georgia between March 28, 1973, and December 31, 1979, who were later convicted of murder or manslaughter either after a trial or a guilty plea, plus 30 additional defendants with death sentences. That included 1,472 voluntary manslaughter cases, 758 murder cases without a penalty trial, 117 murder cases that resulted in a life sentence and 128 with a death sentence. Thus, this second data set added cases arising during an additional 18-month period and included, for the original study period and for the additional 18-month period, more homicide cases that did not result in a death sentence.

Neither data set included cases in which the homicide charges were dismissed, resulted in an acquittal, or resulted in a sentence of probation.

In this broader range of cases, 49 percent involved white victims and 51 percent involved only black victims. Thirteen percent of the cases with white victims and 2 percent of the cases with only black victims resulted in death sentences.

Sources: Same as for the first set.

The researchers subjected the cases to a regression analysis for more than 200 independent variables. Their analysis of the first data set did not include consideration of the strength of the evidence in the cases, but the researchers have apparently developed statistical measurement techniques for including that important information in their analysis of at least some stages of the second data set. They have made available accounts of their analysis of the first data set and preliminary accounts of their analysis of the second data set. They have not yet published their final report.

Analytic method: Logistic regression analysis; "two *a priori* measures, one based on the number of statutory aggravating factors in the case and another based on an intuitive weighing of aggravating and mitigating circumstances."[107]

Finding: A homicide defendant was more likely to be sentenced to death in a case with a white victim than in a case with a black victim only, controlling for the aggravating and mitigating circumstances in the cases.

2. *Researcher*: Barnett.[108]

Data: The first set of data in the Baldus, Pulaski, and Woodworth study.

Source: The Baldus, Pulaski, and Woodworth files.

Analytic method: Cross-tabulation and comparison of percentages.

Rather than use a statistical measurement methodology to control for the strength of a case, Barnett read the files individually and subjectively rated the cases on a scale of 0, 1, or 2 for each of three factors: (*a*) the certainty that the defendant was a deliberate killer; (*b*) the closeness of the relationship between the defendant and the victim; and (*c*) the heinousness of the killing. On the basis of that rating, the cases were divided into three groups. The largest group was one in which a death sentence was rare. A second group consisted of cases in which it was unusual for a defendant to be spared the death penalty. The third group, about one-fifth of the cases, fell into an intermediate range in which death sentences were neither rare nor common.

Findings: Overall, there was a high degree of consistency in the death penalty decisions. Nevertheless, there were cases for which there was no meaningful difference between some that resulted in death sentences and others that did not. For "murders whose facts make the death penalty a serious possibility, the defendant's prior record seems important, as does sometimes the race-of-the-victim."[109] Barnett's analysis assigned the race-of-the-victim factor a smaller explanatory role than did Baldus, Pulaski, and Woodworth, but found that it was especially pronounced for felony murder cases.[110]

3. *Researchers*: Bowers and Pierce.[111]

Data: All persons actually sentenced to death between 1973 and 1977 in four states: Georgia, Florida, Texas, and Ohio. The researchers studied the cases according to the race of the victim and of the defendant. To impose some control over the circumstances of the offense, they gave special attention to cases that involved felony murders.

Source: The Supplementary Homicide Reports submitted by local law enforcement agencies to the FBI.

Analytic method: Cross-tabulation with comparison of percentages.

Findings: A death sentence was significantly more likely in a case with a white victim than in a case with a black victim.[112]

Reviewing the Florida and Georgia Supreme Court decisions in the cases, the researchers found that those decisions did not change the race-of-the-victim effect.

The researchers also studied the geographical patterns for the death sentence in Florida and Georgia. They divided the circuits into regional groupings and found significant variations.[113]

4. *Researcher*: Bowers.[114]

Data: Cases involving criminal homicide charges in 21 Florida counties in 1973–1976 and in 20 Florida counties in 1976–1977.[115]

Source: The Supplementary Homicide Reports submitted by local law enforcement agencies to the FBI.

Analytic method: Ordinary least squares regression analysis.

Findings: Death sentences appeared more likely in cases with white victims, but the difference did not have statistical significance.[116] Dividing the counties into four regions, there were highly significant regional disparities.[117]

5. *Researcher*: Zeisel.[118]

Data: The 114 men on death row in Florida in September 1977. Eighty-five of the 114 had been convicted of murder committed in the course of the felonies of rape, robbery, or burglary. Ninety-four percent of them killed white victims; 2 percent killed white and black victims only; 4 percent killed only black victims.

Sources: The Supplementary Homicide Reports submitted by local law enforcement agencies to the FBI; additional unpublished data.[119]

Analytic method: Cross-tabulation with comparison of percentages.

Finding: The race of the victim was an important factor in the death penalty decision.[120] For interracial killings, a death sentence was more likely for a black defendant with a white victim than a white defendant with a black victim.

6. *Researcher*: Radelet.[121]

Data: 326 homicide cases in 20 Florida counties between 1976 and 1977 in which the defendant and the victim were strangers or only vague acquaintances.

Sources: Court records and, occasionally, defense attorneys and newspapers.[122]

Analytic method: Loglinear logit analysis of crosstabulations.

Finding: There was a substantial race-of-the-victim effect. Defendants in cases with white victims were more likely to be sentenced to death than defendants in cases with black victims, regardless of the race of the defendant.[123]

7. *Researcher*: Bentele.[124]

Data: All cases decided by the Georgia Supreme Court in 1981 involving defendants who had death or life imprisonment sentences.

Source: The state supreme court opinions.

Analytic method: Subjective review.

Findings: There were comparable cases with different sentences without any meaningful explanation.[125] The facts of four sets of cases were contrasted to illustrate the absence of any reason for conflicting results in comparable cases.[126]

8. *Researchers*: Foley and Powell.[127]

Data: Cases from 19 Florida counties,[128] studying the race and sex of the defendant and the victim and several other factors about the offense: very general circumstances of the crime, whether there were additional charges or accomplices, the relationship between the defendant and the victim, and the kind of weapon used.

Source: Court records.[129]

Analytic method: Ordinary least squares regression analysis.

Findings: The jury in making its sentencing recommendation and the judge in making the sentencing decision were both influenced by the number of offenses and the number of victims involved. Both were more likely to opt for the death penalty for male than for female defendants. The judges, but not the juries in their nonbinding recommendations, were influenced by the race of the victim.[130]

9. *Researcher*: Arkin.[131]

Data: 142 felony murder cases in Dade County, Florida, between 1973 and 1976. Fifty-four of the cases resulted in first degree murder convictions; 10 of those cases resulted in death sentences that were not later reduced.

Sources: The prosecuting attorneys' grand jury memoranda; the court files; in cases of special interest, interviews with prosecuting and defense attorneys and judges.[132]

Analytic method: Subjective review.

Findings: Twenty-four of the cases without a death sentence were clearly distinguishable from the 10 death penalty cases. Another 14 cases were arguably distinguishable from the 10 death penalty cases. For the remaining 6 cases, there was no meaningful distinction.[133]

In the cases that involved felony murders, there was only a slight race-of-the-victim effect.[134]

10. *Researcher*: Radelet.[135]

Data: All cases in Florida between December 8, 1972, and September 20, 1984, in which the judge imposed a death sentence. There were 326 death penalties imposed on 316 men (8 with two death sentences) and 2 women.

Sources: A form filled out by the defendants; the judges' sentencing memoranda; news clippings; and appellate decisions. There was no information on the seriousness of the cases.[136]

Analytic method: Cross-tabulation with comparison of proportions.

Findings: White-victim cases were more likely to result in the death penalty.[137]

11. *Researchers*: Gross and Mauro.[138]

Data: The death penalty experience of eight states over the five-year period between January 1, 1976, and December 31, 1980. Three of the states had a high number of death sentences and received primary attention in the report: Florida, Georgia, and Illinois. The other five states were Arkansas, Mississippi, North Carolina, Oklahoma, and Virginia. The factors studied were the age, sex, and race of the victim and the defendant; the weapon used; whether a separate felony was involved; the relationship between the defendant and the victim; and the urban or rural character of the county of the homicide.[139]

Sources: The Supplementary Homicide Reports that local law enforcement agencies file with the FBI; the *Death Row USA* publication of the NAACP Legal Defense and Educational Fund.[140]

Analytic method: Cross-tabulation with comparison of percentages and logistic regression analysis.

Findings: For felony murder cases, the race of the victim had a sizable effect on the likelihood that a defendant received the death penalty in Florida, Georgia, Illinois, Mississippi, North Carolina, and Oklahoma, but not in Arkansas or Virginia.[141]

The researchers also studied the state supreme court decisions in the death penalty cases in Florida and Georgia. They observed that the race-of-the-victim disparities survived the appellate review process.[142]

Conviction Stage

Researcher: Bowers (see Sentencing Stage [4]) also evaluated 613 of the 1,045 cases indicted for first degree murder in the selected Florida counties between 1973 and 1977. Those cases resulted in 305 first degree murder convictions.

Findings: "[T]he variables of felony circumstance, number of offenders, and female victim are statistically significant predictors."[143] There were also "substantial regional disparities in the likelihood that a person indicted for first degree murder will actually be convicted on that charge, and this pattern is compounded when we consider the indictment and conviction stages together."[144] In addition, the race of the victim was a strong determinant independently of those factors; that was especially true for a black defendant in the case with a white victim.[145] "[T]he race of the defendant has a nearly significant effect ($p = .067$) on the likelihood of a first degree murder conviction, controlling for legally relevant factors."[146]

Charging Stage

1. Researcher: Bowers (see Sentencing Stage [4] and Conviction Stage) also considered the indictment decisions in the sample of persons charged with criminal homicide in 20 Florida counties in 1976–1977.

Findings: Although the aggravating circumstances had a significant effect on whether a defendant was indicted for first degree murder, so did the race of the victim. Although cases with white victims were more aggravating then cases with black victims, the race-of-the-victim effect figured prominently beyond that consideration. This was true regardless of the race of the defendant.

2. Researchers: Bowers and Pierce (see Sentencing Stage [3]) also found that for felony murder cases there was a race-of-the-victim effect at the indictment stage.

They also noted another phenomenon. Comparing the charges suggested in the police reports with those recommended by the prosecutors, they determined that prosecutors tended to upgrade some cases by alleging an aggravating felony circumstance or charging the defendant with an accompanying felony, and downgrade others, depending on the race of the defendant and the victim.[147]

3. Researchers: Radelet and Pierce.[148]

Data: The same data used by Bowers and Pierce (see Sentencing Stage [3]) and by Radelet (see Sentencing Stage [6]). One thousand seventeen of the defendants indicted for first degree murder in 21 selected Florida counties for homicides that occurred between 1973 and 1977 or indicted for first, second, or third degree murder in 20 selected Florida counties for homicides that occurred in 1976 or 1977.

Sources: Court records; letters to defense attorneys; the Supplemental Homicide Reports.

Analytic method: Loglinear logit analysis of crosstabulations.

Findings: Comparing the police records and the court records on the basis of whether they charged a felony murder, a possible felony murder, or no felony murder, the researchers found changes made by the prosecutors that "are associated with both the defendant's and the victim's races, and are not explained by factors such as the victim-offender relationship, number of offenders, or number of victims."[149]

4. Researcher: Paternoster.[150]

In South Carolina, if the prosecutor decides to request the death penalty in a case, he or she must notify defense counsel and the state supreme court administrator at least 30 days before trial. Paternoster studied the decisions of the prosecutor whether to seek the death penalty.

Data: Homicides with an arrest in South Carolina between June 8, 1977, and December 31, 1981.

Sources: The Supplementary Homicide Reports; police reports; the attorney general's indictment and disposition reports; and the prosecutors' notices of intent to seek a death sentence.

Analytic method: Cross-tabulation with comparison of percentages and loglinear logit analysis.

Findings: For over 300 cases that had at least one aggravating circumstance, defendants in cases with white victims had a significantly greater chance of having the prosecutor pursue the death penalty than defendants in cases with black victims.[151] In addition, cases processed in rural jurisdictions were more likely than cases processed in urban jurisdictions to receive a death sentence.[152]

The researcher also noted that at the penalty stage, 7 of the 169 armed robbery–murder cases in the study resulted in death sentences. All of those cases had white victims, and 5 cases had black defendants.[153]

5. Researcher: Radelet (see Sentencing Stage [6]) also evaluated the indictment stage for all cases in 20 Florida counties in 1976–1977 that were indicted for first, second, or third degree murder.

Findings: The probability of a first degree murder indictment, as well as the probability of a death sentence, varied with the race of the victim and the relationship between the defendant and the victim. That effect occurred for white and black defendants.[154]

Some of these studies are undergoing further refinement or analysis. Other valuable research projects are currently under way. Shortly after the 1976 death penalty decisions, we began to undertake a study of the implementation of the death penalty under the new procedures. In the rest of this chapter, we describe the project that we conducted. In Chapter IV, we report the results of that project, and in Chapter V we analyze those results in the light of the constitutional principles discussed in Chapter II.

PART 5.

The Design of the Empirical Study

We chose North Carolina as the jurisdiction for our study. The North Carolina capital punishment procedure is a modified version of the Model Penal Code proposal that served as a model for two of the statutes that the Supreme Court upheld in 1976. It is relatively typical of those enacted by most capital states in response to the Supreme Court's death penalty decisions. We studied homicide cases that arose during the first year of the operation of that procedure, from June 1, 1977, to May 31, 1978.

The research staff collected information about the homicide cases that occurred during the relevant year from the files of the state medical examiner, court records, police reports, and interviews with the prosecuting and defense attorneys. The information sought included all the statutorily relevant factors, including the quality of the evidence for both the prosecution and the defense on the issues relevant to the determination of the defendant's guilt or innocence of first degree murder and the presence or absence of aggravating and mitigating circumstances. The study developed a complex strategy for quantitatively measuring the quality of the evidence. It also gathered information about factors that should not be relevant to the outcome, including the judicial district where the case was processed and the race and sex of the defendant and the victim. The study followed the cases from the medical examiner's certification of a case as a homicide through the pretrial, trial, postconviction, and clemency procedures to ascertain for each stage and for the system as a whole whether the discretion of the decision makers was sufficiently controlled so that the decisions reached at each stage were made in accordance with the statutory standards.

During the study period, 661 persons were homicide victims in 645 events. (Fifteen of the events involved multiple victims.) For committing those homicides, 611 defendants were arrested and the study obtained information about the race and sex of 604 of those defendants. Of those 604 *defendants*, 213 were white males, 52 white females, 278 nonwhite males, and 61 nonwhite females. Of the 661 *victims*, 235 were white males, 74 white females, 270 nonwhite males, and 82 nonwhite females.

Nine defendants were sentenced to death, one of them twice for two separate homicides. Those nine persons were three white males, two white females, and four nonwhite males (three Indians and one black). One white male committed suicide on death row. All the others except one white female had their death sentences reversed on appeal. She was executed on November 2, 1984, after unsuccessfully proceeding through all the state and federal remedies available to her and being denied executive clemency.

The first impression from those figures is that the total number of death sentences seems small. In comparison with the preceding years, when North Carolina operated under a mandatory death penalty scheme that it devised, first judicially and then legislatively, in an effort to save a capital punishment system that the Supreme Court later decided was misguided, the total number is small.[155] The change from the mandatory to the discretionary death sentencing system naturally decreased the annual number of death sentences, but a grand total of only 9 such sentences still seems unusually small. Any impression that this number was an aberration resulting from the process of adjusting to the new procedures was dispelled in subsequent years, however. According to information supplied by the North Carolina Department of Correction, the state's death row received 7 persons under the sentence of death in calendar year 1979, 8 in 1980, 5 in 1981 (one of them with two death sentences), 12 in 1982, and 11 in 1983. Only two other persons, both white males, have been executed in the state, one in 1985 and one in 1986. Thus, the first year's experience under the new death penalty law yielded a representative number of death sentences.[156] Obviously the new law brought a major change in the North Carolina death penalty picture. The state tumbled from the top of the death penalty statistics [157] to a position of less prominence.

The second impression from the 1977–1978 death sentence figures is that those sentenced to death were disproportionately male and nonwhite. Four out of the nine death sentences were given to nonwhites, three of them Indians, and seven of the nine were given to males. Thus, the proportion of nonwhites sent to death row, 44 percent, and the proportion of males sent to death row, 77 percent, was substantially greater than the proportion of each of those groups in the general population. According to 1980 census figures for North Carolina, 24 percent of the population was nonwhite and 48.6 percent was male. Looking, not to the whole population, but to the particular population of persons arrested for homicides, which is the special interest of the judicial process, the picture is very different. The figures for the study year reveal that of all 604 persons arrested for all homicides for whom race and sex information was available, 56.1 percent (339 persons) were nonwhite, and 43.9 percent (265 persons) were white. Those racial proportions are roughly equivalent to national figures for the same period.[158] Narrowing the group to cases with capital characteristics, the figures for the study year show that of all persons arrested with strong evidence of first degree murder (see Table 2 in this chapter, Categories 1A and 1B) and at least one aggravating circumstance, 65.6 percent (126 persons) were nonwhite and 34.4 percent (66 persons) were white.

Although the study data cannot show whether the people arrested actually committed the crimes, two factors suggest that this disproportionate arrest rate reflects the actual homicide rate for nonwhites and whites rather than discretionary arrest practices. The first factor is that the person arrested rarely disputed responsibility for the killing: only 52 raised that as a defense. The second factor is the breakdown for the racial characteristics of the victims.

The victims of all homicides in the study were 52 percent nonwhite and 48 percent white. Nationally, during the same period, the victims of all homicides were around 47 percent nonwhite and 53 percent white.[159] Thus nonwhites were homicide victims far out of proportion to their presence in the general population. For the victims of all homicides in the study for which there were arrests, the comparable figures were also 52 percent nonwhite victims, 48 percent white victims. In the cases where arrests were made so that a match-up of victim and defendant is possible, the study shows that homicides were overwhelmingly intraracial. For nonwhite defendants, 89 percent of the victims in their cases were also nonwhite. For white defendants, 95 percent of the victims of the homicides in their cases were also white. The essentially intraracial character of homicides means that although in a particular case the race of the victim may be only a tenuous indicator of the race of the perpetrator, in the range of cases the race of the victim is a guide to the race of the killer.

Comparison of those sentenced to death with those eligible for a death sentence reliably yields a different perspective from comparison with the general population. Nonwhites were arrested for homicide, and for capital murder, well out of proportion to their share of the general population. From this perspective, nonwhites appear to be *under*represented on death row—44 percent versus a 56.1 percent arrest rate for homicides in general and a 65.6 percent arrest rate for cases with evidence qualifying them for capital consideration. These figures seem to contradict the contention that the judicial process discriminates against nonwhites in the death penalty process. Based on these figures, the conclusion would be that if there is any discrimination, it appears to be against *whites*.

This analysis demonstrates the flaw in any argument that relies on comparing the proportions of any group on death row with the proportions of the same group in the general population. Neither arbitrariness nor discrimination can be proved simply by looking at the total number of people by race on death row compared to the general population. Even the analysis above, comparing the proportions of a group on death row with its proportions in the arrest population for the proper capital crime, is too simplistic. Such gross figures overlook the dynamics of the criminal justice process, where decisions affecting the fate of the arrested persons are made in a series of discretionary stages by a number of officials in a decentralized network. As a result, such an analysis is inadequate to show an absence of discrimination against nonwhites. A more sensitive analysis tracing each discretionary stage of the judicial process is necessary.

Because the subject of the study is the judicial process of selecting homicide cases for capital punishment, it includes all homicide cases for which an arrest was made. Of course, the study has no information about the perpetrator of any homicide where no arrest was made, but the absence of an arrest also means that the homicide was never within the judicial process. Accordingly, the study focuses on the pool of homicide arrests and follows them through the discretionary decisions within the judicial process. By following the pool of homicide arrests through the process, the study avoids any bias that might be introduced by sample selection. At every stage of the process, the study includes not only all cases that reached that stage but also all cases with an arrest that were earlier diverted from the process.

In addition, the study considers each discretionary stage separately. That permits observation of the role of each discretionary decision maker.

The discretionary stages can conveniently be divided into those that arise before trial and those that arise during or after trial. The pretrial discretionary stages are largely under the control of the prosecutor,[160] while the later stages are under the control of a succession of additional officials (the trial judge, the trial jury, the sentencing jury, the state supreme court, and the governor). The prosecutor alone exercises the discretion at some of the pretrial stages, but must share the discretionary power at others. Thus the decision whether to reduce or dismiss the first degree murder charge before submission to the grand jury or after indictment is exclusively within the control of the prosecutor. The decision whether to indict for first degree murder is, theoretically, for the grand jury to make.[161] Nevertheless, the prosecutor exercises considerable control over the grand jury in the overwhelming majority of cases.[162] Although in North Carolina the prosecutor is not permitted to be present in the grand jury room during any of the grand jury proceedings, including the taking of testimony and the deliberations and voting, the prosecutor has considerable formal and informal control mechanisms. For example, the prosecutor determines whether to submit a charge to the grand jury[163] and what witnesses the grand jury will hear,[164] and signs the indictment[165] along with the foreperson of the grand jury.[166] The prudent technique, therefore, is to evaluate this stage in two ways: both as a discrete stage of grand jury or grand jury–prosecuting attorney discretion and as part of the prosecutor's package of pretrial discretion. Similarly, at the stage of deciding whether to dismiss the first degree murder charge in exchange for a plea of guilty to a less serious offense, the prosecutor shares the decision making with the defendant and the defense attorney. The decision regarding plea reflects interplay between the decision of the prosecutor about what leniency to offer, if any, and the decision of the defendant about what terms to accept, if any. Accordingly, the study again adopts the technique of evaluating this stage in two ways: this time, both as a discrete stage of prosecutor–defense attorney–defendant discretion and as part of the prosecutor's package of pretrial discretion.

Thus, to evaluate the prosecutor's package of pretrial discretion, the study looks at the pool of arrested defendants and compares the cases brought to trial for first degree murder with the cases that were not. To evaluate separately the prosecutor's dismissal discretion, the study looks also at the pool of arrested defendants and compares the cases dismissed at any stage with those that were not. To evaluate the shared grand jury–prosecuting attorney discretion at the indictment stage, the study looks to the pool of cases indicted at any level and compares the cases indicted for first degree murder with those not indicted at that level. Finally, to evaluate the shared prosecuting attorney–defense attorney–defendant discretion at the guilty plea stage, the study evaluates both the pool of homicide indictments and the pool of first degree murder indictments, comparing for both pools the defendants brought to trial for first degree murder with those who were not.

Ideally, at the trial and later stages, each discretionary actor should be separately studied as well. The number of cases that progressed this far, however, is too small for that. Accordingly, the study evaluates the decision of the judge whether to submit the case to the jury on first degree murder and of the jury whether to convict on that charge on the larger pools of arrests, indictments, and first degree murder indictments. That technique blends the judge's discretion with that of the prosecutor and that of the prosecutor and grand jury (for the pool of indictments) and the prosecuting attorney–defense attorney–defendant (for the pool of first degree murder indictments). It represents the combined effect of the jury's discretion with those and with the trial judge's. The size of the data base would not allow a more discrete analysis. What the study was able to evaluate was the results of the entire process at each of those stages.

There were only 18 first degree murder convictions during the study year, too small for any kind of further evaluation by statistical method. Nevertheless, the study does review those cases individually.

The results of the analysis based on the pool of homicide arrests are generally consistent with the results based on the narrower pools of homicide indictments and first degree murder indictments. For that reason, and to minimize the complexity of the discussion, the text includes only tables based on the pool of homicide arrests. The tables based on the narrower pools are all set out in Appendix B for completeness of the analysis.

PART 6.

The Data Collection Process

The first requirement in the data collection process is to identify all cases that qualify for entry into the process. Homicides furnish a more comprehensive laboratory for study than most other crimes. Most homicides are identified as such; many instances of other crimes, by contrast, go unreported. In addition, law enforcement authorities generally devote substantial resources to homicide investigations and are able to develop considerable physical and scientific evidence. Accordingly, homicide has the highest detection and resolution rates of any crime.[167]

North Carolina provides a central source for information about homicide cases in the office of the Chief Medical Examiner. By statute:

> Upon the death of any person resulting from violence, poisoning, accident, suicide or homicide; occurring suddenly when the deceased had been in apparent good health or when unattended by a physician; occurring in a jail, prison, correctional institution or in police custody, or occurring under any suspicious, unusual or unnatural circumstances, the medical examiner of the county in which the body of the deceased is found shall be notified by a physician in attendance, hospital employee, law-enforcement officer, funeral home employee, emergency medical technician, relative or by any other person having suspicion of such a death.[168]

That medical examiner is required to investigate the cause and manner of death.[169] "If the death was from external causes, the medical examiner shall state on the certificate of death the means of death, and whether, in the medical examiner's opinion, the manner of death was accident, suicide, homicide or undetermined."[170] The medical examiner is also required to make a full report to the Chief Medical Examiner.[171]

Accordingly, the files of the Chief Medical Examiner provide the initial data base for the study. The study focuses on the one-year period from June 1, 1977, to May 31, 1978, the first year of the death penalty statute that North Carolina enacted in response to the 1976 death penalty decisions. It includes all cases certified by that office as homicides and no other cases.

The initial criterion for the inclusion of a case in the study is the medical examiner's determination that the case presents a homicide.[172] The study then excludes all cases in which no arrest was made, all cases certified as "death by vehicle,"[173] and all cases in which the defendant was 14 years old or younger.[174] Thus, the study includes all homicide cases that were subject to felony processing during the study year except death by vehicle cases.

After identifying all North Carolina homicides that occurred during the study year, the study collected information on them from six sources:

- Files of the Chief Medical Examiner
- Court records

- Police reports
- Police Information Network records of previous arrests and convictions
- Interviews with the prosecuting attorneys
- Interviews with the defense attorneys

The research staff reviewed the files of the Chief Medical Examiner in all cases. Those files consistently contained considerable information about the victim. They often contained information as well about the defendant and the homicidal incident, although that was generally also available from the investigating law enforcement agency. The staff also reviewed the court records in all cases. They read or obtained copies of the police reports in the great majority of cases. Where they could not get the reports, the researchers interviewed the investigating officers. The quality and completeness of those reports varied among police departments, but most were at least satisfactory for the purposes of the study. The researchers obtained the prior criminal history information for each defendant from the North Carolina Police Information Network, which is the principal source for such information for the prosecutors. Whatever deficiencies in reporting, recording, or identification those data might suffer, they are the data that were available to the prosecutors and courts. Accordingly, they are a satisfactory data source for an evaluation of the discretionary decisions by the prosecutors; it permits testing of those decisions using the information, and only the information, generally available to them. Finally, the researchers interviewed most of the prosecuting and defense attorneys. In the majority of cases the interviewers talked to both attorneys. In nearly all cases, they talked to one attorney or the other. The researchers conducted their inquiries using a data collection instrument designed for the study. The instrument is available from the authors. It contains questions about nearly every aspect of the background of the victims and the defendants, the facts of the case, and the judicial processing of the case from arrest to final disposition. The only question relevant to the study that the instrument did not include was the quality of counsel. The research staff was able to ascertain for most cases whether the defendant was represented by retained or appointed counsel, but that distinction does not provide a reliable guide to the effectiveness of counsel. The researchers despaired of being able to devise an objective standard for this purpose, especially in view of the fact that most cases were resolved by guilty plea, or dismissal, rather than trial. Even such quantitative factors as the number of pretrial motions filed would necessarily be unreliable guides. The attorney who obtains voluntary file disclosure from the prosecuting attorney, for example, may well be more effective than one who files a formal motion for discovery.[175]

PART 7.

The Relevant Variables for the Empirical Study

In North Carolina, as in other states, today the only crime qualifying for capital punishment is first degree murder. North Carolina General Statutes section 14–17 defines that crime as murder committed in any of the following circumstances:

- If "perpetrated by means of poison, lying in wait, imprisonment, starving, torture"
- If perpetrated "by any other kind of willful, deliberate, and premeditated killing"
- If "committed in the perpetration or attempted perpetration of any arson, rape or a sex offense, robbery, kidnapping, burglary, or other felony committed or attempted with the use of a deadly weapon"

The North Carolina Constitution provides that the only means of charging a person with a capital offense is indictment by a grand jury.[176] An indictment is sufficient to charge first degree murder if it specifies that offense or if it simply alleges "that the accused person feloniously, willfully, and of his malice aforethought, did kill and murder (naming the person killed). . . ,"[177] even without allegations of the special requirements for first degree murder.[178] The prosecutor need not "determine, before the return of the indictment, whether he will ultimately prosecute a defendant for murder in the first or second degree."[179] The indictment may specify that it is for second degree murder, or the prosecutor may later confine the charge to second degree murder. Otherwise, an open murder indictment is sufficient to charge first degree murder. In the discussion, the term *first degree murder indictments* includes indictments that specify that degree and open murder indictments.

North Carolina law at the time of the study defined first degree murder as a "murder which shall be perpetrated by means of poison, lying in wait, imprisonment, starving, torture, or by any other kind of willful, deliberate, and premeditated killing, or which shall be committed in the perpetration or attempted perpetration of any arson, rape, robbery, kidnapping, burglary, or other felony committed or attempted with the use of a deadly weapon." Premeditation means simply thought beforehand for some length of time, however short. Deliberation means a cool state of mind in furtherance of a fixed design. It does not require brooding or reflection for any appreciable length of time. A defendant can deliberate even if he or she was in an emotional state at the time as long as the emotion was not such as to disturb the faculties and reason.[180] Voluntary intoxication may negate the existence of premeditation and deliberation if it is so great that the defendant is utterly unable to form a deliberate and premeditated purpose to kill.[181]

The North Carolina Supreme Court recently summarized the mental element standards for the other categories of homicide and for the defense of self-defense as follows:

> Murder in the second degree is the unlawful killing of a human being with malice but without premeditation and deliberation.
>
> Voluntary manslaughter is the unlawful killing of a human being without malice and without premeditation and deliberation. For example, a killing by reason of anger suddenly aroused by provocation which the law deems adequate to dethrone reason temporarily and thus to displace malice is voluntary manslaughter. Likewise, a killing resulting from the use of excessive force in the exercise of the right of self-defense is manslaughter.
>
> Involuntary manslaughter is the unlawful killing of a human being without malice, without premeditation and deliberation, and without intention to kill or inflict serious bodily injury. Stated somewhat differently, involuntary manslaughter is the unintentional killing of a human being without malice by (1) some unlawful act not amounting to a felony or naturally dangerous to human life, or (2) an act or omission constituting culpable negligence.
>
> The law of perfect self-defense excuses a killing altogether if, at the time of the killing, these four elements existed:
>
> (1) it appeared to defendant and he believed it to be necessary to kill the deceased in order to save himself from death or great bodily harm; and
>
> (2) defendant's belief was reasonable in that the circumstances as they appeared to him at the time were sufficient to create such a belief in the mind of a person of ordinary firmness; and
>
> (3) defendant was not the aggressor in bringing on the affray, *i.e.*, he did not aggressively and willingly enter into the fight without legal excuse or provocation; and
>
> (4) defendant did not use excessive force, *i.e.*, did not use more force than was necessary or reasonably appeared to him to be necessary under the circumstances to protect himself from death or great bodily harm.

The existence of these four elements gives the defendant a *perfect right of self-defense* and requires a verdict of not guilty, not only as to the charge of murder in the first degree but as to all lesser included offenses as well.

On the other hand, if defendant believed it was necessary to kill the deceased in order to save herself from death or great bodily harm, and if defendant's belief was reasonable in that the circumstances as they appeared to her at the time were sufficient to create such a belief in the mind of a person of ordinary firmness, but defendant, although without murderous intent, was the aggressor in bringing on the difficulty, or defendant used excessive force, the defendant under those circumstances has only the *imperfect right of self-defense*, having lost the benefit of perfect self-defense, and is guilty at least of voluntary manslaughter.[182]

The statute provides that any person who commits first degree murder "shall be punished with death or imprisonment in the State's prison for life as the court shall determine pursuant to G.S. 15A–2000." Thus, not all first degree murder convictions result in capital punishment. Section 15A– 2000 establishes procedures by which a jury should determine the sentence and establishes standards for that determination. It is a modified version of the Model Penal Code proposal that served as a model for the Georgia and Florida death penalty statutes upheld by the U.S. Supreme Court in the 1976 death penalty decisions. It provides, in the event of a first degree murder conviction, for "a separate sentencing proceeding to determine whether the defendant should be sentenced to death or life imprisonment."[183] If the defendant was convicted after a trial, the sentencing proceeding is to be conducted before the trial jury unless it is unable to reconvene. If the defendant was convicted on a guilty plea or if the trial jury is unavailable, the court is required to empanel a jury to determine punishment.[184] A sentence of death may be imposed only on the basis of a unanimous vote for such a penalty by 12 jurors.[185] "If the jury cannot, within a reasonable time, unanimously agree to its sentence recommendation, the judge shall impose a sentence of life imprisonment."[186]

The jury recommendation[187] as to sentence must be based on the following matters:

1. Whether any sufficient aggravating circumstance or circumstances as enumerated in subsection (e) exist;[188]
2. Whether any sufficient mitigating circumstance or circumstances as enumerated in subsection (f), which outweigh the aggravating circumstance or circumstances found, exist;[189] and
3. Based on these considerations, whether the defendant should be sentenced to death or to imprisonment in the State's prison for life.[190]

The provisions and standards provided by section 15A–2000 apply to the jury sentencing stage of the capital punishment process only. By the terms of the statute, they do not apply to any of the other discretionary stages.

Thus, under the statutory standards, the available evidence on the issues of guilt or innocence of first degree murder and the available aggravating and mitigating circumstances, including the defendant's prior criminal record, should have determined the outcomes. In contrast, such factors as the sex and race of the defendant or victim or the judicial district where the case was tried, which are not relevant to the statutory standards, should not have any effect on the outcomes.[191] The categories of information from the data collection instrument that are therefore relevant to the present inquiry are the following:

- The court proceedings and determinations
- The evidence available to each side on the issues relating to guilt or innocence
- The evidence available to each side on the aggravating and miti-gating circumstances
- The defendant's prior criminal record
- The judicial district in which the case was processed
- The race and sex of the victim and of the defendant

Information about the court proceedings, the judicial district, the race and sex of the victim, and the defendant's prior record was universally available in documented form. Information about the race and sex of the defendant was available for most of the defendants. The study developed each of those factors as a complete item.

The available evidence factor presents a special challenge. Obviously, the quality of the available evidence is an important consideration in the discretionary decision-making processes. The study developed strategies for gathering the information and for including it in the analysis. The information about the available evidence was obtained from three sources: police reports, interviews with the prosecuting attorneys, and interviews with the defense attorneys. There was general congruence between the reports of the police and the prosecuting attorneys, but these often differed in some respects from those of the defense attorneys. The study reconciles these differences using the following policy. In those instances where direct discrepancies exist between the evaluations of the prosecuting and defense attorneys, the study uniformly accepts the evaluations of the prosecuting attorneys. In contrast, if either attorney reported evidence that the other did not mention but would be peculiarly available only to that attorney, the study credits that account. For example, if the defense attorney advised that the defendant would present an alibi witness, but the prosecuting attorney expressed no knowledge of such a witness, the study includes that witness in the evaluation.

In this way, the study strives to achieve consistency in two respects. First, the study attempts to include all the evidence that was available to the decision makers in the judicial process, and only that evidence. Second, if there were going to be any bias in the evaluation of the quality of the evidence, the study endeavors to maintain a consistent direction to that bias, here in favor of the prosecution perspective because the study is directed at the judicial process and its official actors. This is done with an understanding that it does not achieve absolute truth in every case, or perhaps any case, and that it does not standardize the quantity or reliability of the relatively subjective aspects of this information. Thus, in any selected case, the study assessment could undoubtedly be challenged.

The available evidence in each case consists of a varying number of separate items. That circumstance presents a measurement challenge that does not exist with regard to the other variables. In order to take the quality of the evidence into account the study needs to develop a quantitative measure of its value. The measure has to be capable of assimilating diverse kinds of evidence into a manageable number of categories. The measure also has to be sensitive to the reduction in probative value of particular items of evidence arising from their cumulative character or their discrediting features.

The measure that the study develops is designed, not to decide the proper outcome in any case, but to provide an objective and quantifiable score for the cases that will provide a reasonably accurate description of them in groups for comparison with other groups of cases measured in the same way. It is designed to assure the validity of the statistical evaluation of the run of cases and not the outline in any particular case. The study results showed considerable correlation between the statistical predictions based on the evidence measure and the actual outcomes, and explained a substantial portion of the variation with extralegal variables. The measure is in a sense validated by those results.

To formulate this measure, the study employs a strategy that involves two stages: a qualitative stage and a quantitative stage.[192]

The Qualitative Stage

Only three factual issues relevant to the question of guilt or innocence for first degree murder were actually raised in the cases during the study year. Two additional issues were in contention at the penalty stage of cases that resulted in a first degree murder conviction.

The guilt or innocence issues correspond to the three traditional aspects of a criminal offense: the act element (*actus reus*), the mental element (*mens rea*), and the affirmative defenses:[193]

1. Identification of the defendant as a perpetrator: whether the defendant was the person, or an accomplice of the person, who committed the killing[194]
2. Degree of culpability: whether the mental state of the defendant at the time of the killing, including consideration of the felony murder doctrine, qualified for first degree murder rather than a lesser degree of homicide[195]
3. Self-defense: whether the defendant acted in self-defense or in defense of others.[196]

All three issues involve the question of guilt or innocence of capital murder. A decision favorable to the defense on any of the three at any stage diverted the defendant from the death penalty track.

For the penalty stage issues, the study looks to the statute for the list of aggravating and mitigating circumstances. The list of aggravating circumstances is exclusive.[197] Although the list of mitigating circumstances is not exclusive, the cases did not raise any mitigating circumstances other than those listed in the statute. The statistical analysis treats the aggravating circumstances together and the mitigating circumstances together as two separate measures, except that two of those circumstances are treated as separate items: prior record and multiple victims. The defendant's prior record is treated as a distinct factor because it could be either a statutory aggravating or a statutory mitigating circumstance. The multiple victims factor is treated distinctly because it does not correspond precisely to a statutory aggravating factor but corresponds closely to two of them.[198]

The Quantitative Stage

The study developed a complex strategy for assigning a numerical score to the quality of the evidence for each of the three guilt or innocence issues. The strategy produces a separate raw score, for each case on each issue, in the following manner. On the basis of a review of the literature on litigation of a criminal case and on the basis of experience, the study estimates the relative probative value of the different kinds of evidence in homicide cases generally. Each item of evidence is assigned a maximum value based on that estimate. From that maximum value, percentage reductions are made on the basis of factors that tend to limit, qualify, or discredit the evidence. The size of the percentage reduction depends on both the category of evidence and the character of the compromising factor. For subsequent impeaching factors for each item, additional reductions are taken from the remaining total, not the amount of the original maximum.

The study identifies seven categories of evidence that might be relevant to an issue: (a) the testimony of an eyewitness to the incident; (b) the testimony of a witness to relevant circumstances (e.g., that the defendant was seen near, or far from, the scene of the crime at about the time of the crime, that the defendant had a motive to commit the crime, or that the defendant had committed similar crimes); (c) the testimony of an accomplice; (d) the statement of a defendant; (e) physical or scientific evidence; (f) character testimony; and (g) electronic wiretap or eavesdrop evidence. Experience indicates that cumulative items of evidence in the same category on any issue tend to have diminishing value. Accordingly, related items of physical evidence are aggregated and given a single score. For example, fingerprint evidence at the site of the crime, regardless of the number of prints, is valued at 60 points for its contribution to the identification of the defendant. Witnesses are treated differently. If a case had more than one witness on a particular fact, the initial maximum value for the second and succeeding witnesses is determined by successively subtracting 10 points from the maximum value for the first. For example, the first eyewitness on the issue of the identity of the defendant as a perpetrator has a maximum value of 50, the second a maximum value of 40, the third of 30, the fourth of 20, and the fifth of 10. If none of them has any impeaching features, the total score for the issue for eyewitness testimony is 150.

The maximum value for a witness therefore varies according to the number of witnesses in the same category and the ranking of the witness within that category. For that reason, the reductions are taken as a percentage of the maximum value for the particular witness rather than as a fixed number. To accomplish this, the witnesses are tentatively ranked. For the tentative ranking, each witness in the same category is assigned the same maximum value. That value is then reduced by the percentage reductions. This process yields a tentative total score for each witness. The actual scoring is then performed; only the highest ranking witness (or one of them, if two or more have the same tentative scoring) is given the maximum value. That value is reduced by any applicable percentage deduction to determine the actual score for that witness. The second ranking witness is given the maximum value less 10 points, and that value is reduced by any applicable percentage deductions to determine that witness's actual score. The same process is performed for each additional witness to a maximum of five. Because the reductions are percentages of the remaining total, the score for a witness can approach, but never reach, zero. For example, if the maximum value for an eyewitness is 50, and the eyewitness is subject to impeachment because he or she is mentally abnormal (percentage reduction of 40 percent) and was intoxicated at the time of the incident (percentage reduction of 40 percent), the maximum value of 50 for that witness is first reduced by 40 percent to 30, then the 30 score is reduced by 40 percent to 18. Mathematically, the order in which impeachment factors are deducted does not affect the results.

The maximum values and their corresponding percentage reductions are largely the same for all three issues. The precise figures that the study uses are set out in Appendix A.

The item scores are added to provide an overall score for each category for each issue. This process is carried out separately for the prosecution evidence and for the defense evidence on each issue. After the total score for each side is calculated, the defense score is subtracted from the prosecution score. The final score for any issue can thus be positive, negative, or zero. The identification of the defendant score ranges from 350 to −90 with an average of 288; the degree of culpability score ranges from 309 to −250 and averages −5; the self-defense score ranges from 300 to

−218 and averages 170. The raw score has no independent significance. There is no point on the range where it can be said, for any particular case, that the prosecution is strong or weak. Instead, the scores are used simply for comparison with the scores of other cases in the statistical analyses performed.

Four additional scores are constructed based on the evidence regarding aggravating circumstances, mitigating circumstances, the defendant's prior record, and the number of victims. The aggravating and mitigating circumstances scores both range from zero to 25, with zero representing the absence of such circumstances. The prior criminal record score ranges from zero to 30, with zero indicating no prior record. The multiple victims' score is either zero, representing one victim, or one, representing more than one victim.

The scores are constructed as follows:

Aggravating circumstances: Each aggravating circumstance is regarded equally. Because cumulative aggravating circumstances tend to have diminishing marginal values, the total score is determined as follows:

Number of aggravating circumstances	Marginal value	Total score
None	0	0
1	10	10
2	8	18
3	5	23
4	1	24
5	1	25

Actual range: 0–25

Mitigating circumstances: Each mitigating circumstance is regarded equally. Because cumulative mitigating circumstances tend to have diminishing marginal values, the total score is determined as follows:

Number of mitigating circumstances	Marginal value	Total score
None	0	0
1	10	10
2	8	18
3	5	23
4	1	24
5	1	25

Actual range: 0–25

Prior record:

10 for one prior capital felony conviction
8 each for a second or third prior capital felony conviction

8 for one prior violent felony conviction

7 each for a second or third prior violent felony conviction

3 for one prior nonviolent felony conviction

2 each for a second or third prior nonviolent felony conviction

1 each for one to three prior misdemeanor convictions

Actual range: 0–30

Multiple victims:

Number of victims	Score
1	0
2 or more	1

In view of the circumstance that some cases had multiple defendants or multiple victims, or both, the study has to define the unit for analysis. Two defendants charged with homicide of the same victim, or one defendant charged with homicide of two victims, may not present truly independent cases. In order to satisfy technical statistical assumptions of independence, the study selects a set of distinct defendant–victim pairs as the units of analysis. This is accomplished as follows:

- Where the homicidal event involved only one defendant and one victim, that pair constitutes the unit of analysis. This is by far the most frequent situation.
- Where the homicidal event involved one defendant with two or more victims, the study randomly pairs the defendant with one of the victims for the unit of analysis, leaving the other victim out of the study.
- Where the homicidal event involved more than one defendant with only one victim, the study randomly pairs one of the defendants with the victim for the unit of analysis, leaving the other defendant out of the study.
- Where the homicidal event involved more than one defendant and more than one victim, the study randomly pairs one defendant with one victim and the other defendant with the other victim. There are only three such events.

This selection process yields a pool of 523 independent defendants, or defendant–victim pairs. The study does not have sufficient information to construct quality-of-evidence scores for 34 of those, including one who received a death sentence. The following list charts the course of the remaining 489 defendants through the judicial process.

489	Defendant–victim units
−45	Dismissed before indictment
444	

$\dfrac{-113}{331}$ Indicted for less than first degree murder

$\dfrac{-12}{319}$ Dismissed after indictment

$\dfrac{-213}{106}$ Guilty pleas to less than first degree murder

$\dfrac{-46}{60}$ Brought to trial on less than first degree murder

$\dfrac{-34}{26}$ Trial judge refused to submit first degree murder charge to jury

$\dfrac{-8}{18}$ Convicted only of less than first degree murder

-10 Sentenced to life

8 Sentenced to death (plus one defendant for whom the study had insufficient data on quality of evidence)

$\dfrac{-2}{6}$ Convictions reversed

$\dfrac{-5}{1}$ Death sentences reversed

-0 Clemency

1 Executed

PART 8.

The Statistical Analysis

Once the data were accumulated, coded, and classified, the study was ready to determine what factors affected the outcome of each discretionary decision stage. The statistical method that the study uses for this purpose is multiple logistic regression analysis.[199]

Multiple regression analysis seeks to describe the variation in the values of an outcome, or dependent, variable, in terms of the effects of several factors, or independent variables, while statistically controlling for the interrelationship or correlation among them. If there is statistical evidence that a factor makes a contribution to the prediction of an outcome beyond that expected by chance, that factor is said to be statistically significant. Only when the probability of the observed contribution of a factor being the result of chance is extremely low can it be said that the factor is statistically significant. Conventionally, a probability of 1 in 20 or less that the result could have occurred by chance is considered low enough to support a conclusion of significance. That is represented as a probability value of .05 or less ($p < .05$). The degree of significance increases, of course, as the probability value decreases. Thus, a probability value of .01 ($p < .01$) indicates that the probability that the result reflected chance is less than 1 in 100, and .001 ($p < .001$) that the probability that the result reflected chance is less than 1 in 1,000.

This statistical significance is assessed by formulating a mathematical model that includes a number of variables that might affect the outcome. A particular variable may have an effect that is either consistent, regardless of the values of other variables, or varied, depending on the values of one or more other variables. If the effect is varied, there is a statistical "interaction" between the variables involved.

The study used logistic multiple regression analysis rather than ordinary least squares multiple regression analysis. Ordinary least squares multiple regression analysis requires a dependent variable that takes on many values, such as weight (e.g., 10 pounds, 20 pounds, 30 pounds) or income (e.g., $10,000, $20,000, $30,000). Logistic multiple regression analysis, in contrast, explains the relationship between a set of factors and the probability of a binary outcome. In this study, all the outcomes (i.e., the dependent variables) have only two possible values and are therefore binary (e.g., first degree murder indictment or no first degree murder indictment; first degree murder trial or no first degree murder trial; conviction or acquittal; death sentence or life sentence). Accordingly, logistic multiple regression analysis is the proper technique. It predicts the odds of the outcome for the various values of the set of independent variables.[200] The odds of an outcome happening are the familiar betting odds derived from the probability that an event will occur divided by the probability that the event will not occur. Thus, if the probability of an event is .5, the odds are .5 ÷ .5 or 1 to 1 or "even," that it will occur. Similarly, if the probability is .75, the odds are .75 ÷ .25, or 3 to 1, that the event will occur.

Although logistic regression analysis is a somewhat different technique from ordinary least squares regression analysis, the method of determining the significance of independent variables is similar. In both, the statistical significance of an independent variable or set of variables is assessed by comparing the amount of error in prediction of a model that does not include the variable or variables of interest with the amount of error in prediction of a model that includes them. For the statistical test of significance, however, logistic regression analysis employs a chi-square probability distribution based on an approximation for moderately large samples rather than the conventional F probability distribution used with ordinary multiple regression analysis.

Table 1 describes the basic set of variables used in the analyses. They include seven evidence variables and four race and sex variables.[201] In

TABLE 1
The Basic Set of Variables

Category of variables	Description	Coding
Basic evidence	Evidence of first degree murder mental element, or felony murder	309 to −250
	Evidence of identification of the defendant as a perpetrator	350 to −90
	Evidence of self-defense	300 to −205
	Evidence of aggravating circumstances	0 to 25
	Evidence of mitigating circumstances	0 to 25
	Evidence of the defendant's prior criminal record	0 to 30
	Multiple victims	0 = no, 1 = yes
Judicial District	District in which case was processed	Dummy variables for eight judicial districts and one judicial district group
Race and sex	Race of the defendant	0 = white, 1 = nonwhite
	Race of the victim	0 = white, 1 = nonwhite
	Sex of the defendant	0 = female, 1 = male
	Sex of the victim	0 = female, 1 = male

addition, they include nine variables representing the 30 judicial districts in which the cases were processed.[202] An interaction between any two of those variables is represented as an additional variable composed of the product of the values of each pair of interacting variables.

The regression analyses in this study consider a sequence of "models." A model is a mathematical equation that relates the odds of an outcome variable to one or more independent variables. In a sequence of models, all the models use the same outcome variable. The first model in the sequence has no independent variables, only a constant, and thus assumes that all cases were treated alike. The next model introduces one or more independent variables to determine the extent to which those variables explain the variations in the outcome. The more complex model tests whether the additional variables significantly reduce the amount of error in predicting the outcome variable—that is, whether by adding the additional variables, the model better fits the data. Each succeeding model builds on the variables in the preceding models and adds additional variables to create a more complicated model in an effort better to explain the outcome variations. Single variables are entered before interactions.[203] Thus, the analysis proceeds in a sequence examining increasingly complex models that successively attempt to explain more and more of the variation of the outcome variable.

The assessment of the significance of a variable may depend on the order in which that variable is introduced in a series of models. In any such assessment, the only proper conclusion that can be drawn is that certain variables explain differences among the odds better than chance, given that certain other variables are already included in the model. Accordingly, careful consideration must be given to the order in which variables are added.

The ordering used in this study was to enter the basic evidence variables before the extralegal variables (the judicial district and the race and sex of the defendant and victim). The race-of-the-defendant variable alone and the race-and-sex-of-the-defendant-and-victim variables as a set were then entered both before and after the judicial district variable, at all stages where the judicial district variable was included, to assure that any significant effects found were independent of order. The interactions were entered only after the simple variables.

The following sequence of models was studied. The simplest model contained only a constant to represent the situation in which every defendant was treated equally regardless of circumstances. Such a trivial model was considered only as a base against which to judge the effect of the factors under study.

At the first step, the scores for the basic evidence variables were added:

- Identification of the defendant as a perpetrator
- Degree of culpability for first degree murder
- Self-defense
- Aggravating circumstances
- Mitigating circumstances
- Defendant's prior criminal record
- Number of victims

These variables were included first because under the legal standards they are the only variables that should be statistically significant in their power to explain outcome differences among the defendants.

The next set of variables added to the model, for pretrial stages only, were those representing differences among the judicial districts. These variables measure whether the outcome for defendants with similar evidence scores varied depending on the judicial district that processed the case.

Next, a set of four variables involving the race and sex of the defendant and victim were added to the model. Effects of race and sex variables entered after the basic evidence and judicial district would indicate that controlling for judicial district differences and for given levels of the evidentiary variables, the outcome tended to vary according to the race or sex of the defendant or the victim. In addition, in a separate model, the race of the defendant was entered as a single variable after judicial district. As explained above, the analysis was repeated with both the race-of-the-defendant variable alone and the set of four variables together added before the judicial district variable.

By this step, the model included all the variables in Table 1. The remaining models added some of the possible interactions among these basic variables. First were added the interactions of the evidentiary variable most frequently in dispute, degree of culpability, with each of the other evidentiary variables.[204] These interactions test whether different levels of degree of culpability had a different effect on the outcome depending on the levels of the other evidentiary variables.[205]

The next steps, for pretrial stages only, added the interactions of the judicial district variable with the degree of culpability variable and the judicial district variable with the aggravating circumstances variable. These two interactions test whether the variations among different districts had the same pattern at all levels of seriousness of the cases.

The last terms added to the model were the interactions of the race-of-the-defendant variable with the degree of culpability and with the aggravating circumstances variables. These interactions test whether the difference between white and nonwhite defendants varied across levels of degree of culpability or aggravating circumstances.

That sequence of models was studied for each of the following outcome variables:

1. The odds of a dismissal at any stage given an arrest (Table 3)
2. The odds of an indictment for first degree murder
   a. given an arrest (Table 6)
   b. given an indictment for some degree of homicide (Table B-2)
3. The odds of a trial for first degree murder
   a. given an arrest (Table 11)
   b. given an indictment for some degree of homicide (Table B-5)
   c. given an indictment for first degree murder (Table B-7)
4. The odds that the judge submitted the case to the jury on the first degree murder charge

     a. given an arrest (Table 17)
     b. given an indictment on any degree of homicide (Table B-9)
     c. given an indictment for first degree murder (Table B-11)
  5. The odds of a guilty verdict on first degree murder
     a. given an arrest (Table 21)
     b. given an indictment on any degree of homicide (Table B-14)
     c. given an indictment for first degree murder (Table B-16)
  6. The odds of a death sentence
     a. given an arrest (Table 24)
     b. given an indictment on any degree of homicide (Table B-18)
     c. given an indictment for first degree murder (Table B-20)

The results are reported in a series of tables, Appendix B, and discussed in the text in Chapter IV. The models for each outcome based on the pool of all arrested defendants enabled the study to analyze each discretionary stage in the context of the entire judicial process up to that stage. Tables based on those models are presented in Chapter IV. The models for each outcome based on the narrower pools of all defendants indicted for either murder or first degree murder enabled the study to evaluate separately discrete units of the process. Those results were not substantially different, so tables based on those models are presented in Appendix B and are not discussed in the text. The main tables used are:

Logistic Regression Analysis Tables

The primary table used to report the results of the study for each stage is titled "Logistic Regression Analysis." Tables 3, 6, 11, 17, 21, and 24 in Chapter IV are logistic regression analysis tables, each reporting the analysis for a different stage of the process. Each of those tables has seven columns, headed as follows:

  1. *Model*
  2. *−Model likelihood*
  3. *Improvement chi-square*
  4. *Model degrees of freedom*
  5. *Improvement degrees of freedom*
  6. *Probability* <
  7. *Number of infinite coefficient estimates*

The logistic regression analysis tables should be read as follows: The first column (*Model*) lists the groups of variables that have been added to the model preceding it. The model for each line, therefore, contains all the variables in the preceding lines plus those listed in that line.

The second column (*−Model likelihood*) presents a measure of the fit of the model to the data. The smaller the number, the better the fit. The addition of new variables will always improve the fit to some extent, so this column is not alone important. The question is whether the improvement in the fit reflects chance or is a result of a true predictive relationship between the independent variables added and the outcome variable. This question is answered using a calculation based on a chi-square statistic presented in the third column.

The third column (*Improvement chi-square*) is the decrease in the model likelihood from the preceding line multiplied by two.

The fourth column (*Model degrees of freedom*) shows the total number of variables in the model.

The fifth column (*Improvement degrees of freedom*) shows the number of variables added to the model in that line alone.

The sixth column (*Probability* <) reports the significance level of the chi-square statistic for the improvement degrees of freedom. This is the probability that the relationship between the variables added and the outcome variables could have occurred by chance. A probability of .05 or less ($p < .05$) is conventionally considered significant.

The final column (*Number of infinite coefficient estimates*) provides an indicator of the validity of the model coefficient estimates and hence the degree of confidence in any conclusion based on the probability shown in the sixth column. The presence of one infinite coefficient estimate in a model does not necessarily invalidate any conclusions based on that model, but suggests that caution should be exercised in interpreting the results. The presence of many infinite coefficient estimates in a model indicates that the number of cases on which the coefficient estimates are based may be insufficient to produce valid results.

Coefficient Tables

The logistic regression analysis tables show which groups of variables have a significant effect on an outcome. They do not show whether a specific variable in a group contributes, or does not contribute, to that effect. The role that individual variables have in predicting an outcome for each stage can be clarified by examining the coefficients of the last model containing a significant group of variables in each table. This examination for each stage is presented in a table titled "Coefficient Estimates for Last Regression Model with a Significant Category of Variables." Tables 4, 8, 12, 18, 22, 23, and 25 in Chapter IV are coefficient tables. Thus, each logistic regression analysis table is followed by one, or in one case two, coefficient tables. Each coefficient table has five columns, headed as follows:

1. *Variable*
2. *Coefficient*
3. *Standard error*
4. *Chi-square*
5. *Probability* <

The coefficient tables should be read as follows: The first column (*Variable*) lists the specific variables making up the prediction equation.

The second column (*Coefficient*) contains the values, rounded to three decimal places, of the coefficients for each variable as estimated by the logistic regression computer program.

The third (*Standard error*) and fourth (*Chi-square*) columns include information that may be used to determine whether a coefficient is significantly different from a value of zero. This reveals whether the contribution of the variable to the prediction of the odds of the outcome is distinguishable from chance.

The probability is found in the fifth column (*Probability* <). Again, conventionally a value of .05 or less ($p < .05$) is taken as indicating a real rather than a chance effect.

Bar Graphs

The first part of the arbitrariness inquiry is the determination of the extent of correlation between the basic evidence variables—representing the legal standards—and the discretionary outcomes in the death penalty process. The logistic regression tables provide that information. Based on that information, the study constructed bar graphs to illustrate the proportion of outcomes that were consistent with the evidence and the propor-

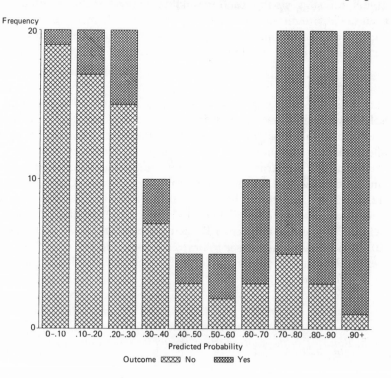

tion that were not. Those bar graphs are presented in Figures 2 and 3 in Chapter IV, in the format of the model bar graph shown here.

The bar graphs should be read as follows: The horizontal line at the base of the bar graphs shows the probability ranges for a selected outcome predicted on the basis of the evidence alone. The predicted values are based on a logistic regression equation that includes only the basic evidence variables. The high probability ranges represent strong cases for first degree murder; the low probability ranges represent weak cases for first degree murder.

The height of each bar reflects the number of cases in each predicted range. The cases with an outcome that continued them on the death penalty track are depicted by the dark cross-hatching pattern. The cases diverted from the death penalty track are depicted by the light pattern. If the basic evidence variables in the cases were highly correlated with the outcomes, the bars for the higher ranges should have only the dark pattern and the bars for the lower ranges should have only the light pattern. The bars in the intermediate ranges could more justifiably mix both patterns.

Relative-Odds Tables

For people not accustomed to reading statistical tables such as the logistic regression analysis and coefficient tables, the significant effects in those tables can be presented in the more familiar terms of "odds." The relative odds are derived mathematically from the coefficients of the variables in a particular regression analysis. This technique facilitates an appreciation of the magnitude of the significant effects. A variable that has a significant effect increases the chances of a particular outcome by multiplying the odds for or against that outcome. If the presence of a given factor changes the odds from 2–1 to 6–1, for example, that can be described as multiplying the odds by 3. Thus, a case with that factor would have three times greater odds than a case without that factor of achieving the outcome.

The relative-odds multipliers for significant judicial district effects are listed at the foot of their coefficient tables. That is done for Tables 8, 12, and 23 in Chapter IV.

The tables titled "Relative Odds" describe significant interactions with racial effects in terms of odds ratios. They are Tables 15, 16, 19, and 20 in Chapter IV, and are set out as follows:

1. (*Variable*)
2. (*Variable*)
3. *Variable combination odds multiplier for white defendants*
4. *Variable combination odds multiplier for nonwhite defendants*
5. *Ratio of odds multiplier for nonwhite defendants to white defendants*

TABLE 2
Assignment of Cases to Evidence-Quality
Categories by Issue Pattern

	Issues		
Case classification	*Degree of culpability*	*Identification of the defendant as perpetrator*	*Self-defense*
Category 1A	High	High	High
Category 1B	High	High	Low
Category 1B	High	Low	High[a]
Category 1B	High	Low	Low
Category 2	Low	High	High
Category 3	Low	High	Low
Category 3	Low	Low	High
Category 3	Low	Low	Low

Note: The logistic regression analysis used the actual quality of evidence scores, not these categories. These categories are for illustrative purposes only.

[a]Any case in the top 30% on the issue of self-defense was not in the top 30% on the issue of the mental element requirement for first degree murder. The same evidence that was relevant to the self-defense claim also disputed the first degree murder mental element.

The relative-odds tables should be read as follows: The first two columns (shown here as *Variable*) present the values of the variables involved in the interaction that is being considered.

The next two columns (*Odds multiplier*) show the amount the odds would be multiplied for the values of those variables for white and nonwhite defendants.[206]

The final column (*Ratio of odds multiplier*) compares the odds multipliers for the two racial groups to show their relative odds. The ratio is calculated by dividing the odds multiplier for nonwhite defendants by the odds multiplier for white defendants.

First Degree Murder and Trial Rate Tables

Although the logistic regression analysis used the raw scores for the quality of evidence—a range of 440 points in the identification of the defendant as a perpetrator, 559 for the degree of culpability, and 518 for self-defense—a table obviously cannot include all those scores. To reduce the scores to a manageable number for descriptive purposes only, the study classified those raw scores into four categories:

Category 1A: strong first degree murder cases
Category 1B: cases with high scores on the first degree murder mental

element evidence but low scores on the identification of the
defendant as a perpetrator evidence

Category 2: cases with high scores on the identification of the defendant
as a perpetrator evidence but low scores on the first degree
murder mental element evidence

Category 3: cases with low scores on the first degree murder mental
element evidence and low scores on the evidence for one or
both other issues as well

For the descriptive purpose of these tables only, each case is assigned
to one of the four evidence-quality categories, based on its pattern of
scores for each issue. This is accomplished in the following manner: First,
the cases are divided according to whether their raw scores for each issue
fall into the top 30 percent of case scores for that issue—identification of
the defendant, degree of culpability, and self-defense. Cases falling into
the upper 30 percent of scores on an issue are deemed to have high evidence quality on that issue; all other cases are deemed to be of lower
quality. Each case is assigned to one of the four quality of evidence categories on the basis of whether it has a "high" or "low" evidence quality
score for each issue, according to the allocation described in Table 2. As
Table 2 shows, a case is classified a Category 1A case only if it falls in the
top 30 percent of scores on all three issues. The evidence in such a case
would clearly identify the defendant as a perpetrator, establish that the
defendant was highly culpable with respect to the mental element requirement for first degree murder, and raise no issue of self-defense. A case is
classified in Category 1B if the available evidence score is in the top 30
percent as to the mental element requirement for first degree murder,
but not as to the identification of the defendant as a perpetrator or self-
defense. A case is classified in Category 2 if the evidence score is in the top
30 percent as to the identification of the defendant and the lack of a complete defense of self-defense, but low as to establishing the requisite mental
element for first degree murder. All other cases have low scores as to the
degree of culpability and at least one other issue, and they are classified in
Category 3.

Tables 10 and 14 in Chapter IV list all the cases according to these
quality-of-evidence categories, by judicial district, and whether they were
indicted for first degree murder or not and whether they were brought to
trial for first degree murder or not.

Additional Tables

Additional tables are used to help explain the data further. These
tables are relatively self-explanatory and are discussed in Chapter IV.

CHAPTER IV

The Results of the Empirical Study

The legal standards defining first degree murder and describing the aggravating and mitigating circumstances should, of course, determine the decisions at all stages of the death penalty process. The results of the empirical study show that the basic evidence on those legal issues was, in fact, the most consistently significant factor in the outcomes. Those same results also show, however, that it was not a controlling factor. The outcomes could not be explained only by the legal standards. Substantial variation in the outcomes was not accounted for by the relevant evidence.

This variation could be caused by the failure of the study to include consideration, or sufficiently accurate consideration, of a relevant legal factor or combination of legal factors, despite the study's efforts to be complete. In addition, if there was a nonlinear relationship between evidence factors and outcomes, the variation could have resulted from failure to take any nonlinearity into account in the statistical models employed. Otherwise, the variation can be explained only as arbitrariness (or discrimination). To determine whether the variation is attributable to methodological difficulties or to arbitrariness, the study tested whether selected extralegal variables that should have no determining effect on the outcomes, under the legal standards, had any responsibility for the variation. The extralegal variables were the judicial district in which the case was processed and the race and sex of the defendant and the victim.

TABLE 3
Logistic Regression Analysis of Probability
of Dismissal after Arrest

Pool: All homicide arrests
489 defendant–victim units
57 dismissed

Model	-Model likelihood	Improve-ment chi-square	Model degrees of freedom	Improve-ment degrees of freedom	Probability <	Number of infinite coefficient estimates
Constant	150.2	—	1	—	—	
Basic evidence	129.9	40.6	8	7	.001	1
Judicial district	126.4	7.0	17	9	.70	2
Race and sex of defendant and victim	126.2	.4	21	4	.99	2
Culpability ° evidence	123.5	5.4	26	5	.50	2
Judicial district ° culpability	119.5	8.0	35	9	.70	2
Judicial district ° aggravating circumstances	112.6	13.9	44	9	.20	10
Defendant's race ° culpability and defendant's race ° aggravating circumstances	111.7	1.8	46	2	.50	13

PART 1.

The Decision to Dismiss

Table 3 shows the logistic regression analysis for the dismissal decision. As should be expected, the evidence variables were the only significant factor at this stage ($p < .001$). Table 4 shows that the stronger the
evidence in a case, the lower the odds of its dismissal. Table 4 also shows
that all three evidence variables relevant to guilt or innocence were significant. As Table 5 shows, no case with more than one victim was dismissed.

TABLE 4

Coefficient Estimates for Last Regression Model with a Significant Category of Variables for Probability of Dismissal after Arrest

Pool: All homicide arrests
489 defendant–victim units
57 dismissed

Variable	Coefficient	Standard error	Chi-square	Probability <
Intercept	−.305	.735	.17	.68
Identity of defendant as a perpetrator	−.005	.002	4.23	.04
Absence of self-defense	−.003	.001	5.69	.02
Degree of culpability	−.005	.002	4.55	.04
Aggravating circumstances	−.088	.052	2.80	.10
Mitigating circumstances	−.023	.059	.16	.70
Prior record	−.070	.067	1.09	.30
Multiple victims	−5.118	†	†	†

Note: The coefficients of a model that omitted the multiple victims variable, but included all other basic evidence variables, were identical to the coefficients for those variables presented in this table.
†The coefficient was infinite.

TABLE 5

Case Dismissal by Number of Victims

Pool: All homicide arrests
489 defendant–victim units

	Number of Victims	
Case dismissal	One	More than one
No	421	11
	88%	100%
Yes	57	0
	12%	0%
Total	478	11
	100%	100%

TABLE 6
Logistic Regression Analysis of Probability
of First Degree Murder Indictment

Pool: All homicide arrests
489 defendant–victim units
331 first degree murder indictments

Model	–Model likelihood	Improvement chi-square	Model degrees of freedom	Improvement degrees of freedom	Probability <	Number of infinite coefficient estimates
Constant	307.7	—	1	—	—	
Basic evidence	278.6	58.2	8	7	.001	0
Judicial district	255.6	46.0	17	9	.001	1
Race and sex of defendant and victim	252.8	5.6	21	4	.30	1
Culpability ° evidence	250.8	4.0	26	5	.70	1
Judicial district ° culpability	247.8	6.0	35	9	.80	1
Judicial district ° aggravating circumstances	239.6	16.4	44	9	.10	3
Defendant's race ° culpability and defendant's race ° aggravating circumstances	237.6	4.0	46	2	.20	3

Otherwise, the aggravating and mitigating circumstances were not significant in the dismissal decision. And, as Table 3 shows, neither were any of the extralegal factors.

PART 2.

The Decision to Indict for First Degree Murder

Table 6 shows the logistic regression analysis for the indictment decision. Again, the basic evidence factor was significant ($p < .001$). Appro-

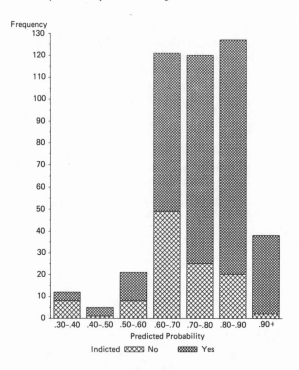

FIGURE 2
Observed Outcomes for Predicted Probability Ranges
for Model Including Only Evidence Variables
for First Degree Murder Indictments

priately, the quality of evidence was an important determinant of the likelihood of an indictment for first degree murder. Table 8 shows that the effective evidence variables were the degree of culpability and the aggravating circumstances.

After accounting for the basic evidence variables, however, considerable variation remained in the indictment decision. This variation is depicted in the bar graph in Figure 2. In that figure, the highest range was for the 90 percent and above probability. As the figure shows, most cases in that range were indicted for first degree murder. In the 80–90 percent and 70–80 percent ranges the bars show that about one-fifth of the cases were not indicted for first degree murder. In the two lowest ranges, 30–40 percent and 40–50 percent, there were a number of first degree murder indictments—indeed, half the cases in those two low ranges were indicted for murder one. In the middle ranges, 50–60 percent and 60–70 percent, the cases were fairly evenly divided.

TABLE 7

**Supplementary Tests of Significance of Race, Sex,
and Judicial District Variables for Probability
of First Degree Murder Indictment**

Pool: All homicide arrests
489 defendant–victim units
331 first degree murder indictments

Model	–Model likelihood	Improve- ment chi- square	Improve- ment degrees of freedom	Probability <	Number of infinite coefficient estimates
Race of defendant entered after basic evidence	276.9	3.4	1	.10	1
Race and sex of defendant and victim entered after basic evidence	276.6	4.0	4	.50	1
Judicial district entered after race and sex of defendant and victim	252.8	47.6	9	.001	1

Why was the first degree murder indictment rate not entirely consistent with the evidence in the cases? Some of the variation is explained by differences among the judicial districts. Table 6 shows that the judicial district factor was significant at the same level ($p < .001$) as the basic evidence. No other factor had a significant predictive effect. The race of the defendant was not a significant factor, regardless of whether it was considered alone or in an interaction with the quality of evidence or aggravating factors. As Table 7 shows, that was true regardless of whether the race of the defendant was entered before or after the judicial district factor.

The significance of the judicial district factor deserves a closer look. Table 8 shows that Districts 5, 12, and 26 were the districts that had the aberrant rates of indictment. These differences are further illustrated in Table 9. Most of the districts had first degree murder indictment rates between 60 percent and 80 percent.[1] Districts 5 and 26 had significantly higher rates of 100 percent and 90 percent, and District 12 had a significantly lower rate of only 37.5 percent. Table 8 shows that, using Judicial District Group B as a reference for comparison purposes, a defendant in District 5 had much higher odds of being indicted for first degree murder

TABLE 8
Coefficient Estimates for Last Regression Model
with a Significant Category of Variables for Probability
of First Degree Murder Indictment

Pool: All homicide arrests
489 defendant–victim units
331 first degree murder indictments

Variable	Coefficient	Standard error	Chi-square	Probability <
Intercept	−.576	.507	1.29	.26
Identity of defendant as a perpetrator	−.000	.001	.04	.85
Absence of self-defense	.000	.001	.21	.65
Degree of culpability	.006	.001	16.83	.001
Aggravating circumstances	.048	.024	3.92	.05
Mitigating circumstances	.009	.023	.17	.68
Prior record	.028	.025	1.27	.26
Multiple victims	−1.095	.751	2.13	.15
Judicial District 3	.328	.599	.30	.59
Judicial District 5	8.24[a]	†	†	†
Judicial District 12	−1.732[b]	.469	13.63	.001
Judicial District 14	.104	.637	.03	.87
Judicial District 16	1.108	.827	1.80	.18
Judicial District 18	.233	.428	.29	.59
Judicial District 26	1.548[c]	.568	7.43	.01
Judicial District 27	.555	.498	1.24	.27

TABLE 8 — Continued
Coefficient Estimates for Last Regression Model
with a Significant Category of Variables for Probability
of First Degree Murder Indictment

Pool: All homicide arrests
489 defendant–victim units
331 first degree murder indictments

Variable	Coefficient	Standard error	Chi-square	Probability <
Judicial District Group A	−.504	.275	3.37	.07

[†]The coefficient was infinite.

[a]The infinite coefficient for Judicial District 5 shows that all the cases in that district were indicted for first degree murder.

[b]The coefficient for District 12 shows that a defendant in that district had only two-tenths the odds of being indicted for first degree murder compared to similar defendants in Judicial District Group B.

[c]The coefficient for District 26 means that a defendant in that district had 4.7 times greater odds of a first degree indictment relative to similar defendants in Judicial District Group B.

TABLE 9
First Degree Murder Indictments by Judicial District

Pool: All homicide arrests
489 defendant–victim units
331 first degree murder indictments

First degree murder indictment	*Judicial District or District Group*									
	3	5	12	14	16	18	26	27	A	B
No	5	0	20	4	2	10	4	7	45	61
	25.0%	0.0%	62.5%	26.7%	12.5%	23.8%	10.3%	26.9%	40.5%	34.7%
Yes	15	12	12	11	14	32	35	19	66	115
	75.0%	100%	37.5%	73.3%	87.5%	76.2%	89.7%	73.1%	59.5%	65.3%
Total	20	12	32	15	16	42	39	26	111	176
	100%	100%	100%	100%	100%	100%	100%	100%	100%	100%

Note: Group A includes districts 7, 10, 11, 13, 20, 21, 22, and 29. Group B includes districts 1, 2, 4, 6, 8, 9, 15, 17, 19, 23, 24, 25, 27, 28, and 30.

TABLE 10
First Degree Murder Indictment Rates
by Judicial District and Quality of Evidence

| Judicial district | Indictment Rate | | Quality of Evidence | | | | | | | |
| | First degree murder | All homicide indictments | First degree murder indictment | | | | No first degree murder indictment | | | |
			1A	1B	2	3	1A	1B	2	3
8	2	19	2	0	0	0	4	2	6	5
21	5	19	3	2	0	0	5	3	4	2
25	6	22	5	1	0	0	6	0	5	8
12	12	28	5	5	1	1	2	1	6	7
13	8	14	2	3	2	1	0	0	2	4
11	11	18	7	4	0	0	3	1	2	1
9	14	18	4	4	3	3	0	1	2	1
14	11	14	1	5	3	2	0	0	1	2
10	8	10	3	2	0	3	0	0	2	0
15	8	10	2	3	2	1	0	2	0	0
18	32	40	12	9	6	5	1	1	3	3
4	19	23	6	2	7	4	0	1	1	2
17	10	12	1	4	2	3	0	1	1	0
23	5	6	2	1	0	2	0	0	1	0
3	15	17	4	3	3	5	2	0	0	0
22	7	8	3	3	0	1	0	0	0	1
29	8	9	4	0	1	3	0	0	0	1
20	9	10	1	3	2	3	0	0	1	0
27	19	21	7	5	2	5	0	0	1	1
7	10	11	6	0	1	3	0	0	0	1
16	14	15	6	4	2	2	0	0	0	1
19	15	16	3	2	4	6	0	1	0	0
26	35	36	9	8	6	12	0	0	1	0
2	1	1	0	0	1	0	0	0	0	0
1	3	3	0	1	1	1	0	0	0	0
24	4	4	2	0	0	2	0	0	0	0
30	4	4	2	1	1	0	0	0	0	0
6	11	11	6	1	1	3	0	0	0	0
5	12	12	3	3	2	4	0	0	0	0
28	13	13	0	4	3	6	0	0	0	0

Total   331   444

than a defendant in District Group B similarly situated as to all other factors. In fact, a defendant in District 26 had 4.7 times greater odds. In contrast, a defendant in District 12 had only two-tenths the odds of a defendant in District Group B.

Table 10 further illustrates the influence of the judicial district factor. It displays the indictment pattern for each of the 30 judicial districts, in ranked order, for the 444 cases with adequate quality-of-evidence information. The tendency for most of the districts was to indict most homicide cases at the first degree murder level. Twenty-four of the districts had first degree murder indictment rates in excess of 75 percent. Six of those had 100 percent rates, and 13 indicted all but 1 or 2 cases for first degree murder. District 26 indicted 35 of 36 cases at the first degree murder level. That was not, however, a uniform pattern. Six districts had significantly lower rates, ranging from 10 percent to 61 percent. In District 8 only 2 of 19 homicide indictments were for first degree murder; in District 21, 5 of 19; in District 25, 6 of 22; and in District 12, 12 of 28.

The natural question is whether this variation can be explained on the basis of differences in the strength of the evidence or seriousness of the homicides, on the basis of differences in the indictment policies of the prosecutors for similar homicides, or on the basis of other extralegal factors. The logistic regression analysis rules out the first explanation. That analysis determined that the differences among the judicial districts cannot be explained by the quality of evidence in the cases. To describe the components of that conclusion, Table 10 classifies the indictment figures by the quality of evidence in the cases according to the four categories described in Table 2 in Chapter III.

Table 10 shows that the 24 districts with high first degree murder indictment rates indicted cases at that level from all four quality of evidence categories, including all of their Category 1A cases. By contrast, all but one of the six districts with low first degree murder indictment rates had Category 1A cases, and all but two had Category 1B cases, that they indicted only at a level less than first degree murder.

District 28, for example, indicted all 13 of its homicide cases for first degree murder, yet none of the cases had Category 1A quality: 4 were Category 1B, 3 Category 2, and 6 Category 3. Similarly, District 26, which indicted 35 of its 36 homicide cases at the first degree murder level, had only 9 Category 1A cases and 8 Category 1B cases. The rest, over half of the total indicted at the high level, were 6 Category 2 cases and 12 Category 3 cases. The one case to escape a murder one indictment in District 26 was a Category 2 case. Look also at District 3. There, 15 of 17 homicide cases, including 3 Category 1B and 5 Category 3 cases, were indicted for first degree murder. Yet the only 2 cases not indicted for murder one were both Category 1A cases. By contrast, in District 8, where only 2 of the 19 homicides were indicted for first degree murder, 4 Category 1A and 2

Category 1B cases escaped that fate. Similarly, District 21, with a 5 for 19 record on murder one indictments in homicide cases, diverted 5 Category 1A and 3 Category 1B cases from the death penalty track at the indictment stage.

Table 10 thus illustrates, by grouping the cases into categories on the basis of quality of evidence, what the logistic regression analysis in Table 6 reports on the basis of the actual quality-of-evidence scores: the data do not readily support a hypothesis that differences in the seriousness of the homicides was responsible for the variability among judicial districts in the first degree murder indictment rates.

PART 3.

The Decisions Leading to a Trial
for First Degree Murder

The indictment stage is only the first opportunity that the prosecutor has to exercise discretion in the processing of homicide cases. After indictment, the prosecutor may still reduce or dismiss the first degree murder charge, on his or her own initiative or after negotiations with the defense. Some prosecutors may be less active than others in their use of the indictment process for effective screening of cases, preserving their flexibility in view of three circumstances: (a) the prosecuting attorney may not have sufficient information at this early stage to make a precise assessment of its severity; (b) ample room for more realistic assessment of the case and corresponding adjustment of the charge remains throughout the later judicial stages; and (c) indicting for first degree murder enhances the prosecutor's plea bargaining posture with the defendant.

Ultimately, only 60 of the 331 cases indicted for first degree murder went to trial on that charge, and only 18 (5.4 percent) resulted in first degree murder verdicts. This shows not only a propensity to indict for the maximum degree but also the considerable exercise of discretion at later stages in the process. If some prosecutors prefer to postpone their screening, their later exercise of discretion could restore the balance among the judicial districts. To determine whether the variation identified at the indictment level was canceled by subsequent discretionary decisions of the prosecutors, the study evaluated the course of all cases to see what factors determined whether they were actually brought to trial on a first degree murder charge.

Table 11 shows the logistic regression analysis for the decisions to bring cases to trial on a first degree murder charge. The quality of evidence maintained its significant effect at the .001 level. Table 12 shows that none of the evidence factors bearing on guilt or innocence was significant

TABLE 11
Logistic Regression Analysis of Probability
of First Degree Murder Trial

Pool: All homicide arrests
489 defendant–victim units
60 first degree murder trials

Model	–Model likelihood	Improvement chi-square	Model degrees of freedom	Improvement degrees of freedom	Probability <	Number of infinite coefficient estimates
Constant	182.0	—	1	—	—	
Basic evidence	167.5	29.0	8	7	.001	0
Judicial district	154.5	26.0	17	9	.01	0
Race and sex of defendant and victim	151.3	6.4	21	4	.20	0
Culpability * evidence	146.7	9.2	26	5	.20	0
Judicial district * culpability	139.7	14.0	35	9	.20	0
Judicial district aggravating factors	132.3	14.8	44	9	.10	1
Defendant's race * culpability and defendant's race * aggravating circumstances	126.0	12.6	46	2	.01	1

at this stage by itself. Instead, two variables relevant to the seriousness of a case—the aggravating circumstances score and whether the defendant allegedly killed more than one victim—were the significant evidence predictors. The involvement of multiple victims had a particularly strong effect. A defendant accused of killing more than one victim had 10 times greater odds of being brought to trial for first degree murder than a defendant charged with killing only one victim.

Although the evidence was therefore a very strong predictor of whether a defendant was brought to trial for first degree murder at this important stage, there was still considerable variation in the decisions unaccounted for by the evidence. The bar graph in Figure 2 provides insight into that variation. The highest predicted probabilities of a trial for first

TABLE 12
Coefficient Estimates for Last Regression Model with a Significant
Category of Variables for Probability of First Degree Murder Trial

Pool: All homicide arrests
489 defendant–victim units
60 first degree murder trials

Variable	Coefficient	Standard error	Chi-square	Probability <
Intercept	−5.096	1.371	13.92	.0002
Identity of defendant as a perpetrator	.002	.003	.38	.54
Absence of self-defense	−.000	.002	.03	.87
Degree of culpability	−.004	.013	.09	.77
Aggravating circumstances	.228	.079	8.36	.004
Mitigating circumstances	−.072	.054	1.76	.19
Prior record	−.056	.053	1.09	.30
Multiple victims	2.336 [a]	.900	6.74	.01
Judicial District 3	3.238	1.842	3.09	.08
Judicial District 5	5.060 [b]	1.440	12.35	.0004
Judicial District 12	−.199	1.477	.02	.89
Judicial District 14	2.913 [c]	1.070	7.42	.007
Judicial District 16	1.213	1.448	.70	.41
Judicial District 18	−1.923	2.129	.82	.37
Judicial District 26	−2.087	2.856	.53	.47
Judicial District 27	2.151 [d]	.864	6.19	.02
Judicial District Group A	1.297	.755	2.95	.09
Race of defendant	1.088	.733	2.20	.14
Race of victim	−.944	.577	2.68	.11

TABLE 12

Coefficient Estimates for Last Regression Model with a Significant Category of Variables for Probability of First Degree Murder Trial

Pool: All homicide arrests
489 defendant–victim units
60 first degree murder trials

Variable	Coefficient	Standard error	Chi-square	Probability <
Sex of defendant	.943	.573	2.70	.10
Sex of victim	.056	.432	.02	.897
Culpability ° identity of defendant as a perpetrator	.000	.000	.31	.58
Culpability ° absence of self-defense	.000	.000	3.82	.05
Culpability ° aggravating circumstances	−.003	.001	9.56	.002
Culpability ° mitigating circumstances	.001	.001	2.50	.12
Culpability ° prior record	.002	.001	5.01	.03
Judicial District 3 ° culpability	−.000	.015	0.00	.98
Judicial District 5 ° culpability	.015	.013	1.36	.24
Judicial District 12 ° culpability	−.010	.017	.33	.57
Judicial District 14 ° culpability	−.014	.018	.67	.41
Judicial District 16 ° culpability	−.012	.009	1.64	.20
Judicial District 18 ° culpability	.024	.018	1.66	.20
Judicial District 26 ° culpability	.028	.031	.81	.37

TABLE 12 — Continued
Coefficient Estimates for Last Regression Model with a Significant Category of Variables for Probability of First Degree Murder Trial

Pool: All homicide arrests
489 defendant–victim units
60 first degree murder trials

Variable	Coefficient	Standard error	Chi-square	Probability <
Judicial District 27 ° culpability	.006	.011	.33	.57
Judicial District Group A ° culpability	.005	.007	.48	.50
Judicial District 3 ° aggravating circumstances	−.278	.146	3.61	.06
Judicial District 5 ° aggravating circumstances	−.249	.116	4.62	.04
Judicial District 12 ° aggravating circumstances	.219	.122	3.20	.08
Judicial District 14 ° aggravating circumstances	.141	.126	1.26	.27
Judicial District 16 ° aggravating circumstances	.110	.128	.74	.39
Judicial District 18 ° aggravating circumstances	.076	.112	.47	.50
Judicial District 26 ° aggravating circumstances	.211	.205	1.06	.31
Judicial District 27 ° aggravating circumstances	−1.062	†	†	†

TABLE 12 — Continued

Coefficient Estimates for Last Regression Model with a Significant Category of Variables for Probability of First Degree Murder Trial

Pool: All homicide arrests
489 defendant–victim units
60 first degree murder trials

Variable	Coefficient	Standard error	Chi-square	Probability <
Judicial District Group A ° aggravating circumstance	−.006	.064	.01	.94
Race ° culpability	.013	.006	5.67	.02
Defendant's race ° aggravating circumstances	−.154	.049	10.02	.002

[†]The coefficient was infinite.

[a]The coefficient for the multiple-victims variable shows that the odds of defendants in cases with more than one victim being brought to trial on a first degree murder charge were about 10 times greater than defendants in similar cases with only one victim.

[b]The coefficient for Judicial District 5 shows that the odds of being brought to trial for first degree murder were 158 times greater for defendants in that district than for defendants in Judicial District Group B.

[c]The coefficient for Judicial District 14 shows that the odds of being brought to trial for first degree murder were 18 times greater for defendants in that district than for defendants in Judicial District Group B.

[d]The coefficient for Judicial District 27 shows that the odds of being brought to trial for first degree murder were 9 times greater for defendants in that district than for defendants in Judicial District Group B.

degree murder based on the evidence are only in the 40–50 percent range. In that range, one-half of the cases actually were brought to trial for first degree murder. In the 30–40 percent range, also about half the cases were brought to trial for first degree murder. Although most cases in the 10 percent or less and the 10–20 percent ranges were not brought to trial for first degree murder, a substantial number were. Although there was a general correspondence between the evidence and the outcomes, the predicted probabilities were all low.

One explanation for the lack of definitiveness in the predictions based on the legal standards, as shown in Table 11, is that although the evidence was a highly significant factor, so was the judicial district. The level of significance for the judicial district factor at this stage was slightly less impressive than it had been at the indictment stage ($p < .01$ versus $p < .001$), but it was substantial nonetheless. Table 12 shows that Districts 5, 14, and 27 had the most aberrant trial rate patterns, higher than the rest of the districts for cases with similar evidence, compared to Judicial District Group B.

TABLE 13
First Degree Murder Trial by Judicial District

First degree murder trial	Judicial District or District Group									
	3	5	12	14	16	18	26	27	A	B
No	17	7	25	9	13	39	36	22	94	167
	85.0%	58.3%	78.1%	60.0%	81.2%	92.9%	92.3%	84.6%	84.7%	94.9%
Yes	3	5	7	6	3	3	3	4	17	9
	15.0%	41.7%	21.9%	40.0%	18.8%	7.1%	7.7%	15.4%	15.3%	5.1%
Total	20	12	32	15	16	42	39	26	111	176
	100%	100%	100%	100%	100%	100%	100%	100%	100%	100%

Note: Group A includes districts 7, 10, 11, 13, 20, 21, 22, and 29. Group B includes districts 1, 2, 4, 6, 8, 9, 15, 17, 19, 23, 24, 25, 27, 28, and 30.

The statistics in the logistic regression table summarize a great deal of complexity. Simplifying, for illustrative purposes, by not controlling for the quality of the evidence, Table 13 shows the first degree murder trial rates for the judicial districts. Districts 5 and 14 were still high. Most of the districts had first degree murder trial rates in the 5–15 percent range, with Districts 12 and 16 slightly higher, at 22 percent and 19 percent. District 5, however, had a rate of 42 percent and District 14 of 40 percent.

In "odds" terms, looking back at Table 12, which does control for the evidence variables, all other factors being equal, the odds for a defendant in District 5 of standing trial on first degree murder were 158 times those of a similarly situated defendant in comparison District Group B; of a defendant in District 14, 18 times greater; and of a defendant in District 27, 9 times greater. This demonstrates a statistically significant differential in the exercise of prosecutorial discretion in different judicial districts, controlling for the quality of evidence in the cases.

This information shows that the judicial district variation that occurred at the indictment level was not in fact balanced by subsequent discretionary decisions by the prosecutor. Districts that engaged in meaningful screening at the indictment level, as well as those that did not, exercised selectivity in deciding which of the indicted cases to bring to trial. Any expectation that the judicial districts that exercised minimal discretion at the indictment stage would undertake considerably more screening during the postindictment, pretrial stage than the judicial districts that had already engaged in extensive screening did not materialize. As Table 14 shows, the judicial districts that screened cases at a substantial level at the indictment stage continued to screen the cases that they did

TABLE 14
First Degree Murder Trial Rates
by Judicial District and Quality of Evidence

Judicial district	Total number of homicide indictments	First degree murder indictments				First degree murder trial				No first degree murder trial			
		1A	1B	2	3	1A	1B	2	3	1A	1B	2	3
8	19	2	0	0	0	0	0	0	0	2	0	0	0
21	19	3	2	0	0	2	0	0	0	1	2	0	0
25	22	5	1	0	0	1	0	0	0	4	1	0	0
12	28	5	5	1	1	2	4	0	1	3	1	1	0
13	14	2	3	2	1	1	1	0	0	1	2	2	1
11	18	7	4	0	0	2	0	0	0	5	3	0	0
9	18	4	4	3	3	0	1	0	0	4	3	3	2
14	14	1	5	3	2	0	3	1	2	1	2	2	0
10	10	3	2	0	3	1	0	0	1	2	2	0	2
15	10	2	3	2	1	0	0	0	0	2	3	2	1
18	40	12	9	6	5	1	2	0	0	11	7	6	5
4	23	6	2	7	4	0	0	0	0	6	2	7	4
17	12	1	4	2	3	0	0	0	0	1	3	2	3
23	6	2	1	0	2	1	0	0	0	1	1	0	1
3	17	4	3	3	5	0	0	2	1	4	3	1	3
22	8	3	3	0	1	2	1	0	0	1	2	0	1
29	9	4	0	1	3	1	0	0	1	3	0	1	2
20	10	1	3	2	3	1	1	0	0	0	2	2	2
27	21	7	5	2	5	1	2	0	1	6	3	2	4
7	11	6	0	1	3	2	0	0	0	4	0	1	3
16	15	6	4	2	2	2	0	0	1	4	4	2	1
19	16	3	2	4	6	1	1	0	0	2	1	4	6
26	36	9	8	6	12	1	2	0	0	7	6	6	9
2	1	0	0	1	0	0	0	1	0	0	0	0	0
1	3	0	1	1	1	0	0	0	0	0	1	1	1
24	4	2	0	0	2	2	0	0	0	0	0	0	1
30	4	2	1	1	0	0	0	0	0	2	1	1	0
6	11	6	1	1	3	0	0	0	1	6	1	1	2
5	12	3	3	2	4	3	0	1	1	0	3	1	3
28	13	0	4	3	6	0	0	0	0	0	4	3	5

Total: 60 first degree murder trials.

indict for first degree murder before bringing them to trial on that charge. Thus the variation among districts at the indictment stage screening maintained its influence on the trial stage.

Table 11 shows one more significant factor in the determination of whether a case was brought to trial for first degree murder. The race of the defendant, in an interaction with the degree of culpability score and

TABLE 15
**Relative Odds of Trial on First Degree Murder
for Nonwhite Defendants to White Defendants
for Aggravating Circumstances Score of Zero
and Selected Degree of Culpability Scores**

Aggravating circumstances score	Degree of culpability score	Variable combination odds multiplier for white defendants	Variable combination odds multiplier for nonwhite defendants	Ratio of odds multiplier for nonwhite defendants to white defendants
0	−100	1.5	1.2	.8:1
0	0	1.0	3.0	3:1
0	100	.7	7.3	10:1

Note: The odds multipliers are rounded to the nearest tenth. The ratios are calculated from the actual odds multipliers and then rounded to the nearest tenth.

in an interaction with the aggravating circumstances score, was significant in determining whether a defendant was brought to trial for first degree murder, at the .01 level. Thus, although the race of the defendant alone was not a significant factor at the dismissal or indictment stages, it did become a significant factor in the decision-making process determining whether the defendant was required to stand trial for a capital offense, in interaction with the evidence regarding degree of culpability and aggravating circumstances. Table 12 reveals that both those interactions were statistically significant. Tables 15 and 16 illustrate the effects that those interactions had by comparing the odds multipliers for selected values of degree of culpability and aggravating circumstances scores for white and nonwhite defendants. Table 15 shows that holding the aggravating circumstances score constant at zero, a nonwhite defendant's odds of being brought to trial on first degree murder are multiplied dramatically relative to those of a white defendant's for cases with medium and high values of degree of culpability. Although for cases with a low degree of culpability score there was almost no relative disadvantage (i.e., the ratio was .8 to 1, almost even), for cases with a mid-level degree of culpability score, the ratio was 3 to 1, and for cases with a high degree of culpability score, the ratio was 10 to 1. That is, nonwhite defendants in cases with no aggravating circumstances but middle or high range degree of culpability scores had 3 or 10 times greater odds, respectively, than white defendants with cases in the same ranges of being brought to trial at risk of the death penalty.

Table 16 shows the same computation for defendants with cases presenting one aggravating circumstance. If the case had one aggravating circumstance, the odds persisted against nonwhite defendants, though at a somewhat lower level, for cases with high degree of culpability scores. For cases with low and medium values of culpability, however, the relative disadvantage was reversed. Holding the aggravating circumstances score

TABLE 16
Relative Odds of Trial on First Degree Murder
for Nonwhite Defendants to White Defendants for
Aggravating Circumstances Score of 10
and Selected Degree of Culpability Scores

Aggravating circumstances score	Degree of culpability score	Variable combination odds multiplier for white defendants	Variable combination odds multiplier for nonwhite defendants	Ratio of odds multiplier for nonwhite defendants to white defendants
10	−100	14.6	2.5	.2:1
10	0	9.8	6.2	.6:1
10	100	6.6	15.3	2.3:1

Note: The odds multipliers are rounded to the nearest tenth. The ratios are calculated from the actual odds multipliers and then rounded to the nearest tenth.

constant at one, for a low degree of culpability score, white defendants had five times the odds, and for a medium degree of culpability score, white defendants had slightly less than twice the odds of a nonwhite defendant of standing trial for first degree murder. But for cases with a high degree of culpability score, the odds substantially disfavored nonwhite defendants, 2.3 to 1.

Accordingly, at a high level of degree of culpability a nonwhite defendant had odds 2.3 times greater than a white defendant of being brought to trial for first degree murder, if the aggravating circumstances scores for both defendants were high and a 10 times greater chance if the aggravating circumstances scores for both were low. These odds were calculated controlling for all other factors, including the quality of the evidence in the cases of both the nonwhite and the white defendants. In serious cases, therefore, a nonwhite defendant stood a much greater chance of being brought to trial at risk of receiving a death sentence, although the disparity was less if both cases had an aggravating circumstance other than prior record or multiple victims. Even in that situation, however, the nonwhite defendant had more than double the odds of the white defendant of standing trial for capital murder.

PART 4.

The Decision to Submit the Case
to the Jury on First Degree Murder

Table 17 shows that the basic evidence again properly played an important role in determining whether the trial judge submitted a case

TABLE 17
Logistic Regression Analysis of
Probability of Trial Judge Submitting
First Degree Murder Charge to Jury

Pool: All homicide arrests
489 defendant–victim units
26 first degree murder submissions

Model	−Model likelihood	Improvement chi-square	Model degrees of freedom	Improvement degrees of freedom	Probability <	Number of infinite coefficient estimates
Constant	101.6	—	1	—	—	
Basic evidence	79.9	43.4	8	7	.001	0
Race and sex of defendant and victim	76.3	6.6	12	4	.20	0
Culpability ° evidence	70.4	11.8	17	5	.05	0
Defendant's race ° culpability and defendant's race ° aggravating factors	66.5	7.8	19	2	.01	0

to the jury for a decision on guilt or innocence of first degree murder. At this stage, both the basic evidence factor and the interaction of the degree of culpability with the other basic evidence variables were significant ($p < .001$ and $p < .05$, respectively). Table 18 shows that the defendant's prior record and the interaction of the prior record factor with the degree of culpability factor were the only two individually significant evidentiary variables.

The significant interactions at this stage made the relationship between the evidence variables and the outcome more complex than the comparable relationship in earlier stages. Nevertheless, after controlling for the effects of the basic evidence variables, some variation in the outcomes was left unaccounted for. Figure 3 compares the predicted probabilities in outcome with the actual outcomes. It shows that the probabilities of any case being submitted to the jury on first degree murder predicted from the evidence were overwhelmingly low. Even in the two lowest ranges, however—10 percent or less and between 10 percent and 20 percent—a number of cases (the actual number was 17) were submitted to the jury on a first degree murder charge.

Tables 17 and 18 show further that the other significant factor predicting the outcome at this stage was the race of the defendant. As at the

TABLE 18
Coefficient Estimates for Last Regression
Model with a Significant Category of
Variables for Probability of Trial Judge Submitting
First Degree Murder Charge to Jury

Pool: All homicide arrests
489 defendant–victim units
26 first degree murder submissions

Variable	Coefficient	Standard error	Chi-square	Probability <
Intercept	−6.088	2.420	6.33	.02
Identity of defendant as a perpetrator	.003	.005	.27	.61
Absence of self-defense	.007	.004	2.65	.11
Degree of culpability	−.008	.022	.14	.70
Aggravating circumstances	.132	.096	1.87	.18
Mitigating circumstances	.034	.088	.15	.70
Prior record	−.294	.140	4.41	.04
Multiple victims	1.090	.977	1.24	.27
Defendant's race	1.965	1.163	2.86	.10
Victim's race	−1.518	.795	3.65	.06
Defendant's sex	.191	.825	.05	.82
Victim's sex	−1.045	.516	4.09	.05
Culpability ° identity of defendant as perpetrator	.000	.000	.01	.92
Culpability ° absence of self-defense	.000	.000	1.84	.18
Culpability ° aggravating circumstances	−.001	.001	.51	.48
Culpability ° mitigating circumstances	−.000	.001	.26	.62

TABLE 18 — Continued
Coefficient Estimates for Last Regression
Model with a Significant Category of
Variables for Probability of Trial Judge Submitting
First Degree Murder Charge to Jury

Pool: All homicide arrests
489 defendant–victim units
26 first degree murder submissions

Variable	Coefficient	Standard error	Chi-square	Probability <
Culpability * prior record	.004	.002	6.39	.02
Defendant's race * culpability	.015	.010	2.13	.15
Defendant's race * aggravating circumstances	−.154	.060	6.52	.02

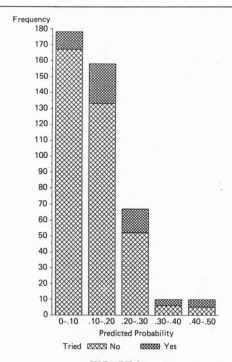

FIGURE 3
Observed Outcomes for Predicted Probability Ranges
for Model Including Only Evidence Variables
for First Degree Murder Trials

TABLE 19

**Relative Odds of Trial Judge Submitting
First Degree Murder Charge to Jury
for Nonwhite Defendants to White Defendants
for Prior Record Score of Zero and
Selected Aggravating Circumstances Scores**

Prior record score	Aggravating circumstances score	Variable combination odds multiplier for white defendants	Variable combination odds multiplier for nonwhite defendants	Ratio of odds multiplier for nonwhite defendants to white defendants
0	0	1.0	3.0	3:1
0	10	3.7	6.2	1.7:1
0	18	10.8	11.2	1:1

Note: The odds multipliers are rounded to the nearest tenth. The ratios are calculated from the actual odds multipliers and then rounded to the nearest tenth.

TABLE 20

**Relative Odds of Trial Judge Submitting
First Degree Murder Charge to Jury
for Nonwhite Defendants to White Defendants
for Prior Record Score of 10 and
Selected Aggravating Circumstances Scores**

Prior record score	Aggravating circumstances score	Variable combination odds multiplier for white defendants	Variable combination odds multiplier for nonwhite defendants	Ratio of odds multiplier for nonwhite defendants to white defendants
10	0	.05	3.0	56:1
10	10	.20	6.2	31.4:1
10	18	.60	11.2	19.8:1

Note: The odds multipliers are rounded to the nearest tenth. The ratios are calculated from the actual odds multipliers and then rounded to the nearest tenth.

trial stage, that factor did not have an independent effect. Instead, the interaction for the race of the defendant with the aggravating circumstances score contributed to the prediction of this outcome ($p < .02$).

The overall effect of the three significant variables—prior record, the race of the defendant, and aggravating circumstances—on the odds of a defendant, once arrested, having his or her case submitted to a jury for a first degree murder verdict is illustrated in Tables 19 and 20. Table 19 shows that, for defendants with no prior record, nonwhites were at a relative disadvantage to whites in cases with no aggravating circumstances or only one aggravating circumstance. That disadvantage decreased with increasing levels of aggravating circumstance scores until the two racial groups were even when both had cases with two aggravating circumstances. The odds of having the trial judge submit the case to a jury on first degree murder were 3.0 times greater for a nonwhite compared to a white defendant where both had cases with no aggravating circumstances. When both had cases with one aggravating circumstance, the odds were only 1.7 times greater. The odds were even when both had cases with two aggravating circumstances. This means that in very aggravated murders, nonwhite and white defendants with no prior record had roughly the same odds of having a jury decide a charge of first degree murder. The odds that the case of a nonwhite defendant with no prior record would be submitted to a jury on a first degree murder charge, however, were 3.0 times those of a similarly situated white defendant when both cases had no aggravating circumstances.

Table 20 reveals that in cases where the defendant had at least some prior record (i.e., a score of 10), nonwhite defendants were at a substantial disadvantage relative to white defendants at this stage regardless of the level of the aggravating circumstances score. The odds for a nonwhite defendant with a prior record but no other aggravating circumstances of having a jury consider a first degree murder charge were 56 times those of a comparable white defendant. The odds for a nonwhite defendant with a prior record and one other aggravating circumstance of having a jury deliberate on the first degree murder charge against him or her at this stage were 31 times greater than those of a similarly situated white defendant. The odds at this stage for a nonwhite defendant with a prior record and two aggravating circumstances were almost 20 times those for a white defendant with a comparable case, including a prior record and two aggravating circumstances.

PART 5.

The Decisions of the Jury

Because of the very small number of defendants convicted of first degree murder (18) and sentenced to death (8), the statistical models that can be tested for the jury verdict and death penalty decision stages are quite simple and involve only two variable groups: the basic evidence and the race and sex of the defendant and victim (see Tables 21–25). Tables 21 and 24 disclose that the basic evidence variable had a significant impact on both the guilt and penalty decisions, at the .001 level. Tables 22 and 25 show that, for both decisions, the degree of culpability score and the de-

TABLE 21
**Logistic Regression Analysis of Probability
of First Degree Murder Conviction**

Pool: All homicide arrests
489 defendant–victim units
18 first degree murder convictions

Model	–Model likelihood	Improve- ment chi- square	Model degrees of freedom	Improve- ment degrees of freedom	Probability <	Number of infinite coefficient estimates
Constant	77.1	—	1	—	—	
Basic evidence	53.1	48.0	8	7	.001	0
Race and sex of defendant and victim	50.0	6.2	12	4	.20	0

TABLE 22
**Coefficient Estimates of Last Regression
Model with a Significant Category of Variables
for Probability of First Degree Murder Conviction**

Pool: All homicide arrests
489 defendant–victim units
18 first degree murder convictions

Variable	Coefficient	Standard error	Chi-square	Probability <
Intercept	−7.699	2.302	11.18	.001
Identity of defendant as a perpetrator	−.001	.002	.05	.83
Absence of self-defense	.011	.007	2.59	.11
Degree of culpability	.022	.007	10.41	.002
Aggravating circumstances	−.023	.042	.31	.59
Mitigating circumstances	.017	.036	.22	.65
Prior record	−.085	.035	5.84	.02
Multiple victims	.778	.900	.75	.39

TABLE 23
Coefficient Estimates of Regression Model
Including Basic Evidence and Race and Sex Variables
for Probability of First Degree Murder Conviction

Pool: All homicide arrests
489 defendant–victim units
18 first degree murder convictions

Variable	Coefficient	Standard error	Chi-square	Probability <
Intercept	−6.160	2.428	6.44	.02
Identity of defendant as a perpetrator	−.000	.003	.05	.83
Absence of self-defense	.010	.007	1.95	.17
Degree of culpability	.023	.007	11.24	.001
Aggravating circumstances	−.032	.042	.58	.45
Mitigating circumstances	.023	.037	.40	.53
Prior record	.081	.036	5.14	.03
Multiple victims	.817	.943	.75	.39
Defendant's race	1.311	.811	2.61	.11
Victim's race	−1.826[a]	.859	4.52	.04
Defendant's sex	.670	.855	.61	.43
Victim's sex	.852	.606	1.98	.16

[a]The coefficient for the race of the victim shows that the odds of a first degree murder verdict were six times greater if the victim was white than if the victim was nonwhite.

fendant's prior criminal record were the only significant predictors in the set of evidence variables.

The race and sex factors for the defendant had no significant effect at the verdict or penalty stages. Table 23 shows that the race of the victim alone did have a significant effect ($p < .04$) at the verdict stage. All other factors being equal, including the quality of evidence and the seriousness of the offense, defendants in cases with white victims were six times more

TABLE 24
Logistic Regression Analysis of Probability of Death Sentence

Pool: All homicide arrests
489 defendant–victim units
8 death sentences

Model	-Model likelihood	Improve- ment chi- square	Model degrees of freedom	Improve- ment degrees of freedom	Probability <	Number of infinite coefficient estimates
Constant	40.8	—	1	—	—	
Basic evidence	26.1	29.4	8	7	.001	1
Race and sex of defendant and victim	22.7	6.8	12	4	.20	1

TABLE 25
**Coefficient Estimates of Last Regression
Model with a Significant Category of
Variables for Probability of Death Sentence**

Pool: All homicide arrests
489 defendant–victim units
8 death sentences

Variable	Coefficient	Standard error	Chi-square	Probability <
Intercept	−7.273	2.380	9.33	.003
Identity of defendant as a perpetrator	.001	.004	.03	.87
Absence of self-defense	.004	.007	.28	.60
Degree of culpability	.024	.009	6.50	.01
Aggravating circumstances	−.012	.067	.03	.86
Mitigating circumstances	.003	.055	.00	.96
Prior record	.122	.051	5.66	.02
Multiple victims	−7.356	†	†	†

†The coefficient was infinite.

TABLE 26
Death Sentences

Pool: All first degree murder convictions
18 defendant–victim units
8 death sentences

	Sentence		Quality of Evidence				Number of aggravating circumstances
	Death	Life	1A	1B	2	3	
1	●		●				6
2	●		●				4
3	●		●				2
4	●		●				2
5	●		●				2
6	●		●				0
7	●			●			4
8	●			●			2
9		●	●				6
10		●	●				3
11		●	●				2
12		●	●				1
13		●	●				1
14		●	●				0
15		●	●				0
16		●		●			6
17		●		●			3
18		●		●			2

likely to be found guilty of first degree murder than defendants in cases with nonwhite victims.

Other studies that did not control for the quality of the evidence or did not include a full complement of cases also found an effect for the race of the victim at the jury verdict stage. These findings confirm that effect after taking into consideration the strength of the evidence for all homicide cases that entered the capital punishment judicial process. The principal weakness in this study is the low number of cases available for analysis at the verdict and later stages. As the judicial process diverted defendants from the death penalty track, it also thinned the data available for analysis. The low number of cases compromises both the capacity of the study to evaluate some factors and the reliability of its evaluation of others. For all stages after the trial began, the study was unable to include the judicial district factor in the analysis. Moreover, the reliability of the results at the later stages is limited by the number of cases for which the study was able to conduct its comprehensive data collection. Nevertheless, the consistency of the findings of an effect for the race of the victim at the verdict stage in this study with that in other studies is noteworthy.

TABLE 27
State Supreme Court
Review of All Death Sentences

Pool: All death sentences[a]
8 defendant–victim units with
9 death sentences

Conviction		Death Sentence	
Reversed	*Affirmed*	*Reversed*	*Affirmed*
2[b]	7	6[c]	1[d]

[a]One defendant committed suicide while on death row before any appellate decision in his case.
[b]*State v. Jones*, 296 N.C. 495, 251 S.E.2d 425 (1979); *State v. Spaulding*, 298 N.C. 149, 257 S.E.2d 391 (1979).
[c]*State v. Goodman*, 298 N.C. 1, 257 S.E.2d 116 (1979); *State v. Johnson*, 298 N.C. 47, 257 S.E.2d 597 (1979); *State v. Cherry*, 298 N.C. 86, 257 S.E.2d 551 (1979); *State v. Johnson*, 298 N.C. 355, 259 S.E.2d 752 (1979); *State v. Detter*, 298 N.C. 604, 260 S.E.2d 567 (1979); *State v. Silhan*, 302 N.C. 223, 275 S.E.2d 450 (1981).
[d]*State v. Barfield*, 298 N.C. 306, 259 S.E.2d 510 (1979).

TABLE 28
Commutations

Pool: All unreversed death sentences
1 defendant–victim unit

Commutation	*Execution*
0	1

PART 6.

The Decisions after the Trial

The number of cases that survived the trial stage on the death penalty track was so small that no statistical analysis could be reliably performed on them at all. Accordingly, their progress through the appeal and commutation stages is simply reported in Tables 26, 27, and 28. As those tables show, the Supreme Court of North Carolina reversed the convictions in two of the nine cases that received a death sentence and reversed only the death penalty in six others. In the one remaining case, the governor refused commutation and the defendant was executed.

The defendant in that case, Velma Barfield, was a grandmother, the first white female and only the third female executed in North Carolina at least since 1910. She was convicted of killing a white male, her boy friend, who died from acute arsenic poisoning after she put ant poison in his tea and beer. She admitted killing another white male and two white females (including her mother) in the same manner, and the prosecution presented evidence that she had earlier done the same to another white male (her husband). These other murders were used as evidence of her guilt but not as aggravating circumstances. The jury found as aggravating circumstances that the crime was committed for pecuniary gain and to prevent the victim from turning her in for forgery of checks on the victim's account, and that the murder was especially heinous, atrocious, or cruel. Although the defendant introduced evidence that she had a history of abuse of prescription drugs that she obtained through five separate doctors, had been hospitalized four times for overdoses, was under the influence of drugs at the time of the poisonings, and forged the checks to obtain funds to pay for her drugs, the jury found no mitigating circumstances. Her case was processed in Judicial District 16.[2]

CHAPTER V

A Legal Analysis of the Empirical Results

The results of the study show that, despite the new procedures, there was arbitrariness in the administration of the capital punishment process in North Carolina. Although the legal standards—represented by the basic evidence variables—were the most consistently significant factor in the outcomes at all stages of the process, a considerable proportion of the outcomes at each stage was at variance with the legal standards. In evaluating the magnitude of the variation, remember that the data deal with homicide. Nearly all the defendants were proper prospects for punishment in the criminal justice process. Even if prosecutors, judges, and juries engaged in rank racial discrimination, they would still have treated all defendants as serious offenders. Any favoritism would therefore be a matter of less-harsh treatment within the context of general criminal treatment. Keep in mind also that the data deal with the processes leading to the death penalty. Although constitutional congruence between the law and its administration need not be a geometric standard demanding an unattainably perfect fit, substantial departure in practice from the legislative norm should not be permitted for capital punishment, even though necessity may require that it be tolerated for prison sentences.

PART 1.

Prosecutorial Discretion

The prosecutor's discretionary decisions had a significant effect on whether a case was brought to trial for first degree murder without regard to the quality of the evidence or the seriousness of the case. That discretion was exercised in connection with the charging, dismissal, and plea bargaining decisions.[1] If the prosecutor took the case to trial, the trial and sentencing juries, the trial judge, the appellate court, and the governor might make important discretionary decisions. The prosecutor's earlier discretion, however, may fairly be singled out as the one with the widest practical impact.[2]

In North Carolina, the prosecuting function is highly decentralized. The state is divided into several judicial districts—30 at the time of the study year—and each district elects its own district attorney, who is "responsible for the prosecution on behalf of the State of all criminal actions."[3] Although each district attorney enjoys considerable autonomy, each acts on behalf of the state and enforces state law. Therefore, if the new procedures effectively control the exercise of discretion within the statutory guidelines throughout the judicial process in homicide cases, there should be no significant variations in the discretionary decisions among judicial districts apart from those resulting from differences in evidence. The outcomes of the decisions should be susceptible of consistent explanation according to the legal standards.

The results of the study, however, showed that the chances of defendants in cases with the same quality of evidence being brought to trial on a first degree murder charge, and therefore at risk of a death sentence, depended to a significant extent ($p < .01$) on what judicial district processed the case. Although most of the districts brought only 5 percent to 15 percent of their cases to trial for first degree murder, at least two districts had aberrantly high rates, one of 42 percent and the other of 40 percent. Controlling for the quality of the evidence in the cases, at least three districts operated outside the norms established by the rest. In one, the odds of a defendant being brought to trial on first degree murder were 158 times those of a similarly situated defendant in a control group; in a second, 18 times greater; and in a third, 9 times greater.

Similar cases were treated differently in different judicial districts within the same jurisdiction, without any meaningful explanation based on legal standards. The state law was thus applied differently in different judicial districts: first degree murder was a significantly different crime for pretrial purposes depending on which district attorney's office prosecuted the case, even though the statutory standards were the same. The new statutory procedures did not expressly apply to the prosecutors, and the prosecutors varied in the way they applied the law. Is the fact that a defendant's exposure to the risk of a death penalty decision at the trial stage depended largely on which prosecutor within the state had responsibility for the defendant's case a matter of constitutional significance?

In *McGautha*, the nature of the defendant's procedural challenges identified the sentencing jury as the locus of the arguably unconstitutional measure of discretion. In *Furman*, however, the focus of the challenge shifted from the process to the outcome. The Court held the death penalty unconstitutional on the basis of impressions about the pattern of its use. Without systematic evidence of that pattern, the Court certainly acted without evidence of the systemic location of responsibility for the pattern. Justice Stewart considered the arbitrariness "the product of [the] legal system" generally.[4] The other swing justices, however, generally assumed that the determining discretionary stage was sentencing. Thus, Justice Douglas wrote: "[W]e know that the discretion of judges and juries in imposing the death penalty enables the penalty to be selectively applied . . . ."[5] Justice White wrote: "[J]udges and juries have ordered the death penalty with such infrequency . . . ."[6]

We have seen that when Justice Stewart wrote the plurality opinion in *Gregg*, he refined his *Furman* opinion, interpreting it as based on an evaluation of death penalty statutes on their face rather than in practice. He made one further refinement that proceeded from the first. In *Furman*, Justice Stewart recognized that the arbitrariness of the death penalty was a result of the "legal system" rather than one specific aspect of the system. In *Gregg*, he narrowed the focus of his criticism to the sentencing stage.[7] The petitioner argued that the new procedures were inadequate because they did not confine the discretion of the prosecutor at the charging and plea negotiation stages, or of the jury at the trial stage where it could convict the defendant of a lesser-included noncapital offense, or of the executive at the commutation stage. Justice Stewart responded that *Furman* dealt only with the sentencing stage, "the decision to impose the death sentence on a specific individual who had been convicted of a capital offense."[8] He referred to no portion of the *Furman* opinions to support that statement. Certainly his own opinion does not. It was clearly result oriented, calculating the incidence of death penalty dispositions and not the process that produced them. The other *Furman* opinions assumed that sentencing was the culprit stage but did not suggest that the decision would be different if it turned out that prosecutors, trial juries, judges, or governors were the discretionary actors who were skewing the capital punishment pattern. In *Gregg*, however, Justice Stewart simply said that under *Furman* "[t]he existence of these discretionary stages is not determinative of the issues before us."[9]

Evidently uncomfortable leaving this important issue with an *ipse dixit* modification of his *Furman* opinion, Justice Stewart added a footnote to try to explain it. Reminiscent of the *McGautha* "it can't be done" rationale, Justice Stewart argued:

> In order to repair the alleged defects pointed to by the petitioner, it would be necessary to require that prosecuting authorities charge a capital offense whenever arguably there had been a capital murder and that they refuse to plea bargain with the defendant. If a jury refused to convict even though the evidence supported the charge, its verdict would have to be reversed and a verdict of guilty entered or a new trial ordered, since the discretionary act of jury nullification would not be permitted. Finally, acts of executive clemency would have to be prohibited.[10]

It may seem ironic that in the same decision where the Court discovered that the states had controlled jury discretion in a way that seven years earlier it had pronounced impossible, the Court also declared impossible any legislative control of the prosecutors' charging and plea negotiation discretion and of the juries' trial decision discretion. Justice Stewart's conclusion—that the only way to control those discretionary decisions would be to prohibit them—may be exaggerated.

Justice White also focused on the sentencing stage,[11] but he discussed the same problem with a more reasoned approach:

> Unless prosecutors are incompetent in their judgments, the standards by which they decide whether to charge a capital felony will be the same as those by which the jury will decide questions of guilt and sentence. Thus defendants will escape the death penalty through prosecutorial charging decisions only because the offense is not sufficiently serious; or because the proof is insufficiently strong. This does not cause the system to be standardless any more than the jury's decision to impose life imprisonment on a defendant whose crime is deemed insufficiently serious or its decision to acquit someone who is probably guilty but whose guilt is not established beyond a reasonable doubt.[12]

Alluding to the specific problem of discretionary plea bargaining in exchange for testimony, Justice White explained that though it "is a grisly trade . . . it is not irrational; for it is aimed at insuring the successful conclusion of a first degree murder case against one or more other defendants. Whatever else the practice may be, it is neither inexplicable, freakish, nor violative of the Eighth Amendment." [13]

In *Williams v. Indiana,*[14] the Court considered an appeal from a death sentence by a defendant whose two co-defendants were sentenced to prison terms after they entered guilty pleas.[15] The defendant challenged the uncontrolled discretion of the prosecutor to determine whether to pursue a capital charge. The state supreme court decided that "[t]here was no constitutional impropriety in extending leniency to the accomplices in exchange for guilty pleas and denying that leniency to defendant."[16] The Supreme Court dismissed the appeal for lack of a substantial federal question.

Williams v. Indiana and Justice Stewart's opinion in *Gregg* can be understood in the light of Justice Stewart's analysis of the statutory procedures on their face. That he would not insist that a death penalty statute include procedures directed at the other discretionary stages does not necessarily mean that he would ignore evidence that those stages produced the same crazy-quilt pattern that he condemned in *Furman*. Justice White was specific on this point:

> Petitioner's argument that prosecutors behave in a standardless fashion in deciding which cases to try as capital felonies is unsupported by any facts. Petitioner simply asserts that since prosecutors have the power not to charge capital felonies they will exercise that power in a standardless fashion. This is untenable. Absent facts to the contrary, it cannot be assumed that prosecutors will be motivated in their charging decision by factors other than the strength of their case and the likelihood that a jury would impose the penalty if it convicts.[17]

By providing standards for the sentencing jury or judge, Justice White argued, the state was also establishing standards to guide the other discretionary actors. Without the kind of experience that informed his *Furman* position, at least, Justice White was "unwilling to assume the contrary."[18] Evidence that the operation of the new statutes produced the same pattern of results as the pre-*Furman* statutes should get a hearing before Justice White.[19]

Were Justice Stewart still on the Court, he would have to do the same to be true to his *Furman* opinion. Unwilling, in *Gregg*, to impose particular procedures on the states under the new statutes, as he was in *McGautha* under the former statutes, Justice Stewart might be expected to be as attentive to data about the effect of the new system as he was in *Furman* to his experience with the former system. If the same kind of crazy-quilt pattern appeared, Justice Stewart could hardly disregard it simply because its cause might be traced to prosecutors rather than juries.

On the other hand, Justice Stewart declared in *Gregg* that his *Furman* opinion had not been designed indirectly to outlaw "capital punishment by placing totally unrealistic conditions on its use."[20] Yet, in *Furman*, Justice Stewart's opinion had expressed no suggestion as to how his objections could be overcome, and *McGautha* certainly had held out no promise that the ALI model was an answer. Still, his opinion in *Gregg* was based simply on the new statutes as written, without any consideration of them in operation, and did not necessarily foreclose testing the results for arbitrariness.

Justice Powell's opinion in *Proffitt v. Florida,* for Justices Stewart and Stevens as well as himself, also focused on the sentencing stage. He wrote that "the requirements of *Furman* are satisfied when the sentencing authority's discretion is guided and channelled . . . ."[21] Justice Powell did not discuss the other discretionary stages. He did emphasize that his favorable assessment of the new procedures was made "on their face"[22] because they "appear to meet the constitutional deficiencies identified in *Furman.*"[23] Justice Stevens signed that opinion as well, and when his turn came to author the plurality opinion, in *Jurek v. Texas,* he maintained the general focus on the sentencing stage.[24]

Outside of the death penalty context, the Supreme Court has accorded broad constitutional berth to all phases of prosecutorial discretion, including charging discretion. The Court recently described and explained this policy as follows:

> In our criminal justice system, the Government retains "broad discretion" as to whom to prosecute. . . . "[S]o long as the prosecutor has probable cause to believe that the accused committed an offense defined by statute, the decision whether or not to prosecute, and what charge to file or bring before a grand jury, generally rests entirely in his discretion. . . ." This broad discretion rests largely on the recognition that the decision to prosecute is particularly ill-suited to judicial review. Such factors as the strength of the case, the prosecution's general deterrence value, the Government's enforcement priorities, and the case's relationship to the Government's overall enforcement plan are not readily susceptible to the kind of analysis the courts are competent to undertake. Judicial supervision in this area, moreover, entails systemic costs of particular concern. Examining the basis of a prosecution delays the criminal proceeding, threatens to chill law enforcement by subjecting the prosecutor's motives and decision-making to outside inquiry, and may undermine prosecutorial effectiveness by revealing the Government's enforcement policy. All these are substantial concerns that make the courts properly hesitant to examine the decision whether to prosecute.[25]

The Court has held that the Constitution does not require any routine review before trial of a prosecutor's decision to institute criminal proceedings.[26] At the same time, however, if pending trial the defendant is confined or released on conditions that effect a significant restraint of liberty, the Fourth Amendment does require an informal, nonadversarial judicial review of the prosecutor's assessment of probable cause.[27] Moreover, "although prosecutorial discretion is broad, it is not 'unfettered.' Selectivity in the enforcement of criminal laws is . . . 'subject to constitutional restraints.' . . . In particular, the decision to prosecute may not be " 'deliberately based upon an unjustifiable standard such as race, religion, or other arbitrary classification.' ' " [28] In addition, prosecutors may not exercise their discretion "vindictively" [29] or through the use of unkept promises.[30] In *Batson v. Kentucky*,[31] the Court held that, although prosecutors, like defense attorneys, may have broad prerogatives in excusing jurors from prospective jury panels, it would be unconstitutional for a prosecutor to excuse blacks from a jury panel solely on account of their race through purposeful discrimination in the exercise of peremptory challenges, and that the courts must inquire into any adequate showing of a violation.

Does the "death is different" doctrine require greater scrutiny of prosecutorial discretion in capital than in noncapital cases, at least on a systemic if not a case-by-case basis?

Since the 1976 decisions, the Court has carefully policed [32] the sentencing stage of the death penalty process.[33] It has held that the sentencing authority must be permitted to consider lesser-included offenses supported by the evidence [34] and all relevant mitigating circumstances,[35] but may not consider information withheld from the defense [36] or utilize vague aggravating factors.[37] It has also held that the double jeopardy clause [38] and the privilege against compulsory self-incrimination, including the *Miranda* requirements,[39] apply to the penalty phase of a capital trial. Although the Court has invalidated the death penalty in two circumstances—for rape [40] and for "accomplice felony murder" [41]—in part because sentencing juries had repudiated the death penalty for these crimes,[42] the Court has never even considered imposing explicit controls on any other discretionary stage.[43]

In *Roberts*, the plurality struck down the Louisiana system because every jury in a first degree murder case was instructed on lesser-included offenses, whether justified by the evidence or not. The Court criticized this aspect of the system, not only because it lacked standards, but also because "it plainly invites the jurors to disregard their oaths and choose a verdict for a lesser offense whenever they feel the death penalty is inappropriate." [44] A prosecutor, of course, is always in that position for plea negotiations. "While limiting or eliminating sentencing discretion can assure that those sentenced to death are a rationally selected subset of those convicted of capital crimes, it cannot assure that those convicted are a rational subset of those who could be charged with a capital crime. Therefore, confining sentencing discretion cannot guarantee that those sentenced to death are a rationally selected subset of all capital offenders." [45]

The *Furman* concern was with the results,[46] and the constitutional position of capital punishment should be affected by an adequate demonstration of arbitrariness in the results of the death penalty process without regard to the stage of the process where the skewing occurs. The Court has never explained why the Constitution would require control of the exercise of discretion at the sentencing stage but permit unrestricted discretion to have an arbitrary effect at other stages. The Court has not limited the need to control discretion to the discretion exercised by sentencing juries, but has applied it as well to judges who perform the capital sentencing responsibility. There seems no reason not to be equally concerned about the discretionary input into the decision by the prosecutor.[47] As the Court recently wrote, "the Fourteenth Amendment protects an accused throughout the proceedings bringing him to justice."[48]

A defendant subject to processing by a more vigorous prosecutor might receive a death sentence that one subject to processing by a less vigorous prosecutor might escape, even though their cases are the same under the legal standards. In essence, the prosecutors are applying different versions of the legal standards, and the defendants are subject to different "laws" depending on the district of the state in which their cases are processed. Although the prosecutors might individually pursue consistent policies, the variations in their contributions to the outcomes for the cases in the jurisdiction results in arbitrariness. The issue is whether the process is equitable, and the question of which discretionary stage or decision maker is responsible for any arbitrariness should not obscure the focus on the arbitrariness of the system for administering capital punishment.

PART 2.

The Measure of Arbitrariness

The results showed arbitrariness at the trial and verdict stages as well as the pretrial stages. They also reliably pinpointed strong relationships between selected extralegal factors and the outcomes at each stage for which the number of cases still in the process provided an adequate data base.

The race of the defendant had a significant effect when the seriousness of the case was controlled for, that is, in interactions of that factor with the degree of culpability factor and also the aggravating circumstances factor. With everything other than the race of the defendant being equal, including the quality of evidence in the cases, in less serious cases a white defendant generally stood a greater chance of being brought to trial on a first degree murder charge than a nonwhite defendant. In more serious cases, however, the nonwhite defendant stood the greater chance of enduring trial on a capital charge. For example, in a case with a low score on both the degree of culpability and aggravating circumstances scores, the odds were almost even for the white and the nonwhite defendant, with the white defendant having slightly greater odds of being brought to trial for first degree murder. If the case had one aggravating circumstance, but the degree of culpability score was still low, the white defendant had 5 times the odds of the similarly situated nonwhite defendant of a murder one trial. In contrast, in a case with one aggravating circumstance and a high degree of culpability score, the nonwhite defendant had the greater odds of risking a first degree murder trial than a similarly situated white defendant, 2.3 to 1. And if their cases had no aggravating circumstances but still a high degree of culpability score, the nonwhite defendant had odds 10 times greater than the white defendant in the same position of having to stand trial on first degree murder.

For the cases that went to trial, the race of the defendant continued to be a significant factor in the determination of whether the first degree murder charge was submitted to the jury, again in interaction with variables regarding the seriousness of the case. At this stage of the trial, if neither the nonwhite or the white defendant had a prior record, their odds of risking a jury verdict on murder one were fairly close. If both defendants had two aggravating circumstances, their odds were even. But if both had one aggravating circumstance the odds of the nonwhite defendant having the murder one charge considered by the jury were 1.7 times those of the white defendant, and if neither had any aggravating circumstances, the odds of the nonwhite defendant were three times greater. The differential was much more dramatic, however, for defendants with a prior record. If both defendants had a prior record score of 10, the odds of having the jury deliberate the first degree murder charge for the nonwhite defendant were much greater than for the similarly situated white defendant: 19.8 times greater if both defendants' cases had two aggravating circumstances, 31.4 times greater if both cases had only one aggravating circumstance, and a striking 56 times greater if they had no aggravating circumstances.

At the verdict stage, the race of the defendant did not have a significant effect, but a new factor did: the race of the victim. Controlling for all factors except the race of the victim, a defendant charged with murder of a white was six times more likely to be convicted than a defendant charged with murdering a nonwhite. In 1975, defending the state's then mandatory capital punishment system before the Supreme Court, a representative of the North Carolina Attorney General's office told the Court that the disproportionate number of nonwhites on death row resulted from the state's diligence in prosecuting the killers of nonwhite victims.[49] These data demonstrate that, in fact, the state was less vigorous in its prosecution of cases with nonwhite victims than with white victims.

At the penalty stage, the only significant factors were the degree of culpability and the defendant's prior record. The number of cases that reached the penalty phase was too small to justify any conclusions from the results at this stage.

The *Furman* opinions did not specify the point at which the accumulation of aberrant results becomes not only statistically but constitutionally significant.[50] Chief Justice Burger and Justice Brennan may have marked out the extremes. Justice Brennan wrote: "It is unlikely that this Court will confront a severe punishment that is obviously inflicted in wholly arbitrary fashion; no state would engage in a reign of blind terror."[51] Chief Justice Burger countered: "There are doubtless prisoners on death row who would not be there had they been tried before a different jury or in a different state. . . . However, this element of fortuity does not stand as an indictment either of the general functioning of juries in capital cases or of the integrity of jury decisions in individual cases."[52]

Certainly the Court would not demand a standard of perfection beyond the reach of human institutions. Since *Furman*, it has recognized that a capital punishment system must tolerate an occasional irregular discretionary decision to divert a murder defendant from the death penalty track. In *Gregg*, the plurality observed that "the isolated decision of a jury to afford mercy does not render unconstitutional death sentences on defendants who were sentenced under a system that does not create a substantial risk of arbitrariness or caprice."[53] In *Pulley v. Harris*,[54] the Court held: "Any capital sentencing scheme may occasionally produce aberrational outcomes. Such inconsistencies are a far cry from the major systemic defects identified in *Furman*."[55] The *Gregg* plurality wrote "that discretion must be suitably directed and limited so as to *minimize* the risk of *wholly* arbitrary and capricious action."[56] In *Proffitt*, the plurality suggested considerable tolerance for a discretionary range of capital sentencing decisions when it expressed satisfaction with the new procedures because they eliminated "total arbitrariness and capriciousness."[57] In *Zant v. Stephens (I)*,[58] the Court explained that *Gregg* "upheld the Georgia death penalty statute because the standards and procedures set forth therein promised to *alleviate to a significant degree* the concern of *Furman*."[59]

Chief Justice Burger, in *Furman*, sarcastically characterized the prevailing opinions as condemning "the flexible sentencing system" because it "has yielded more mercy than the Eighth Amendment can stand."[60] Justice Stewart later wrote, in *Gregg*, "Nothing in any of our cases suggests that the decision to afford an individual defendant mercy violates the Constitution."[61] Justice White wrote in *Gregg* that the state should be allowed to permit "the jury to dispense mercy on the basis of factors too intangible to write into a statute . . . ."[62]

Certainly, the injustice of an unjust dispensation of mercy is different from the injustice of an unjust execution. *Furman*, however, held that at some point the disparity becomes systemic, not merely incidental. The diversion decisions then effectively modify the law in practice for some defendants, while others remain subject to the law as written.

Selective or erratic mercy for some who qualify for the death penalty results in a system that is unfair to those denied such mercy, even if they do qualify for the penalty they received and therefore could not complain about its imposition on them in the abstract.[63] If District A applies different death penalty standards from District B, if District C applies different standards to nonwhite and white defendants, and if District D applies different standards depending on whether the victim is nonwhite or white, what measure can be used to determine whether any defendant "qualifies" for the death penalty? What, then, are the standards?

Arbitrary favoritism of a degree that undermines the standards as they appear on the statute books cheats those denied such favoritism even if they may be equally undeserving of the leniency improperly afforded others. As John Merrick, the "Elephant Man," said, "If your mercy is so cruel, what do you have for justice?"[64] *Furman,* as well as *Woodson* and *Roberts,* therefore accorded standing[65] to capital defendants to complain about the abstract unfairness of the system that sentenced them without inquiring whether they individually could show that the unfairness had an impact on their own cases. In a sense, capital defendants may be in competition for a limited measure of mercy. Each dose doled out unfairly reduces the supply remaining for equitable distribution. Justice White's infrequency theory would entertain some such concept of leniency as a finite resource. Even if the supply of mercy is not thus limited, and even if an executed defendant would have been executed regardless of whether another had been spared, the system of justice cannot tolerate arbitrary decision making. A capital punishment system that provides arbitrary leniency for some defendants by definition is responsible for arbitrary execution of others.

A condemned defendant who complains about this state of capital punishment affairs does not demand that whatever statutorily irrelevant consideration saved the spared defendant be applied as well to his or her case. That defendant challenges, not simply the decision in his or her own case, but the validity of the system to make the judgment about who meets the death penalty standards. The irregular application of the statutory standards drains the standards of significant meaning.

A mathematical measure of arbitrariness need not be precisely calculated for present purposes. The Supreme Court in 1976 upheld the capital punishment systems on the assumption that the new procedures might be capable of confining capital punishment decisions within the statutory standards. The results are at least sufficient to cast considerable doubt on that critical assumption.[66] Because that assumption is no longer warranted in view of the results of this study, the Supreme Court should impose on the states that are the proponents of the new procedures the burden of showing that they do work, or of developing additional procedures that will be effective. Until the states accomplish that, the Court should no longer permit capital punishment to be carried out on the basis of the assumption that has been discredited by these data.

APPENDICES AND NOTES

APPENDIX A

Outline for Scoring the Quality of the Evidence

**Scoring Outline for Whether the Defendant
Was a Perpetrator of the Homicide**

I. Prosecution evidence

    A. Eyewitness evidence

        1. Maximum value for each of the first five witnesses: 50, 40, 30, 20, 10

        2. Value reduction for each witness who

	knew defendant before occurrence	did not know defendant before occurrence
a) Qualified his or her identification of the defendant	−50%	−50%
b) Qualified his or her description of the defendant's activity	−50%	−50%
c) Had a brief or poor view or poor eyesight	−40%	−20%
d) Identified somebody else or did not identify the defendant in a pretrial identification	−40%	−20%

e) Made a prior inconsistent statement about the defendant's activity	−40%	−40%
f) Provided the police with a description that did not fit the defendant	−40%	−40%
g) Had a prior conviction	−20%	−20%
h) Identified the defendant on the basis of voice, speech, or walk but not appearance	−40%	−20%
i) Had a motive to make a false identification	−40%	−40%
j) Was subject to suggestive identification procedures	−40%	−20%
k) Was a child or mentally abnormal	−40%	−20%
l) Was under the influence of alcohol or drugs at the time of the homicide	−40%	−20%
m) Had evidence of bad character other than a prior conviction	−10%	−10%

B. Statement of the defendant

   1. Maximum value for a statement

	made to a law en-forcement officer	*made to others than an officer*
a) Written statement admitting involvement in the homicidal act	75	70
b) Written statement denying involvement in the homicidal act but admitting presence at the scene of the act where innocent bystanders would not be expected	35	30
c) Written statement denying involvement in the homicidal act but admitting aiding the perpetrator	65	55
d) Written statement admitting involvement in the homicidal act but raising a defense	75	70
e) Oral statement admitting involvement in the homicidal act	65	60
f) Oral statement denying involvement in the homicidal act but admitting presence at the scene of the act	25	20

g) Oral statement denying involvement in the homicidal act but admitting aiding the perpetrator	55	50
h) Oral statement admitting involvement in the homicidal act but raising a defense	65	60

2. Value reductions: none

C. Accomplice evidence

  1. Maximum value for each of the first five accomplices: 50, 40, 30, 20, 10

  2. Value reductions for

    a) Promise made to accomplice in exchange for testimony

      (1) Reduced charge or sentence with prison time   −40%

      (2) Reduced charge or sentence without prison time   −60%

      (3) Unspecified leniency   −10%

      (4) Other   −10%

    b) Accomplice who

      (1) Made a prior statement denying role of the defendant   −50%

      (2) Was vague, evasive, or inconsistent about role of the defendant   −30%

D. Electronic wiretap or eavesdrop evidence

  1. Maximum values

    a) Heard defendant plan or admit involvement in the homicidal act   100

    b) Heard defendant admit presence at the scene of the act   10

    c) Heard statement by defendant demonstrating knowledge of the act in advance   75

    d) Heard statement by defendant demonstrating knowledge of unpublicized fact about the act after its occurrence   50

    e) Heard statement by defendant admitting involvement in the act but raising a defense   100

  2. Value reductions: none

E. Scientific evidence

   1. Fingerprints

      a) Maximum values

(1) In a place at scene where the defendant was unlikely to be at any reasonable time before the occurrence unless he or she was involved in the homicide	60
(2) In a place at scene to which the defendant had reasonable access at times other than during the occurrence	10
(3) In a place associated with the homicide but not alone establishing the defendant's involvement in the homicide	40

      b) Value reductions

         (1) Qualified identification: -50%
         (2) Disputed by defense:[†] -33%

   2. Footprints

      a) Maximum values

(1) In a place at scene where the defendant was unlikely to be at any reasonable time before the occurrence unless he was involved in the homicide	50
(2) In a place at scene to which the defendant had reasonable access at times other than during the homicide	5
(3) In a place associated with the homicide but not alone establishing defendant's involvement in the homicide	40

      b) Value reductions

         (1) Qualified identification: -50%
         (2) Disputed by defense: -33%

   3. Weapons evidence

      a) Maximum value: 75 points
      b) Value reductions

         (1) Weapon established as used in homicide

            (*a*) Qualified identification: -50%
            (*b*) Disputed by defense: -33%

[†] For scientific evidence, value reductions were applied for defense disputes only if the scientific evidence was unqualified.

(2) Weapon in the defendant's possession, owned by the defendant, found in the defendant's home, or fingerprint of the defendant found on weapon

(*a*) Qualified identification: −50%
(*b*) Disputed by defense: −33%

(3) Defendant shown to have fired gun at or near time of homicide

(*a*) Qualified identification: −50%
(*b*) Disputed by defense: −33%

4. Trace evidence (hair, fiber, blood stain, dirt, etc.)

a) Maximum value: 50
b) Value reductions

(1) Qualified identification: −50%
(2) Disputed by defense: −33%

5. Physical evidence

a) Defendant's possession of goods taken from victim

(1) Maximum value: 30
(2) Value reduction if disputed by defense: −33%

b) Defendant's contemporaneous injury

(1) Maximum values

(*a*) Medical or other evidence that defendant had an injury sustained by perpetrator: 40
(*b*) Medical or other evidence that accused had an injury consistent with involvement: 20

(2) Value reduction if disputed by defense: −33%

F. Circumstantial evidence

1. Defendant seen at or near scene of homicide at or about time of homicide where innocent bystanders would not be expected

a) Maximum value for each of the first three witnesses: 25, 15, 5
b) Value reduction for each witness who

	knew defendant before occurrence	*did not know defendant before occurrence*
(1) Qualified his or her identification of the defendant	−50%	−50%
(2) Had brief or poor view or poor eyesight	−40%	−20%
(3) Identified somebody else or did not identify the defendant in a pretrial identification procedure	−40%	−50%

	knew defendant before occurrence	did not know defendant before occurrence
(4) Provided the police with a description that did not fit the defendant	−40%	−40%
(5) Had a prior conviction	−20%	−20%
(6) Identified the defendant on the basis of voice, speech, or walk, but not appearance	−40%	−20%
(7) Had a motive to make a false identification	−40%	−40%
(8) Was subjected to suggestive identification procedures	−40%	−20%
(9) Was a child or mentally abnormal	−40%	−20%
(10) Was under the influence of alcohol or drugs at the time of the homicide	−40%	−20%
(11) Had evidence of bad character other than a prior conviction	−10%	−10%

2. Victim was last seen in company of the defendant shortly before his or her disappearance or death

   a) Maximum value for each of the first three witnesses: 25, 15, 5

   b) Value reduction for each witness who

	knew defendant before occurrence	did not know defendant before occurrence
(1) Qualified his or her identification	−50%	−50%
(2) Had a brief or poor view or poor eyesight	−40%	−20%
(3) Identified somebody else or did not identify the defendant in a pretrial identification procedure	−40%	−50%
(4) Provided the police with a description that did not fit the defendant	−40%	−40%
(5) Had a prior conviction	−20%	−20%
(6) Identified the defendant on the basis of voice, speech, or walk, but not appearance	−40%	−20%
(7) Had a motive to make a false identification	−40%	−40%
(8) Was subjected to suggestive identification procedures	−40%	−20%
(9) Was a child or mentally abnormal	−40%	−20%

(10) Was under the influence of alcohol or drugs at the time of the homicide	−40%	−20%
(11) Had evidence of bad character other than a prior conviction	−10%	−10%

3. Evidence of motive, preparation, or intent of the defendant to kill this victim

    a) Maximum value for each of the first witnesses as to

        (1) Motive: 20, 10
        (2) Preparation or intent: 40, 30, 20, 10

    b) Value reduction for each witness who

        (1) Was a close relative of the victim: −30%
        (2) Was a friend of the victim: −30%
        (3) Had a prior conviction: −20%
        (4) Had a motive to testify falsely: −40%
        (5) Was a child or mentally abnormal: −40%
        (6) Made a prior inconsistent statement: −50%
        (7) Had evidence of bad character other than a prior conviction: −10%

4. Evidence of similar crimes by the defendant

    a) Prior homicide with common characteristics

        (1) Maximum value for each of the first four prior homicides: 40, 20, 10, 5
        (2) Value reduction if disputed by defense: −33%

    b) Prior predicate offense with common characteristics

        (1) Maximum value for each of the first four priors: 40, 20, 10, 5
        (2) Value reduction if disputed by defense: −33%

5. Defendant seen engaging in activities that would tend to make him or her an accessory after the fact

    a) Maximum value for each of the first four witnesses

        For homicide: 40, 20, 10, 5
        For predicate offense: 40, 20, 10, 5

    b) Value reduction for each witness who

	knew defendant before occurrence	*did not know defendant before occurrence*
(1) Qualified his or her identification	−50%	−50%
(2) Had a brief or poor view or poor eyesight	−40%	−40%
(3) Identified somebody else or did not identify the defendant in a pretrial identification procedure	−40%	−40%

(4) Provided the police with a description that did not fit the defendant   −40%   −40%

(5) Had a prior conviction   −20%   −20%

(6) Identified the defendant on the basis
of voice, speech, or walk, but not
appearance   −40%   −40%

(7) Had a motive to make a false
identification   −40%   −40%

(8) Was subjected to suggestive
identification procedures   −40%   −40%

(9) Was a child or mentally abnormal   −40%   −40%

(10) Was under the influence of alcohol or
drugs at the time of the homicide   −40%   −40%

(11) Had evidence of bad character other
than a prior conviction   −10%   −10%

(12) Qualified his or her description of the
defendant's activity   −50%   −50%

(13) Gave a prior inconsistent statement   −40%   −40%

6. Evidence that defendant was seen with a co-defendant shortly before
or after the incident where there was independent evidence against the
co-defendant   (Not used)

7. Character evidence (use only if defendant raised the issue of
character)   (Not used)

II. Defense evidence

A. Eyewitness evidence (other than co-defendant)

1. Maximum value for each of the first five witnesses: 50, 40, 30, 20, 10

2. Value reduction for each witness who

	denied defendant was present	denied defendant was involved in homicide
a) Qualified his or her identification or their description of the defendant's activity	−50%	−50%
b) Had a brief or poor view or poor eyesight	−30%	−30%
c) Previously identified the defendant as a perpetrator or accomplice	−40%	−40%
d) Was a close relative of the defendant	−40%	−40%

e) Was a friend of the defendant	-40%	-40%
f) Had other motive to testify falsely	-40%	-40%
g) Was a child or mentally abnormal	-40%	-40%
h) Never saw the defendant before the incident	-20%	0%
i) Was a co-defendant who admitted involvement	-20%	-20%
j) Was a co-defendant who denied involvement	-40%	-40%
k) Was the defendant (use only if no alibi evidence by the defendant)	0%	-50%

B. Alibi evidence

1. Maximum value for each of the first five witnesses: 50, 40, 30, 20, 10

2. Value reduction for each witness who

	was positive regarding time and place	*was qualified regarding time and place*
a) Was spouse of the defendant	-50%	-50%
b) Was other close relative of the defendant	-40%	-40%
c) Was an employer, co-worker or business acquaintance of the defendant	-20%	-20%
d) Was a co-defendant	-40%	-40%
e) Was the defendant	-50%	-50%
f) Was a friend of the defendant	-40%	-40%
g) Had other motive to testify falsely	-40%	-40%
h) Made a prior inconsistent statement	-40%	-40%
i) Had a prior conviction	-20%	-20%
j) Was a child or mentally abnormal	-30%	-30%
k) Was under the influence of drugs or alcohol at the time of the homicide	-20%	-20%
l) Had evidence of bad character other than a prior conviction	-10%	-10%

C. Character evidence

1. Maximum value for each of the first three witnesses: 25, 15, 5

2. Value reduction for each witness who was

  a) A relative of the defendant   −40%

  b) A friend of the defendant   −40%

  c) An employer, co-worker, or business   −20%
   acquaintance of the defendant

 D. Scientific evidence

  1. Defendant did not fire the gun at the time of the homicide (when the homicide was committed with a gun)

   a) Maximum value: 75

   b) Value reduction if

    (1) Scientific evidence was qualified: −50%
    (2) Scientific evidence was disputed by prosecution (do not use if scientific evidence was qualified): −33%

  2. Gun or other weapon involved was shown to belong to someone else and not linked to the defendant

   a) Maximum value: 75
   b) Value reduction if disputed by prosecution: −33%

  3. Fingerprint, footprint, or trace evidence of person not linked to defendant (whether or not identified as belonging to named individual) found on victim's body or in other incriminating place

   a) Maximum value: 75

   b) Value reduction if

    (1) Scientific evidence was qualified: −50%
    (2) Scientific evidence was disputed by prosecution (do not use if scientific evidence is qualified): −33%

  4. No fingerprint, footprint, or other trace evidence of defendant found at scene despite forensic search

   a) Maximum value: 75
   b) Value reduction if disputed by prosecution: −33%

III. Final score on whether defendant was a perpetrator of the homicide

 A. Add prosecution and defense scores separately

1. Prosecution = Eyewitness + Statement of + Accomplice + Scientific
 score   evidence   the defendant   evidence   evidence

         + Circumstantial
          evidence

2. Defense   = Eyewitness + Alibi   + Character + Scientific
 score   evidence   evidence   evidence   evidence

 B. Subtract defense score from prosecution score to obtain final score on whether the defendant was a perpetrator of the homicide

Scoring Outline for
Whether the Defendant Acted with the
Mental Element for First Degree Murder

I. Prosecution evidence

    A. Eyewitnesses to premeditation and deliberation or contemporaneous involvement in a predicate felony

        1. Maximum value for each of the first five witnesses: 50, 40, 30, 20, 10 [†]

        2. Value reductions for each witness who

a) Gave a qualified or inconclusive statement	−50%
b) Had a brief or poor view or poor eyesight	−40%
c) Knew the victim before the occurrence and was	
(1) In the victim's family only	−40%
(2) In the victim's family and in the defendant's family or a friend of the defendant	−10%
(3) A friend of the victim only	−40%
(4) A friend of the victim and in the defendant's family or a friend of the defendant	−10%
(5) A co-worker or business acquaintance of the victim only	−20%
(6) A co-worker or business acquaintance of the victim and the defendant	0%
d) Had a prior conviction	−20%
e) Had a motive to testify falsely	−40%
f) Was a child or mentally abnormal	−40%
g) Gave a prior inconsistent statement	−40%
h) Was under the influence of drugs or alcohol at the time of the homicide	−40%
i) Had evidence of bad character other than a prior conviction	−10%

    B. Statement of the defendant admitting premeditation and deliberation or involvement in a predicate felony

        1. Maximum value: 75

        2. Value reductions for

          a) Oral statement: −10
          b) Statement made to others than police: −5

[†] Deduct five points from the value for each witness with a statement about the circumstances surrounding the homicidal event but not the event itself.

C. Accomplice evidence of premeditation and deliberation or involvement in a predicate felony

  1. Maximum value for each of the first five accomplices: 50, 40, 30, 20, 10

  2. Value reduction for prosecution inducement of accomplice to testify with promise of

a) Reduced charge with prison sentence	−40%
b) Reduced charge without prison sentence	−60%
c) Unspecified leniency	−20%

  3. Value reduction for each witness who

a) Gave a qualified or inconclusive statement	−50%
b) Had a brief or poor view or poor eyesight	−40%

    c) Knew the victim before the occurrence and was

(1) In the victim's family only	−40%
(2) In the victim's family and in the defendant's family or a friend of the defendant	−10%
(3) A friend of the victim only	−40%
(4) A friend of the victim and in the defendant's family or a friend of the defendant	−10%
(5) A co-worker or business acquaintance of the victim only	−20%
(6) A co-worker or business acquaintance of the victim and the defendant	0%

d) Had a prior conviction	−20%
e) Had a motive to testify falsely	−40%
f) Was a child or mentally abnormal	−40%
g) Gave a prior inconsistent statement	−40%
h) Was under the influence of drugs or alcohol at the time of the homicide	−40%
i) Had evidence of bad character other than a prior conviction	−10%

D. Scientific evidence

  1. Distance of shots inconsistent with lesser level of culpability

    a) Maximum value: 75
    b) Value reduction if there was a substantive challenge by the defense: −50%

  2. Angle or location of shots or wounds inconsistent with lesser level of culpability

a) Maximum value: 75

b) Value reduction if there was a substantive challenge by the defense: −50%

3. Number of shots or wounds inconsistent with lesser level of culpability

a) Maximum value: 75

b) Value reduction if there was a substantive challenge by the defense: −50%

4. Other aspect of victim's condition inconsistent with lesser level of culpability

a) Maximum value: 75

b) Value reduction if there was a substantive challenge by the defense: −50%

5. Other aspect of defendant's weapon inconsistent with lesser level of culpability

a) Maximum value: 75

b) Value reduction if there was a substantive challenge by the defense: −50%

6. Aspect of victim's weapon inconsistent with lesser level of culpability

a) Maximum value: 75

b) Value reduction if there was a substantive challenge by the defense: −50%

7. Aspect of defendant's condition inconsistent with lesser level of culpability

a) Maximum value: 75

b) Value reduction if there was a substantive challenge by the defense: −50%

8. Aspect of scene inconsistent with lesser level of culpability

a) Maximum value: 75

b) Value reduction if there was a substantive challenge by the defense: −50%

E. Circumstantial evidence

1. Witnesses to prior threats by the defendant against the victim

a) Maximum value for strongest witness to each distinct threat: 10

b) Value reduction for each witness who

(1) Knew the victim before the occurrence and was

(*a*) In the victim's family only   −40%

(*b*) In the victim's family and in the   −10%
defendant's family or a friend of the
defendant

(c) A friend of the victim only	−40%
(d) A friend of the victim and in the defendant's family or a friend of the defendant	−10%
(e) A co-worker or business acquaintance of the victim only	−20%
(f) A co-worker or business acquaintance of the victim and the defendant	0%
(2) Had a prior conviction	−20%
(3) Had a motive to testify falsely	−40%
(4) Was a child or mentally abnormal	−40%
(5) Gave a prior inconsistent statement	−40%
(6) Was under the influence of drugs or alcohol at the time of the homicide	−40%
(7) Had evidence of bad character other than a prior conviction	−10%

2. Witnesses to prior acts of aggression by the defendant against the victim

   a) Maximum value for strongest witness to each distinct act: 15

   b) Value reduction for each witness who

(1) Knew the victim before the occurrence and was	
(a) In the victim's family only	−40%
(b) In the victim's family and in the defendant's family or a friend of the defendant	−10%
(c) A friend of the victim only	−40%
(d) A friend of the victim and in the defendant's family or a friend of the defendant	−10%
(e) A co-worker or business acquaintance of the victim only	−20%
(f) A co-worker or business acquaintance of the victim and the defendant	0%
(2) Had a prior conviction	−20%
(3) Had a motive to testify falsely	−40%
(4) Was a child or mentally abnormal	−40%
(5) Gave a prior inconsistent statement	−40%
(6) Was under the influence of drugs or alcohol at the time of the homicide	−40%

(7) Had evidence of bad character other than a   −10%
prior conviction

3. Evidence of similar homicides or attempted homicides by the
defendant with a different victim

   a) Maximum value for each of the first four similar homicides or
attempts: 40, 30, 20, 10

   b) Value reductions

      (1) Conviction record: 0%
      (2) Disputed by defense: −50%
      (3) Undisputed by defense: −20%

4. Witnesses to the violent character of the defendant

   a) Maximum value for each of the first two witnesses: 20, 10

   b) Value reduction for each witness who knew the defendant before
the occurrence and was

      (1) In the victim's family only   −40%

      (2) In the victim's family and in the defendant's   −10%
family or a friend of the defendant

      (3) A friend of the victim only   −40%

      (4) A friend of the victim and in the defendant's   −10%
family or a friend of the defendant

      (5) A co-worker or business acquaintance of the   −20%
victim only

      (6) A co-worker or business acquaintance of the   0%
victim and the defendant

5. Witnesses to the peaceful character of the victim

   a) Maximum value for each of the first two witnesses: 20, 10

   b) Value reduction for each witness who knew the victim before the
occurrence and was

      (1) In the victim's family only   −40%

      (2) In the victim's family and in the defendant's   −10%
family or a friend of the defendant

      (3) A friend of the victim only   −40%

      (4) A friend of the victim and in the defendant's   −10%
family or a friend of the defendant

      (5) A co-worker or business acquaintance of the   −20%
victim only

      (6) A co-worker or business acquaintance of the   0%
victim and the defendant

6. Witnesses that defendant planned or prepared to kill the victim before the occurrence

   a) Maximum value for each of the first four witnesses: 40, 30, 20, 10

   b) Value reduction for each witness who

   (1) Knew the victim before the occurrence and was

(*a*) In the victim's family only	−40%
(*b*) In the victim's family and in the defendant's family or a friend of the defendant	−10%
(*c*) A friend of the victim only	−40%
(*d*) A friend of the victim and in the defendant's family or a friend of the defendant	−10%
(*e*) A co-worker or business acquaintance of the victim only	−20%
(*f*) A co-worker or business acquaintance of the victim and the defendant	0%

(2) Had a prior conviction	−20%
(3) Had a motive to testify falsely	−40%
(4) Was a child or mentally abnormal	−40%
(5) Gave a prior inconsistent statement	−40%
(6) Was under the influence of drugs or alcohol at the time of the homicide	−40%
(7) Had evidence of bad character other than a prior conviction	−10%

7. Witnesses that the defendant had a motive for killing the victim

   a) Maximum value for each of the first two witnesses: 20, 10
   b) Value reductions: none

II. Defense evidence

   A. Eyewitness evidence that the defendant did not act with premeditation and deliberation or was not involved in a predicate felony or committed a homicide of less than first degree murder

   1. Maximum value for each of the first five witnesses: 50, 40, 30, 20, 10

   2. Value reduction for each witness who

a) Gave qualified or inconclusive testimony	−50%
b) Had a brief or poor view or poor eyesight	−40%

   c) Knew the defendant before the occurrence and was

(1) In the victim's family only	−40%

(2) In the defendant's family and in the victim's family or a friend of the victim   −10%

(3) A friend of the defendant only   −40%

(4) A friend of the defendant and in the victim's family or a friend of the victim   −10%

(5) A co-worker or business acquaintance of the defendant only   −20%

(6) A co-worker or business acquaintance of the victim and the defendant   0%

d) Had a prior conviction   −20%

e) Had a motive to testify falsely   −40%

f) Was a child or mentally abnormal   −40%

g) Gave a prior inconsistent statement   −40%

h) Was under the influence of drugs or alcohol at the time of the homicide   −40%

i) Had evidence of bad character other than a prior conviction   −10%

j) Was the defendant   −50%

B. Circumstantial evidence

  1. Witnesses to prior threats by the victim against the defendant

    a) Maximum value for strongest witness to each distinct threat: 10

    b) Value reduction for each witness who

      (1) Knew the defendant before the occurrence and was

        (*a*) In the defendant's family only   −40%

        (*b*) In the defendant's family and in the victim's family or a friend of the victim   −10%

        (*c*) A friend of the defendant only   −40%

        (*d*) A friend of the defendant and either in the victim's family or a friend of the victim   −10%

        (*e*) A co-worker or business acquaintance of the defendant only   −20%

        (*f*) A co-worker or business acquaintance of the victim and the defendant   0%

      (2) Had a prior conviction   −20%

      (3) Had a motive to testify falsely   −40%

        (4) Was a child or mentally abnormal —   −40%

        (5) Gave a prior inconsistent statement —   −40%

        (6) Was under the influence of drugs or alcohol —   −40%
            at the time of the homicide

        (7) Had evidence of bad character other than a —   −10%
            prior conviction

  2. Witnesses to prior acts of aggression by the victim against the defendant

    a) Maximum value for strongest witness to each distinct act: 15

    b) Value reduction for witness who

      (1) Knew the defendant before the occurrence and was

        (*a*) In the defendant's family only —   −40%

        (*b*) In the defendant's family and either in —   −10%
            the victim's family or a friend of the victim

        (*c*) A friend of the defendant only —   −40%

        (*d*) A friend of the defendant and either in —   −10%
            the victim's family or a friend of the victim

        (*e*) A co-worker or business acquaintance of —   −20%
            the defendant only

        (*f*) A co-worker or business acquaintance of —   0%
            the victim and the defendant

      (2) Had a prior conviction —   −20%

      (3) Had a motive to testify falsely —   −40%

      (4) Was a child or mentally abnormal —   −40%

      (5) Gave a prior inconsistent statement —   −40%

      (6) Was under the influence of drugs or alcohol —   −40%
         at the time of the homicide

      (7) Had evidence of bad character other than a —   −10%
         prior conviction

C. Scientific evidence

  1. Condition of the defendant consistent with lesser level of culpability

    a) Maximum value: 40
    b) Value reduction for substantive challenge by the prosecutor: −50%

  2. Condition of the defendant's weapon consistent with lesser level of culpability

    a) Maximum value: 40

    b) Value reduction for substantive challenge by the prosecutor: −50%

3. Condition of victim consistent with lesser level of culpability

    a) Maximum value: 40

    b) Value reductions for substantive challenge by the prosecutor: −50%

4. Condition of the victim's weapon consistent with lesser level of culpability

    a) Maximum value: 40

    b) Value reduction for substantive challenge by the prosecutor: −50%

5. Condition of scene consistent with lesser level of culpability

    a) Maximum value: 40

    b) Value reduction for substantive challenge by the prosecutor: −50%

III. Final score on whether the defendant acted with the mental element for first degree murder

    A. Weight prosecution's circumstantial evidence score categories as follows to obtain overall prosecution circumstantial evidence score

$$\text{Prosecution circumstantial score} = .67 \times \text{Prior threat} + .67 \times \text{Prior assault} + .5 \times \text{Similar homicides or attempts}$$
$$+ .75 \times \text{Violent character of defendant} + 1.0 \times \text{Planning, preparation, or motive}$$

    B. Add prosecution and defense scores separately by combining scores for each evidence category

$$\text{Prosecution score} = \text{Eyewitness evidence} + \text{Statement of the defendant} + \text{Accomplice evidence} + \text{Scientific evidence}$$
$$+ \text{Circumstantial evidence}$$

$$\text{Defense score} = \text{Eyewitness evidence} + \text{Circumstantial evidence} + \text{Scientific evidence}$$

    C. Subtract defense score from prosecution score to obtain final score on whether the defendant acted with the mental element for first degree murder

Scoring Outline for
Whether the Defendant Acted in Self-Defense
or in Defense of Others

I. Prosecution evidence

  A. Eyewitness evidence

   1. Maximum value for each of the first eyewitnesses [†] who

     a) Denied any threat by the victim: 50, 40, 30, 20, 10

     b) Confirmed threat by the victim but denied that it involved danger of bodily injury or death: 40, 30, 20, 10

     c) Confirmed threat by the victim but stated that the defendant provoked it or was the aggressor: 40, 30, 20, 10

     d) Confirmed that the defendant did not take advantage of an avenue of retreat: 40, 30, 20, 10

     e) Supported a conclusion that any threat was not of imminent danger: 40, 30, 20, 10

     f) Supported a conclusion that the defendant used excessive force: 30, 20, 10

   2. Value reduction for each witness who

     a) Knew the victim before the occurrence and was

(1) In the victim's family only	−40%
(2) In the victim's family and in the defendant's family or a friend of the defendant	−10%
(3) A friend of the victim only	−40%
(4) A friend of the victim and in the defendant's family or a friend of the defendant	−10%
(5) A co-worker or business acquaintance of the victim only	−20%
(6) A co-worker or business acquaintance of the victim and the defendant	0%

b) Had a prior conviction	−20%
c) Had a motive to testify falsely	−40%
d) Was a child or mentally abnormal	−40%
e) Gave a prior inconsistent statement	−40%
f) Was under the influence of drugs or alcohol at the time of the homicide	−40%

[†] The initial maximum value for each circumstantial eyewitness is 5 points less than the maximum value for the comparable direct eyewitness.

     g) Had evidence of bad character other than a   −10%
        prior conviction

B. Statement of the defendant

  1. Maximum value for each statement of the defendant that

     a) Included facts inconsistent with any theory of   75
        self-defense

     b) Included facts inconsistent with the defendant's   60
        evidence of the need for self-defense

     c) Omitted facts consistent with the defendant's   50
        need for self-defense

     d) Admitted that the victim's threat did not involve   50
        danger of death or serious bodily harm

     e) Admitted that the defendant provoked the threat   50
        or was the aggressor

     f) Admitted that the force used was excessive   40

  2. Value reduction

     a) Deduct 10 from the value of a statement made
        orally rather than in writing
     b) Deduct 5 from the value of a statement not
        made to the police

C. Scientific evidence

  1. Maximum value for evidence that

     a) Distance of shots was inconsistent with   50
        self-defense

     b) Angle or location of shots or wounds was
        inconsistent with self-defense

     c) Number of shots or wounds was inconsistent   50
        with self-defense

     d) Number of shots or wounds suggested excessive   30
        force

     e) Other aspect of victim's condition was   40
        inconsistent with self-defense

     f) Other aspect of defendant's weapon was   40
        inconsistent with self-defense

     g) Aspect of victim's weapon was inconsistent with   40
        defendant acting in self-defense

     h) Aspect of defendant's condition was inconsistent   40
        with self-defense

   i) Aspect of scene was inconsistent with   40
    self-defense

  2. Value reduction: Deduct 50% of maximum value for any evidence
  substantively challenged by the defense

 D. Circumstantial evidence

  1. Witnesses to prior threats by the defendant against the victim

   a) Maximum value for strongest witness to each
   distinct threat: 10

   b) Value reduction for each witness who
    (1) Knew the victim before the occurrence and was

     (*a*) In the victim's family only   −40%

     (*b*) In the victim's family and in the defen-   −10%
     dant's family or a friend of the defendant

     (*c*) A friend of the victim only   −40%

     (*d*) A friend of the victim and either in the   −10%
     defendant's family or a friend of the
     defendant

     (*e*) A co-worker or business acquaintance of
     the victim only   −20%

     (*f*) A co-worker or business acquaintance of   0%
     the victim and the defendant

    (2) Had a prior conviction   −20%

    (3) Had a motive to testify falsely   −40%

    (4) Was a child or mentally abnormal   −40%

    (5) Gave a prior inconsistent statement   −40%

    (6) Was under the influence of drugs or alcohol   −40%
    at the time of the homicide

    (7) Had evidence of bad character other than a   −10%
    prior conviction

  2. Witnesses to prior acts of aggression by the defendant against the
  victim

   a) Maximum value for strongest witness to each distinct act: 15

   b) Value reduction for witness who

    (1) Knew the victim before the occurrence and was

     (*a*) In the victim's family only   −40%

     (*b*) In the victim's family and either in the   −10%
     defendant's family or a friend of the
     defendant

  (*c*) A friend of the victim only   −40%

  (*d*) A friend of the victim and either in the   −10%
    defendant's family or a friend of the
    defendant

  (*e*) A co-worker or business acquaintance of   −20%
    the victim only

  (*f*) A co-worker or business acquaintance of   0%
    the victim and the defendant

 (2) Had a prior conviction   −20%

 (3) Had a motive to testify falsely   −40%

 (4) Was a child or mentally abnormal   −40%

 (5) Gave a prior inconsistent statement   −40%

 (6) Was under the influence of drugs or alcohol   −40%
   at the time of the homicide

 (7) Had evidence of bad character other than a   −10%
   prior conviction

3. Witnesses to the violent character of the defendant

 a) Maximum value for each of the first three witnesses: 25, 15, 5

 b) Value reduction for each witness who was

  (1) In the victim's family only   −40%

  (2) In the victim's family and in the defendant's   −10%
    family or a friend of the defendant

  (3) A friend of the victim only   −40%

  (4) A friend of the victim and in the defendant's   −10%
    family or a friend of the defendant

  (5) A co-worker or business acquaintance of the   −20%
    victim only

  (6) A co-worker or business acquaintance of the   0%
    victim and the defendant

4. Witnesses to the peaceful character of the victim

 a) Maximum value for each of the first three witnesses: 25, 15, 5

 b) Value reduction for each witness who was

  (1) In the victim's family only   −40%

  (2) In the victim's family and in the defendant's   −10%
    family or a friend of the defendant

  (3) A friend of the victim only   −40%

  (4) A friend of the victim and in the defendant's   −10%
    family or a friend of the defendant

    (5) A co-worker or business acquaintance of the   −20%
        victim only

    (6) A co-worker or business acquaintance of the   0%
        victim and the defendant

5. Witnesses that defendant planned or prepared to kill the victim before the occurrence

   a) Maximum value for each of the first four witnesses: 40, 30, 20, 10

   b) Value reduction for each witness who

     (1) Knew the victim before the occurrence and was

       (*a*) In the victim's family only   −40%

       (*b*) In the victim's family and in the defen-   −10%
           dant's family or a friend of the defendant

       (*c*) A friend of the victim only   −40%

       (*d*) A friend of the victim and in the defen-   −10%
           dant's family or a friend of the defendant

       (*e*) A co-worker or business acquaintance of   −20%
           the victim only

       (*f*) A co-worker or business acquaintance of   0%
           the victim and the defendant

     (2) Had a prior conviction   −20%

     (3) Had a motive to testify falsely   −40%

     (4) Was a child or mentally abnormal   −40%

     (5) Gave a prior inconsistent statement   −40%

     (6) Was under the influence of drugs or alcohol   −40%
       at the time of the homicide

     (7) Had evidence of bad character other than a   −10%
       prior conviction

6. Witnesses that the defendant had a motive for killing the victim

   a) Maximum value for each of the first two witnesses: 20, 10
   b) Value reductions: none

II. Defense evidence

  A. Eyewitnesses that victim threatened the defendant or others with death or serious bodily harm

    1. Maximum value for each of the first five witnesses: 50, 40, 30, 20, 10 [†]

[†] The maximum value for each circumstantial eyewitness is five points less than the maximum value for the comparable direct eyewitness.

2. Value reductions

   a) For each defense eyewitness whose statement was qualified regarding

(1) Whether the threat by the victim involved danger of death or serious bodily harm	−50%
(2) Whether the defendant provoked the threat or was the aggressor	−40%
(3) Whether the defendant failed to take advantage of an avenue of retreat	−40%
(4) Whether the threat was of imminent danger	−40%
(5) Whether the use of force was excessive	−20%

   b) For each defense eyewitness who

     (1) Knew the defendant before the occurrence and was

(*a*) In the defendant's family only	−40%
(*b*) In the defendant's family and in the victim's family or a friend of the victim	−10%
(*c*) A friend of the defendant only	−40%
(*d*) A friend of the defendant and either in the victim's family or a friend of the victim	−10%
(*e*) A co-worker or business acquaintance of the defendant only	−20%
(*f*) A co-worker or business acquaintance of the victim and the defendant	0%
(2) Had a prior conviction	−20%
(3) Had a motive to testify falsely	−40%
(4) Was a child or mentally abnormal	−40%
(5) Gave a prior inconsistent statement	−40%
(6) Was under the influence of drugs or alcohol at the time of the homicide	−40%
(7) Had evidence of bad character other than a prior conviction	−10%
(8) Was the defendant	−50%

B. Circumstantial evidence

   1. Witnesses to prior threats by the victim against the defendant

     a) Maximum value for strongest witness to each distinct threat: 20

b) Value reduction for each witness who

(1) Knew the defendant before the occurrence and was

    (*a*) In the defendant's family only   −40%

    (*b*) In the defendant's family and in the victim's family or a friend of the victim   −10%

    (*c*) A friend of the defendant only   −40%

    (*d*) A friend of the defendant and in the victim's family or a friend of the victim   −10%

    (*e*) A co-worker or business acquaintance of the defendant only   −20%

    (*f*) A co-worker or business acquaintance of the victim and the defendant   0%

(2) Had a prior conviction   −20%

(3) Had a motive to testify falsely   −40%

(4) Was a child or mentally abnormal   −40%

(5) Gave a prior inconsistent statement   −40%

(6) Was under the influence of drugs or alcohol at the time of the homicide   −40%

(7) Had evidence of bad character other than a prior conviction   −10%

(8) Was the defendant   −50%

2. Witnesses to prior acts of aggression by the victim against the defendant

a) Maximum value for strongest witness to each distinct threat: 30

b) Value reduction for each witness who

(1) Knew the defendant before the occurrence and was

    (*a*) In the defendant's family only   −40%

    (*b*) In the defendant's family and in the victim's family or a friend of the victim   −10%

    (*c*) A friend of the defendant only   −40%

    (*d*) A friend of the defendant and in the victim's family or a friend of the victim   −10%

    (*e*) A co-worker or business acquaintance of the defendant only   −20%

    (*f*) A co-worker or business acquaintance of the victim and the defendant   0%

(2) Had a prior conviction	− 20%
(3) Had a motive to testify falsely	− 40%
(4) Was a child or mentally abnormal	− 40%
(5) Gave a prior inconsistent statement	− 40%
(6) Was under the influence of drugs or alcohol at the time of the homicide	− 40%
(7) Had evidence of bad character other than a prior conviction	− 10%
(8) Was the defendant	− 50%

3. Witnesses to the violent character of the victim

 a) Maximum value for each of the first three witnesses: 25, 15, 5

 b) Value reduction for each witness who was

(1) In the defendant's family only	− 40%
(2) In the defendant's family and in the victim's family or a friend of the victim	− 10%
(3) A friend of the defendant only	− 40%
(4) A friend of the defendant and in the victim's family or a friend of the victim	− 10%
(5) A co-worker or business acquaintance of the defendant only	−20%
(6) A co-worker or business acquaintance of the victim and the defendant	0%

4. Witnesses to the peaceful character of the defendant

 a) Maximum value for each of the first three witnesses: 25, 15, 5

 b) Value reduction for each witness who was

(1) In the defendant's family only	−40%
(2) In the defendant's family and in the victim's family or a friend of the victim	−10%
(3) A friend of the defendant only	−40%
(4) A friend of the defendant and in the victim's family or a friend of the victim	−10%
(5) A co-worker or business acquaintance of the defendant only	−20%
(6) A co-worker or business acquaintance of the victim and the defendant	0%

5. Witnesses that defendant knew or had reason to believe that the victim had plans or made preparations to kill him or her

   a) Maximum value for each of the first four witnesses: 40, 30, 20, 10

   b) Value reduction for each witness who

   (1) Knew the defendant before the occurrence and was

(*a*) In the defendant's family only	−40%
(*b*) In the defendant's family and in the victim's family or a friend of the victim	−10%
(*c*) A friend of the defendant only	−40%
(*d*) A friend of the defendant and in the victim's family or a friend of the victim	−10%
(*e*) A co-worker or business acquaintance of the defendant only	−20%
(*f*) A co-worker or business acquaintance of the victim and the defendant	0%

(2) Had a prior conviction	−20%
(3) Had a motive to testify falsely	−40%
(4) Was a child or mentally abnormal	−40%
(5) Gave a prior inconsistent statement	−40%
(6) Was under the influence of drugs or alcohol at the time of the homicide	−40%
(7) Had evidence of bad character other than a prior conviction	−10%
(8) Was the defendant	−50%

C. Scientific evidence

   1. Maximum values

a) Condition of the defendant was consistent with self-defense	35
b) Condition of the defendant's weapon was consistent with self-defense	35
c) Condition of the victim was consistent with self-defense	35
d) Condition of the victim's weapon was consistent with self-defense	35
e) Condition of the scene was consistent with self-defense	35

   2. Value reductions: Deduct 20 points from any category against which the prosecution raised a substantive challenge.

III. Final score on whether the defendant acted in self-defense or in defense of others

A. Add prosecution and defense scores separately

1. Prosecution = Eyewitness + Statement of + Scientific
score   evidence   the defendant   evidence

    + Circumstantial
      evidence

2. Defense   = Eyewitness + Circumstantial + Scientific
score   testimony   evidence   evidence

B. Subtract defense score from prosecution score to obtain final score for whether the defendant acted in self-defense or in defense of others

APPENDIX B

Supplementary Tables

TABLE B-1
Supplementary Tests of Significance of
Race, Sex, and Judicial District Variables
for Probability of Dismissal

Pool: All homicide arrests
489 defendant–victim units
57 dismissed

Model	–Model likelihood	Improve- ment chi- square	Improve- ment degrees of freedom	Probability <	Number of infinite coefficient estimates
Race of defendant entered after basic evidence	129.8	.2	1	.99	1
Race and sex of victim and defendant entered after basic evidence	129.7	.4	4	.99	1
Judicial district entered after race and sex of defendant and victim	126.2	7.0	9	.70	2

194

TABLE B-2
Logistic Regression Analysis of Probability
of First Degree Murder Indictment

Pool: All homicide indictments
444 defendant–victim units
331 first degree murder indictments

Model	-Model likelihood	Improve-ment chi-square	Model degrees of freedom	Improve-ment degrees of freedom	Probability <	Number of infinite coefficient estimates
Constant	251.9	—	1	—	—	0
Basic evidence	233.3	37.2	8	7	.001	0
Judicial district	208.8	48.9	17	9	.001	0
Race and sex of defendant and victim	205.8	6.0	21	4	.20	0
Culpability ° evidence	203.9	3.8	26	5	.70	0
Judicial district ° culpability	200.8	6.2	35	9	.80	0
Judicial district ° aggravating circumstances	185.0	31.6	44	9	.001	10
Defendant's race ° culpability and defendant's race ° aggravating circumstances	182.5	5.0	46	2	.10	10

TABLE B-3
Coefficient Estimates for Last Regression Model
with a Significant Category of Variables
for Probability of First Degree Murder Indictment

Pool: All homicide indictments
444 defendant–victim units
331 first degree murder indictments

Variable	Coefficient	Standard error	Chi-square	Probability <
Intercept	1.456	.587	6.16	.02
Identity of defendant as a perpetrator	−.002	.002	1.25	.27
Absence of self-defense	−.000	.001	.18	.68
Degree of culpability	.005	.002	12.30	.001
Aggravating circumstances	.039	.026	2.21	.14
Mitigating circumstances	−.015	.024	.40	.53
Prior record	.013	.026	.26	.62
Multiple victims	−1.216	.761	2.56	.11
Judicial District 1	.903	.809	1.25	.26
Judicial District 2	7.191	19.785	.13	.72
Judicial District 3	−1.655	.477	12.02	.001
Judicial District 4	.148	.703	.04	.84
Judicial District 5	1.552	1.080	2.07	.16
Judicial District 6	.161	.461	.12	.73
Judicial District 7	2.601	1.038	6.27	.02
Judicial District 8	1.385	.781	3.14	.08
Judicial District 9	−.439	.297	2.18	.14

TABLE B-4
Supplementary Tests of Significance of Race,
Sex, and Judicial District Variables
for Probability of First Degree Murder Trial

Pool: All homicide arrests
489 defendant–victim units
60 first degree murder trials

Model	−Model likelihood	Improve- ment chi- square	Improve- ment degrees of freedom	Probability <	Number of infinite coefficient estimates
Race of defendant entered after basic evidence	166.5	2.0	1	.20	0
Race and sex of defendant and victim entered after basic evidence	163.9	7.2	4	.20	0
Judicial district entered after race and sex of defendant and victim	151.3	25.2	9	.01	0

TABLE B-5
Logistic Regression Analysis of Probability
of First Degree Murder Trial

Pool: All homicide indictments
444 defendant–victim units
60 first degree murder trials

Model	–Model likelihood	Improve-ment chi-square	Model degrees of freedom	Improve-ment degrees of freedom	Probability <	Number of infinite coefficient estimates
Constant	172.7	—	1	—	—	0
Basic evidence	162.3	20.8	8	7	.01	0
Judicial district	149.3	26.0	17	9	.01	0
Race and sex of defendant and victim	146.0	6.6	21	4	.20	0
Culpability ° evidence	140.9	10.2	26	5	.10	0
Judicial district ° culpability	132.4	17.0	35	9	.05	0
Judicial district ° aggravating factors	125.1	14.6	44	9	.20	1
Defendant's race ° culpability and defendant's race ° aggravating factors	119.7	10.8	46	2	.01	1

TABLE B-6
Coefficient Estimates for Last Logistic Regression
Model with a Significant Category of Variables
for Probability of First Degree Murder Trial

Pool: All homicide indictments
444 defendant–victim units
60 first degree murder trials

Variable	Coefficient	Standard error	Chi-square	Probability <
Intercept	−4.740	1.458	10.58	.01
Identity of defendant as a perpetrator	−.001	.003	.13	.72
Absence of self-defense	−.001	.002	.35	.55
Degree of culpability	−.008	.015	.32	.57
Aggravating circumstances	.219	.080	7.44	.01
Mitigating circumstances	−.068	.055	1.49	.22
Prior record	−.064	.054	1.41	.24
Multiple victims	2.445	.902	7.35	.01
Judicial District 1	3.460	2.030	2.90	.09
Judicial District 2	4.624	1.415	10.67	.002
Judicial District 3	−.415	1.484	.08	.78
Judicial District 4	2.955	1.119	6.98	.01
Judicial District 5	.573	1.613	.13	.73
Judicial District 6	−2.085	2.129	.96	.33
Judicial District 7	−1.987	2.853	.48	.49
Judicial District 8	2.021	.876	5.32	.03
Judicial District 9	1.238	.760	2.65	.11
Defendant's race	1.062	.763	1.94	.17

TABLE B-6 — Continued
Coefficient Estimates for Last Logistic Regression
Model with a Significant Category of Variables
for Probability of First Degree Murder Trial

Pool: All homicide indictments
444 defendant–victim units
60 first degree murder trials

Variable	Coefficient	Standard error	Chi-square	Probability <
Victim's race	−.784	.586	1.79	.19
Defendant's sex	1.082	.613	3.12	.08
Victim's sex	.014	.437	.00	.98
Culpability * identity of defendant as perpetrator	.000	.000	.37	.55
Culpability * absence of self-defense	.000	.000	5.38	.02
Culpability * aggravating circumstances	−.002	.001	8.75	.004
Culpability * mitigating circumstances	.001	.001	2.30	.13
Culpability * prior record	.002	.001	5.21	.03
Judicial District 1 * culpability	−.010	.019	.25	.62
Judicial District 2 * culpability	.016	.013	1.57	.22
Judicial District 3 * culpability	−.010	.018	.31	.58
Judicial District 4 * culpability	−.009	.018	.29	.60
Judicial District 5 * culpability	−.009	.010	.81	.37
Judicial District 6 * culpability	.025	.018	1.85	.18

TABLE B-6 — Continued
Coefficient Estimates for Last Logistic Regression
Model with a Significant Category of Variables
for Probability of First Degree Murder Trial

Pool: All homicide indictments
444 defendant–victim units
60 first degree murder trials

Variable	Coefficient	Standard error	Chi-square	Probability <
Judicial District 7 ° culpability	.027	.031	.76	.39
Judicial District 8 ° culpability	.007	.011	.46	.50
Judicial District 9 ° culpability	.006	.007	.75	.39
Judicial District 1 ° aggravating circumstances	−.276	.152	3.28	.07
Judicial District 2 ° aggravating circumstances	−.227	.115	3.87	.05
Judicial District 3 ° aggravating circumstances	.242	.128	3.60	.06
Judicial District 4 ° aggravating circumstances	.118	.130	.82	.37
Judicial District 5 ° aggravating circumstances	.132	.137	.93	.34
Judicial District 6 ° aggravating circumstances	.080	.112	.50	.48
Judicial District 7 ° aggravating circumstances	.233	.205	1.30	.26

TABLE B-6 — Continued
Coefficient Estimates for Last Logistic Regression
Model with a Significant Category of Variables
for Probability of First Degree Murder Trial

Pool: All homicide indictments
444 defendant–victim units
60 first degree murder trials

Variable	Coefficient	Standard error	Chi-square	Probability <
Judicial District 8 ° aggravating circumstances	−1.066	†	†	†
Judicial District 9 ° aggravating circumstances	−.004	.065	.00	.95
Defendant's race ° culpability	.011	.006	3.97	.05
Defendant's race ° aggravating circumstances	−.148	.050	8.95	.003

†The coefficient was infinite.

TABLE B-7
Logistic Regression Analysis of
Probability of First Degree Murder Trial

Pool: All first degree murder indictments
331 defendant–victim units
60 first degree murder trials

Model	–Model likelihood	Improve- ment chi- square	Model degrees of freedom	Improve- ment degrees of freedom	Probability <	Number of infinite coefficient estimates
Constant	155.0	—	1	—	—	
Basic evidence	147.7	14.6	8	7	.10	0
Judicial district	132.7	30.0	17	9	.001	0
Race and sex of defendant and victim	129.8	5.8	21	4	.30	0
Culpability ° evidence	126.3	7.0	26	5	.30	0
Judicial district ° culpability	120.5	11.6	35	9	.30	0
Judicial district ° aggravating factors	112.3	16.4	44	9	.10	1
Defendant's race ° culpability and defendant's race ° aggravating circumstances	106.9	10.8	46	2	.01	1

TABLE B-8
Coefficient Estimates for Last Regression
Model with a Significant Category of Variables for
Probability of First Degree Murder Trial

Pool: All first degree murder indictments
331 defendant–victim units
60 first degree murder trials

Variable	Coefficient	Standard error	Chi-square	Probability <
Intercept	−5.626	1.593	12.46	.000
Identity of defendant as a perpetrator	.003	.003	1.00	.32
Absence of self-defense	.001	.002	.10	.76
Degree of culpability	−.008	.015	.26	.61
Aggravating circumstances	.232	.083	7.82	.006
Mitigating circumstances	−.072	.059	1.49	.222
Prior record	−.109	.064	2.85	.10
Multiple victims	2.516	.959	6.88	.009
Judicial District 3	1.183	2.462	.23	.64
Judicial District 5	4.371	1.450	9.09	.003
Judicial District 12	−5.365	4.603	1.36	.25
Judicial District 14	3.289	1.267	6.73	.01
Judicial District 16	.384	1.558	.06	.81
Judicial District 18	−1.046	2.183	.23	.64
Judicial District 26	−2.440	2.867	.72	.40
Judicial District 27	1.998	.898	4.95	.03
Judicial District Group A	1.541	.772	3.98	.05
Race of defendant	.977	.778	1.58	.21
Race of victim	−.612	.612	1.00	.32

TABLE B-8 — Continued
Coefficient Estimates for Last Regression
Model with a Significant Category of Variables for
Probability of First Degree Murder Trial

Pool: All first degree murder indictments
331 defendant–victim units
60 first degree murder trials

Variable	Coefficient	Standard error	Chi-square	Probability <
Sex of defendant	1.001	.617	2.63	.11
Sex of victim	.366	.495	.55	.46
Culpability * identity of the defendant as perpetrator	.000	.000	.19	.67
Culpability * absence of self-defense	.000	.000	4.05	.05
Culpability * aggravating circumstances	−.002	.001	7.06	.008
Culpability * mitigating circumstances	.001	.001	2.15	.15
Culpability * prior record	.002	.001	4.55	.04
Judicial District 3 * culpability	−.020	.021	.89	.35
Judicial District 5 * culpability	.014	.014	1.07	.31
Judicial District 12 * culpability	−.105	.052	4.01	.05
Judicial District 14 * culpability	−.020	.022	.76	.39
Judicial District 16 * culpability	−.010	.010	1.13	.29
Judicial District 18 * culpability	.027	.020	1.80	.18
Judicial District 26 * culpability	.030	.031	.98	.33

TABLE B-8 — Continued
Coefficient Estimates for Last Regression
Model with a Significant Category of Variables for
Probability of First Degree Murder Trial

Pool: All first degree murder indictments
331 defendant–victim units
60 first degree murder trials

Variable	Coefficient	Standard error	Chi-square	Probability <
Judicial District 27 * culpability	.006	.011	.32	.57
Judicial District Group A * culpability	.003	.007	.14	.71
Judicial District 3 * aggravating circumstances	−.068	.214	.10	.76
Judicial District 5 * aggravating circumstances	−.203	.120	2.86	.10
Judicial District 12 * aggravating circumstances	.821	.399	4.24	.04
Judicial District 14 * aggravating circumstances	.130	.147	.78	.38
Judicial District 16 * aggravating circumstances	.129	.136	.90	.35
Judicial District 18 * aggravating circumstances	.001	.134	.00	.99
Judicial District 26 * aggravating circumstances	.225	.204	1.21	.28
Judicial District 27 * aggravating circumstances	−1.05	†	†	†

TABLE B-8 — Continued
Coefficient Estimates for Last Regression
Model with a Significant Category of Variables for
Probability of First Degree Murder Trial

Pool: All first degree murder indictments
331 defendant–victim units
60 first degree murder trials

Variable	Coefficient	Standard error	Chi-square	Probability <
Judicial District Group A ° aggravating circumstances	−.007	.067	.01	.92
Race ° culpability	.012	.006	4.07	.05
Defendant's race ° aggravating circumstances	−.514	.052	8.91	.003

†The coefficient was infinite.

TABLE B-9
Logistic Regression Analysis of Probability of Trial Judge
Submitting First Degree Murder Charge to Jury

Pool: All homicide indictments
444 defendant–victim units
26 first degree murder submissions

Model	−Model likelihood	Improve- ment chi- square	Model degrees of freedom	Improve- ment degrees of freedom	Probability <	Number of infinite coefficient estimates
Constant	97.7	—	1	—	—	0
Basic evidence	78.9	17.6	8	7	.02	0
Race and sex of defendant and victim	75.4	7.0	12	4	.20	0
Culpability ° evidence	69.5	11.8	17	5	.05	0
Defendant's race ° culpability and defendant's race ° aggravating factors	65.6	7.8	19	2	.05	0

TABLE B-10
Coefficient Estimates of Last Regression Model
with a Significant Category of Variables
for Probability of Trial Judge Submitting
First Degree Murder Charge to Jury

Pool: All homicide indictments
444 defendant–victim units
26 first degree murder submissions

Variable	Coefficient	Standard error	Chi-square	Probability <
Intercept	−5.713	2.436	5.50	.02
Identity of defendant as a perpetrator	−.003	.005	.25	.62
Absence of self-defense	.007	.004	2.40	.12
Degree of culpability	−.010	.022	.20	.66
Aggravating circumstances	.122	.096	1.61	.21
Mitigating circumstances	.036	.089	.16	.69
Prior record	−.298	.142	4.41	.04
Multiple victims	1.137	.975	1.36	.24
Defendant's race	1.904	1.164	2.68	.11
Victim's race	−1.487	.792	3.52	.06
Defendant's sex	.058	.828	.00	.95
Victim's sex	−1.080	.518	4.35	.04
Culpability ° identity of defendant as perpetrator	.000	.000	.01	.95
Culpability ° absence of self-defense	.000	.000	1.82	.18
Culpability ° aggravating circumstances	−.001	.001	.40	.53
Culpability ° mitigating circumstances	−.000	.001	.25	.62

TABLE B-10 — Continued
**Coefficient Estimates of Last Regression Model
with a Significant Category of Variables
for Probability of Trial Judge Submitting
First Degree Murder Charge to Jury**

Pool: All homicide indictments
444 defendant–victim units
26 first degree murder submissions

Variable	Coefficient	Standard error	Chi-square	Probability <
Culpability * prior record	.004	.002	6.31	.02
Defendant's race * culpability	.015	.010	2.22	.14
Defendant's race * aggravating circumstances	−.154	.061	6.41	.02

TABLE B-11
**Logistic Regression Analysis of Probability of Trial Judge
Submitting First Degree Murder Charge to Jury**

Pool: All first degree murder indictments
331 defendant–victim units
26 first degree murder submissions

Model	−Model likelihood	Improvement chi-square	Model degrees of freedom	Improvement degrees of freedom	Probability <	Number of infinite coefficient estimates
Constant	90.1	—	1	—	—	
Basic evidence	74.0	32.2	8	7	.001	0
Race and sex of defendant and victim	71.3	5.4	12	4	.30	0
Culpability * evidence	66.5	9.6	17	5	.10	0
Defendant's race * culpability and defendant's race * aggravating circumstances	62.1	6.8	19	2	.05	0

TABLE B-12
Coefficient Estimates of Last Regression Model
with a Significant Category of Variables
for Probability of Trial Judge Submitting
First Degree Murder Charge to Jury

Pool: All first degree murder indictments
331 defendant–victim units
26 first degree murder submissions

Variable	Coefficient	Standard error	Chi-square	Probability <
Intercept	−4.884	2.365	4.26	.04
Identity of defendant as a perpetrator	.002	.005	.10	.75
Absence of self-defense	.007	.004	2.67	.11
Degree of culpability	−.019	.024	.62	.44
Aggravating circumstances	.067	.110	.38	.54
Mitigating circumstances	.072	.099	.53	.47
Prior record	−.231	.150	2.36	.13
Multiple victims	1.315	1.014	1.68	.20
Defendant's race	1.781	1.165	2.34	.13
Victim's race	−1.343	.795	2.85	.10
Defendant's sex	−.139	.856	.03	.88
Victim's sex	−1.028	.540	3.62	.06
Culpability ° identity	.000	.000	.12	.74
Culpability ° self-defense	.000	.000	1.71	.20
Culpability ° aggravating circumstances	−.000	.001	.00	.96
Culpability ° mitigating circumstances	−.001	.001	.54	.47
Culpability ° prior record	.003	.002	3.99	.05

TABLE B-12 — Continued
**Coefficient Estimates of Last Regression Model
with a Significant Category of Variables
for Probability of Trial Judge Submitting
First Degree Murder Charge to Jury**

Pool: All first degree murder indictments
331 defendant–victim units
26 first degree murder submissions

Variable	Coefficient	Standard error	Chi-square	Probability <
Defendant's race ° culpability	.017	.010	2.74	.10
Defendant's race ° aggravating circumstances	−.163	.061	7.02	.01

TABLE B-13
Supplementary Coefficient Estimates of Last Regression
Model with a Significant Category of Variables
for Probability of First Degree Murder Conviction

Pool: All homicide arrests
489 defendant–victim units
18 first degree murder convictions

Variable	Coefficient	Standard error	Chi-square	Probability <
Intercept	−6.160	2.428	6.44	.02
Identity of defendant as a perpetrator	−.000	.003	.05	.83
Absence of self-defense	.010	.007	1.95	.17
Degree of culpability	.023	.007	11.24	.001
Aggravating circumstances	−.032	.042	.58	.45
Mitigating circumstances	.023	.037	.40	.53
Prior record	.081	.036	5.14	.03
Multiple victims	.817	.943	.75	.39
Defendant's race	1.311	.811	2.61	.11
Victim's race	−1.826	.859	4.52	.04
Defendant's sex	−.670	.855	.61	.43
Victim's sex	−.852	.606	1.98	.16

TABLE B-14
Logistic Regression Analysis of
Probability of First Degree Murder Conviction

Pool: All homicide indictments
444 defendant–victim units
18 first degree murder convictions

Model	−Model likelihood	Improve- ment chi- square	Improve- ment degrees of freedom	Probability <	Number of infinite coefficient estimates
Constant	74.4	—	1	—	—
Basic evidence	52.6	43.6	8	7	.001
Race and sex of defendant and victim	49.6	6.0	12	4	.20

TABLE B-15
Coefficient Estimates of Last Regression
Model with a Significant Category
of Variables for Probability
of First Degree Murder Conviction

Pool: All homicide indictments
444 defendant–victim units
18 first degree murder convictions

Variable	Coefficient	Standard error	Chi-square	Probability <
Intercept	−7.531	2.300	10.75	.01
Identity of defendant as a perpetrator	−.001	.002	.09	.76
Absence of self-defense	.011	.007	2.56	.11
Degree of culpability	.022	.007	9.86	.002
Aggravating circumstances	−.024	.042	.32	.57
Mitigating circumstances	.018	.036	.27	.61
Prior record	.083	.035	5.45	.02
Multiple victims	.768	.898	.73	.40

TABLE B-16
Logistic Regression Analysis of
Probability of First Degree Murder Conviction

Pool: All first degree murder indictments
331 defendant–victim units
18 first degree murder convictions

Model	–Model likelihood	Improvement chi-square	Model degrees of freedom	Improvement degrees of freedom	Probability <
Constant	69.2	—	1	—	—
Basic evidence	50.2	38.0	8	7	.001
Race and sex of defendant and victim	47.6	5.2	12	4	.30

TABLE B-17
Coefficient Estimates of Last Regression
Model with a Significant Category of Variables
for Probability of First Degree Murder Conviction

Pool: All homicide arrests
489 defendant–victim units
18 first degree murder convictions

Variable	Coefficient	Standard error	Chi-square	Probability <
Intercept	−7.321	2.472	10.61	.001
Identity of defendant as a perpetrator	−.000	.002	.00	.97
Absence of self-defense	.011	.007	2.68	.11
Degree of culpability	.019	.007	7.76	.006
Aggravating circumstances	−.025	.042	.35	.56
Mitigating circumstances	.027	.037	.52	.48
Prior record	.082	.036	5.21	.03
Multiple victims	.982	.918	1.14	.28

TABLE B-18
Logistic Regression Analysis
of Probability of Death Sentence

Pool: All homicide indictments
444 defendant–victim units
8 death sentences

Model	-Model likelihood	Improve-ment chi-square	Model degrees of freedom	Improve-ment degrees of freedom	Probability <	Number of infinite coefficient estimates
Constant	39.6	—	1	—	—	
Basic evidence	26.0	27.2	8	7	.001	1
Race and sex of defendant and victim	22.6	6.8	12	4	.20	1

TABLE B-19
Coefficient Estimates for Last Regression
Model with a Significant Category of Variables
for Probability of Death Sentence

Pool: All homicide indictments
444 defendant–victim units
8 death sentences

Variable	Coefficient	Standard error	Chi-square	Probability <
Intercept	−7.168	2.404	8.89	.003
Identity of defendant as a perpetrator	.001	.004	.02	.89
Absence of self-defense	.004	.007	.27	.60
Degree of culpability	.023	.009	6.25	.02
Aggravating circumstances	−.013	.067	.04	.85
Mitigating circumstances	.004	.055	.01	.95
Prior record	.120	.052	5.44	.02
Multiple victims	−6.777	†	†	†

†The coefficient was infinite.

TABLE B-20
Logistic Regression Analysis
of Probability of Death Sentence

Pool: All first degree murder indictments
331 defendant–victim units
8 death sentences

Model	−Model likelihood	Improve- ment chi- square	Model degrees of freedom	Improve- ment degrees of freedom	Probability <	Number of infinite coefficient estimates
Constant	37.4	—	1	—	—	
Basic evidence	25.4	24.0	8	7	.01	1
Race and sex of defendant and victim	22.0	6.8	12	4	.20	1

TABLE B-21
Coefficient Estimates for Last Regression Model
with a Significant Category of Variables
for Probability of Death Sentence

Pool: All first degree murder indictments
331 defendant–victim units
8 death sentences

Variable	Coefficient	Standard error	Chi-square	Probability <
Intercept	−6.999	2.384	8.62	.004
Identity of defendant as a perpetrator	.001	.004	.05	.83
Absence of self-defense	.004	.007	.30	.59
Degree of culpability	.022	.010	5.35	.03
Aggravating circumstances	−.010	.068	.02	.88
Mitigating circumstances	.001	.057	.00	.99
Prior record	.114	.052	4.74	.03
Multiple victims	−6.815	†	†	†

†The coefficient was infinite.

Notes

Chapter I

1. Lewis, THE DEVELOPMENT OF AMERICAN PRISON AND PRISON CUSTOMS 1776–1845 at 16 (Patterson Smith 1967); McKelvey, AMERICAN PRISONS: A STUDY IN AMERICAN SOCIAL HISTORY PRIOR TO 1915 at 2, 7, 16–17 (University of Chicago 1936); Rothman, THE DISCOVERY OF THE ASYLUM: SOCIAL ORDER AND DISORDER IN THE NEW REPUBLIC 61, 79 (Little, Brown 1971).

2. U.S. Department of Justice, National Prisoner Statistics, CAPITAL PUNISHMENT 1979 at 18, reprinted in Bedau, THE DEATH PENALTY IN AMERICA 56 (3d ed. Oxford 1982). *See also* Bowers, EXECUTIONS IN AMERICA 33–35, 200–401 (Heath 1974). This work contains a compilation, prepared by Teeters and Zibulka, of all executions at state prisons going back to the first date that executions in each state were conducted according to state rather than local authority.

3. U.S. Department of Justice, National Prisoner Statistics, CAPITAL PUNISHMENT 1977 at 12 (1978).

4. The Teeters and Zibulka compilation goes back earlier than the federal data because it is based on information from each state. Different states centralized their executions at different times, however, so the compilation does not include all states before about 1930 either. With the caveat, then, that the data is not comprehensive, the annual average execution rates that it shows for the four decades before the 1930s are as follows: the 1920s, 116; the 1910s, 110; the 1900s, 118; the 1890s, 121. Bowers, *supra* note 2, at 40; *see also* Bye, CAPITAL PUNISHMENT

IN THE UNITED STATES 1, 56–58 (Committee of Philanthropic Labor of Philadelphia Yearly Meeting of Friends 1919); Hartung, "Trends in the Use of Capital Punishment," 284 Annals of the Am. Acad. of Pol. and Soc. Sci. 8, 13 (1952).

The execution rate for England and Wales during the same period was also low. During the 1900s the annual rate was 16; during the 1910s, 12; during the 1920s, 14; during the 1930s, 9; and during the 1940s, 13. Great Britain Royal Commission on Capital Punishment, REPORT 298–301 (1953).

5. U.S. Department of Justice, National Prisoner Statistics, *supra* note 3, at 12 (1978).

6. *Id.*

7. *Id.*

8. U.S. Department of Justice, Federal Bureau of Investigation, Uniform Crime Reports, CRIME IN THE UNITED STATES 1983 at 43 (1984).

9. U.S. Department of Justice, Bureau of Justice Statistics, CAPITAL PUNISHMENT 1984 at 7 (1985).

10. *Id.*

11. According to the Teeters and Zibulka compilation, Georgia held 417 electrocutions between 1917 and 1964, for an annual average of just under 9.

12. According to the Teeters and Zibulka compilation, New York electrocuted 695 persons between 1890 and 1963, for an annual average of just over 9 executions.

13. According to the Teeters and Zibulka compilation, Texas had 361 executions between 1924 and 1964, for an annual average close to 9. Bowers, *supra* note 2, at 372.

14. According to the Teeters and Zibulka compilation, California carried out 500 executions between 1893 and 1967, for an annual average of fewer than 7.

15. According to the Teeters and Zibulka compilation, North Carolina executed 362 persons between 1910 and 1961, for an annual average of 7. That information is confirmed by data from the North Carolina Department of Correction. Behre, A BRIEF HISTORY OF CAPITAL PUNISHMENT IN NORTH CAROLINA (Office of Correction, Sept. 1973). The Department of Correction information shows that there were only three years in which the total number of executions in North Carolina was as high as 20: 1934, with 20; 1936, with 23; and 1947, with 23. In only six other years did the number exceed 10: 1925 (12), 1935 (11), 1937 (12), 1939 (15), 1944 (15), and 1946 (13). There were only 2 executions in 1912, 1915, and 1958, only 1 in 1910, 1924, 1952, 1955, 1956, and 1961, and none in 1913, 1954, 1959, and 1960. The racial breakdown for those executed during those years was 290 nonwhite (285 black and five Indian) and 72 white. *See also* Hartung, *supra* note 4, at 15.

16. U.S. Department of Justice, Bureau of Justice Statistics, *supra* note 9, at 7.

17. Treason consisted of a variety of offenses that constituted betrayal of one's lord, a breach of the bond of allegiance, including killing him, committing adultery with his wife, violating his daughter, and forging his seal, as well as fleeing from battle or supporting his enemies. Later, petty treason was distinguished as a betrayal of one's lord and high treason as a betrayal of one's king. The punishment for treason included "drawing," or dragging by a horse, before execution, and for high treason, drawing, hanging, disemboweling, burning, be-

heading, and quartering. 2 Pollock and Maitland, THE HISTORY OF ENGLISH LAW 500–508 (2d ed. 1899).

18. The early common law did not distinguish between murder and manslaughter. *Id.* at 485.

19. 1 Stephen, A HISTORY OF THE CRIMINAL LAW IN ENGLAND 463 (1883); 1 Radzinowicz, A HISTORY OF ENGLISH CRIMINAL LAW 4 (Macmillan 1948); 2 Pollock and Maitland, *supra* note 17, at 470.

20. 4 Blackstone, COMMENTARIES 18 (1769).

21. 1 Radzinowicz, *supra* note 19, at 4; 1 Stephen, *supra* note 19, at 466; REPORT FROM THE SELECT COMMITTEE ON CAPITAL PUNISHMENT vii–viii (House of Commons 1931) ("It was during that period that Edmund Burke declared that he could obtain the consent of the House of Commons to any Bill imposing the punishment of death. Our legislation then proceeded in the spirit of Draco himself, the Archon of Athens, whose laws, published in 621 B.C., were said to be 'written not in ink, but in blood,' and who declared that 'the smallest crime deserved death, and he could find no other punishment for the greatest'"); Laurence, A HISTORY OF CAPITAL PUNISHMENT 13–14 (Sampson Low, Manton & Co. 1932) ("Property even more than person, was under the guardianship of the gallows").

22. 1 Stephen, *supra* note 19, at 470–471; *see also* 1 Radzinowicz, *supra* note 19, at 5–6 and n.14.

23. Hartung, *supra* note 4, at 10, 12.

24. Bedau, *supra* note 2, at 7; Bye, *supra* note 4, at 2–3; Hartung, *supra* note 4, at 10; Filler, "Movements to Abolish the Death Penalty in the United States," 284 Annals of Am. Acad. of Pol. and Soc. Sci. 124, 124 (1952).

25. Bye, *supra* note 4, at 2.

26. Revised Statutes of North Carolina, Ch. 34, §§ 1–8, 10–15, 17–18, 20–23 (1837). Horse-stealing and bigamy were the only offenses that were made subject to the benefit of clergy.

27. Revised Code of North Carolina, Ch. 34, §§ 1–8, 10–12, 14, 16–17 (1855).

28. Battle's Revisal of the Public Statutes of North Carolina, Ch. 32, §§ 1–2, 4 (1873).

29. Bye, *supra* note 4, at 5.

30. Approximately 86% (3,334) of the 3,859 persons executed between 1930 and 1967 were executed for murder, 12% (455) for rape, and 2% for six crimes: armed robbery (25), kidnapping (20), burglary (11), sabotage (6), aggravated assault (6), and espionage (2). U.S. Department of Justice, National Prisoner Statistics, *supra* note 3, at 12 (1978).

31. Mullaney v. Wilbur, 421 U.S. 684, 698 (1975).

32. Aristotle, THE RHETORIC, Bk. I, Ch. 13.

33. 3 Stephen, *supra* note 19, at 17; *see also* Great Britain Royal Commission on Capital Punishment, *supra* note 4, at 6.

34. McGautha v. California, 402 U.S. 183, 197–199 (1971).

35. *Id.* at 199.

36. "All through this period the law is only feeling its way tentatively towards this classification. . . . The production of the finished picture will require many centuries of judicial labour, with occasional assistance from the legislature." 3 Holdsworth, A HISTORY OF ENGLISH LAW 256 (1909).

37. 3 Stephen, *supra* note 19, at 21; Kaye, "The Early History of Murder and Manslaughter," 83 L. Q. Rev. 365 (1967).

38. 3 Stephen, *supra* note 19, at 22; Plucknett, A CONCISE HISTORY OF THE COMMON LAW 446 (5th ed. Little, Brown 1956).

39. Wechsler and Michael, "A Rationale of the Law of Homicide," 37 Colum. L. Rev. 701, 707 (1937).

40. Today, this may be limited to dangerous felonies or to specified felonies. *See* LaFave and Scott, CRIMINAL LAW 623–625 (West 2d ed. 1986).

41. 3 Stephen, *supra* note 19, at 22; Wechsler and Michael, *supra* note 39, at 721. Today, this would not provide an independent basis for malice aforethought. *See* LaFave and Scott, *supra* note 40, at 641–642.

42. 3 Stephen, *supra* note 19, at 22–23; Wechsler and Michael, *supra* note 39, at 721.

43. 3 Stephen, *supra* note 19, at 44.

44. Plucknett, *supra* note 38, at 446; 3 Stephen, *supra* note 19, at 42–43.

45. Plucknett, *supra* note 38; 3 Stephen, *supra* note 19, at 44; Perkins, "The Law of Homicide," 36 J. Cr. L. & C. 391, 444 (1946).

46. 1 Stephen, *supra* note 19, at 459–460; Plucknett, *supra* note 38, at 439. Blackstone reported:

> This trial was held before the bishop in person, or his deputy; and by a jury of twelve clerks: and there, first, the party himself was required to make oath of his own innocence; next, there was to be the oath of twelve compurgators, who swore they believed he spoke the truth; then, witnesses were to be examined upon oath, but on behalf of the prisoner only; and, lastly, the jury were to bring in their verdict upon oath, which usually acquitted the prisoner; otherwise, if a clerk, he was degraded, or put to penance. A learned judge, in the beginning of the last century, remarks with much indignation the vast complication of perjury and subornation of perjury, in this solemn farce of a mock trial; the witnesses, the compurgators, and the jury, being all of them partakers in the guilt; the delinquent party also, though convicted before on the clearest evidence, and conscious of his own offence, yet was permitted and almost compelled to swear himself not guilty: nor was the good bishop himself, under whose countenance this scene of wickedness was daily transacted, by any means exempt from a share of it. And yet by this purgation the party was restored to his credit, his liberty, his lands, and his capacity of purchasing afresh, and was entirely made a new and an innocent man.

4 Blackstone, *supra* note 20, at 361; *see also* 1 Pollock and Maitland, *supra* note 17, at 443–444.

47. 1 Stephen, *supra* note 19, at 462–463; Plucknett, *supra* note 38, at 440.

48. 1 Stephen, *supra* note 19, at 461.

49. 4 Blackstone, *supra* note 20, at 360.

50. Dalzell, BENEFIT OF CLERGY IN AMERICA 24 (Blair 1955).

51. 1 Radzinowicz, *supra* note 19, at 8, 83–86.

52. 1 Stephen, *supra* note 19, at 461; Dalzell, *supra* note 50, at 24.

53. 1 Stephen, *supra* note 19, at 461; *see also* 1 Pollock and Maitland, *supra* note 17, at 445.

54. 4 Blackstone, *supra* note 20, at 363; 1 Stephen, *supra* note 19, at 462.

In the United States, the benefit of clergy appears to have been universally available. Case reports record the according of this privilege to slaves. *See* Dalzell, *supra* note 50, at 100–109, 125–127, 248. In 1806, the North Carolina Supreme Court ruled: "No reason can at this date exist, why Females shall not be entitled to the benefit of Clergy, as well as Males." State v. Gray, 5 N.C. 147, 147 (1806). A North Carolina statute later expressly conferred it on women: "In every case where a man, being convicted of any felony, may demand the benefit of his clergy, if a woman be convicted of the same or like offence, upon her prayer, judgment of death shall not be given against her, but she shall suffer the same punishment as a man would suffer, who has the benefit of his clergy allowed him in the like case." Revised Statutes of North Carolina, Ch. 34, § 29 (1837).

55. 4 Blackstone, *supra* note 20, at 365.

In the United States also, no person could claim the benefit of clergy more than once. *See* Dalzell, *supra* note 50, at 138, 221. A North Carolina statute expressly provided: "No person, who hath once been admitted to the benefit of his clergy, and shall afterward be arraigned or convicted for any clergiable offence, subsequently committed, shall be admitted to have privilege or benefit of his clergy." Revised Statutes of North Carolina, Ch. 34, § 25 (1837). "[W]here clergy has once been regularly allowed to a person, it operates as a pardon to him of all clergyable felonies committed by him anterior to the time of such allowance of clergy." State v. Carroll, 27 N.C. 139, 143 (1844).

56. 4 Blackstone, *supra* note 20, at 374.

57. *Id.* at 362, 364, 365, 367; 1 Stephen, *supra* note 19, at 463; Plucknett, *supra* note 38, at 440.

58. 4 Blackstone, *supra* note 20, at 360, 365; 1 Stephen, *supra* note 19, at 463; Plucknett, *supra* note 38, at 441.

North Carolina provided by statute for the consequences of a successful interposition of a benefit of clergy claim:

Where any person, upon conviction of any felony, be allowed his clergy, he shall, if it be manslaughter,* be marked with an M upon the brawn of the left thumb, and if any other felony, with a T on the same place of the thumb—these marks to be made by the sheriff openly in the court before the judge, before such person be discharged; or it shall be in the power of the court, before which such conviction was had, instead of burning the hand of such convict, to order and adjudge him or her to receive one or more public whippings, or to pay a moderate pecuniary fine, in the discretion of said court under all of the circumstances of the case, the entry of which judgment shall have the same legal effects and consequences, to all intents and purposes, as if the person so convicted had been burned in the hand in presence of the court.

Every person, that shall be allowed or admitted to have the benefit or privilege of his clergy, shall, after such clergy allowed and burning in the hand, or other punishment, according to the preceding section of this act, be forthwith enlarged and delivered out of prison by the court before whom such clergy shall be granted: *Provided nevertheless,* that the court, before whom any such allowance of clergy shall be had, shall and may, for the further correction of such person, to whom such clergy shall be allowed, detain and keep him in prison for such convenient time, as the said court in its discretion shall think proper, so as the same do not exceed one year's imprisonment.

Revised Statutes of North Carolina, Ch. 34, §§ 26–27 (1837).

° The codification ascribes the origin of these sections to the English statutes, "4 Hen. 7, c. 13—1816, c. 918; 18 Eliz. c. 7, s. 2 and 3." The 1854 codification expressly provided that the punishment for manslaughter should be branding or a fine and imprisonment up to one year.

59. 4 Blackstone, *supra* note 20, at 366.

60. 1 Stephen, *supra* note 19, at 465–467.

61. *Id.* at 463–465; 3 Stephen, *supra* note 19, at 44–45; Plucknett, *supra* note 38, at 446.

62. 1 Stephen, *supra* note 19, at 463–464.

63. Murder (Abolition of Death Penalty) Act, 1965, 13 & 14 Eliz. 2 (Nov. 8, 1965) Deb., H.L. 1317–1322 (1969).

64. *See* 793 Parl. Deb., H. C. (5th Ser.) 1294–1298 (1969); 306 Parl. Deb., H.L. 1317–1322 (1969).

65. *See generally* LaFave and Scott, *supra* note 40, at 605.

66. Friedman, A HISTORY OF AMERICAN LAW 61–62 (Simon & Schuster 1973). "Connecticut has the distinction of being the only colony in which benefit of clergy was wholly unknown." Dalzell, *supra* note 50, at 215, 233.

67. *See* Commonwealth v. Gable, 7 Sergeant & Rawle 422, 424 (Pa. 1821).

68. Act of April 30, 1790; 1 Stat. L. 119; sec. 5329 R.S.

69. *See* Dalzell, *supra* note 50, at 234–235.

70. Lewis, *supra* note 1, at 25–32; McKelvey, *supra* note 1, at 6–7.

71. Wechsler and Michael, *supra* note 39, at 703; Friedman, *supra* note 66, at 249; Hartung, *supra* note 4, at 10.

72. *Id.*

73. *Id.* at 704.

74. *Id.* at 705.

75. McGautha v. California, 402 U.S. 183, 198 (1971); LaFave and Scott, *supra* note 40, at 642. North Carolina did so in 1893. State v. Benton, 276 N.C. 641, 657, 174 S.E.2d 793 (1970).

76. Wechsler and Michael, *supra* note 39, at 707–708; *see* State v. Daniels, 134 N.C. 671, 676, 46 S.E. 991, 993 (1904):

> The line which separates felonious homicides committed . . . without premeditation, from those accompanied by the additional mental condition called "premeditation," is shadowy and difficult to fix. The law cannot safely prescribe any uniform and universal rule in regard thereto. As in questions of negligence and the like, it can only define the term, and submit the question of its existence to the jury.

77. McGautha v. California, *supra* note 75, at 198–199; *see also* Cardozo, LAW AND LITERATURE 99–101 (Harcourt, Brace 1931); Geimer, "The Law of Homicide in North Carolina: Brand New Cart Before Tired Old Horse," 19 Wake Forest L. Rev. 331, 334–379 (1983).

78. Woodson v. North Carolina, 428 U.S. 280, 290–299 (1976); McGautha v. California, *supra* note 75, at 183, 199; Friedman, *supra* note 66, at 250. *Consider* State v. Fuller, 114 N.C. 885, 19 S.E. 797, 802 (1894) (Justice Avery):

> The passage of the Act of 1893 [dividing murder into two degrees] marks an era in the judicial history of the state. . . . The theory upon which this change has been made is that the law will always be executed more faithfully when it is in accord with an enlightened idea of justice.
>
> Heretofore public opinion has approved, and often applauded, the conduct of juries in disregarding the instructions of judges as to the technical weight to be given to the use of a deadly weapon. The consequence has been that, a lax administration of the law being tolerated in such cases, other juries have constituted themselves judges of the law as well as of the facts, when proof has shown a more heinous offense. The experience of a few years will probably demonstrate here, as elsewhere, that fewer criminals will escape under a law which is in accord with the public sense of justice than under one which makes no discrimination between offenses differing widely in the degree of moral turpitude exhibited.

Blackstone reported that the harshness of the death penalty had a deleterious effect upon the enforcement of the law:

> The injured, through compassion, will often forbear to prosecute: juries, through compassion, will sometimes forget their oaths, and either acquit the guilty or mitigate the nature of the offence: and judges, through compassion, will respite one half of the convicts, and recommend them to the royal mercy. Among so many chances of escaping, the needy or hardened offender overlooks the multitude that suffer; he boldly engages in some desperate attempt, to relieve his wants or supply his vices; and, if unexpectedly the hand of justice overtakes him, he deems himself peculiarly unfortunate, in falling at last a sacrifice to those laws, which long impunity has taught him to contemn.

4 Blackstone, *supra* note 20, at 19.

79. *McGautha*, 402 U.S. at 200.

80. *Id.* at 199.

North Carolina in 1949 gave the jury discretion to recommend mercy. *See* Patrick, "Capital Punishment and Life Imprisonment in North Carolina, 1946 to 1968: Implications for Abolition of the Death Penalty," 6 Wake Forest L. Rev. 417, 419 (1970).

81. 402 U.S. 183 (1971).

82. 408 U.S. 238 (1972).

83. *Id.* at 309 (Stewart, J.).

84. *Id.* at 313 (White, J.); 291–295 (Brennan, J.).

85. *Id.* at 257 (Douglas, J.); 364–366 (Marshall, J.).

86. In North Carolina, if there is evidence from which the jury could find one or more aggravating circumstances beyond a reasonable doubt, the prosecutor must seek the death penalty in the event of a first degree murder conviction. State v. Jones, 299 N.C. 298, 308, 261 S.E.2d 860, 867 (1980). Of course, the prose-

cutor may exercise discretion concerning the degree of vigor to exercise in that pursuit.

87. Davis, DISCRETIONARY JUSTICE: A PRELIMINARY INQUIRY 4 (Louisiana State Univ. 1969). This definition has been criticized in Pepinsky, "Better Living Through Police Discretion," 47 Law & Contemp. Probs. 249, 250 (1984); Fletcher, "Some Unwise Reflections About Discretion," 47 Law & Contemp. Probs. 269, 274–275 (1984); Reiss, "Research on Administrative Discretion and Justice," 23 J. Leg. Ed. 69, 73 (1970).

88. Allen, "Foreword; The Nature of Discretion," 47 Law & Contemp. Probs. 1, 13 (1984).

89. Dworkin, TAKING RIGHTS SERIOUSLY 31 (Harvard 1978).

90. "Discretion, like the hole in a doughnut, does not exist except as an area left open by a surrounding belt of restriction." *Id. See* 4 Blackstone, *supra* note 20, at 372:

> Our statute law has not therefore often ascertained the quantity of fines, nor the common law ever; it directing such an offence to be punished by fine, in general, without specifying the certain sum: which is fully sufficient, when we consider, that however unlimited the power of the court may seem, it is far from being wholly arbitrary; but it's [*sic*] discretion is regulated by law. For the bill of rights has particularly declared, that excessive fines ought not to be imposed, nor cruel and unusual punishments inflicted.

91. Dworkin, *supra* note 89, at 33.

92. *See* Wright, "Beyond Discretionary Justice," 81 Yale L. J. 575, 594 (1972); Fletcher, *supra* note 87, at 283–284.

93. Fletcher, *supra* note 87, at 270.

94. Blackstone reflected this ambivalence:

> And it is moreover one of the glories of our English law, that the nature, though not always the quantity or degree, of punishment is *ascertained* for every offence; and that it is not left in the breast of any judge, nor even of a jury, to alter that judgment, which the law has beforehand ordained, for every subject alike, without respect of persons. For, if judgments were to be the private opinions of the judge, men would then be slaves to their magistrates; and would live in society, without knowing exactly the conditions and obligations which it lays them under. And besides, as this prevents oppression on the one hand, so on the other it stifles all hopes of impunity or mitigation; with which an offender might flatter himself, if his punishment depended on the humour or discretion of the court. Whereas, where an established penalty is annexed to crimes, the criminal may read their certain consequence in that law, which ought to be the unvaried rule, as it is the inflexible judge, of his actions.
>
> The discretionary fines and discretionary length of imprisonment, which our courts are enabled to impose, may seem an exception to this rule. But the general nature of the punishment, *viz.* by fine or imprisonment, is in these cases fixed and determinate: though the duration and quantity of each must frequently vary, from the aggravations or otherwise of the offence, the quality and condition of the parties, and from innumerable other circum-

stances. The *quantum*, in particular, of pecuniary fines neither can, nor ought to be, ascertained by any invariable law. The value of money itself changes from a thousand causes; and, at all events, what is ruin to one man's fortune, may be matter of indifference to another's.

4 Blackstone, *supra* note 20, at 371. But *see* 1 Radzinowicz, *supra* note 19, at 89:

Yet Romilly doubted whether it could be said "that the species of punishment is ascertained for every offence, when in so great a number of felonies it remains in practice with the judge to say whether the criminal shall suffer death, transportation or imprisonment." He condemns the practice of selecting offenders to be executed instead of those to be recommended for mercy, adding that since the aggravating circumstances on the strength of which the judges based their decision were necessarily variable and unpredictable, the operation of capital statutes was thus made even more indeterminate and their deterrent value more doubtful.

95. *Cf.* Great Britain Royal Commission on Capital Punishment, *supra* note 4, at 173.

96. Pepinsky, *supra* note 87, at 253.

97. Vorenberg, "Narrowing the Discretion of Criminal Justice Officials," 1976 Duke Law J. 657, 662.

See Bacigal, "Some Observations and Proposals on the Nature of the Fourth Amendment," 46 Geo. Wash. L. Rev. 529, 559–560 (1978):

Complete elimination of discretion and the potential for arbitrariness, however, is both undesirable and impossible. It is undesirable because mechanical application of rules frequently leads to injustice. It is impossible because rules always lack sufficient detail to resolve every problem. Officials can use their discretion properly to furnish justice or improperly to frustrate justice. The remedy for the potential abuse of discretion is to employ checks and balances to control the exercise of discretion and to prevent arbitrary action.

See also Breitel, "Controls in Criminal Law Enforcement," 27 U. Chi. L. Rev. 427, 428 (1960) ("[C]rime control, at least in some of its phases, inevitably requires that discretion be exercised."); Goodheart, "The Rule of Law and Absolute Sovereignty," 106 U. Pa. L. Rev. 943, 949 (1958) ("It is obvious that under no conceivable legal system can there be complete rule under the law, as a large degree of freedom of action must be left to those who exercise the power of government. On the other hand, there is hardly any political system, however tyrannical, which can function without placing some legal limitations on the powers of its officers.") *See also* Frank, LAW AND THE MODERN MIND 129 (Anchor Books 1963); Pound, AN INTRODUCTION TO THE PHILOSOPHY OF LAW 70–71 (Yale 1961).

98. Pattenden, THE JUDGE, DISCRETION, AND THE CRIMINAL TRIAL 35 (Clarendon Press 1982).

The need for discretion also arises because public attitudes change over time, and it is not always possible immediately to adapt the statutory law to these changes. The exercise of discretion may also function as an informal means of testing public reaction to a change in enforcement practice that may lead to legislative revision in the area. Abrams, "Internal Policy: Guiding the Exercise of Prosecutorial Discretion," 19 U.C.L.A. L. Rev. 1, 3 (1971).

   99. Aristotle, THE ETHICS, Bk. V, Ch. X:

> The next thing to speak of is the subject of "the equitable" and equity, and the relation that the equitable bears to the just, and equity to justice; for when we examine the subject, they do not seem to be absolutely the same, nor yet generally different. And we sometimes praise "the equitable," and the man of that character; so that we even transfer the expression, for the purpose of praise, to other cases, showing by the use of the term "equitable" instead of "good," that equity is better. Sometimes, again, if we attend to the definition, it appears absurd that equity should be praiseworthy, when it is something different from justice, for either justice must be not good, or equity must be not just, that is, if it is different from justice; or, if they are both good, they must be both the same.
>
> From these considerations, then, almost entirely arises the difficulty on the subject of the equitable. But all of them are in one sense true and not inconsistent with each other; for "the equitable" is just, being better than a certain kind of "just"; and it is not better than "the just," as though it were of a different genus. Just and equitable, therefore, are identical; and both being good, "the equitable" is the better. The cause of the ambiguity is this, that "the equitable" is just, but not that justice which is according to law, but the correction of the legally just. And the reason of this is, that law is in all cases universal, and on some subjects it is not possible to speak universally with correctness. In those cases where it is necessary to speak universally, but impossible to do so correctly, the law takes the most general case, though it is well aware of the incorrectness of it. And the law is not, therefore, less right; for the fault is not in the law, nor in the legislator, but in the nature of the thing; for the subject-matter of human actions is altogether of this description.
>
> When, therefore, the law speaks universally, and something happens different from the generality of cases, then it is proper where the legislator falls short, and has erred, from speaking generally, to correct the defect, as the legislator would himself direct if he were then present, or as he would have legislated if he had been aware of the case. Therefore the equitable is just, and better than some kind of "just"; not indeed better than the "absolute just," but better than the error which arises from universal enactments.

See also Aristotle, *supra* note 32:

> Unwritten law makes up for the defects of a community's written code of law. This is what we call equity; people regard it as just; it is, in fact, the sort of justice which goes beyond the written law. Its existence partly is and partly is not intended by legislators; not intended, where they have noticed no defect in the law; intended, where they find themselves unable to define things exactly, and are obliged to legislate as if that held good always which in fact only holds good usually; or where it is not easy to be complete owing to the endless possible cases presented, such as the kinds and sizes of weapons that may be used to inflict wounds—a lifetime would be too short to

make out a complete list of these. If, then, a precise statement is impossible and yet legislation is necessary, the law must be expressed in wide terms; and so, if a man has no more than a finger-ring in his hand when he lifts it to strike or actually strikes another man, he is guilty of a criminal act according to the written words of the law, but he is innocent really, and it is equity that declares him to be so. From this definition of equity it is plain what sort of actions, and what sort of persons, are equitable or the reverse. Equity must be applied to forgivable actions, and it must make us distinguish between criminal acts on the one hand, and errors of judgement, or misfortunes, on the other. . . . Equity bids us be merciful to the weakness of human nature; to think less about the laws than about the man who framed them, and less about what he said than about what he meant; not to consider the actions of the accused so much as his intentions; nor this or that detail so much as the whole story; to ask not what a man is now but what he has always or usually been. It bids us remember benefits rather than injuries, and benefits received rather than benefits conferred; to be patient when we are wronged; to settle a dispute by negotiation and not by force; to prefer arbitration to litigation —for an arbitrator goes by the equity of a case, a judge by the strict law, and arbitration was invented with the express purpose of securing full power for equity.

100. Schmidhauser, "Judicial Discretion," 8 INT. ENCY. OF THE SOC. SCIS. 320 (1968).

101. Gulliver, "Negotiations as a Mode of Dispute Settlement," 7 Law and Soc. Rev. 667, 684 (1973); *see also* Hoebel, THE LAW OF PRIMITIVE MAN (Harvard 1961).

102. Packer, THE LIMITS OF THE CRIMINAL SANCTION 290 (Stanford 1968); *see also* Lord Camden in Hindson v. Kersey (1680), reported in The King v. Alman, 8 Howell St. Tr. 54, 57 n.* (1765) ("The discretion of a Judge is the law of tyrants: it is always unknown. It is different in different men. It is casual, and depends upon constitution, temper, passion. In the best it is oftentimes caprice; in the worst it is every vice, folly and passion to which human nature is liable."); United States v. Wunderlich, 342 U.S. 98, 101 (1951) (Douglas, J., dissenting) ("Absolute discretion is a ruthless master. It is more destructive of freedom than any of man's other inventions.").

103. Fuller, THE MORALITY OF LAW 81 (Yale 1964).

104. Selznick, "The Sociology of Law," 9 INT. ENCY. OF THE SOC. SCIS. 50, 52 (1968).

105. Davis, *supra* note 87, at 25.

106. Packer, *supra* note 102, at 290; *see also* Vorenberg, *supra* note 97, at 655, 671, 673.

107. Ross, SETTLED OUT OF COURT: THE SOCIAL PROCESS OF INSURANCE CLAIMS ADJUSTMENTS 6–7 (Aldine 1970).

108. Ross, "Insurance Claims Complaints: A Private Appeals Procedure," 9 Law and Soc. 275, 275 (1975).

109. Baker, "The Prosecutor—Initiation of Prosecution," 23 J. Crim. L. & C. 770, 796 (1933).

110. Friedman, "Legal Rules and the Process of Social Change," 19 Stan. L. Rev. 786, 789 (1967).

111. *Id.* at 789–790.

112. Wasby, SMALL TOWN POLICE AND THE SUPREME COURT 6 (Lexington 1976).

113. Davis, *supra* note 87, at 52–161.

Even these procedures may not take adequate account of the effect on the exercise of discretion of the personal goals of the decision makers and the needs of the institutions that they serve. Feeley argued that although such procedural reforms would help, they may not get decision makers to "assume stronger commitments to the formal goals and rules of the systems and act accordingly." Feeley, "Two Models of the Criminal Justice System: An Organizational Perspective," 7 Law and Soc. Rev. 407, 421–422 (1973). The suggestion that they could, Feeley has argued, "tends to underestimate the very real and strong individual and subgroup incentives, goals, and values, and underestimates as well the 'crime control model' as the operative normative ideal among many persons involved in the system." *Id.* at 422. He said: "The task of institutionalized reform rests squarely on the generation of mechanisms which strengthen the position of the organizational goals and norms vis-à-vis the competing subgroup and individual goals." *Id.*; *see also*, Mayhew, "Institutions of Representation: Civil Justice and the Public," 9 Law and Soc. 401, 410 (1975).

Pepinsky has gone so far as to contend that the technique of confining discretion may be counterproductive. His argument is that more detailed law increases discretion. Pepinsky, CRIME AND CONFLICT 13 (Academic Press 1976). He reasons that each legal specification simply increases the areas of discretion open to the public officer by presenting more options as to courses of action to follow. *Id.* at 14–23. This reasoning seems to be semantic only. All of the options available under a more specific statute are also available under a more general statute; they just do not stand out as clearly.

114. "Without an objective standard [by which to evaluate culpability and mitigating circumstances], a comparative analysis might prove the best alternative. Thus, cases in which similar killings have been considered to be more blameworthy by one sentencing authority than another can be regarded as ones in which the death penalty is disproportionate." Dix, "Appellate Review of the Decision to Impose Death," 68 Geo. L. Rev. 97, 107 (1979).

115. *See generally* Arkin, "Discrimination and Arbitrariness in Capital Punishment: An Analysis of Post-Furman Murder Cases in Dade County, Florida, 1973–1976," 33 Stan. L. Rev. 75, 76 (1980); Bowers and Pierce, "Arbitrariness and Discrimination Under Post-*Furman* Capital Statutes," 26 Crime and Delinq. 563, 572–573 (1980); Messinger, "Introduction," in ALDINE CRIME AND JUSTICE ANNUAL xxi (1973); Paternoster, "Race of Victim and Location of Crime: The Decision to Seek the Death Penalty in South Carolina," 74 J. Crim. L. and Crim. 754, 758 n.27 (1983).

116. *See generally* Lempert, "Dessert and Deterrence, Assessment of the Moral Bases of the Case for Capital Punishment," 79 Mich. L. Rev. 1177 (1981).

117. Radin, "Proportionality, Subjectivity, and Tragedy," 18 U.C. Davis L. Rev. 1165 (1985), argued: "Whether someone is guilty of a crime or deserves to die for it is not of concern to the pure utilitarian. But no one in her right mind is a pure utilitarian." *Id.* at 1170. Random executions can create a reign of terror, but they cannot target particular undesired activity for deterrence. If a citizen were

subject to capital punishment without regard to the commission of crime, capital punishment would be irrelevant to crime control or any legitimate utilitarian purpose. *See* Bentham, AN INTRODUCTION TO THE PRINCIPLES OF MORALS AND LEGISLATION, Ch. XIII (1780).

118. U.S. Const., Amend. XIV.

119. *Id.*, Amend. VIII.

120. The history of the death penalty in England includes some instances of *de jure* discrimination. Even after availability of benefit of clergy was expanded beyond clerks in orders, it was long denied to women. Moreover, true clergy could claim it without limit; lords and peers were limited to claiming it for their first offense but were not branded upon exercising the privilege; commoners could claim it only once also, but that limit was enforced by branding them if they did exercise the privilege to establish that they had exhausted their quota. 4 Blackstone, *supra* note 20, at 365. The relationship of the privilege to the official church may have excluded members of other faiths, but Blackstone disputed that suggestion:

> It hath been said, that Jews, and other infidels and heretics, were not capable of the benefit of clergy, till after the statute 5 Ann. c.6 as being under a legal incapacity for orders. But, with deference to such respectable authorities, I much question whether this was ever ruled for law, since the reintroduction of the Jews into England, in the time of Oliver Cromwell. For, if that were the case, the Jews are still in the same predicament, which every day's experience will contradict: the statute of queen Anne having certainly made no alteration in this respect; it only dispensing with the necessity of reading in those persons, who, in case they could read, were before the act entitled to the benefit of their clergy.

Id. There does not seem to be any history of discrimination expressly written into capital punishment statutes in the United States since the Civil War. *Cf.* Dalzell, *supra* note 50, at 126; Bowers, EXECUTIONS IN AMERICA 173 (Heath 1974). Of course, southern lynch mobs in the late nineteenth century acted out of "naked racism, no more." Friedman, *supra* note 66, at 506; Bowers, *supra*, at 175; Bye, *supra* note 4, at 68–69.

121. Hunter v. Underwood, 105 S.Ct. 1916, 1920 (1985); Village of Arlington Heights v. Metropolitan Housing Development Corp., 429 U.S. 252, 265–266 (1977); Washington v. Davis 426 U.S. 229, 240 (1976).

122. *See* Prejean v. Maggio, 765 F.2d 482, 486 (5th Cir. 1985).

123. *See* Turner v. Murray, 106 S.Ct. 1683, 1687 (1986); McCleskey v. Kemp, 753 F.2d 877, 925 n.24 (11th cir. 1985) (Clark, J., dissenting) *cert. granted* 106 S.Ct. 3331 (1986): "The majority opinion notes that the Baldus study ignores quantitative difference in cases: 'looks, age, personality, education, profession, job, clothes, demeanor, and remorse. . . .' However, it is these differences that often are used to mask, either intentionally or unintentionally, racial prejudice."

124. Hunter v. Underwood, 105 S.Ct. 1916, 1920 (1985).

125. *Cf.* Castaneda v. Partida, 430 U.S. 482, 493 (1977): ("'[s]ometimes a clear pattern, unexplainable on grounds other than race, emerges from the effect of state action even when the governing legislation appears neutral on its face.'") In *Castaneda*, the evidence showed that in a county with a 79.1% Hispanic popula-

tion, over an 11-year period only 39% of the persons summoned for grand jury service were Hispanic. The evidence also showed that the system of selecting grand jurors was highly subjective. The Supreme Court held that evidence sufficient to make out a prima facie case of discrimination. 430 U.S. at 496–497.

126. U.S. Const., Amend. VIII.

Chapter II

1. Meltsner, CRUEL AND UNUSUAL 23–24 (Random House 1973).
2. 390 U.S. 570 (1968).
3. 391 U.S. 510 (1968).
4. A.L.I., MODEL PENAL CODE § 201.6 (Tent. Draft No. 9 [1959]). At its May 1959 meeting, the American Law Institute effected minor revisions in the tentative draft. The proposal, with those revisions, was included in the 1962 Proposed Official Draft as section 210.6, as follows:

(1) *Death Sentence Excluded.* When a defendant is found guilty of murder, the Court shall impose sentence for a felony of the first degree if it is satisfied that:

(a) none of the aggravating circumstances enumerated in Subsection (3) of this Section was established by the evidence at the trial or will be established if further proceedings are initiated under Subsection (2) of this Section; or

(b) substantial mitigating circumstances, established by the evidence at the trial, call for leniency; or

(c) the defendant, with the consent of the prosecuting attorney and the approval of the Court, pleaded guilty to murder as a felony of the first degree; or

(d) the defendant was under 18 years of age at the time of the commission of the crime; or

(e) the defendant's physical or mental condition calls for leniency; or

(f) although the evidence suffices to sustain the verdict, it does not foreclose all doubt respecting the defendant's guilt.

(2) *Determination by Court or by Court and Jury.* Unless the Court imposes sentence under Subsection (1) of this Section, it shall conduct a separate proceeding to determine whether the defendant should be sentenced for a felony of the first degree or sentenced to death. The proceeding shall be conducted before the Court alone if the defendant was convicted by a Court sitting without a jury or upon his plea of guilty or if the prosecuting attorney and the defendant waive a jury with respect to sentence. In other cases it shall be conducted before the Court sitting with the jury which determined the defendant's guilt or, if the Court for good cause shown discharges that jury, with a new jury empanelled for the purpose.

In the proceeding, evidence may be presented as to any matter that the Court deems relevant to sentence, including but not limited to the nature and circumstances of the crime, the defendant's character, background, history, mental and physical condition and any of the aggravating or mitigating circumstances enumerated in Subsections (3) and (4) of this Section. Any such evidence which the Court deems to have probative force may be received, regardless of its admissibility under the exclusionary rules of evidence, provided that the defendant's counsel is accorded a fair opportunity to rebut any hearsay statements. The prosecuting attorney and the defendant or his counsel shall be permitted to present argument for or against sentence of death.

The determination whether sentence of death shall be imposed shall be in the discretion of the Court, except that when the proceeding is conducted before the Court sitting with a jury, the Court shall not impose sentence of death unless it submits to the jury the issue whether the defendant should be sentenced to death or to imprisonment and the jury returns a verdict that the sentence should be death. If the jury is unable to reach a unanimous verdict the Court shall dismiss the jury and impose sentence for a felony of the first degree.

The Court, in exercising its discretion as to sentence, and the jury, in determining upon its verdict, shall take into account the aggravating and mitigating circumstances enumerated in Subsections (3) and (4) and any other facts that it deems relevant, but it shall not impose or recommend sentence of death unless it finds one of the aggravating circumstances enumerated in Subsection (3) and further finds that there are no mitigating circumstances sufficiently substantial to call for leniency. When the issue is submitted to the jury, the Court shall so instruct and also shall inform the jury of the nature of the sentence of imprisonment that may be imposed, including its implication with respect to possible release upon parole, if the jury verdict is against sentence of death.

(3) *Aggravating Circumstances.*

(a) The murder was committed by a convict under sentence of imprisonment.

(b) The defendant was previously convicted of another murder or of a felony involving the use or threat of violence to the person.

(c) At the time the murder was committed the defendant also committed another murder.

(d) The defendant knowingly created a great risk of death to many persons.

(e) The murder was committed while the defendant was engaged or was an accomplice in the commission of, or an attempt to commit, or flight after committing or attempting to commit robbery, rape or deviate sexual intercourse by force or threat of force, arson, burglary or kidnapping.

(f) The murder was committed for the purpose of avoiding or preventing a lawful arrest or effecting an escape from lawful custody.

(g) The murder was committed for pecuniary gain.

(h) The murder was especially heinous, atrocious or cruel, manifesting exceptional depravity.

(4) *Mitigating Circumstances.*

(a) The defendant has no significant history of prior criminal activity.

(b) The murder was committed while the defendant was under the influence of extreme mental or emotional disturbance.

(c) The victim was a participant in the defendant's homicidal conduct or consented to the homicidal act.

(d) The murder was committed under circumstances which the defendant believed to provide a moral justification or extenuation for his conduct.

(e) The defendant was an accomplice in a murder committed by another person and his participation in the homicidal act was relatively minor.

(f) The defendant acted under duress or under the domination of another person.

(g) At the time of the murder, the capacity of the defendant to appreciate the criminality [wrongfulness] of his conduct or to conform his conduct to the requirements of law was impaired as a result of mental disease or defect or intoxication.

(h) The youth of the defendant at the time of the crime.

5. 402 U.S. 183, 185–186 (1971).

6. *Id.* at 207 (emphasis added). Justice Black, in a concurring opinion, wrote that the procedure does not "offend the Due Process Clause of the Fourteenth Amendment. Likewise, I do not believe that petitioners have been deprived of any other rights explicitly or implicitly guaranteed by the other provisions of the Bill of Rights." *Id.* at 223. *See also* note 14, *infra.*

7. *Id.* at 186.

8. *Id.* at 197.

9. *Id.* at 204.

10. *Id.* at 207. *See* Black, CAPITAL PUNISHMENT: THE INEVITABILITY OF CAPRICE AND MISTAKE 66–76, 100, 101 (2d ed. Norton 1981).

11. 446 U.S. 420 (1980).

12. *Id.* at 442.

13. *Id.* at 440.

14. The *McGautha* dissenting opinion was premised solely on the due process clause. In a footnote, Justice Brennan noted that the eighth amendment issue of whether the death penalty was cruel and unusual punishment was not presented. 402 U.S. at 310 n.74. In *Furman v. Georgia,* Justices Brennan and Marshall took the position that the death penalty does constitute cruel and unusual punishment. That eighth amendment position was the basis for their dissent in *Gregg.* *Cf.* note 6, *supra,* and accompanying text.

15. 402 U.S. at 252.

16. *Id.* at 270.

17. *Id.* at 280.

18. *Id.* at 249.

19. *Id.* at 285.

20. *Id.* at 284.

21. *Id.* at 249.

22. *Id.* at 285.

23. *Id.* at 265, 268, 275, 280. Justice Brennan identified two other interests also. He summarized all three as follows:

First, due process requires the states to protect individuals against the arbitrary exercise of state power by assuring that the fundamental policy choices underlying any exercise of state power are explicitly articulated by some responsible organ of state government. *Second,* due process of law is denied by state procedural mechanisms that allow for the exercise of arbitrary power without providing any means whereby arbitrary action may be reviewed or corrected. *Third,* where federally protected rights are involved due process of law is denied by state procedures which render inefficacious the federal judicial machinery that has been established for the vindication of those rights. *Id.* at 270.

24. 408 U.S. 238 (1972).

25. *Furman,* 408 U.S. at 274, 286, 291–295 (Brennan, J., concurring); *id.* at 364–366 (Marshall, J., concurring).

26. Lockett v. Ohio, 438 U.S. 586, 599 (1978).

27. *Furman* involved three cases: one was a murder conviction in Georgia; two were rape convictions, one in Georgia and one in Texas. 408 U.S. at 239.

28. *Id.*

29. Justices Brennan and Marshall have consistently reaffirmed that their position was that the death penalty, in all circumstances, violates the eighth and fourteenth amendments. *E.g.,* Beck v. Alabama, 447 U.S. 625, 646 (1980).

30. *See* Lockett v. Ohio, 438 U.S. 586, 622 (White, J., concurring and dissenting); *id.* at 599 (Burger, C.J., with Stewart, Powell, and Stevens, JJ.); *Gregg,* 428 U.S. at 220–221 (White, J., with Burger, C.J., and Rehnquist, J.); *Furman,* 408 U.S. at 396–397, 398–399 (Burger, C.J., with Blackmun, Powell, and Rehnquist, JJ., dissenting); Black, *supra* note 10; Ely, DEMOCRACY AND DISTRUST 173–174, 176 (Harvard 1980) (focusing on the Douglas opinion); Murphy, RETRIBUTION, JUSTICE AND THERAPY 238 (Reidel 1979); Bentele, "The Death Penalty in Georgia: Still Arbitrary," 62 Wash. U. L. Q. 573, 574 n.3 (1985); Gillers, "Deciding Who Dies," 129 U. Pa. L. Rev. 1, 10 n.35, 27 (1980); Goodpaster, "The Trial for Life: Effective Assistance of Counsel in Death Penalty Cases," 58 N.Y.U. L. Rev. 299, 307 (1983); Paternoster, "Prosecutorial Discretion in Requesting the Death Penalty: A Case of Victim-Based Racial Discrimination," 18 Law. and Soc. Rev. 437, 438 (1984); Radin, "The Jurisprudence of Death: Evolving Standards for the Cruel and Unusual Punishments Clause," 126 U. Pa. L. Rev. 989, 995, 998 (1978); Note, 87 Harv. L. Rev. 1690, 1690–1691, 1692 (1974); Note, "Capital Punishment in 1984: Abandoning the Pursuit of Fairness and Consistency," 69 Cornell L. Rev. 1129, 1134, 1142–1145 (1984).

31. *E.g.,* Beck v. Alabama, 447 U.S. 625, 639 (1980); Harry Roberts v. Louisiana, 431 U.S. 633, 644 (1977) (Rehnquist, J., dissenting).

32. *Furman,* 408 U.S. at 360, quoting United States v. Rosenberg, 195 F.2d 583, 608 (2d Cir.) (Frank, J.), *cert. den.,* 344 U.S. 838 (1952).

33. 408 U.S. at 309.

34. *Id.* at 308 and nn.8, 9.

35. *Id.* at 309.

36. *Id.*

37. *Id.* at 309–310.

38. *Id.* at 293–295.

39. *Id.* at 257.

40. *See id.* at 249.

41. *Id.* at 245.

42. *Id.* at 249–250, quoting from President's Commission on Law Enforcement and the Administration of Justice, THE CHALLENGE OF CRIME IN A FREE SOCIETY 143 (1967).

43. 408 U.S. at 250–251, quoting from Koeninger, "Capital Punishment in Texas, 1924–1968," 15 Crime & Delin. 132, 141 (1969).

44. 408 U.S. at 251, quoting from Lawes, LIFE AND DEATH IN SING SING 155–160 (Sun Dial 1928).

45. *Id.* at 251, quoting from Clark, CRIME IN AMERICA 335 (Simon & Schuster 1970).

46. *Id.* at 251–252.

47. *Id.* at 364–366. He supported that statement about racial discrimination with the following footnote:

> Alexander, The Abolition of Capital Punishment, Proceedings of the 96th Congress of Correction of the American Correctional Association, Baltimore, Md., 57 (1966); Criminal Justice: The General Aspects, in Bedau, *supra*, n.45, at 405, 411–414; Bedau, Death Sentences in New Jersey, 1907–1960, 19 Rutgers L. Rev. 1, 18–21, 52–53 (1964); R. Clark, Crime in America 335 (1970); Hochkammer, The Capital Punishment Controversy, 60 J. Crim. L. C. & P. S. 360, 361–362 (1969); Johnson, The Negro and Crime, 217 Annals Am. Acad. Pol. & Soc. Sci. 93, 95, 99 (1941); Johnson, Selective Factors in Capital Punishment, 36 Social Forces 165 (1957); United Nations, *supra*, n.77, ¶ 69, at 98; Williams, The Death Penalty and the Negro, 67 Crisis 501, 511 (1960); M. Wolfgang & B. Cohen, Crime & Race: Conceptions and Misconceptions 77, 80–81, 85–86 (1970); Wolfgang, Kelly, & Nolde, Comparison of the Executed and Commuted Among Admissions to Death Row, 53 J. Crim. L. C. & P. S. 301 (1962). 408 U.S. at 364–365 n.152.

48. *Id.* at 389 n.12; *see also* Gillers, *supra* note 30, at 27 n.117, 99 (1980) ("none provides facts to support his argument").

49. 408 U.S. at 390 n.12. Chief Justice Burger nevertheless joined Justice Powell's dissent conceding the discriminatory impact of the penalty: "Certainly the claim is justified that this criminal sanction falls more heavily on the relatively impoverished and underprivileged elements of society. The 'have-nots' in every society always have been subject to greater pressure to commit crimes and to fewer constraints than their more affluent fellow citizens. This is, indeed, a tragic byproduct of social and economic deprivation, but it is not an argument of constitutional proportions under the Eighth or Fourteenth Amendment." *Furman,* 408 U.S. at 447; *see also id.* at 388–389 (Burger, C.J., dissenting).

50. *Id.* at 310.

51. Chief Justice Burger observed that all "five opinions in support of the judgments . . . share a willingness to make sweeping factual assertions, unsupported by empirical data, concerning the manner of imposition and effectiveness of capital punishment in this country." *Furman,* 408 U.S. at 405.

52. *See* notes 60 and 61 and accompanying text.

53. 408 U.S. at 313.

54. *Id.* at 314.

55. *Id.* at 313.

56. *Id.* at 311–312.

57. *Id.* at 312.

58. *Id.* at 311–312; *see* Palmer, "Two Perspectives on Structuring Discretion: Justices Stewart and White on the Death Penalty," 70 J. Crim. L. and Crim. 194, 194, 198–199 (1979).

59. *See* Lockett v. Ohio, 438 U.S. 586, 599 (1978)(Burger, C.J.): In *Furman* three justices "concluded that discretionary sentencing, unguided by legislatively defined standards, violated the Eighth Amendment because it was 'pregnant with discrimination' (Douglas), because it permitted the death penalty to be 'wantonly' and 'freakishly' imposed (Stewart), and because it imposed the death penalty with 'great infrequency' and afforded 'no meaningful basis for distinguishing the few cases in which it [was] imposed from the many cases in which it [was] not' (White)."

60. Moore v. Illinois, 408 U.S. 786, 800 (1972).

61. Alabama: *E.g.*, McCants v. Alabama, 408 U.S. 933 (1972).
Arizona: *E.g.*, Sims v. Eyman, 408 U.S. 934 (1972).
Connecticut: *E.g.*, Davis v. Connecticut, 408 U.S. 935 (1972).
Delaware: Seeney v. Delaware, 408 U.S. 939 (1972).
Florida: *E.g.*, Thomas v. Florida, 408 U.S. 935 (1972).
Kentucky: Williams v. Kentucky, 408 U.S. 938 (1972).
Louisiana: *E.g.*, Marks v. Louisiana, 408 U.S. 933 (1972).
Maryland: *E.g.*, Miller v. Maryland, 408 U.S. 934 (1972).
Massachusetts: *E.g.*, Stewart v. Massachusetts, 408 U.S. 845 (1972).
Mississippi: *E.g.*, Yates v. Cook, 408 U.S. 934 (1972).
Missouri: *E.g.*, Duisen v. Missouri, 408 U.S. 935 (1972).
Nebraska: *E.g.*, Alvarez v. Nebraska, 408 U.S. 937 (1972).
Nevada: Walker v. Nevada, 408 U.S. 935 (1972).
New Jersey: *E.g.*, In re Reynolds, 408 U.S. 934 (1972).
North Carolina: *E.g.*, Hamby v. North Carolina, 408 U.S. 937 (1972).
Ohio: *E.g.*, Eaton v. Ohio, 408 U.S. 935 (1972).
Oklahoma: *E.g.*, Koonce v. Oklahoma, 408 U.S. 934 (1972).
Pennsylvania: *E.g.*, Scoleri v. Pennsylvania, 408 U.S. 934 (1972).
South Carolina: Fuller v. South Carolina, 408 U.S. 937 (1972).
Tennessee: Herron v. Tennessee, 408 U.S. 937 (1972).
Utah: Kelback v. Utah, 408 U.S. 935 (1972).
Virginia: *E.g.*, Williams v. Slayton, 408 U.S. 935 (1972).
Washington: *E.g.*, Smith v. Washington, 408 U.S. 934 (1972).

62. Justice Blackmun wrote in his dissenting opinion: "Not only are the capital punishment laws of 39 states and the District of Columbia struck down, but also all those provisions of the federal statutory structure that permit the death penalty are voided." *Furman*, 408 U.S. at 411. Justice Powell suggested in his dissenting opinion that "the constitutionality of a very few mandatory statutes remains undecided. . . . Since Rhode Island's only capital statute—murder by a life prisoner—is mandatory, no law in that State is struck down by virtue of the Court's decision today." *Id.* at 417 n.2. But *see* Harry Roberts v. Louisiana, 431 U.S. 633 (1977) (holding unconstitutional a statute requiring the death penalty for the murder of a law enforcement officer in the performance of duty).

63. *See* Pulley v. Harris, 104 S.Ct. 871, 876 (1984): "In response to that

decision, roughly two-thirds of the States promptly redrafted their capital sentencing statutes in an effort to limit jury discretion and avoid arbitrary and inconsistent results."

64. 282 N.C. 431, 194 S.E.2d 19 (1973).

65. 194 S.E.2d at 29.

66. *Id.* at 28–29.

67. *See* Woodson v. North Carolina, 428 U.S. 284, 286–287 (1976).

68. A.L.I., MODEL PENAL CODE § 210.6 (Proposed Official Draft 1962). *See* note 4, *supra.* Before *Furman,* no state had adopted this MODEL PENAL CODE recommendation, except for the bifurcated trial.

69. *See* Proffitt v. Florida, 428 U.S. 242, 247–248 (1966); Gregg v. Georgia, 428 U.S. 153, 163–164, 194 (1966).

70. *See* Gregg v. Georgia, 428 U.S. at 164.

71. Proffitt v. Florida, 428 U.S. at 248.

72. *Id.* at 248–250; *see also* Spaziano v. Florida, 104 S.Ct. 3154, 3158 n.4 (1984); Barclay v. Florida, 103 S.Ct. 3418, 3426 (1983); *id.* at 3442 n.17 (Marshall, with Brennan, JJ., dissenting); Zant v. Stephens, 103 S.Ct. 2733, 2741 (1983). In Florida, "[t]he jury's verdict is advisory only; the actual sentence is determined by the trial judge." *Proffitt,* 428 U.S. at 248–249. *Cf.* Baldwin v. Alabama, 105 S.Ct. 2727 (1985); Stebbing v. Maryland, 105 S.Ct. 276 (1984) (denial of certiorari to review Maryland statute directing a death sentence unless the mitigating factors outweigh the aggravating factors).

73. Proffitt v. Florida, 428 U.S. at 250–251; Gregg v. Georgia, 428 U.S. at 166–167. *See* discussion in Chapter II, Part 7.

74. Jurek v. Texas, 428 U.S. 262, 270–271 (1966). But *see* Black, *supra* note 10, at 66–78, 114–126.

In Zant v. Stephens, 103 S.Ct. 2733 (1983), the Supreme Court upheld a death sentence that the jury based on three aggravating circumstances, one of which was invalid. In finding the sentence adequately supported by the remaining aggravating circumstances, the Court seemed to view the constitutional role of the aggravating circumstance as narrowing the definition of the capital crime. Under Georgia law, the finding of one aggravating circumstance qualifies the case for the discretionary sentencing decision of the jury without any required weighing of mitigating circumstances. *Id.* at 2741 n.12. Thus, the theory of *Zant* must be that within the range narrowed by an aggravating circumstance unguided jury discretion is constitutionally acceptable. *See* Barclay v. Florida, 103 S.Ct. 3383 3429 (1983)(Stevens, J., with Powell, J., concurring). This was confirmed in California v. Ramos, 103 S.Ct. 3446, 3457 n.22 (1983):

> [T]he fact that the jury is given no specific guidance on how the commutation factor is to figure into its determination presents no constitutional problem. As we held in *Zant v. Stephens, supra,* the constitutional prohibition on arbitrary and capricious sentencing determinations is not violated by a capital sentencing scheme that permits the jury to exercise unbridled discretion in determining whether the death penalty should be imposed after it has found that the defendant is a member of the class made eligible for the penalty by statute.

Presumably, that language should be understood as assuming that the statute narrows the eligible class, compared to the pre-*Furman* statutes, by aggravating circumstances or their equivalent. *Cf.* Weisberg, "Deregulating Death," 1983 S.Ct. Rev. 305, 349–350.

75. Jurek v. Texas, 428 U.S. at 269.

76. *Id.*

77. *See* Bedau, "Social Science Research in the Aftermath of *Furman v. Georgia*: Creating New Knowledge About Capital Punishment in the United States," in Riedel and Chappel, eds., Issues in Criminal Justice: Planning and Evaluation 75, 82 (1976); White, "The Role of the Social Sciences in Determining the Constitutionality of Capital Punishment," 45 Am. J. of Orthopsychiatry 581, 587–590 (1975).

78. *See* Arkin, "Discrimination and Arbitrariness in Capital Punishment: An Analysis of Post-Furman Murder Cases in Dade County, Florida, 1973–1976," 33 Stan. L. Rev. 75, 101 n.148 (1980); Hubbard, "'Reasonable Levels of Arbitrariness' in Death Sentencing Patterns: A Tragic Perspective on Capital Punishment," 18 U.C. Davis L. Rev. 1113, 1136 (1985); Kopeny, "Capital Punishment—Who Should Choose?" 12 West. State U. L. Rev. 383, 395–416 (1985).

79. Gregg v. Georgia, 423 U.S. 1082 (1976); Jurek v. Texas, 423 U.S. 1082 (1976); Woodson v. North Carolina, 423 U.S. 1082 (1976); Proffitt v. Florida, 423 U.S. 1082 (1976); Roberts v. Louisiana, 423 U.S. 1082 (1976).

80. At the same time that it granted certiorari in the five cases, on January 22, 1976 the Court issued the following order:

> Briefs for petitioners in all of the foregoing cases . . . shall be filed with the Clerk on or before February 25, 1976. Briefs for respondents shall be filed on or before March 25, 1976. Cases set for oral argument at 1 p.m. on March 30, 1976, subject to further order of the Court. The Solicitor General is invited to file a brief in these cases expressing the views of the United States. 423 U.S. at 1083.

81. 428 U.S. 153 (1976).

82. 428 U.S. 242 (1976).

83. 428 U.S. 262 (1976).

84. 428 U.S. 280 (1976).

85. 428 U.S. 325 (1976).

86. *Gregg,* 428 U.S. at 169, 198; *see also id.* at 187; *Proffitt, id.* at 251, 253.

87. In his *Furman* dissent, Chief Justice Burger had written, "I had thought that nothing was clearer in history . . . than the American abhorrence of the 'common-law rule imposing a mandatory death sentence on all convicted murderers.' . . . [T]he 19th century movement away from mandatory death sentences marked an enlightened introduction of flexibility into the sentencing process. . . . This change in sentencing practice was greeted by the Court as a humanizing development." *Furman,* 408 U.S. at 402. He used that argument, not in opposition to a mandatory death penalty but in opposition to the apparent requirement that he perceived as a possible thrust of *Furman* to require the death penalty to be mandatory. Yet he voted in *Woodson* and *Roberts* to uphold mandatory capital punishment systems.

88. The four dissenters in *Furman* all joined in opinions written by three of them. Justice Blackmun also wrote a separate dissent to express his personal abhorrence for the death penalty. 408 U.S. at 405.

89. *See, e.g.*, Petersilia, RACIAL DISPARITIES IN THE CRIMINAL JUSTICE SYSTEM (Rand 1983); *cf.* Langan, "Racism on Trial: New Evidence to Explain the Racial Composition of Prisons in the United States," 76 J. Crim. L. & Crim. 666 (1985).

90. *Furman*, 408 U.S. at 447; *see also id.* at 445–446: "Much also is made of the undeniable fact that the death penalty has a greater impact on the lower economic strata of society, which include a relatively higher percentage of persons of minority racial and ethnic group backgrounds." *Id.* at 450: "I agree that discriminatory application of the death penalty in the past, admittedly indefensible . . . ."

91. *Furman*, 408 U.S. at 447. In his opinion in *Furman*, Justice Douglas wrote: "It is 'cruel and unusual' to apply the death penalty — *or any other penalty* — selectively to minorities whose numbers are few, who are outcasts of society, and who are unpopular, but whom society is willing to see suffer though it would not countenance general application of the same penalty across the board." 408 U.S. at 245 (emphasis added).

Cf. Gideon v. Wainwright, 372 U.S. 335 (1963) (Clark, J., concurring):

[T]he Constitution makes no distinction between capital and noncapital cases. The Fourteenth Amendment requires due process of law for the deprival of 'liberty' just as for the deprival of 'life,' and there cannot constitutionally be a difference in the quality of the process based merely upon a supposed difference in the sanction involved. How can the Fourteenth Amendment tolerate a procedure which it condemns in capital cases on the ground that deprival of liberty may be less onerous than deprival of life — a value judgment not universally accepted — or that only the latter deprival is irrevocable? I can find no acceptable rationalization for such a result, and I therefore concur in the judgment of the Court [holding that the right to counsel applies to noncapital felonies]. *Id.* at 349.

92. 408 U.S. 471, 481 (1972); *see also* Kent v. United States, 383 U.S. 541, 557 (1966); Reid v. Covert, 354 U.S. 1, 77 (1957) (Harlan, J., concurring in result) (quoted in note 94, *infra*). In United States v. Raddatz, 447 U.S. 667 (1980), the Court later summarized that the procedural demands of due process may require greater or less protection depending on "(a) the private interests affected; (b) the risk of an erroneous determination through the process accorded and the probable value of added procedural safeguards; and (c) the public interest and administrative burdens, including costs that the new procedures would involve." 447 U.S. at 677; *see also* Schall v. Martin, 104 S.Ct. 2403, 2415–2417 (1984); Matthews v. Eldridge, 424 U.S. 319 (1976); Gerstein v. Pugh, 420 U.S. 103, 114 (1975); Gagnon v. Scarpelli, 411 U.S. 778 (1973); Friendly, "Some Kind of Hearing," 123 U. Pa. L. Rev. 1267, 1267–1273 (1975).

Justice Powell recently stated, in the context of recommending less than a "full scale 'sanity trial'" for the determination of sanity for execution: "Due process is a flexible concept, requiring only 'such procedural protections as the particular situation demands.'" Ford v. Wainwright, 106 S.Ct. 2595, 2610 (1986).

93. *See Gregg*, 428 U.S. at 188: "Because of the uniqueness of the death penalty, *Furman* held . . . ." *See generally* Black, *supra* note 10, at 29–30.

94. In Furman v. Georgia, 408 U.S. 238 (1972), Justice Brennan reviewed some of the earlier cases:

> "That life is at stake is of course another important factor in creating the extraordinary situation. The difference between capital and non-capital offenses is the basis of differentiation in law in diverse ways in which the distinction becomes relevant." *Williams v. Georgia*, 349 U.S. 375, 391 (1955) (Frankfurter, J.). "When the penalty is death, we, like state court judges, are tempted to strain the evidence and even, in close cases, the law in order to give a doubtfully condemned man another chance." *Stein v. New York*, 346 U.S. 156, 196 (1953) (Jackson, J.). "In death cases doubts such as those presented here should be resolved in favor of the accused." *Andres v. United States*, 333 U.S. 740, 752 (1948) (Reed, J.). Mr. Justice Harlan expressed the point strongly: "I do not concede that whatever process is due an offender faced with a fine or a prison sentence necessarily satisfies the requirements of the Constitution in a capital case. The distinction is by no means novel, . . . nor is it negligible, being literally that between life and death." *Reid v. Covert*, 354 U.S. 1, 77 (1957) (concurring in result). And, of course, for many years this Court distinguished death cases from all others for purposes of the constitutional right to counsel. See *Powell v. Alabama*, 287 U.S. 45 (1932); *Betts v. Brady*, 316 U.S. 455 (1942); *Bute v. Illinois*, 333 U.S. 640 (1948).

In Parker v. North Carolina, 397 U.S. 790, 809–810 (1970), Justice Brennan earlier wrote, in a separate opinion joined by Justices Douglas and Marshall:

> The penalty schemes involved here are also distinguishable from most plea bargaining because they involve the imposition of death—the most severe and awesome penalty known to our law. This Court has recognized that capital cases are treated differently in some respects from noncapital cases. See, *e.g.*, *Williams v. Georgia*, 349 U.S. 375, 391 (1955). We have identified the threat of a death penalty as a factor to be given considerable weight in determining whether a defendant has deliberately waived his constitutional rights.

In support of that last sentence, Justice Brennan discussed Green v. United States, 335 U.S. 184 (1957); Fay v. Noia, 372 U.S. 391 (1963); and United States v. Jackson, 390 U.S. 570 (1968).

95. In Gardner v. Florida, Justice Stevens wrote in his plurality opinion for three Justices: "In 1949 . . . no significant constitutional difference between the death penalty and lesser punishments for crime had been expressly recognized by the Court." 430 U.S. at 357. In McGautha v. California, 402 U.S. 183 (1967), the Court wrote: "Nor does the fact that capital, as opposed to any other, sentencing is in issue seem to distinguish this case. *See* Williams v. New York, 337 U.S. 241, 251–252 (1949)." *McGautha*, 402 U.S. at 217.

96. Woodson v. North Carolina, 428 U.S. 280, 303–304 (1976) (Stewart, J., with Powell and Stevens, JJ.); *see also* California v. Ramos, 103 S.Ct. 3446, 3451

n.9 (1983) ("The Court . . . has recognized . . . the qualitative difference of death from all other punishments . . . .").

97. Gardner v. Florida, 430 U.S. 349, 357–358 (1977) (Stevens, J., with Stewart and Powell, JJ.).

98. 397 U.S. 790, 809–810 (1970).

99. McGautha v. California, 402 U.S. 183, 311 (1971).

Justice Douglas in his later opinion in *Furman* argued that the same kind of discrimination he found fatal for the death penalty would also be unacceptable if it existed in regard to other penalties. *See* note 91, *supra*.

100. *Furman*, 408 U.S. at 306. *See also* McCleskey v. Kemp, 753 F.2d 877, 927 (11th Cir. 1985) (Clark, J., dissenting) (suggesting that a random incidence of racial bias in the criminal justice system might have to be tolerated, subject to correction in a particular case where it manifests itself, because we have no alternative to that system, but that the death penalty could not be permitted under the same circumstances); Hubbard, *supra* note 78, at 1139.

101. 408 U.S. at 286–292. Justice Brennan reasoned as follows:

> The only explanation for the uniqueness of death is its extreme severity. Death is today an unusually severe punishment, unusual in its pain, in its finality, and in its enormity. No other existing punishment is comparable to death in terms of physical and mental suffering. . . . The unusual severity of death is manifested most clearly in its finality and enormity. . . . The calculated killing of a human being by the State involves by its very nature, a denial of the executed person's humanity. . . . A prisoner remains a member of the human family [with constitutional rights]. . . . His punishment is not irrevocable. . . . In comparison to all other punishments today, then, the deliberate extinguishment of human life by the State is uniquely degrading to human dignity. 408 U.S. at 287–291.

Justice Brennan identified six societal circumstances as demonstrating a consensus about the uniqueness of death as a punishment: (*a*) "There has been no national debate about punishment . . . comparable to the debate about the punishment of death"; (*b*) "no other punishment has been so continuously restricted"—some states have abolished the death penalty, but none has yet abolished imprisonment; (*c*) the death penalty is reserved for the most heinous crimes; (*d*) some states have special procedures for death penalty cases; (*e*) juries and governors treat death penalty cases differently; and (*f*) the Supreme Court treats death penalty cases as a class apart. 408 U.S. at 286.

The validity of Justice Brennan's first point (*a*) is probably not undermined by either the fact that the outcome of the debate has been popular support for the death penalty, or the fact that the purposes and methods of imprisonment and its alternatives have undergone considerable public discussion and change from the repentance ideal to the rehabilitation ideal to the developing punishment model.

102. 408 U.S. at 271–279, 291–304.

103. *Id.* at 309.

104. *Id.* at 293–294.

105. *See* Gregg v. Georgia, 428 U.S. 153, 188 (1976).

106. "Death is irrevocable, life imprisonment is not. Death, of course,

makes rehabilitation impossible . . . . [D]eath has always been viewed as the ultimate sanction." 408 U.S. at 346.

107. 408 U.S. at 347.

108. 451 U.S. 949 (1981).

109. 451 U.S. at 955 (dissenting from denial of certiorari).

110. 105 S.Ct. 2633 (1985).

111. *Id.* at 2636, 2639; *see also* Ford v. Wainwright, 106 S.Ct. 2595, 2604 (1986).

112. 428 U.S. at 187 (citing his own and Justice Brennan's opinions in *Furman*).

113. 428 U.S. at 303–304 (again citing his own and Justice Brennan's opinions in *Furman*).

114. 408 U.S. at 447.

115. Gardner v. Florida, 430 U.S. 349, 357 (1977).

Justice Stevens, concurring in the denial of certiorari in Coleman v. Balkcom, 451 U.S. 949 (1981), wrote: "We must, however, also be as sure as possible that novel procedural shortcuts have not permitted error of a constitutional magnitude to occur. For, after all, death cases are indeed different in kind from all other litigation. The penalty, once imposed, is irrevocable." *Id.* at 953. In a concurring opinion for himself and Justice Powell in Barclay v. Florida, 103 S.Ct. 3418 (1983), Justice Stevens wrote: "Death as a punishment is unique in its severity and irrevocability. Since *Furman v. Georgia*, this Court's decisions have made clear that the States may impose this ultimate sentence only if they follow procedures that are designed to assure reliability in sentencing determinations." *Id.* at 3429.

116. 103 S.Ct. 3001, 3009 (1983). Justice Powell also joined the Court's opinion in California v. Ramos, 103 S.Ct. 3446 (1983), which listed him as a supporter of the doctrine on the basis of his subscribing to the Stewart opinion in *Woodson*, the Stevens opinions in *Gardner* and *Beck*, and the Burger opinion in Lockett v. Ramos, 103 S.Ct. at 3451 n.9. In Stephens v. Kemp, 104 S.Ct. 562 (1983), Justice Powell wrote an opinion dissenting from the granting of a stay of execution in which he recognized "that the death sentence is qualitatively different from all other sentences, and therefore special care is exercised in judicial review." *Id.* at 565.

117. 438 U.S. 586 (1978).

118. *Id.* at 604. Chief Justice Burger also wrote in that opinion: "Given that the imposition of death by public authorities is so profoundly different from all other penalties, we cannot avoid the conclusion that an individualized decision is essential in capital cases." *Id.* at 605; *see also id.* n.13: "We emphasize that in dealing with standards for imposition of the death sentence we intimate no view regarding the authority of a State or of the Congress to fix mandatory, minimum sentences for non-capital crimes." In Ake v. Oklahoma, 105 S.Ct. 1087 (1985), Chief Justice Burger wrote in a concurring opinion:

This is a capital case in which the Court is asked to decide whether a State may refuse an indigent defendant "any opportunity whatsoever" to obtain psychiatric evidence for the preparation and presentation of a claim of insanity by way of defense when the defendant's legal sanity at the time of the offense was "seriously in issue."

The facts of the case and the question presented confine the actual holding of the Court. In capital cases the finality of the sentence imposed warrants protections that may or may not be required in other cases. Nothing in the Court's opinion reaches non-capital cases. _Id._ at 1099.

119. 447 U.S. 625 (1980).

120. _Id._ at 637.

121. 103 S.Ct. 3383 (1983).

122. 103 S.Ct. at 3406; _see also id._ at 3410, 3411. Justice Blackmun has also joined a majority of the Court in setting aside some death sentences on procedural grounds that probably would not require reversal in nondeath cases. Turner v. Murray, 106 S.Ct. 1683 (1986); Zant v. Stephens, 456 U.S. 410 (1982); Hopper v. Evans, 456 U.S. 605 (1982); Bullington v. Missouri, 451 U.S. 430 (1981); Presnell v. Georgia, 439 U.S. 14 (1978); Godfrey v. Georgia, 446 U.S. 420 (1980); Lockett v. Ohio, 438 U.S. 586, 616 (1978); Gardner v. Florida, 430 U.S. 349, 364 (1977); _see also_ Gilmore v. Utah, 429 U.S. 1012, 1019 (1976); Green v. Georgia, 442 U.S. 95 (1979). He has written little about the death penalty. Although professing personal opposition to it, _Furman,_ 408 U.S. at 405–406, quoted in note 234 _infra,_ he voted to uphold its constitutionality in _Furman_ and _Gregg._

123. 455 U.S. 104 (1982).

124. _Id._ at 117–118.

125. 103 S.Ct. 3446, 3451 (1983). In Zant v. Stephens, 103 S.Ct. 2733 (1983), Justice O'Connor also subscribed to the Court's opinion, written by Justice Stevens for himself, Chief Justice Burger, and Justices Blackmun and Powell, as well as O'Connor, which explained in dictum that "there is a qualitative difference between death and any other form of permissible punishment." 103 S.Ct. at 2747.

126. "Petitioner has argued, in effect, that no matter how effective the death penalty may be as a punishment, government, created and run as it must be by humans, is inevitably incompetent to administer it. This cannot be accepted as a proposition of constitutional law. . . . Mistakes will be made and discriminations will occur which will be difficult to explain." 408 U.S. at 226.

127. 106 S.Ct. 1683, 1687–1688 (1986). In Gardner v. Florida, Justice White concurred in the decision invalidating a death sentence because it was imposed on the basis of information that was not disclosed to the defendant. He wrote specially to emphasize that he would limit the disclosure requirement to death penalty cases because the constitutional rationale for it was the eighth amendment. 430 U.S. at 364; _see also_ Zant v. Stephens, 103 S.Ct. 2733, 2751 (1983) (White, J., concurring). Justice White also joined in the opinion for the Court in California v. Ramos, 103 S.Ct. 3446 (1983), in which Justice O'Connor cited his opinion in _Gardner_ as casting his lot with the "death is different" doctrine. 103 S.Ct. at 3451 n.9. He also joined Justice Powell's dissent from the granting of a stay in Stephens v. Kemp, 104 S.Ct. 562, 565 (1983), which recognized the doctrine as requiring special care in judicial review. _Cf._ Zant v. Stephens, 103 S.Ct. 2733, 2750–2751 (White, J., concurring).

128. 430 U.S. at 371.

129. 428 U.S. at 322-323. Chief Justice Rehnquist has also voted, each time

in dissent, to uphold the death penalty for (*a*) the crime of felony murder for the driver of the getaway car who did not kill the victim, was not present at the killing, and did not intend the killing or anticipate the use of deadly force in the robbery, Enmund v. Florida, 458 U.S. 782, 801 (1982); and (*b*) the crime of rape for a repeat offender. Coker v. Georgia, 433 U.S. 584, 610–611 (1977).

The attraction of the doctrine is evidently too strong even for Chief Justice Rehnquist to reject it entirely. In Zant v. Stephens, 103 S.Ct. 2733 (1983), in a concurring opinion denying relief to a capital defendant, he said, "Of course, a more careful application of this standard is appropriate in capital cases," 103 S.Ct. at 2757. In Ake v. Oklahoma, 105 S.Ct. 1087 (1985), Chief Justice Rehnquist dissented from the Court's decision reversing a capital conviction because the indigent defendant was denied the assistance of a psychiatrist for his insanity defense and for his challenge to the state's showing of his future dangerousness. He wrote, "I would limit the rule to capital cases . . . ." *Id*. at 1099. He then disagreed with the application of the rule in that case. In Rummel v. Estelle, 445 U.S. 263 (1980), Chief Justice Rehnquist, writing for the Court, invoked the "death is different" doctrine to argue that "our decisions applying the prohibition of cruel and unusual punishments to capital cases are of limited assistance in deciding the constitutionality" of a prison sentence challenged as disproportionate. *Id*. at 272. He also joined in the dissenting opinion written by Chief Justice Burger in another noncapital disproportionality case, Solem v. Helm, 103 S.Ct. 3001 (1983), that asserted that the death penalty is different, 103 S.Ct. at 3019, 3021 n.4, 3022, and in the opinion by Justice Powell dissenting from the granting of a stay of execution in Stephens v. Kemp, 104 S.Ct. 562, 565 (1983), which recognized that doctrine as requiring special care in judicial review.

It might also be worth noting that in Scott v. Illinois, 440 U.S. 367 (1979), Chief Justice Rehnquist, writing the opinion for the Court, said: "[W]e believe that the central premise of *Argersinger*—that actual imprisonment is a penalty different in kind from fines or the mere threat of imprisonment—is eminently sound and warrants adoption of actual imprisonment as the line defining the constitutional right to appointment of counsel." 440 U.S. at 373. Interestingly, the Court much earlier had drawn that line at the death penalty. Hamilton v. Alabama, 368 U.S. 52, 55 (1961); Uveges v. Pennsylvania, 335 U.S. 437, 441 (1948); Bute v. Illinois, 333 U.S. 640, 674 (1948).

Chief Justice Rehnquist has voted to set aside the conviction or sentence in a capital case on only 2 occasions out of some 33 such cases in which he has participated. In Estelle v. Smith, 451 U.S. 454 (1981), the Court unanimously vacated the death penalty because of a constitutional violation at the penalty hearing. Chief Justice Rehnquist concurred on the basis of Massiah v. United States, 377 U.S. 201 (1964). In Skipper v. South Carolina, 106 S.Ct. 1669 (1986), the Court vacated a death penalty because the trial court had refused to allow the defendant to present evidence regarding his good behavior in jail. Chief Justice Rehnquist joined an opinion by then Chief Justice Burger concurring only because that evidence directly rebutted evidence and argument presented by the prosecution. In 4 cases, Chief Justice Rehnquist has been the lone dissenter to approve a death sentence. Adams v. Texas, 448 U.S. 38, 52 (1980); Green v. Georgia, 442 U.S. 95, 98 (1979); Bell v. Ohio, 438 U.S. 637, 644 (1978) and Lockett v. Ohio, 438 U.S. 586, 628 (1978); Gardner v. Florida, 430 U.S. 349, 371 (1977).

130. *See* California v. Ramos, 103 S.Ct. 3446, 3451 (1983).

131. *See Gregg*, 428 U.S. at 187; *see also* Eddings v. Oklahoma, 455 U.S. 104, 117–118 (1982); Coleman v. Balkcom, 451 U.S. 949 (1981) (opinions of Justice Stevens concurring in, and Chief Justice Rehnquist dissenting from, the denial of certiorari); Beck v. Alabama, 447 U.S. 625, 638 (1980); Gardner v. Florida, 430 U.S. 349, 358 (1977); *see also* Barefoot v. Estelle, 103 S.Ct. 3404–3405 (1983) (Marshall, J., dissenting).

State courts as well as federal courts have given special attention to capital cases. *See* Stein v. New York, 346 U.S. 156, 196 (1953) ("When the penalty is death, we, like state court judges, are tempted to strain the evidence and even, in close cases, the law, in order to give a doubtfully condemned man another chance"). This phenomenon is not new. One 1801 North Carolina decision, for example, "voided a death sentence solely because the indictment contained the following misspelling in the description of the place of the fatal wound: 'in and upon the aforesaid left *brest* of him.'" Nakell, "The Cost of the Death Penalty," 14 Crim. L. Bull. 69, 74 (1978).

At common law:

> Compassionate judges abetted the juries by devising technicalities to bring the defendant within clergyable status or to acquit him; such as holding that a heifer was not a cow (*King v. Cook*, 168 E.R. 155; 1774) a colt was not a horse, (168 E.R. 917), and a drake was not a duck (*Rex v. Holloway*, 171 E.R. 1131 n., reporter's note); or that a charge of larceny from the person would not be maintained if the victim was asleep (*King v. Thompson*, 168 E.R. 323); that a theft of a pair of stockings was not supported by evidence of taking two odd ones (do); that the stealing of an article at 9:30 P.M., in summer, was not committed at night (168 E.R. 231); that an indictment for stealing a brace of partridges could not be sustained unless it was proved that the birds were alive; and that a presentment upon the *oath* of the grand jury was bad because the plural form *oaths* was not used.

Dalzell, BENEFIT OF CLERGY IN AMERICA 38 (John F. Blair 1955).

In the biblical era, procedural obstacles substantially ameliorated the apparent harshness of the death penalty of that time, perhaps with the design of largely eliminating it. *See* Krivosha, Copple, and McDonough, "A Historical and Philosophical Look at the Death Penalty—Does It Serve Society's Needs?" 16 Creighton L. Rev. 1, 5–6 (1982):

> The procedures developed by the Sanhedrin, and required to be followed before the death penalty could be imposed, made the imposition of the death penalty virtually impossible. One could not be convicted of a capital offense upon his or her own admission but could be convicted only upon the testimony of two witnesses, both of whom were required to testify exactly alike as to every material fact; discrepancies in the testimony required acquittal. Both witnesses were further required to testify that they had warned the accused just before he committed the crime that his proposed act was a capital offense. In addition, in order to convict one of a capital offense, at least one member of the Sanhedrin had to vote in favor of the accused. If all the members of the Sanhedrin voted for conviction, the accused was acquitted. This rule was based upon the notion that at least

one person on the Sanhedrin should have presented the position of the accused, and all sides should have been considered.

Capital cases provided further that testimony of blood or marriage relatives was forbidden. Witnesses were not allowed to testify to anything based on inference or secondhand knowledge, circumstantial evidence being prohibited. A witness giving false testimony against the accused would himself be subjected to the death penalty.

There even remained an avenue of acquittal virtually to the very end. While a condemned was led to the place of execution, if indeed he ever was, it was required that he be preceded by a herald who was to call out, requesting anyone who possessed evidence which might clear or excuse the accused to come forth. If such a witness came forward or even if the accused himself maintained that his innocence could still be proved, an opportunity to present the evidence was given. Finally, the prohibition against placing one twice in jeopardy was employed, and once an individual was acquitted, he could not again be tried for the same crime regardless of any new evidence discovered.

132. Adams v. Texas, 448 U.S. 38, 44 (1980); Witherspoon v. Illinois, 391 U.S. 510 (1968).

133. Davis v. Georgia, 429 U.S. 122, 123 (1976).

134. *E.g.*, Miles v. United States, 103 U.S. 304, 310 (1980) (The Court upheld the exclusion for cause, in a polygamy trial, of a juror who believed that polygamy was ordained of God, even though he believed that Congress had a right to prohibit polygamy and that he would consider it his duty, if satisfied by the evidence, to find the defendant guilty of polygamy). Of course, *Witherspoon* rationalized its result because the death penalty decision calls for the jury not simply to apply a fixed legal standard to the facts found but to "express the conscience of the community on the ultimate question of life or death." 391 U.S. at 519; *see also* Adams v. Texas, *supra* note 132, at 46; Wainwright v. Witt, 105 S.Ct. 844, 851 (1985). That is not decisively different from "[t]he purpose of the jury trial" generally, which "is to prevent oppression by the Government. . . . [T]he essential feature of a jury obviously lies in the interposition between the accused and his accuser of the commonsense judgment of a group of laymen . . . ." Williams v. Florida, 399 U.S. 78, 100 (1970).

135. Adams v. Texas, *supra* note 132, at 44.

136. Wainwright v. Witt, 105 S.Ct. 844, 852 (1985); *see also* Darden v. Wainwright, 106 S.Ct. 2464, 2469 (1986).

137. Wainwright v. Witt, 105 S.Ct. at 852. The Court also held that a state trial judge's finding that a prospective juror should be disqualified for anti-capital punishment bias is a factual finding that is entitled to a presumption of correctness on federal habeas corpus. *Id.* at 855.

138. Turner v. Murray, 106 S.Ct. 1683, 1688 (1986).

139. *Id.* at 1686–1687; Ristaino v. Ross, 424 U.S. 589 (1976); Ham v. South Carolina, 409 U.S. 524 (1973).

140. Turner v. Murray, 106 S.Ct. at 1687.

141. *Id.* at 1688.

142. 447 U.S. 625 (1980).

143. *Id.* at 638 n.14.

144. Harry Roberts v. Louisiana, 428 U.S. 325 (1976); Woodson v. North Carolina, *supra* note 67.

145. Harry Roberts v. Louisiana, 431 U.S. 633 (1977).

146. Lockett v. Ohio, 438 U.S. 586, 604 (1978); Harry Roberts v. Louisiana, 431 U.S. 633, 637 (1977).

147. *Lockett*, 438 U.S. at 605 n.13.

148. Godfrey v. Georgia, 446 U.S. 420, 428 (1980); Gregg v. Georgia, *supra* note 70.

149. Gregg v. Georgia, *supra* note 70; Proffitt v. Florida, *supra* note 69; Jurek v. Texas, *supra* note 74. In Zant v. Stephens, 103 S.Ct. 2733 (1983), the Court ruled that "the Constitution does not require a state to adopt specific standards for instructing the jury in its consideration of aggravating and mitigating circumstances." 103 S.Ct. at 2750.

150. *See* Gregg v. Georgia, 428 U.S. at 195; Pulley v. Harris, 104 S.Ct. 871 (1984).

151. Godfrey v. Georgia, 446 U.S. at 428; California v. Ramos, 103 S.Ct. 3446, 3452 (1983).

152. Estelle v. Smith, 451 U.S. 454, 462–463 (1981).

153. *Id.* at 466–467.

154. Bullington v. Missouri, 451 U.S. 430 (1981); *see also* Arizona v. Rumsey, 104 S.Ct. 2305 (1984).

155. Strickland v. Washington, 104 S.Ct. 2052 (1984).

156. *Id.* at 2064 (1984) (holding that the same standard for ineffective assistance of counsel that applies to a trial applies to the sentencing stage of a death penalty proceeding although it might not to "an ordinary sentencing, which may involve informal proceedings and standardless discretion in the sentence"). *Cf.* United States v. DiFrancesco, 449 U.S. 117, 134–139 (1980); North Carolina v. Pearce, 395 U.S. 711, 719–721, 723 (1969).

157. Gardner v. Florida, 430 U.S. at 357, 358, 360; *see* California v. Ramos, 103 S.Ct. 3446, 3453 (1983).

In *Gardner v. Florida*, the Court reviewed a death sentence imposed by a judge after the jury recommended life. The judge relied in part on a presentence report prepared on his order after the jury made its recommendation. The report was not disclosed to the defense. The Court held that if the information in a report "is the basis for a death sentence, the interest in reliability plainly outweighs the State's interest in preserving the availability of comparable information in the cases." 430 U.S. at 359.

158. United States v. Jackson, 390 U.S. 570 (1968).

159. *See* Corbitt v. New Jersey, 439 U.S. 12 (1978); Parker v. North Carolina, 397 U.S. 790 (1970); Brady v. United States, 397 U.S. 742 (1970).

160. Zant v. Stephens, 103 S.Ct. 2733, 2747 (1983).

161. *Id.* In dissent, in Caldwell v. Mississippi, 105 S.Ct. 2633 (1985), Justice Rehnquist made the same point, suggesting that he might be changing his approach from rejecting the "death is different" doctrine to limiting it: "Although the Eighth Amendment requires certain processes designed to prevent the arbitrary imposition of capital punishment, it does not follow that every proceeding that strays from the optimum is *ipso facto* constitutionally unreliable. *Zant* and *Barclay* hold as much." *Id.* at 2651; *see also id.* at 2649.

162. 104 S.Ct. 2052 (1984); *see also* Darden v. Wainwright, 106 S.Ct. 2464, 2473 (1986); Messer v. Kemp, 106 S.Ct. 864, 866 (1986) (Marshall with Brennan, JJ., dissenting from denial of certiorari).

163. 103 S.Ct. 3383 (1983).

164. Two psychiatrists testified for the prosecution. One was Dr. James P. Grigson, the psychiatrist whose interviewing procedure in Estelle v. Smith, 451 U.S. 454 (1981) was held to violate the privilege against compulsory self-incrimination.

165. 103 S.Ct. at 3406, 3410 (Blackmun, J., with Brennan and Marshall, JJ., dissenting).

166. *Id.* at 3400.

167. 432 U.S. 282, 303 (1977).

168. 104 S.Ct. 819 (1984).

169. *Id.* at 824 n.9. The case involved, not the defendant's appeal, but an appeal by the press seeking a transcript of the *voir dire*, which had been closed.

170. 103 S.Ct. 3418 (1983).

171. *Id.* at 3428.

172. 104 S.Ct. 752 (1984).

173. 103 S.Ct. 3383, 3391 (1983). *See also* Smith v. Murray, 106 S.Ct. 2661, 2668 (1986) ("We reject the suggestion that the principles of *Wainwright v. Sykes* apply differently depending on the nature of the penalty a State imposes for the violation of its criminal laws.")

174. 28 U.S.C. § 2253.

175. 103 S.Ct. at 3394.

176. *Id.*

177. *Id.*

178. *Id.* at 3391. This point is literally accurate. It should be noted, however, that during the time that the outstanding issues are being litigated, the defendant will be imprisoned, generally in the isolated and relatively harsh conditions of death row. The state is, therefore, vindicating to a substantial, if not the ultimate, extent its interests in its criminal justice system.

179. *Id.* at 3394–3395.

180. *Id.* at 3395.

181. *Id.*

182. *Id.*

183. 103 S.Ct. at 3406.

184. 456 U.S. 605 (1982). The chief justice wrote for seven members of the Court, all but Justices Brennan and Marshall.

185. 456 U.S. at 611. In *Furman*, Chief Justice Burger wrote:

> But even assuming that suitable guidelines can be established, there is no assurance that sentencing patterns will change so long as juries are possessed of the power to determine the sentence or to bring a verdict of guilt on a charge carrying a lesser sentence; juries have not been inhibited in the exercise of these powers in the past. Thus, unless the Court in *McGautha* misjudged the experience of history, there is little reason to believe that sentencing standards in any form will substantially alter the discretionary character of the prevailing system of sentencing in capital cases. That sys-

> tem may fall short of perfection, but it is yet to be shown that a different
> system would produce more satisfactory results.

408 U.S. at 401.

186. *See* Kent v. United States, 383 U.S. 541, 555 (1966) ("But the admoni-
tion to function in a 'parental' relationship is not an invitation to procedural arbitrariness"); Leeper v. Texas, 139 U.S. 462, 468 (1891) ("that law in its regular
course of administration through courts of law is due process, and when secured
by the law of the State the requirement is satisfied; and that due process is so
secured by laws operating on all alike, and not subjecting the individual to the
arbitrary exercise of the powers of government unrestrained by the established
principles of private right and distributive justice"); Hurtado v. California, 110
U.S. 516, 536–537 (1884).

187. *See also* In re Gault, 387 U.S. 1, 18 (1967): "Juvenile Court history has
again demonstrated that unbridled discretion, however benevolently motivated,
is frequently a poor substitute for principle and procedure."

188. Batson v. Kentucky, 106 S.Ct. 1712, 1718 (1986).

189. Godfrey v. Georgia, 446 U.S. 420, 428 (1980) (Stewart, J., joined by
Blackmun, Powell, and Stevens, JJ.). The full quotation is: "This means that if a
State wishes to authorize capital punishment it has a constitutional responsibility
to tailor *and apply* its law in a manner that avoids the arbitrary and capricious
infliction of the death penalty." (Emphasis added.)

As the Court explained in *Zant v. Stephens I, Gregg* "recognized that the
constitutionality of Georgia death sentences ultimately would depend on the
Georgia Supreme Court's construing the statute and reviewing capital sentences
consistently with" the *Furman* concern "that the death penalty not be imposed
capriciously or in a freakish manner." Zant v. Stephens I, 456 U.S. 410, 413 (1982)
(*Per curiam* opinion joined by Chief Justice Burger and Justices White, Blackmun, Rehnquist, Stevens, and O'Connor).

190. 105 S.Ct. 2727 (1985).

191. 428 U.S. at 303.

192. 105 S.Ct. at 2737.

193. 446 U.S. 420 (1980).

194. *Id.* at 433.

195. Dissenting in *Furman*, however, Chief Justice Burger, joined by Justices Blackmun, Powell, and Rehnquist, criticized the Douglas, Stewart, and
White positions on several grounds, but one was the inadequacy of their "empirical basis." 408 U.S. at 389. His opinion suggested that he believed statistical evidence had a legitimate role in this question, phrased in equal protection rather
than cruel and unusual punishment terms, and that he might be receptive to a
more systematic and relevant empirical demonstration than he thought the studies
had so far presented, 408 U.S. at 399, but he made clear that he would be very
demanding of such studies. He also wrote: "This claim of arbitrariness is not only
lacking in empirical support, but also it manifestly fails to establish that the death
penalty is a 'cruel and unusual' punishment. The Eighth Amendment was included in the Bill of Rights to assure that certain types of punishments would
never be imposed, not to channelize the sentencing process." 408 U.S. at 399; *see
also id.* at 397.

196. 106 S.Ct. 689 (1986).

197. *Id.* at 706. Justice Blackmun has also demonstrated an appreciation for the role of social science research in informing the Court about the factual premises for constitutional issues. *See* Ballew v. Georgia, 435 U.S. 223 (1978); Chapter III, Part 1, *infra.*

198. Counting votes is critical to the analysis of the Court's application of the cruel and unusual punishment clause of the Constitution. Many of the important decisions have been rendered by coalitions of plurality opinions rather than by clear majority vote. *See* Gillers, *supra* note 30, at 129; *see also* Tribe, GOD SAVE THIS HONORABLE COURT 31–40 (Random House 1985). All the justices seem inclined to persevere in their personal positions in this area even when they do not command a Court, rather than to join ranks once their dissenting position has been stated. *See* Brennan, "In Defense of Dissents," 37 Hastings L. J. 427, 436–437 (1986). The Court itself has often pursued the vote-counting approach. *See* California v. Ramos, 103 S.Ct. 3446, 3451 n.9 (1983); Gardner v. Florida, 430 U.S. 349, 357 (1977). Recently the Court, fragmented in other areas as well as the death penalty, has increasingly taken a similar tack in those areas. *E.g.,* Cleveland Board of Education v. Loudermill, 105 S.Ct. 1487, 1492 (1985); Garcia v. San Antonio Metro. Transit Authority, 105 S.Ct. 1005, 1021–1022 (1985) (Powell, J., dissenting); Welsh v. Wisconsin, 104 S.Ct. 2091, 2098 n.12 (1984); Members of the City Council v. Taxpayers for Vincent, 104 S.Ct. 2118, 2129 n.24, 2130 n.26, 2131 n.27 (1984); *cf. id.* at 2130 n.25; *see also* Florida Dept. of Health and Rehabilitative Services v. Florida Nursing Home Ass'n, 410 U.S. 147, 153–154 (1981). *See generally* Easterbrook, "Ways of Criticizing the Court," 95 Harv. L. Rev. 802, 832 (1982).

199. *See Woodson,* 428 U.S. at 302–303 (Stewart, J., with Powell and Stevens, JJ.).

200. 428 U.S. at 169; *see also id.* at 187.

201. *See also Proffitt,* 428 U.S. at 251: "*On their face,* these procedures, like those used in Georgia, *appear to meet* the constitutional deficiencies identified in *Furman*" (emphasis added); *id.* at 253: "*On its face* the Florida system thus satisfies the constitutional deficiencies identified in *Furman*" (emphasis added); Pulley v. Harris, 104 S.Ct. 871, 881 (1984) ("On its face, this system . . . cannot successfully be challenged under *Furman* and our subsequent cases"); Zant v. Stephens I, 456 U.S. 410, 413 (1982) (*Gregg* "upheld the Georgia death penalty statute because the standards and procedures set forth therein promised to alleviate to a significant degree the concern of *Furman*"); Hertz and Weisberg, "In Mitigation of the Penalty of Death," 69 Cal. L. Rev. 317, 322 n.24 (1981).

In *Gregg,* Justice Stewart expressed considerable confidence in the new procedures. He summarized his decision as follows: "No longer can a jury wantonly and freakishly impose the death sentence; it is always circumscribed by the legislative guidelines." 428 U.S. at 206–207.

202. 428 U.S. at 198.

203. *Id.* at 188. In Woodson v. North Carolina, Justice Stewart wrote: "The issue, like that explored in *Furman,* involves the procedure employed by the State to select persons for the unique and irreversible penalty of death." 428 U.S. at 287.

204. 402 U.S. at 207. In *Furman,* Chief Justice Burger in dissent wrote: "[I]t would be disingenuous to suggest that today's ruling has done anything less than overrule *McGautha* in the guise of an Eighth Amendment adjudication." *Furman,*

408 U.S. at 400; *see also id.* at 448–449 (Powell, J., dissenting); *Woodson*, 428 U.S. at 319 (Rehnquist, J., dissenting). In *Furman*, Justice Douglas wrote: "We are now imprisoned in the *McGautha* holding." 408 U.S. at 248.

205. 408 U.S. at 310.

206. *Id.* at 309–310. *Cf.* Note, 87 Harv. L. Rev. 1690, 1692–1697 (1974).

207. 428 U.S. at 199; *see* Geimer, "Death at Any Cost: A Critique of the Supreme Court's Recent Retreat from Its Death Penalty Standards," 12 Fla. State L. Rev. 737, 745 (1985).

208. 408 U.S. at 313.

209. *Gregg*, 428 U.S. at 222–223. In *Roberts v. Louisiana*, Justice White also made clear that his *Furman* judgment was based on the death penalty in practice and not on the absence of procedures: In *McGautha*, "we specifically rejected the claims that a defendant's 'constitutional rights were infringed by permitting the jury to impose the death penalty without governing standards' . . . . For myself, I see no need to reconsider *McGautha* and would not invalidate the Louisiana statute for its failure to provide what *McGautha* held it need not provide." *Roberts*, 428 U.S. at 356; *see also* Gillers, *supra* note 30, at 9 n.35 ("The then administration of the death penalty was found unconstitutional because of its results . . .").

210. 428 U.S. at 195.

211. 402 U.S. at 207. *See* text at notes 8–10.

212. 428 U.S. at 193.

213. *Id.*

214. *Id.* at 194–195.

215. *See* Baldwin v. Alabama, 105 S.Ct. 2727, 2732 (1985).

216. 428 U.S. at 293.

217. *Id.* at 302–303.

218. *Id.* at 303–304.

219. *Id.* at 304.

220. *Furman*, 408 U.S. at 310 n.12.

221. 402 U.S. at 207 (emphasis added).

222. *Cf. Furman*, 408 U.S. at 397 (Burger, C.J., dissenting): The Eighth "Amendment is not concerned with the process by which a State determines that a particular punishment is to be imposed in a particular case." *See also id.* at 399. If Justice Stewart's interpretation of *Furman* in *Gregg* is correct, *Furman* was the first case in which the Court used the eighth amendment to set procedural standards. *See* Gillers, *supra* note 30, at 11–12.

223. *Furman*, 408 U.S. at 400.

224. *Id.* at 448–449.

225. *Woodson*, 408 U.S. at 319.

226. 428 U.S. at 195 n.47.

227. *Id.* at 193.

228. *Id.*

229. *Id.* at 195 n.47.

230. 446 U.S. 420 (1980).

231. *Id.* at 433.

232. *See* Turner v. Bass, 753 F.2d 342, 353 (4th Cir. 1985).

233. *See* Gillers, *supra* note 30, at 24 n.108 (1980).

234. Justice Stewart never expressed his personal agonizing about capital punishment in any of his opinions. Justice Blackmun, who resolved the struggle differently, did confess it:

> Cases such as these provide for me an excruciating agony of the spirit. I yield to no one in the depth of my distaste, antipathy, and, indeed, abhorrence, for the death penalty, with all its aspects of physical distress and fear and of moral judgment exercised by finite minds. That distaste is buttressed by a belief that capital punishment serves no useful purpose that can be demonstrated. For me, it violates childhood's training and life's experiences, and is not compatible with the philosophical convictions I have been able to develop. It is antagonistic to any sense of "reverence for life." *Furman*, 408 U.S. at 405–406.

Chief Justice Burger also expressed personal opposition to capital punishment, though without any indication that voting to uphold it caused him any similar anguish:

> If we were possessed of legislative power, I would either join with Mr. Justice Brennan and Mr. Justice Marshall or, at the very least, restrict the use of capital punishment to a small category of the most heinous crimes. Our constitutional inquiry, however, must be divorced from personal feelings as to the morality and efficacy of the death penalty, and confined to the meaning and applicability of the uncertain language of the Eighth Amendment. *Furman*, 408 U.S. at 375 (dissenting opinion joined by Justices Blackmun, Powell, and Rehnquist).

See also State v. Woodson, 287 N.C. 578, 597–598, 215 S.E.2d 607, 619 (1975) (Exum, J., concurring).

235. In his *Furman* dissent, Justice Powell wrote that the improvement of trial procedures generally, and especially the elimination of segregation in jury selection, minimized the likelihood of discriminatory imposition of the death penalty.

236. 104 S.Ct. 562 (1983).

237. *Id.* at 564 n.2.

238. *Id.* at 564–565.

239. *See* Turner v. Murray, 106 S.Ct. 1683, 1695–1696 (1986) (Powell, J., dissenting); *see* England, "Capital Punishment in the Light of Constitutional Evolution: An Analysis of Distinctions Between Furman and Gregg," 52 Notre Dame Law. 596, 606–607 (1977). *Cf.* Spinkellink v. Wainwright, 578 F.2d 582, 604 (5th Cir. 1978): One statement by the plurality in *Gregg* that "'[o]n its face the Florida system thus satisfies the constitutional deficiencies identified in *Furman*' . . . implies that on its face Section 921.141 conclusively removes the arbitrariness and capriciousness which *Furman* held violative of the Eighth and Fourteenth Amendments. If this is so, our concern here in this attack on Section 921.141 as applied would be whether the Florida courts have followed the statute in imposing Spenkelink's death sentence, and a comparison of Spenkelink's case with other Florida death penalty cases would be unnecessary." *See also id.* at 605 and n.26,

613–614. In Smith v. Balkcom, 660 F.2d 573, 584–585 (5th Cir. 1981), modified, 671 F.2d 858 (5th Cir.), *cert. den.* 459 U.S. 882 (1982), however, the Fifth Circuit held that *Spinkellink* did not preclude a constitutional attack on the application of a guided discretion death penalty statute. Instead, it merely requires some evidence of purposeful discrimination against the particular defendant to initiate the inquiry. *Id.* at 585. *See also* McCleskey v. Kemp, 753 F.2d 877, 890–891 (11th Cir. 1985) (*en banc*), *cert. granted*, 106 S.Ct. 3331 (1986).

240. *Furman*, 408 U.S. at 448.

241. *Id.* at 448–449.

242. 433 U.S. 584 (1977).

243. *Cf. Furman*, 408 U.S. at 461 (Powell, J., dissenting): "Specific rape cases (and specific homicides as well) can be imagined in which the conduct of the accused would render the ultimate penalty a grossly excessive punishment."

Other than *Coker*, Justice Powell voted after *Furman* in a manner entirely consistent with Justice Stewart in every capital case while Justice Stewart was on the Court, except Presnell v. Georgia, 439 U.S. 14 (1978). In *Presnell*, Justice Powell wrote a dissenting opinion recommending a remand to the state supreme court for clarification of its opinion, but not necessarily disagreeing with the majority on the law. In Gilmore v. Utah, 429 U.S. 1012 (1976), Justice Powell wrote a separate opinion, which took the same ultimate position as did the two opinions that Justices Stewart and Stevens signed, that the defendant had competently waived his federal rights.

244. 458 U.S. 782 (1982).

245. The Court used the phrase "accomplice felony murder" in *Enmund*, 458 U.S. at 796; it used the phrase "vicarious felony murder" at pages 791 and 799.

246. *Enmund*, 458 U.S. at 829–830.

247. 455 U.S. 104 (1982).

248. *Id.* at 110.

249. 103 S.Ct. 3418 (1983).

250. *Id.* at 3429.

251. 451 U.S. 430 (1981). Justice Powell later concurred in a decision applying *Bullington*. Arizona v. Rumsey, 104 S.Ct. 2305 (1984).

252. 103 S.Ct. 3446 (1983).

253. 104 S.Ct. 752 (1984).

254. 408 U.S. at 430, 457.

255. But *see* 408 U.S. at 445: "While there might be particular cases in which capital punishment would be regarded as excessive and shocking to the conscience of the community . . . ."

In Pulley v. Harris, 104 S.Ct. 871, 875–876 (1984), the Court distinguished two proportionality issues: the abstract proportionality of the punishment for the nature of the crime, and the comparative proportionality of the punishment for similar occurrences of the same crime. Theoretically those two issues may be distinct. *See Gregg*, 428 U.S. at 173:

> When a form of punishment in the abstract (in this case, whether capital punishment may ever be imposed as a sanction for murder) rather than in the particular (the propriety of death as a penalty to be applied to a specific defendant for a specific crime) is under consideration, the inquiry into "excessiveness" has two aspects. First, the punishment must not involve the

unnecessary and wanton infliction of pain . . . . Second, the punishment must not be grossly out of proportion to the severity of the crime.

See also Baldus, Pulaski, and Woodworth, "Comparative Review of Death Sentences: An Empirical Study of the Georgia Experience," 74 J. Crim. L. and Crim. 661, 665–667 (1983); Baldus, Pulaski, Woodworth, and Kyle, "Identifying Comparatively Excessive Sentences of Death: A Quantitative Approach," 33 Stan. L. Rev. 1, 3–4 and n.8 (1980); Van Duizend, "Comparative Proportionality Review in Death Sentence Cases," 8 State Ct. J. 9, 9–10 (1984); Dix, "Appellate Review of the Decision to Impose Death," 68 Geo. L. Rev. 97, 107 (1979); Radin, supra note 30, 993, 994 n.16, 1057–1062. The comparative proportionality concept is the essence of the arbitrariness standard in practice requiring a meaningful distinction between cases that are treated differently for death penalty purposes. That issue arises only in connection with offenses that survive an abstract proportionality analysis. Both abstract and comparative proportionality are part of the same moral scheme, however, see Radin, "Proportionality, Subjectivity and Tragedy," 18 U.C. Davis L. Rev. 1165, 1166–1167 (1985), and the decisions have tended to blend the two issues as a practical matter. The abstract proportionality analysis looks to the judgments of other juries for part of its guidance. The comparative proportionality analysis categorizes the individual crime to render it suitable for comparison with others. Enmund, for example, could fit into either proportionality issue: accomplice felony–murder analyzed either as a separate crime or as a specific fact situation under the crime of murder. Either perspective could yield the same result. Although purportedly making an abstract proportionality ruling, the Court compared the death penalty for the accomplice with the sentences for the man who committed the killings (the jury recommended death; neither the U.S. Supreme Court nor the Florida Supreme Court specified whether the trial judge imposed that penalty) and his wife who accompanied him into the farmhouse for the holdup (life imprisonment): "Enmund did not kill or intend to kill and thus his culpability is plainly different from that of the robbers who killed; yet the state treated them alike and attributed to Enmund the culpability of those who killed . . . . This was impermissible under the Eighth Amendment." Enmund, 458 U.S. at 798. The effect of either kind of proportionality review is the same: to prevent any jury from ever imposing the death penalty in the particular category of case and therefore to set a substantive limit on the definition of a capital crime. See Gregg, 428 U.S. at 206; id. at 224 (White, J., concurring).

Consider also Godfrey v. Georgia, 446 U.S. 420 (1980). In that case the Supreme Court held that Georgia's "outrageously or wantonly vile, horrible or inhuman" aggravating circumstance was unconstitutionally vague. The decision, however, suggests the question whether a killing in the circumstances of that case —an instantaneous killing of family members who were causing the defendant extreme emotional trauma—could ever qualify for the death penalty if other capital sentences do not arise out of similar killings. The question could be resolved under either an abstract or comparative proportionality analysis in the same way, for the category of emotional family crisis killings.

256. 433 U.S. at 603–604.

257. 458 U.S. at 815, 823; see also Cabana v. Bullock, 106 S.Ct. 689, 697 (1986).

258. 428 U.S. 465 (1976).

259. 428 U.S. at 490. The context of Justice Powell's comment was his discussion of the exclusionary rule. He wrote that the "rule deflects the truthfinding process and often frees the guilty," then added: "The disparity in particular cases between the error committed by the police and the windfall afforded a guilty defendant by application of the rule is contrary to the idea of proportionality that is essential to the concept of justice." 428 U.S. at 490.

260. 103 S.Ct. 3001 (1983).

261. *Id.* at 3009; *see also* Cabana v. Bullock, 106 S.Ct. 689, 697 (1986); *see also id.* at 706 (Blackmun with Brennan and Marshall, JJ., dissenting). Justice Powell also wrote the opinion for the Court in Ingraham v. Wright, 430 U.S. 651 (1977), in which he said that "the Cruel and Unusual Punishments Clause circumscribes the criminal process in three ways: . . . second, it proscribes punishment grossly disproportionate to the severity of the crime . . . ."

262. The decision involved the abstract proportionality rather than the comparative proportionality issue. 103 S.Ct. at 3010–3011. As discussed in note 255, however, the two issues are not materially distinguishable in theory or in effect.

263. 455 U.S. 104 (1982).

264. *Id.* at 112; *see also* Ford v. Wainwright, 106 S.Ct. 2595, 2610 (1986) (Powell, J., concurring): "[T]he determination of petitioner's sanity appears to have been made *solely* on the basis of the examinations performed by the state-appointed psychiatrists. Such a procedure invites arbitrariness and error . . . ."

265. Justices Stevens and Stewart voted together in: The five 1976 cases; Davis v. Georgia, 429 U.S. 122 (1976); Coker v. Georgia, 433 U.S. 584 (1977); Gardner v. Florida, 430 U.S. 349 (1977); Lockett v. Ohio, 438 U.S. 586 (1978) and Bell v. Ohio, 438 U.S. 637 (1978); Presnell v. Georgia, 439 U.S. 14 (1978); Green v. Georgia, 442 U.S. 97 (1979); Godfrey v. Georgia, 446 U.S. 420 (1980); Bullington v. Missouri, 451 U.S. 430 (1981) and Arizona v. Rumsey, 104 S.Ct. 2305 (1984).

In Estelle v. Smith, 451 U.S 454 (1981), both voted to reverse the death penalty on the basis of an improper interview of the defendant. Justice Stevens signed the majority opinion. Justice Stewart wrote a separate concurring opinion, agreeing with one of the majority's rationales and declining to reach the other. In Gilmore v. Utah, 429 U.S. 1012 (1976), Justice Stewart joined the unsigned majority order finding that the defendant had waived all his federal rights. Justice Stevens wrote a separate opinion to the same effect. Otherwise, the two justices were together in all the death penalty cases that came before the Court during their shared tenure.

266. 104 U.S. 871, 881–884 (1984).

267. Wainwright v. Witt, 105 S.Ct. 844 (1985); Strickland v. Washington, 104 S.Ct. 2052 (1984); Pulley v. Harris, 104 S.Ct. 871 (1984); Barclay v. Florida, 103 S.Ct. 3418 (1983); Zant v. Stephens, 103 S.Ct. 2733 (1983); Barefoot v. Estelle, 103 S.Ct. 3383 (1983); Hopper v. Evans, 456 U.S. 605 (1982); Gilmore v. Utah, 429 U.S. 1012 (1976); Jurek v. Texas, *supra* note 74; Proffitt v. Florida, *supra* note 69; Gregg v.Georgia, *supra* note 70.

268. 428 U.S. 325, 334 (1976).

269. *Id.* at 335.

270. 428 U.S. 262 (1976).

271. 430 U.S. 349 (1977); *see also* Cabana v. Bullock, 106 S.Ct. 689, 708 (1986); Spaziano v. Florida, 104 S.Ct. 3154, 3167 (1984). He also has joined opinions written by other justices supporting special death penalty safeguards. Darden v. Wainwright, 106 S.Ct. 2464, 2476 (1986) (Blackmun, J., dissenting, with Brennan, Marshall, and Stevens, JJ.).

272. 104 S.Ct. at 884.

273. *Id.* at 882.

274. *Id.*

275. Dissenting in Baldwin v. Alabama, 105 S.Ct. 2727 (1985), Justice Stevens expressed concern about the adequacy of the procedure challenged in that case:

> The arbitrariness and uncertainty of the message conveyed by a mandatory jury death sentence makes such a sentence a constitutionally impermissible factor in a sentencing judge's deliberations. [*Id.* at 2740. He also expressed concern about the way the procedure had worked in the case before the Court:] The record in this case plainly indicates that the jury's sentence was, in fact, on the mind of the judge that sentenced Baldwin in 1977.[4]
>
> [4]Cf. *Eddings v. Oklahoma,* 455 U.S. 104, 112–114 (1982) (considering record evidence of judge's actual application of Oklahoma capital sentencing law). *Id.* at 2741.

The question is whether Justice Stevens would also be concerned about evidence that procedures that appear fair on their face result in arbitrary outcomes, regardless of whether the outcome in a particular case can be demonstrated to be contrary to the legal standards.

276. 455 U.S. 104, 117 (1982).

277. *Id.* at 118.

278. 104 S.Ct. 2305 (1984).

279. 105 S.Ct. 2633, 2646 (1985).

280. Darden v. Wainwright, 106 S.Ct. 2464 (1986); Lockhart v. McCree, 106 S.Ct. 1758 (1986); Poland v. Arizona, 106 S.Ct. 1749 (1986); Cabana v. Bullock, 106 S.Ct. 689 (1986); Baldwin v. Alabama, 105 S.Ct. 2727 (1985); Wainwright v. Witt, 105 S.Ct. 844 (1985); Spaziano v. Florida, 104 S.Ct. 3154 (1986); Pulley v. Harris, 104 S.Ct. 871 (1984); Maggio v. Williams, 104 S.Ct. 311 (1983); Barclay v. Florida, 103 S.Ct. 3418 (1983); Barefoot v. Estelle, 103 S.Ct. 3383 (1983); Zant v. Stephens, 103 S.Ct. 2733 (1983); Hopper v. Evans, 456 U.S. 605 (1982); *see* Strickland v. Washington, 104 S.Ct. 2595, 2612 (1986); *cf.* Ford v. Wainwright, 106 S.Ct. 2595, 2612 (1986).

281. 103 S.Ct. 3446 (1983).

282. 458 U.S. 782 (1982).

283. *See* notes 236–238 and accompanying text.

284. 458 U.S. 782 (1982).

285. Justice Blackmun wrote separately in each of the cases to base his vote on his opinion in *Furman.* He joined Justice White's opinion only in *Roberts v. Louisiana.*

286. 428 U.S. at 220.

287. *Gregg,* 428 U.S. at 221.

288. *Proffitt*, 428 U.S. at 260.
289. *Gregg*, 428 U.S. at 220–221.
290. *Id*. at 222.
291. Justice Blackmun remained aloof from the *Furman* rationale.
292. 428 U.S. at 221–222.
293. *Id*. at 2?4.
294. Justice Stewart in *Gregg* rejected the pure infrequency theory: "But the relative infrequency of jury verdicts imposing the death sentence does not indicate rejection of capital punishment *per se*. Rather, the reluctance of juries in many cases to impose the sentence may well reflect the humane feeling that this most irrevocable of sanctions should be reserved for a small number of extreme cases." 428 U.S. at 182. He went on, however, to point out that "by the end of March 1976, more than 460 persons were subject to death sentences," *id*. at 182, apparently implying that the penalty was no longer imposed infrequently though without referring to any standard of infrequency. *See also Woodson*, 428 U.S. at 303: "While a mandatory death penalty statute may reasonably be expected to increase the number of persons sentenced to death, it does not fulfill *Furman's* basic requirement . . . ."
295. *See Roberts*, 428 U.S. at 360: "[I]f there is danger of freakish and too infrequent imposition of capital punishment under a mandatory system such as Louisiana's, there is very little ground for believing that juries will be any more faithful to their instructions under the Georgia and Florida systems where the opportunity is much, much greater for juries to practice their own brand of unbridled discretion." In *Woodson*, Justice Stewart agreed that a mandatory death penalty may increase the number of death sentences, but argued that it still presented an intolerable danger of arbitrariness. *Woodson*, 428 U.S. at 303.
296. Perhaps it was their position on these statutes that led Justice White to maintain independence from them in the three cases in which they agreed, though such a difference regarding the application of the governing principles to situations where they disagree has not necessarily kept a justice from signing a contemporaneous opinion applying those same principles to reach a more agreeable result in a different situation.
297. Roberts v. Louisiana, 428 U.S. at 346. Justice White might have added that the same considerations had led the Court to invalidate all other death penalty statutes without any published evaluation of their administration.
298. *Jurek*, 428 U.S. at 279: "As of February of this year, 33 persons, including petitioner, had been sentenced to death under the Texas murder statute."
299. "I cannot conclude at this juncture that the death penalty under this system will be imposed so seldom and arbitrarily as to serve no useful penological function . . . ." *Jurek*, 428 U.S. at 279.
300. *Gregg*, 428 U.S. at 222.
301. 428 U.S. at 223. The power of the state supreme court on review of sentence is limited to setting aside the death penalty in a case in which it has been imposed out of proportion to sentences of life or less in similar cases. It is not given the power to correct the disproportionality problem by meting out death sentences in the similar cases. "An error on the side of mercy is not reversible." State v. Fowler, 151 N.C. 731, 733, 66 S.E. 567, 567 (1909). The exercise of this

appellate review function will reduce the frequency of the death penalty generally. It will accomplish that result in two ways: by overturning particular death sentences and by withdrawing certain categories of crimes from eligibility for the death penalty altogether. Justice White noted that the Georgia Supreme Court on the second basis had effectively foreclosed the death penalty from being used for the crime of robbery and for certain classes of rape. *Gregg*, 428 U.S. at 224.

Notwithstanding the consequent reduction in the frequency of the imposition of the death penalty, Justice White believed that the effect of appellate review could be to further the narrowing of the category of capital crimes "to those which are particularly serious or for which the death penalty is peculiarly appropriate," *Gregg*, 428 U.S. at 221, so that juries "will impose the death penalty in a substantial portion of the cases so defined." *Id.* Justice White thus appeared concerned not about the absolute frequency of death sentences, but the frequency of such sentences within an appropriate category of capital crimes. The category of capital murder in each of the five states whose statutes were before the Court was sufficiently broad that Justice White seemed to expect a large number of cases to arise under them. He did not, therefore, address the question of whether he would approve capital punishment for a category of crime so narrow that its incidence would be rare, so that convictions and therefore death penalties for its commission would necessarily be infrequent. Presumably Justice White would insist only on frequency commensurate with the incidence of the crime. That circumstance could certainly be consistent with a general deterrence rationale. Otherwise, the effectiveness of the death penalty as a general deterrent, if that should ever be manifested, would render it unconstitutional.

302. 428 U.S. at 224.

303. *Id.*

304. Roberts v. Louisiana, 428 U.S. at 360.

305. *Id.* at 356.

306. *See* 428 U.S. at 347–348, 356–358.

307. 438 U.S. 586, 621 (1978).

308. Chief Justice Burger joined Justices Stewart, Powell, and Stevens and wrote the plurality opinion in *Lockett*. Justices White, Marshall, and Blackmun concurred in separate opinions that shared a common rationale that anticipated the decision in Enmund v. Florida, 458 U.S. 782 (1982). Justice Brennan did not participate. Chief Justice Rehnquist cast the lone vote to uphold the death penalty.

309. 438 U.S. at 604. Chief Justice Rehnquist misstated the scope of this holding when he wrote in his dissent in *Lockett* that "[w]e are now told, in effect, that in order to impose a death sentence the judge or jury must receive in evidence whatever the defense attorney wishes them to hear." 438 U.S. at 629; *see also id.* at 632 (White, J., concurring and dissenting) ("any and all mitigating circumstances"). As the majority explained: "Nothing in this opinion limits the traditional authority of a court to exclude, as irrelevant, evidence not bearing on the defendant's character, prior record, or the circumstances of his offense." 438 U.S. at 604 n.12. *But see* Weisberg, "Deregulating Death," 1983 Sup. Ct. Rev. 305, 324–325.

310. 438 U.S. at 605.

311. *Id.* at 597.

312. *Id.* at 622.

313. *Id.* at 623.

314. 402 U.S. at 207.

315. *See* Radin, "Cruel Punishment and Respect for Persons: Super Due Process For Death," 53 So. Cal. L. Rev. 1143, 1149–1155 (1980).

316. *See* 428 U.S. at 197.

317. *See* 428 U.S. at 248; *see also* Barclay v. Florida, 103 S.Ct. 3418, 3426 (1983).

318. 446 U.S. 420 (1980).

319. The plurality consisted of Justices Stewart, Blackmun, Powell, and Stevens. Justices Marshall and Brennan concurred on the basis of their opinion that the death penalty constitutes cruel and unusual punishment.

320. 446 U.S. at 433.

321. *Id.* at 450.

322. *Id.* at 428.

323. 103 S.Ct. 3418 (1983).

324. 103 S.Ct. at 3446 (1983).

325. 104 S.Ct. 378 (1983).

326. 103 S.Ct. at 3427.

327. 103 S.Ct. at 3456–3457.

328. *Id.* at 3457.

329. *Id.* at 3457 n.22.

Justice White joined Chief Justice Rehnquist's dissent in Caldwell v. Mississippi, 105 S.Ct. 2633 (1985), in which they said that if a prosecutor "argued to a jury that it should go ahead and impose the death sentence because it did not really matter—the appellate court would correct any 'mistake' the jury might make in choice of sentence . . . I might well agree that the process afforded did not comport with some constitutional norm related to procedural fairness. But . . . the argument here fell far short of telling the jury that it would not be responsible for imposing the death penalty." *Id.* at 2649.

330. 103 S.Ct. 3383 (1983).

331. In addition, Justice White wrote a dissenting opinion in Gilmore v. Utah, 429 U.S. 1012 (1976), in which the U.S. Supreme Court upheld the waiver of his right to appeal by a defendant sentenced to death. Justice White argued that the Utah death penalty statute was subject to "substantial questions under *Furman*," 429 U.S. at 1017–1018, and "the consent of a convicted defendant in a criminal case does not privilege a State to impose a punishment otherwise forbidden by the Eighth Amendment." 429 U.S. at 1018.

332. 442 U.S. 95 (1979).

333. 451 U.S. 454 (1981).

334. Miranda v. Arizona, 384 U.S. 436 (1966).

335. 448 U.S. 38, 46 (1980).

336. 408 U.S. at 399 n.28.

337. 408 U.S. at 310.

338. 428 U.S. at 260.

339. 428 U.S. at 279.

340. 428 U.S. at 307.

341. *Cf. Furman*, 408 U.S. at 376 (Burger, C.J., dissenting): "[T]he Constitution prohibits all punishments of extreme and barbarous cruelty, regardless of how frequently or infrequently imposed." *See* Murphy, *supra* note 30, at 224.

342. 433 U.S. 584 (1977).

343. 458 U.S. 782 (1982).

344. 433 U.S. at 592.

345. 458 U.S. at 800.

346. *Id.* at 798–799.

347. 428 U.S. at 355.

348. *Id.* at 354; *Enmund*, 458 U.S. at 798.

349. *Gregg*, 428 U.S. at 163, 190–191, 195; *Proffitt*, 428 U.S. at 248, 259.

350. *Gregg*, 428 U.S. at 164–165, 192–195; *Proffitt*, 428 U.S. at 248–250, 255–258.

351. *Gregg*, 428 U.S. at 195. In Pulley v. Harris, 104 S.Ct. 871 (1984), the Court later explained *Gregg* as follows: "The bifurcated proceedings, the limited number of capital crimes, the requirement that at least one aggravating circumstance be present, and the consideration of mitigating circumstances minimized the risk of wholly arbitrary, capricious, or freakish sentences." 104 S.Ct. at 876–877.

352. *Jurek*, 428 U.S. at 276.

353. *Gregg*, 428 U.S. at 195.

354. Turner v. Murray, 106 S.Ct. 1683, 1687 (1986) ("Because of the range of discretion entrusted to a jury in a capital sentencing hearing . . . ."). *Cf. McGautha*, 402 U.S. at 217: Jury guidelines "provide no protection against the jury determination to decide on whimsy or caprice."

355. *Gregg*, 428 U.S. at 194–195; *see also Proffitt*, 428 U.S. at 252–253: "The Florida capital sentencing procedures thus seek to assure that the penalty will not be imposed in an arbitrary or capricious manner. Moreover, to the extent that any risk to the contrary exists, it is minimized by Florida's appellate review system . . . ." *See also id.* at 252: "[J]udicial sentencing should lead, if anything, to even greater consistency in the imposition at the trial court level of capital punishment, since a trial judge is more experienced in sentencing than a jury, and therefore is better able to impose sentences similar to those imposed in analogous cases."

356. *Gregg*, 428 U.S. at 204; *Proffitt*, 428 U.S. at 258.

357. *Gregg*, 428 U.S. at 166–167, 204–206; *Proffitt*, 428 U.S. at 258–259.

358. *Proffitt*, 428 U.S. at 250–251.

359. *Id.* at 251.

360. *Id.* at 258.

361. *Gregg*, 428 U.S. at 204; *see also* Baldus, Pulaski, and Woodworth, *supra* note 255, at 672–678; Baldus, Pulaski, Woodworth, and Kyle, *supra* note 255, at 1–2 n.1.

The North Carolina Supreme Court's comparative proportionality review in capital cases is described in Note, 63 N.C. L. Rev. 1146 (1985).

362. *See* Tichnell v. State, 297 Md. 1, 468 A.2d 1, 24–25 (1983) (Eldridge, J., concurring); *id.* at 26 (Cole, J., concurring); *id.* at 30–36 (Davidson, J., dis-

senting). "Of the thirty-seven states that presently permit the death penalty, thirty-one require comparative proportionality review of death sentences." Note, 69 Cornell L. Rev. 1129, 1189, 1242–1243 (1984).

363. Chief Justice Rehnquist, dissenting in *Woodson*, argued that

> it is not at all apparent that appellate review of death sentences, through a process of comparing the facts of one case in which a death sentence was imposed with the facts of another in which such a sentence was imposed, will afford any meaningful protection against whatever arbitrariness results from jury discretion. All that such review of death sentences can provide is a comparison of fact situations which must in their nature be highly particularized if not unique . . . . The Georgia Supreme Court cannot know. . . , when it is reviewing jury sentences for life in capital cases, whether the jurors found aggravating circumstances present, but nonetheless decided to recommend mercy, or instead found no aggravating circumstances at all and opted for mercy. So the "proportionality" type of review, while it would perhaps achieve its objective if there were no possible factual lacunae in the jury verdicts, will not achieve its objective because there are necessarily such lacunae.

428 U.S. at 316, 318; *see also* Tichnell v. State, 297 Md. 1, 468 A.2d 1, 17 (1983). Chief Justice Rehnquist, however, joined Justice White's opinion in *Gregg* with its praise for proportionality review.

364. *Cf.* Enmund v. Florida, 458 U.S. 782, 796 (1982); Woodson v. North Carolina, 428 U.S. 280, 316 (1976) (Rehnquist, J., dissenting). *See* Van Duizend, *supra* note 255, at 11.

365. *Gregg*, 428 U.S. at 204 n.56.

366. *Id.*; *see also* Zant v. Stephens, 103 S.Ct. at 2733, 2744 n.19 (1983).

367. *Gregg*, 428 U.S. at 204 n.56.

368. *Id.*

369. *Proffitt*, 428 U.S. at 258–259; *see generally* Dix, *supra* note 255.

370. *Gregg*, 428 U.S. at 205–206; *Proffitt*, 428 U.S. at 259.

371. *Roberts*, 428 U.S. at 335–336.

372. Of course, it may take a long time for a state supreme court to recognize a change in the capital sentencing pattern, especially if the court does not regularly include non-death penalty cases in its survey.

On the other hand, the proportionality review will prevent juries from beginning to impose death sentences in cases previously perceived by other juries as not qualifying for that severe sentence. The prior practice will require the state supreme court to treat the first case in a potentially developing new pattern as aberrant and to stifle the development. *Cf.* Coker v. Georgia, 433 U.S. 584, 613 (1977) (Burger, C.J., dissenting). This, of course, is a consequence of the feature of proportionality review that permits the state supreme court to correct inconsistent patterns only by setting aside the death penalties in those cases where it was not provided, and not permitting it to impose the death penalty in cases where the sentencing authority rejected it. *See Woodson*, 428 U.S. at 318–319 (Rehnquist, J., dissenting) ("Appellate review affords no correction whatever with respect to those fortunate few who are the beneficiaries of random discretion exercised by juries. . . . It may make corrections at one end of the spectrum, but cannot at the other)." This course is prudent and may be constitutionally necessary. *Cf.* United States v. DiFrancesco, 449 U.S. 117 (1980). Because the sentencing judge or jury has a discretionary role in the death penalty determination, a decision favoring leniency may be determined by mitigating circumstances unique to a particular case. *Cf.* Lockett v. Ohio, *supra* note 26. Any procedure to permit appellate imposition of a death sentence would have to be carefully tailored to accommodate the constitutionally required broad scope given the effect of individualized consideration of mitigating circumstances. This requirement may distinguish capital from other cases, where a sentence may constitutionally be enhanced on appeal. United States v. DiFrancesco, *supra.*

373. *Gregg,* 428 U.S. at 206; *see also id.* at 195: "Where the sentencing authority is required to specify the factors it relied on in reaching its decision, the further safeguard of meaningful appellate review is available to ensure that death sentences are not imposed capriciously or in a freakish manner."

374. *Proffitt,* 428 U.S. at 258–259. Here the plurality shifts from assessing the statute purely on its face to including consideration of its administration in practice. Although this shift enhances the image the Court creates about the Florida statute, *Jurek* demonstrates that it is not at all decisive. *See* text following this note.

375. *Jurek,* 428 U.S. at 276.

376. *See* Dix, *supra* note 255, at 102–103, 106.

377. *See id.* at 107.

378. *Proffitt,* 428 U.S. at 253.

379. *Gregg,* 428 U.S. at 211. Chief Justice Rehnquist and then Chief Justice Burger also signed this opinion.

380. *Gregg,* 428 U.S. at 222–223.

381. *Cf.* note 301, *supra.*

382. 428 U.S. at 223.

383. *Id.*

384. *Proffitt,* 428 U.S. at 260.

385. *Jurek,* 428 U.S. at 278.

386. *See Woodson,* 428 U.S. at 316–317 (Rehnquist, J., dissenting): "By definition, of course, there can be no separate appellate review of the factual basis for the sentencing decision in a mandatory system."

387. 430 U.S. 349 (1977).

388. The plurality (Justice Stevens, with Justices Stewart and Powell) excused the Florida Supreme Court because it "decided petitioner's case before our decision in *Proffitt v. Florida, supra* [note 69], and before its own consideration of *Proffitt,* 315 So.2d 461 (1975), or of *Tedder v. State,* 322 So.2d 908 (1975)." 430 U.S. at 361 n.12.

389. 430 U.S. at 365.

390. *Id.* at 367.

391. *Id.* at 368.

392. 433 U.S. 584 (1977).

393. *Id.* at 592.

394. *Id.* at 597–600.

395. *Id.* at 593–596.

396. *Id.* at 596–597.

397. *Id.* at 597.
398. *Id.*
399. *Gregg*, 428 U.S. at 224.
400. Coker v. State, 234 Ga. 555, 216 S.E.2d 782, 797 (1975).
401. *Gregg*, 428 U.S. at 204–205 n.56.
402. *See also* Enmund v. Florida, 458 U.S. 782 (1982).
403. 446 U.S. 420 (1980).
404. *Id.* at 433.
405. Godfrey v. State, 243 Ga. 302, 253 S.E.2d 710, 718 (1979).
406. 446 U.S. at 449–451.
407. *Id.* at 451. Justice White also compared the facts in *Godfrey* with the facts in other cases where the death penalty had been imposed. Like the majority, he did not look at any cases where the death penalty had not been imposed, even though the aspect of his standard revolving around a "meaningful basis for distinguishing the few cases in which it is imposed from the many cases in which it is not" would seem to recommend such an inquiry.
408. 446 U.S. at 439.
409. *See* Beck v. Alabama, 447 U.S. 625, 638 (1980).
410. 103 S.Ct. 2733 (1983).
411. *Id.* at 2744.
412. *Id.*
413. *Id.* at 2744 n.19.
414. *Id.* at 2749–2750.
415. 103 S.Ct. 3418 (1983).
416. *Id.* at 3428.
417. *Id.* at 3436.
418. *Id.* at 3441–3442, 3444.
419. 104 S.Ct. 871 (1984).
420. 104 S.Ct. 311 (1984).
421. 104 S.Ct. at 881.
422. *See* Dix, *supra* note 255, at 108–109 n. 87 (1979).
423. *See* Zant v. Stephens, 103 S.Ct. 2733, 2747 (1983) ("factors that are constitutionally impermissible or totally irrelevant to the sentencing process, such as for example the race, religion, or political affiliation of the defendant"); *see also* Baldwin v. Alabama, 105 S.Ct. 2727, 2733 (1985).
424. 408 U.S. at 390 n.12.
425. *Id. See also* Justice Powell's dissenting opinion for the same four justices: "[A] different argument, premised on the Equal Protection Clause, might well be made. If a Negro defendant, for instance, could demonstrate that members of his race were being singled out for more severe punishment than others charged with the same offense, a constitutional violation might be established." *Id.* at 449; *see also id.* at 450.
426. Hunter v. Underwood, 105 S.Ct. 1916, 1920 (1985); Village of Arlington Heights v. Metropolitan Housing Development Corp., 429 U.S. 252, 265–266 (1977); Washington v. Davis, 426 U.S. 229, 240 (1976).
427. 408 U.S. at 390 n.12.
428. 104 S.Ct. 562 (1983).

429. *Id.* at 563 (Powell, J., dissenting).

430. *Id.* at 564–565.

431. 104 S.Ct. at 564 n.2. *Cf. Furman,* 408 U.S. at 253, 255–256 (Douglas, J., concurring); *see also* Smith v. Balkcom, 660 F.2d 573, 585 (5th Cir. 1981), *modified,* 671 F.2d 858 (5th Cir.), *cert. den.,* 459 U.S. 882 (1982).

432. 104 S.Ct. 3498 (1984).

433. *Id.* at 3499.

434. 104 S.Ct. 2183 (1984).

435. 104 S.Ct. 450 (1984).

436. *Id.* at 451.

In Hitchcock v. Wainwright, 745 F.2d 1332 (11th Cir. 1984), *affirmed en banc,* 770 F.2d 1514 (11th Cir. 1985), the Eleventh Circuit decided that the defendant was not entitled to an evidentiary hearing on his "claim that the death penalty is applied in a racially discriminatory manner in Florida." 745 F.2d at 1342; 770 F.2d at 1516. Observing that his claim "depends on the same statistical study rejected by this Court in *Sullivan v. Wainwright,* 721 F.2d 316, 317 (11th Cir.), *aff'd,* 104 S.Ct. 450 (1983)," the court held: "The Supreme Court has held this argument to be without merit. *Wainwright v. Ford,* 104 S.Ct. 3498 (1984)." *Id.*

On June 9, 1986, the Supreme Court granted certiorari in that case on that issue and two others. 106 S.Ct. 2888 (1986). *See also* Griffin v. Wainwright, 760 F.2d 1505, 1518 (11th Cir. 1985), *vacated and remanded,* 106 S.Ct. 1964 (1986).

437. Roach v. Martin, 757 F.2d 1463, 1471 (4th Cir. 1985); Briley v. Booker, 746 F.2d 225, 227 (4th Cir. 1984); Shaw v. Martin, 733 F.2d 304, 311–313 (4th Cir. 1984).

438. McCleskey v. Kemp, 753 F.2d 877 (11th Cir. 1985), *cert. granted,* 106 S.Ct. 3331 (1986); *see also* Griffin v. Wainwright, *supra* note 436.

439. 753 F.2d at 890.

The Court did recognize that "race discrimination in the imposition of the death penalty was not the basis of" *Furman. Id.* It also said, however:

Although conceivably the level or amount of disparate racial impact that would render a state's capital sentencing system arbitrary and capricious under the Eighth Amendment might differ slightly from the level or amount of disparate racial impact that would compel an inference of discriminatory intent under the equal protection clause of the Fourteenth Amendment, we do not need to decide whether there could be a difference in magnitude that would lead to opposite conclusions on a system's constitutionality depending on which theory a claimant asserts.

Id. at 891. Focusing on the racial factor blinded the court to the more general nature of the arbitrariness inquiry. *See id.* at 892.

440. *Id.* at 892.

441. *Id.; see also id.* at 893: "'Disparate impact alone is insufficient to establish a violation of the fourteenth amendment. There must be a showing of an intent to discriminate.'" *See also* Griffin v. Wainwright, *supra* note 436.

The Supreme Court granted certiorari in McCleskey v. Kemp on July 7, 1986. 106 S.Ct. 3331 (1986).

442. *Furman*, 408 U.S. at 249, 257.

443. *Id.* at 313.

444. *See* notes 60–61, *supra*.

445. Even in that event, the state courts might interpret state constitutional provisions similar to the eighth amendment in a manner analogous to *Furman*. For example, Article I, Section 27 of the North Carolina Constitution provides: "Excessive bail shall not be required, nor excessive fines imposed, nor cruel and unusual punishments inflicted." The North Carolina Supreme Court has held that a decision of the United States Supreme Court construing a federal constitutional provision with a parallel in the state constitution, "though persuasive by reason of our respect for the views of that Court, does not control our interpretation of the" state constitutional provision. Horton v. Gulledge, 277 N.C. 353, 359, 177 S.E.2d 885, 889 (1970); *see also* Henry v. Edmisten, 315 N.C. 474, 480, 340 S.E.2d 720, 725 (1986); State v. Lane, 301 N.C. 382, 384, 271 S.E.2d 273, 275 (1980); State v. Jarrette, 284 N.C. 625, 655, 202 S.E.2d 721, 741 (1974). *See generally* McGraw, ed., DEVELOPMENTS IN STATE CONSTITUTIONAL LAW (West 1985) (Collection of papers presented at the Williamsburg Conference sponsored by the Conference of Chief Justices of the National Center for State Courts); Brennan, "State Constitutions and the Protection of Individual Rights," 90 Harv. L. Rev. 489 (1977); Nettik Simmons, "Towards a Theory of State Constitutional Jurisprudence," 46 Mont. L. Rev. 261 (1985); Symposium, "The Emergence of State Constitutional Law," 63 Tex. L. Rev. 959 (1985); "Special Project: The Constitutionality of the Death Penalty in New Jersey," 15 Rutgers L. Rev. 261, 323–324, 342–347, 384–385 (1984); Exum, "Dusting Off Our State Constitution," 33 N.C. State Bar Quarterly 6 (Spring 1986).

446. 753 F.2d at 905. Judge Johnson, in a dissenting opinion joined by Judges Hatchett and Clark, also observed: "The fact that a system mishandles a sizable subset of cases is persuasive evidence that the entire system operates improperly." *Id.* at 914. He further pointed out:

> The Supreme Court in Pulley v. Harris . . . emphasized the importance of factors other than appellate proportionality review that would control jury discretion and assure that sentences would not fall into an arbitrary pattern. The decision in *Pulley* deemphasizes the importance of evidence of arbitrariness in individual cases and looks exclusively to "systemic" arbitrariness. *Id.* at 909 n.3.

Chapter III

1. These may be called *legislative facts* or *constitutional facts*. *See* Lockhart v. McCree, 106 S.Ct. 1758, 1762 n.3 (1986); 2 Davis, ADMINISTRATIVE LAW TREATISE 353, 363 (West 1958); Shaman, "Constitutional Fact: The Perception of Reality by the Supreme Court," 35 U. Fla. L. Rev. 236, 236 (1983); Miller and Barron, "The Supreme Court, the Adversary System and the Flow of Information to the Justices: A Preliminary Inquiry," 61 Va. L. Rev. 1187 (1975); Alfange, "The Relevance of Legislative Facts in Constitutional Law," 114 U. Pa. L. Rev. 637, 640 (1966); Karst, "Legislative Facts in Constitutional Law," 1960 Sup. Ct. Rev. 75, 77; Biklé, "Judicial Determination of Questions of Fact Affecting the Constitutional

Validity of Legislative Action," 38 Harv. L. Rev. 6, 7–8 (1924); Traynor, "What Domesday Books for Emerging Law?" 15 U.C.L.A. L. Rev. 1105, 1111 (1968); *see also* Federal Election Com'n v. Nat. Conserv. Pol. Action, 105 S.Ct. 1459, 1470 (1985). Horowitz and Marvell prefer the term *social facts* suggested in Note, 61 Harv. L. Rev. 692, 693 (1948). Horowitz, THE COURTS AND SOCIAL POLICY 45 (Brookings 1977); Marvell, APPELLATE COURTS AND LAWYERS 150, 339, 344 (Greenwood 1978). Monaghan recently used the term *constitutional facts* to refer less precisely to the historical facts specific to a particular case raising a constitutional issue. Monaghan, "Constitutional Fact Review," 85 Colum. L. Rev. 229, 238 (1985). Monahan and Walker more recently recommended that it would be more useful to consider social science research as *social authority* rather than fact. Monahan and Walker, "Social Authority: Obtaining, Evaluating, and Establishing Social Science in Law," 134 U. Pa. L. Rev. 477, 488 (1986).

2. Shaman, *supra* note 1; Karst, *supra* note 1. These may be called *adjudicative facts*. Davis, *supra* note 1.

3. *See* Cardozo, THE GROWTH OF THE LAW 85–86 (Yale 1924); Cardozo, THE NATURE OF THE JUDICIAL PROCESS 30–31, 67, 73, 80–81 (Yale 1921); Karst, *supra* note 1, at 104; Pound, "The Theory of Judicial Decision," 36 Harv. L. Rev. 940, 951 (1923).

4. *See* Furman v. Georgia, 408 U.S. 238, 309–310 nn.12 and 14 (1972) (Stewart, J.); *id.* at 313 (White, J.); *see also id.* at 364–366 nn.152–155 (Marshall, J.); Chapter IV, Part 4, *infra*.

5. In Enmund v. Florida, Justice White wrote the opinion for the Court holding the death penalty unconstitutional for accomplice felony–murder. One factor he considered was that "the death penalty is rarely imposed on one only vicariously guilty of the murder." 458 U.S. at 800. In dissent, Justice O'Connor, for four justices, pointed out that "the data do not reveal the number or fraction of homicides that were charged as felony murders, or the number or fraction of cases in which the State sought the death penalty for an accomplice guilty of felony murder. Consequently, we cannot know the fraction of cases in which juries rejected the death penalty for accomplice felony murder." 458 U.S. at 818–819. Justice White responded that the Court doubted "whether it is possible to gather such information, and at any rate, it would be relevant if prosecutors rarely sought the death penalty for accomplice felony murder, for it would tend to indicate that prosecutors, who represent society's interest in punishing crime, consider the death penalty excessive for accomplice felony murder." 458 U.S. at 796.

6. Smith, JURISPRUDENCE 21 (Columbia 1909), quoted in Cardozo, THE NATURE OF THE JUDICIAL PROCESS, *supra* note 3, at 23.

7. Cardozo, THE GROWTH OF THE LAW, *supra* note 3, at 85–86.

8. *See* Posner, "The Present Situation in Legal Scholarship," 90 Yale L. Rev. 1113, 1120–1121 (1981).

9. *See* Marvell, *supra* note 1, at 173.

10. Lempert and Sanders, AN INVITATION TO LAW AND SOCIAL SCIENCE (Longman 1986); Rosenblum, "A Place for Social Science Along the Judiciary's Constitutional Law Frontier," 66 Nw. U. L. Rev. 455, 456 (1971); *see* Beutel, EXPERIMENTAL JURISPRUDENCE 113–114 (University of Nebraska 1957).

11. *See generally* Barnes and Conley, STATISTICAL EVIDENCE IN LITIGATION 10–14, 545–595 (Little, Brown 1986).

12. *See* Lockhart v. McCree, 106 S.Ct. 1758, 1761 (1986); Ballew v. Georgia, 435 U.S. 223, 246 (1978) (Powell, J., concurring in the judgment); Horowitz, *supra* note 1, at 47–50, 279–283; Zeisel and Diamond, "'Convincing Empirical Evidence' on the Six Member Jury," 41 U. Chi. L. Rev. 281, 292–293 (1974); Sperlich, "Social Science Evidence and the Courts: Reaching Beyond the Adversary Process," 63 Judicature 280, 286–289 (1980).

13. *See* Marvell, *supra* note 1, at 172–204, 216, 220; Note, 61 Harv. L. Rev. 692, 696–702 (1948).

In a recent article, Walker and Monahan argue that social science research relevant to the policy premises for a rule of law should be treated as a source of authority rather than a source of facts. Monahan and Walker, *supra* note 1. Their thesis is that "social science research, when used to create a legal rule, is more analogous to 'law' than to 'fact,' and hence should be treated much as courts treat legal precedent." *Id.* at 478.

14. For example, in Gregg v. Georgia, 428 U.S. 153, 184–185 n.31 (1976), the Court cited the published scholarly debate about the validity of econometric studies of whether the death penalty has a marginal deterrent effect. *See* Ballew v. Georgia, 435 U.S. 223, 232–239 (1978); *see also* Monahan and Walker, *supra* note 1, at 500–501.

In Lockhart v. McCree, 106 S.Ct. 1758, 1762 n.3 (1986), the Supreme Court suggested that an appellate court might review evidence of social science research and reach its own conclusions about the factual premises treated in that research without being bound by the factual findings of the trial court.

15. Muller v. Oregon, 208 U.S. 412, 419 (1908) ("In the brief filed by Mr. Louis D. Brandeis, for the defendant in error, is a very copious collection of all these matters, an epitome of which is found in the margin").

Modern research has discredited the aspect of Brandeis's submission based on the "special physical organization," *id.* at 420 n.1, of women. *See* Strumm, Louis D. Brandeis 128–131 (Harvard University Press 1984); *see also* Monahan and Walker, Social Science in Law 9 (Foundation Press 1985):

> [T]oday its contents would not be accepted as social science evidence. . . .
> [T]he brief was a collection of broad, value-laden statements supported largely by casual observation and opinion. This was typical of social science scholarship at the time. During the next several decades, however, social science became more positivistic and naturalistic, reflecting new beliefs that knowledge about people and society should be gathered "scientifically," through experimental and empirical means.

See also Rosen, The Supreme Court and Social Science 85–86 (Illinois 1972).

A more recent example of a Supreme Court decision relying on a brief by counsel for a party for empirical information relevant to a policy judgment is Bounds v. Smith, 430 U.S. 817, 830–831 (1977) ("Nearly half of the States and the District of Columbia provide some degree of professional or quasi-professional legal assistance to prisoners").

16. Davis, *supra* note 1, at 357–358; Rosen, *supra* note 15, at xi, 12–14.

The Court has even reasonably relied on circumstantial evidence outside the record for its information. For example, in Miranda v. Arizona, 384 U.S. 436

(1966), the Court assumed that actual police practices were in accordance with the recommendations in leading police manuals and texts. The Court noted:

> These texts are used by law enforcement agencies themselves as guides. It should be noted that these texts professedly present the most enlightened and effective means presently used to obtain statements through custodial interrogation. By considering these texts and other data, it is possible to describe procedures observed and noted around the country. *Id.* at 448–449; *see* Rosen, *supra* note 15, at 205–211.

17. 387 U.S. 1 (1967).

18. *Id.* at 14–27 and nn.14, 23, 24, 25, 26, 30, 31, 34, 35; *see also id.* at 74–75 and nn.3–5 (Harlan, J., concurring and dissenting).

19. *Id.* at 60 (Black, J., concurring).

20. 435 U.S. 223 (1978).

21. *Id.* at 232–239; *see also* Brown v. Louisiana, 447 U.S. 323, 332 (1980).

22. 399 U.S. 78 (1970).

23. *Id.* at 87–89.

24. *Id.* at 92–99.

25. *Id.* at 90–92.

26. *Id.* at 99–100.

27. *Id.* at 100–101: "But we find little reason to think that these goals are in any meaningful sense less likely to be achieved when the jury numbers six, than when it numbers 12—particularly if the requirement of unanimity is retained. And, certainly the reliability of the jury as a factfinder hardly seems likely to be a function of its size."

28. *Id.* at 101–102 and nn.48, 49: "What few experiments have occurred—usually in the civil area—indicate that there is no discernible difference between the results reached by the two different-sized juries. In short, neither currently available evidence nor theory suggest that the 12-man jury is necessarily more advantageous to the defendant than a jury composed of fewer members." *See also* Colegrove v. Battin, 413 U.S. 149, 158 (1973).

29. 413 U.S. 149 (1973).

30. *Id.* at 159–160 n.15.

31. *Id.* at 159 n.15.

32. Ballew v. Georgia, 435 U.S. 223, 231 (1978).

33. 435 U.S. at 232–239; *see also* Brown v. Louisiana, 447 U.S. 323, 332 (1980).

34. 435 U.S. at 239.

35. *Id.* at 246.

36. *Id.* at 232 n.10.

37. *See* Horowitz, *supra* note 1, at 279.

38. 104 S.Ct. 3405 (1984).

39. *Id.* at 3413 n.6.

40. *Id.* at 3418 n.14.

41. 347 U.S. 483, 494–495 n.11 (1954).

42. *See* Wechsler, "Toward Neutral Principles of Constitutional Law," 73 Harv. L. Rev. 1, 33 (1959); Doyle, "Can Social Science Data Be Used in Judicial Decisionmaking?" J. of Law and Ed. 13, 16–18 and n.26 (1977).

43. Schwartz, SUPER-CHIEF: EARL WARREN AND HIS SUPREME COURT—A JUDICIAL BIOGRAPHY 106–108 (NYU Press 1983); *see also* Rosen, *supra* note 15, at 164–165, 169–172; Davis, THE UNITED STATES SUPREME COURT AND THE USES OF SOCIAL SCIENCE DATA 115 (MSS Information Corp. 1973).

44. In Tennessee v. Garner, 105 S.Ct. 1694 (1985), the Supreme Court determined the constitutional limits on police use of deadly force against a fleeing suspect. In the process it relied on social science data for the proposition that "while the meaningful threat of deadly force might be thought to lead to the arrest of more live suspects by discouraging escape attempts, the presently available evidence does not support this thesis." 105 S.Ct. at 1700–1701 and n.10. In dissent, Justice O'Connor wrote for three justices: "[T]he fact that police conduct pursuant to a state statute is challenged on constitutional grounds does not impose a burden on the State to produce social science statistics or to dispel any possible doubts about the necessity of the conduct." 105 S.Ct. at 1710.

See also Evans v. Jeff D., 106 S.Ct. 1531, 1542 n.28 (1986) ("This is the experience of every judge and a majority of the members of the Third Circuit Task Force which concluded that that Circuit's ban on fee negotiations 'tends to discourage settlement in some cases and, on occasion, makes it impossible'").

In *Holbrook v. Flynn*, 106 S.Ct. 1340, 1347 n.4 (1986), the Court recently said:

> The only social science study to which respondent has pointed us addresses the effects of prison clothes and courtroom guards upon jury verdicts. Its tentative conclusion is that defendants clad in prison garb or accompanied by guards are more likely to be found guilty than unsupervised defendants wearing their own clothes. However, the study also found that favored treatment was accorded defendants who had *both* supervision *and* prison clothing. Fontaine & Kiger, The Effects of Defendant Dress and Supervision on Judgments of Simulated Jurors: An Exploratory Study, 2 Law and Human Behavior 63, 69–70 (1978). In view of these curious and concededly tentative results, we will, at least for now, rely on our own experience and common sense.

And in *Shea v. Louisiana*, 105 S.Ct. 1065, 1070–1071 (1985), the Court observed: "[I]t is said that the application of *Edwards* to cases pending on direct review will result in the nullification of many convictions and will relegate prosecutors to the difficult position of having to retry cases concerning events that took place years ago. We think this concern is overstated. We are given no empirical evidence in its support . . . ." *See also* Ponte v. Real, 105 S.Ct. 2192, 2209 n.21 (1985) (Marshall, J., dissenting).

45. Cardozo, "The Bench and the Bar," 34 N.Y.S. B.J. 444, 454 (1962). *See also* Adams v. Tanner, 244 U.S. 500, 600 (1917) (Brandeis, J., dissenting) ("Whether a measure relating to the public welfare is arbitrary or unreasonable . . . is obviously not to be determined by assumptions or by *a priori* reasoning. The judgment should be based on a consideration of relevant facts . . .").

46. Davis, *supra* note 1, at 354.

47. Burns Baking Co. v. Bryan, 264 U.S. 504, 520 (1924) (Brandeis, J., dissenting). *See also* Chastleton Corp. v. Sinclair, 264 U.S. 543, 548 (1924) (Holmes, J.) ("[T]he court may ascertain as it sees fit any fact that is merely a ground for

laying down a rule of law"); Prentis v. Atlantic Coast Line, 211 U.S. 210, 227 (1908) (Holmes, J.) ("A judge sitting with a jury is not competent to decide issues of fact; but matters of fact that are merely premises to a rule of law he may decide. . . . As the judge is bound to declare the law he must know or discover the facts that establish the law").

48. Brennan, "Law and Social Sciences," 24 Vital Speeches 143 (1957), reprinted in Westin, ed., THE SUPREME COURT: VIEWS FROM INSIDE 143, 144, 149 (Norton 1961); *see also* Horowitz, *supra* note 1, at 19, 46.

49. 429 U.S. 190, 204 (1976).

50. Rosenblum, *supra* note 10, at 479; *see also id.* at 480: "The social sciences have the breadth, depth and sophistication today to serve as spurs to reform of outmoded or misdirected legal rules, as integrators of knowledge about the consequences of judicial actions, and as responsible informants and aides to the courts where the courts invoke norms to which their expertise is relevant."

51. 429 U.S. at 208 n.22. Davis wrote that courts "often resolve questions of fact by discovering or inventing propositions of law which answer the questions of fact." 2 Davis, *supra* note 1, at 364.

52. See Lockhart v. McCree, 106 S.Ct. 1758, 1764–1766 (1986).

An example of a use of social science data misdirected at an apparent but not true legal question outside of the constitutional realm might be the construction of a will. The basic principle for construction of a will is to give effect to the intention of the testator. 4 Page, WILLS 3–4 (Anderson 1961). If a testator omits any mention of a spouse or child in his or her will, this principle suggests that a court construing the will should seek to ascertain whether the omission was intentional or accidental. Psychology would teach that the omission was intentional. *See, e.g.,* Freud, "Introductory Lectures on Psychoanalysis," in 15 Strachey (ed.), THE STANDARD EDITION OF THE COMPLETE WORKS OF SIGMUND FREUD 21–79 (Hogarth Press 1963). Nevertheless, the law generally provides that the spouse or child should take, despite the will, perhaps unless the testator expressly writes a contrary intention into the will. *See* 2 Page, WILLS 529 (Anderson 1960); N.C. Gen. Stat. §§ 29–14, 29–30, 30–3, 31–5.5. *See also* Sussman, Cates, and Smith, THE FAMILY AND INHERITANCE (1970); Beckstrom, "Sociobiology and Intestate Wealth Transfers," 76 Nw. U. L. Rev. 216 (1981); Dunham, "The Method, Process and Frequency of Wealth Transmission at Death," 30 U. Chi. L. Rev. 241, 251–257 (1963). Fidelity to the intention of the testator as a principle of testamentary construction need not be carried so far as to upset the salutary social policy preferring to divide an estate among a spouse and all the children, in order to provide for them and perhaps also to reduce the concentration of assets. The Freudian theory will respond only to the question about the intent of the testator. The law must decide whether that is truly the determinative question. For other examples, *see* Davis, *supra* note 1, at 364–365.

53. 428 U.S. at 184.

54. *Id.* at 184–185 nn.31, 32.

55. *Id.* at 186–187; *see also* Holbrook v. Flynn, 106 S.Ct. 1340, 1347 (1986).

56. *See* Sperlich, *supra* note 12, at 283–284.

57. *See* Lockhart v. McCree, 106 S.Ct. 1758, 1762–1764 (1986).

58. Traynor, *supra* note 1, at 1108; *see also* Ballew v. Georgia, 435 U.S. 223, 232 n.10 (1978) (Blackmun, J.). *See generally* Horowitz and Willging, THE PSYCHOLOGY OF LAW 307–368 (Little, Brown 1984).

59. *See* Dix, "Appellate Review of the Decision to Impose Death," 68 Geo. L. Rev. 97, 108–109 (1979): "The opinions of Stewart, Powell and Stevens and those of White in *Gregg, Proffitt* and *Jurek* strongly suggest that even the schemes in the cases before the Court might not survive if empirical evidence indicated that their procedural devices did not, in fact, work as anticipated." *See also* Dix, "Administration of the Texas Death Penalty Statutes: Constitutional Infirmities Related to the Prediction of Dangerousness," 55 Tex. L. Rev. 1343 (1977).

60. *See* Maxwell v. Bishop, 398 F.2d 138, 142 (8th Cir. 1968) (Blackmun, J.) ("The witness conceded that some data potentially pertinent were not collected as, for example, that 'with respect to the strength of the prosecution's case' for 'we had no information of that sort that we could objectively collect'"); *see also* Prejean v. Maggio, 765 F.2d 482, 486 (5th Cir. 1985); Shaw v. Martin, 733 F.2d 304, 312–313 (4th Cir.), *cert. den.*, 105 S.Ct. 230 (1984) (criticizing the statistical validity of a study because it did not control for the quality of the evidence or the seriousness of the offense).

61. No other study has attempted the task of including this essential information. Some other research has relied on selected undifferentiated items of evidence as surrogates for the overall quality of the evidence. For example:

a. Whether the defendant was arrested on the same day that the crime occurred. Clarke and Koch, "The Influence of Income and Other Factors on Whether Criminal Defendants Go to Prison," 11 Law and Soc. Rev. 57, 68–69 (1977). This study assumed that the prosecution had a strong case only if the arrest was on the same day. Recognizing the artificial nature of that standard, the authors observed: "A better perspective on the pattern of court dispositions could be obtained if there were some way to determine the likelihood that the defendant is in fact guilty, or at least the strength of the evidence for the prosecution and the defense. In the present study, the only available measure of the strength of the case is arrest promptness. . . . In future research, the authors hope to be able to measure the strength of the case for and against the defendant more sensitively." Parenthetically, the strength of the evidence is more relevant to a study of arbitrariness or discrimination than the actual guilt or innocence of the accused. That is the information that the decision makers at each stage must rely on, and the quality of their decisions in the light of the information known to them is the subject of the study.

b. Whether the defendant testified and the number of co-defendants who testified against the defendant. Note, 21 Stan. L. Rev. 1297 (1969). This study also considered whether the defendant raised the insanity defense, but in evaluating the data showing that a greater percentage of those who did than those who did not got the death penalty, the study appears to have overlooked the likelihood that those whose crimes made them likely candidates for death sentences were more likely to attempt to escape that outcome by raising an insanity defense than those who committed less heinous murders. *See* Goldstein, THE INSANITY DEFENSE 167–168 (Yale 1967).

c. Number of nonpolice witnesses; whether stolen property, weapon, or other tangible evidence was recovered; the number of days between offense and arrest; whether the defendant and victim knew each other; the defendant's age; and the number of co-defendants. Forst and Brosi, "A Theoretical and Empirical Analysis of the Prosecutor," 6 J. Leg. Studies 177, 185, 186 n.14 (1977).

d. The number of charges; the number of witnesses; eyewitness identifications of the defendant; expert testimony; statement by the defendant or alleged accomplices; and the amount of physical evidence. Myers and LaFree, "Sexual Assault and Its Prosecution: A Comparison with Other Crimes," 73 J. Crim. L. and Crim. 1282, 1288–1290 (1982).

e. The number of counts, "to reflect the seriousness of the offense." Rhodes, "A Study of Sentencing in the Hennepin County and Ramsey County District Courts," 6 J. Leg. Studies 333, 337 (1977).

f. Aggravating and mitigating circumstances, considering only cases that resulted in a conviction. Baldus, Pulaski, and Woodworth, "Comparative Review of Death Sentences: An Empirical Study of the Georgia Experience," 74 J. Crim. L. & Crim. 661 (1983); Baldus, Woodworth, and Pulaski, "Monitoring and Evaluating Death Sentencing Systems: Lessons from Georgia," 18 U.C. Davis L. Rev. 1375, 1382 n.16, 1382–1383, 1391 n.30 (1985).

62. 433 U.S. 584 (1977).

63. 458 U.S. 782 (1982).

64. 433 U.S. at 593 (emphasis added).

65. *Id.* at 593–596.

66. *Id.* at 596–597.

67. *Id.* at 597.

68. 458 U.S. at 789–793.

69. *Id.* at 794–796.

70. *See* note 255 in Chapter II.

71. As a corollary to that proposition, note that *Coker* and *Enmund* did not hold that the fact that most states reject the death penalty for a particular crime means that no state may impose it for that crime. Instead, the Court in both cases held that the ultimate question of constitutionality requires the Court to bring its own judgment to bear on the issue. *Coker*, 433 U.S. at 584. Thus, a state that imposes the death penalty evenhandedly within its own jurisdiction for a category of murder that is not capital in other states could see its unique harshness sustained.

72. U.S. Const., Amend. XIV, sec. 1; *cf. Gregg*, 428 U.S. at 205: The standard for the Georgia Supreme Court's proportionality review "is whether 'juries generally throughout the state have imposed the death penalty.'"

In *Baldwin v. Alabama*, 105 S.Ct. 2727 (1985), the Supreme Court implicitly endorsed this position. The Court looked to the experience of the one state in which the death sentence under review had been reached, and held: "'The Alabama scheme, however, has not resulted in such arbitrariness." *Id.* at 2737.

In *Prejean v. Blackburn*, 743 F.2d 1091 (5th Cir. 1984), the Fifth Circuit held that the focus should be each individual judicial district: "'That one or more districts might produce juries that persistently discriminate against black defendants in violation of their sworn duty as jurors does not reflect the actions of juries impaneled in another district whose citizens return jury verdicts which cannot be so faulted." *Id.* at 1101. The Fifth Circuit made this argument as it also contended that any discrimination in the system would have to be identified with a particular case to win any relief for that case. That argument overlooks the point that what is at issue is the sufficiency of the system to safeguard defendants against such discrimination. The experience of the discriminating district would undermine the validity of the system, which would as a result be unconstitutional statewide. It could hardly be approved for most of the state but rejected only for use in the offending district. Not surprisingly, the Court later withdrew that portion of its opinion. Prejean v. Maggio, 765 F.2d 482, 486–487 (5th Cir. 1985).

73. 347 U.S. 483 (1954).

74. Gideon v. Wainwright, 372 U.S. 335 (1963) (right to counsel in all felony prosecutions); *see also* Powell v. Alabama, 287 U.S. 45 (1932) (right to counsel in capital cases); Argersinger v. Hamlin, 407 U.S. 25 (1972) (right to counsel in all cases where defendant was sentenced to jail); Scott v. Illinois, 440 U.S. 367 (1979) (no right to counsel in misdemeanor unless defendant is actually sentenced to jail or prison).

75. Duncan v. Louisiana, 391 U.S. 145 (1968); *see also* Baldwin v. New York, 399 U.S. 66 (1970) (right to jury trial applies to all offenses punishable by a possible prison term of over six months, fine of over $500, or probation of five years); Muniz v. Hoffman, 422 U.S. 454 (1975) (no right to jury trial for a labor union fined $10,000 for criminal contempt).

76. Taylor v. Louisiana, 419 U.S. 522 (1975); Apodaca v. Oregon, 406 U.S. 404 (1972).

77. Alexander v. Louisiana, 405 U.S. 625 (1972); Turner v. Fouche, 396 U.S. 346 (1970); Whiters v. Georgia, 385 U.S. 545 (1967); *see also* Castaneda v. Partida, 430 U.S. 482 (1977). The Court has recently made additional improvements in the jury selection process. Batson v. Kentucky, 106 S.Ct. 1712 (1986); Turner v. Murray, 106 S.Ct. 1683 (1986).

78. Taylor v. Louisiana, 419 U.S. 522 (1975); *see also* Duren v. Missouri, 439 U.S. 357 (1979).

79. *See* Hankerson v. North Carolina, 432 U.S. 233 (1977); Mullaney v. Wilbur, 421 U.S. 684 (1975); *cf.* Patterson v. New York, 432 U.S. 197 (1977); *see also* Sandstrom v. Montana, 442 U.S. 510 (1979).

80. In *Furman*, Chief Justice Burger, in his dissent joined by Justice Blackmun as well as Justices Powell and Rehnquist, made the same point: "[I]t is not enough to show how [the death penalty] was applied in the distant past. The statistics that have been referred to us cover periods when Negroes were systematically excluded from jury service and when racial segregation was the official policy in many States. Data of more recent vintage are essential." 408 U.S. at 390 n.12.

Justice Powell further explained, in his dissent:

> The possibility of racial bias in the trial and sentencing process has diminished in recent years. The segregation of our society in decades past, which contributed substantially to the severity of punishment for interracial crimes, is now no longer prevalent in this country. Likewise, the day is past when juries do not represent the minority group elements of the community. . . . Because standards of criminal justice have "evolved" in a manner favorable to the accused, discriminatory imposition of capital punishment is far less likely today than in the past. 408 U.S. at 450

See also Maxwell v. Bishop, 398 F.2d 138, 147 (8th Cir. 1968) (Blackmun, J.), vacated and remanded on other grounds, 398 U.S. 262 (1970); Zeisel, "Race Bias in the Administration of the Death Penalty: The Florida Experience," 95 Harv. L. Rev. 456, 457, 468 (1981).

81. U.S. Department of Justice, Bureau of Justice Statistics, CAPITAL PUNISHMENT 6–7 (1984).

82. *Cf.* Hazelwood School Dist. v. United States, 433 U.S. 299, 308 (1977). This fallacy appears more frequently in popular than in scholarly discussion. But *cf.* Furman v. Georgia, 408 U.S. 238, 364–366 (Marshall, J., concurring): "A look at the bare statistics regarding executions is enough to betray much of the discrimination. . . . Negroes were executed far more often than whites in proportion to their percentage of the population. Studies indicate that while the higher rate of execution among Negroes is partially due to a higher rate of crime, there is evidence of racial discrimination"; Black, CAPITAL PUNISHMENT: THE INEVITABILITY OF CAPRICE AND MISTAKE 94 (2d ed. Norton 1981); Dike, "Capital Punishment in the United States, Part II: Empirical Data," 13 Crim. J. Abstracts 426, 440, 444, 447 (1981); Foley and Powell, "The Discretion of Prosecutors, Judges, and Juries in Capital Cases," 7 Crim. J. Rev. 16, 16 (1982); Radelet and Pierce, "Race and Prosecutorial Discretion in Homicide Cases," 19 Law and Soc. Rev. 587, 588–589 (1985); Riedel, "Discrimination in the Imposition of the Death Penalty: A Comparison of the Characteristics of Offenders Sentenced Pre-*Furman* and Post-*Furman*," 49 Temp. L. Q. 261, 270–283 (1976); ACLU Policy #236, "Capital Punishment" (ACLU Board Minutes, October 2–3, 1976):

> The existence of the death penalty for crimes results in discrimination against the poor, the uneducated, and members of minority communities. Its imposition as the result of racial bias is easily demonstrated by the statistics on executions from 1930 to the present.*
>
> *Of the 3,589 persons executed for all crimes since 1930, 54.6% have been black or members of other racial minority groups. Of the 455 executed for rape alone, 89.5% have been non-white. As census data clearly reveal, blacks in American society have consistently represented approximately 10% of the United States population. (Source: Bureau of Prisons, National Prisoner Statistics, Bulletin No. 45, *Capital Punishment 1930–68*, August 1969). Of the 392 persons on death row on August 1, 1977, 50.8% were non-white, continuing the classic pattern of racially discriminatory imposition of the death penalty. (Source: Death-row Census, August 1, 1977, National Coalition Against the Death Penalty).

83. *Cf.* State v. Jarrette, 284 N.C. 625, 661, 202 S.E.2d 744–745 (1974); Ely, DEMOCRACY AND DISTRUST 258–259 n.109 (Harvard 1980); Note, 87 Harv. L. Rev. 1690, 1694 n.23 (1974); *see also* Furman v. Georgia, 408 U.S. at 365 n.154 (Marshall, J.) (in arguing that the death penalty discriminates against men, acknowledging that the disparity should be measured against the number of men who kill rather than the general population).

84. *See* Klepper, Nagin, and Tierney, "Discrimination in the Criminal Justice System: A Critical Appraisal of the Literature," in Bernstein, Cohen, Martin, and Torny, eds., RESEARCH ON SENTENCING: THE SEARCH FOR REFORM, vol. II (National Academic Press 1983); Berk, "An Introduction to Sample Selection Bias in Sociological Data," 48 Am. Soc. Rev. 386 (1983); Gross and Mauro, "Patterns of Death: An Analysis of Racial Disparities in Capital Sentencing and Homicide Vic-

timization," 37 Stan. L. Rev. 27, 46–48 (1984); Thompson and Zingraff, "Detecting Sentencing Disparity: Some Problems and Evidence," 86 Am. J. Soc. 869, 873 n.6 (1981); Zeisel, *supra* note 80, at 459 n.19 (1981) ("arrests are the relevant statistic to consider here, because . . . the decision whether or not to impose the death penalty may be made at many different points prior to trial or conviction").

85. *See also* Horowitz, *supra* note 1, at 46, 97, 268 ("What is true in the individual case may be false in the generality of cases, and vice versa").

86. This problem has been noted by several researchers. Professor John Hagan, after reviewing critically sentencing research in general explained the importance of a longitudinal approach: "What is required is longitudinal data, based on observation of the defendants' experience in transit through the criminal justice system." With reference to capital cases, Bowers, EXECUTIONS IN AMERICA 105 (Heath 1974), observed: "To have a full view of the extent of discrimination in capital punishment, it would be important to examine and compare those who moved on and those who moved out at each stage of the legal process leading to execution." In addition, two reports have pointed out that "differences between offenses of capital offenders probably function to the greatest extent before sentencing . . . ." Johnson, "Selective Factors in Capital Punishment," 36 Soc. Forces 165 (1957); Wolfgang, Kelly, and Nolde, "Comparison of the Executed and Commuted among Admissions to Death Row," 53 J. Crim. L., Crim. and P. S. 301, 311 (1962); *see also* Wolfgang and Riedel, "Race, Judicial Discretion and the Death Penalty," 407 Annals of the Am. Acad. of Pol. and Soc. Sci. 119, 133 (1973); Chiricos and Waido, "Socioeconomic Status and Criminal Sentencing: An Empirical Assessment of a Conflict Proposition," 40 Am. Soc. Rev. 753, 756 (1975).

87. *Furman*, 408 U.S. at 364–366 and n.152 (Marshall, J., concurring); Bowers and Pierce, "Arbitrariness and Discrimination Under Post-*Furman* Capital Statutes," 26 Crime and Delinq. 563, 575–586, 593 (1980); Dike, CAPITAL PUNISHMENT IN THE UNITED STATES: A CONSIDERATION OF THE EVIDENCE 45–48 (National Council on Crime and Delinquency 1982); Dike, *supra* note 82, at 441–444; Gross and Mauro, *supra* note 84, at 38–42; Kleck, "Racial Discrimination in Criminal Sentencing: A Critical Review of the Evidence with Additional Evidence on the Death Penalty," 46 Am. Soc. Rev. 783, 786–788 (1981).

Many of the pre-*Furman* studies include offenses other than murder, particularly rape. A study of the punishment imposed on defendants convicted of rape in 25 sample counties in Georgia between 1945 and 1965 produced a strong showing that black defendants in cases with white victims were the most likely to be sentenced to death. Wolfgang and Riedel, "Rape, Race, and the Death Penalty in Georgia," 45 Am. J. Orthopsychiatry 658, 666–667 (1975); Wolfgang and Riedel, *supra* note 86, at 126–133.

88. *See* Pulley v. Harris, 104 S.Ct. 871, 887–888 (1984) (Marshall, J., dissenting).

89. Streib, "Executions under the Post-*Furman* Capital Punishment Statutes: The Halting Progression from 'Let's Do It' to 'Hey, There Ain't No Point in Pulling so Tight,'" 15 Rutgers L. J. 443 (1984).

90. *Id.* at 475–478.

91. *Id.* at 485–486.

92. Dix, "Appellate Review of the Decision to Impose Death," *supra* note 59.

93. *Id.* at 159.

94. Rosen, "The 'Especially Heinous' Aggravating Circumstance in Capital Cases—The Standardless Standard," 64 N.C.L. Rev. 941 (1986).

In Prejean v. Blackburn, 743 F.2d 1091 (5th Cir. 1984), *modified sub nom.* Prejean v. Maggio, 765 F.2d 482 (5th Cir. 1985), the Court—in the course of upholding a death sentence based on a more specific aggravating circumstance—observed of Louisiana's "especially heinous, atrocious, or cruel manner" aggravating circumstance: "Offenses within this category of aggravating circumstances are subject to an individual's or group's subjective intents and biases, including racial prejudice." 743 F.2d at 1102. The modified opinion withdrew the portion of the original opinion with that statement.

95. 64 N.C.L. Rev. at 945.

96. Radelet and Vandiver, "The Florida Supreme Court and Death Penalty Appeals," 74 J. Crim. L. and Crim. 913 (1983).

97. *Id.* at 919–921.

98. *Id.* at 921–922.

99. Baldus, Pulaski, and Woodworth, *supra* note 61.

100. *Id.* at 728.

101. *Id.* at 681–683, 703; *see also* Baldus, Pulaski, Woodworth, and Kyle, "Identifying Comparatively Excessive Sentences of Death: A Quantitative Approach," 33 Stan. L. Rev. 1, 22–48 (1980).

102. 74 J. Crim. L. and Crim. at 728.

103. *Id.* at 714–715, 728.

104. *Id.* at 715, 728.

105. Baldus, Pulaski, and Woodworth have not yet issued a final report on their studies. They have discussed them in Baldus, Woodworth, and Pulaski, *supra* note 61; Baldus, Pulaski, and Woodworth, "The Differential Treatment of White and Black Victim Homicide Cases in Georgia's Capital Charging and Sentencing Process: Preliminary Findings" (June 1982); Baldus, Pulaski, and Woodworth, *supra* note 61. In addition, their preliminary findings were discussed in McCleskey v. Zant, 580 F.Supp. 338, 353–370 (N.D. Ga. 1984), *affirmed sub nom.* McCleskey v. Kemp, 753 F.2d 877, 887–897 (11th Cir. 1985); *see also* Gross, "Race and Death: The Judicial Evaluation of Evidence of Discrimination in Capital Sentencing," 18 U. C. Davis L. Rev. 1275, 1289–1313 (1985).

106. 74 J. Crim. L. and Crim. at 680 n.81.

107. 18 U.C. Davis L. Rev. at 1382 n.16, 1383 n.19.

108. Barnett, "Some Distribution Patterns for the Georgia Death Sentence," 18 U. C. Davis L. Rev. 1327 (1985).

109. *Id.* at 1363.

110. *Id.* at 1351, 1362.

111. Bowers, LEGAL HOMICIDE 193–269 (Northeastern 1984); Bowers and Pierce, *supra* note 87.

112. *Id.* at 598–600.

113. *Id.* at 603–604.

114. Bowers, *supra* note 111, at 337–375; Bowers, "The Pervasiveness of Arbitrariness and Discrimination Under Post-*Furman* Capital Statutes," 74 J. Crim. L. and Crim. 1067 (1983).

115. *Id.* at 1079 n.22, 1083.

116. *Id.* at 1084–1085.

117. *Id.*

118. Zeisel, *supra* note 80.

119. *Id.* at 458–459 nn.18, 20.

120. *Id.* at 459–460.

121. Radelet, "Racial Characteristics and the Imposition of the Death Penalty," 46 Am. Soc. Rev. 918 (1981).

122. *Id.* at 920.

123. *Id.* at 922, 924, 925–926.

124. Bentele, "The Death Penalty in Georgia: Still Arbitrary," 62 Wash. U.L.Q. 573 (1985).

125. *Id.* at 589–591.

126. *Id.* at 585–588.

127. Foley and Powell, *supra* note 82.

128. *Id.* at 17–18.

129. *Id.* at 17.

130. *Id.* at 21.

131. Arkin, "Discrimination and Arbitrariness in Capital Punishment: An Analysis of Post-*Furman* Murder Cases in Dade County, Florida, 1973–1976," 33 Stan. L. Rev. 75 (1980).

132. *Id.* at 86 n.85.

133. *Id.* at 98–100.

134. *Id.* at 85–89.

135. Radelet, "Rejecting the Jury: The Imposition of the Death Penalty in Florida," 18 U. C. Davis L. Rev. 1409 (1985).

136. *Id.* at 1412.

137. *See also* Riedel, *supra* note 82, at 285–286 (tables 7 and 10).

138. Gross and Mauro, *supra* note 84.

139. *Id.* at 49–50.

140. *Id.* at 49–50, 53.

141. *Id.* at 56–65, 75–83, 93–96, 134–136.

142. *Id.* at 87–92.

143. Bowers, "The Pervasiveness of Arbitrariness and Discrimination Under Post-*Furman* Capital Statutes," *supra* note 114, at 1080.

144. *Id.*

145. *Id.*

146. *Id.*

147. 26 Crime and Delinq. at 612–614; *see also* Bowers, *supra* note 114, at 341 n.1.

148. Radelet and Pierce, *supra* note 82.

149. *Id.* at 615.

150. Paternoster, "Prosecutorial Discretion in Requesting the Death Penalty: A Case of Victim-Based Racial Discrimination," 18 Law and Soc. Rev. 437 (1984); Paternoster, "Race of Victim and Location of Crime: The Decision to Seek the Death Penalty in South Carolina," 74 J. Crim. L. and Crim. 754 (1983); *see also* Jacoby and Paternoster, "Sentencing Disparity and Jury Packing: Further Challenges to the Death Penalty," 73 J. Crim. L. and Crim. 379 (1982).

151. 18 Law and Soc. Rev. at 449–454, 469; 74 J. Crim. L. and Crim. at 768, 770–774, 776–778.

152. 74 J. Crim. L. and Crim. at 780–783.

153. 18 Law and Soc. Rev. at 476.

154. 46 Am. Soc. Rev. at 921–923.

155. According to the North Carolina Department of Correction, in 1974, 47 people were sentenced to death: 34 for murder, 11 for rape, 1 for burglary, and 1 for arson; in 1975, 51 people were sentenced to death: 46 for murder and 5 for rape.

156. *See* Exum, "The Death Penalty in America," 8 Campbell L. Rev. 1, 6–7 (1985):

How has the statute been working in North Carolina? To date [March 1, 1986], one hundred nineteen cases in which the jury determined whether to impose death or life imprisonment have been tried under the new death penalty statute and reviewed by our [North Carolina Supreme] court. Of these one hundred nineteen, juries recommended death in forty-eight. In these forty-eight, the court has affirmed the death sentence in twenty-three. Four were given new trials on the issue of guilt. Fourteen were given new sentencing hearings for error in the sentencing phase of the case. Three were reduced to life imprisonment because of the insufficiency of the evidence to support any aggravating circumstances. Four were reduced to life because the court concluded that death was excessive and disproportionate in the particular case at bar. And one was reduced to life because the court concluded that the evidence would not support a first degree murder conviction, but would support only a conviction for accessory before the fact to murder for which the maximum penalty was life.

No accurate figures are presently available on whether the fourteen cases that were remanded for new sentencing hearings or for new trials ultimately concluded with a death sentence or life imprisonment. According to some unofficial information which I have received from the clerk's offices throughout the state, I think it's fairly accurate to say that only two or three of these cases resulted in death sentences on remand. Most resulted in life imprisonment.

The thirty-one cases in which the jury recommended death and which were finally disposed of on appeal come from twenty-two different counties in the state. Cabarrus County has three, while Edgecombe, Gaston, Mecklenburg, New Hanover, Robeson, Surry, and Union have two each. The other counties represented have only one. Of these cases, thirty defendants were men, only one was a woman. Seventeen defendants were white, one was an Indian, thirteen were black. Sixteen were over thirty years old, and fifteen were under thirty; the youngest was nineteen. Only two people have been executed in North Carolina. Both were white. One was a man, Robert Hutchins; the other, Thelma Barfield, a woman.

157. *See* Black, *supra* note 82, at 66; Patrick, "Capital Punishment and Life Imprisonment in North Carolina, 1946 to 1968; Implications for Abolition of the Death Penalty," 6 Wake Forest L. Rev. 417, 418 (1970).

158. U.S. Department of Justice, Federal Bureau of Investigation, UNIFORM CRIME REPORTS 1977 at 10 (1978) (1977 arrest rate for murder: 54% nonwhite, 46% white); U.S. Department of Justice, Federal Bureau of Investigation, UNIFORM CRIME REPORTS 1978 at 13 (1979) (1978 arrest rate for murder: 53% nonwhite, 47% white). Blumstein, "On the Racial Disproportionality of United States' Prison Populations," 73 J. Crim. L. & C. 1259, 1266 (1982), found that 59% of the arrests for murder and attempted murder nationwide in 1974 were of black defendants.

159. U.S. Department of Justice, Federal Bureau of Investigation, UNIFORM CRIME REPORTS 1977 at 12 (1978); U.S. Department of Justice, Federal Bureau of Investigation, UNIFORM CRIME REPORTS 1978 at 9 (1979).

160. Some dismissals technically were entered by a district court judge as a result of a finding at a probable cause hearing that the prosecution had not presented a sufficient case to hold the defendant for further proceedings. That judicial dismissal did not, however, preclude the prosecutor from presenting the case to a grand jury to revive it. N.C. Gen. Stat. § 15–612(b) (1983). If the prosecutor nevertheless acquiesced in the dismissal by not attempting to take the case to a grand jury, it is fair to attribute the dismissal action itself to the prosecutor. Thus, no distinction between dismissals was drawn on this basis.

161. *See* N.C.G.S. § 15A–623(a): "The finding of an indictment . . . requires the concurrence of at least 12 members of the grand jury"; § 15A–624(a): "The grand jury is the exclusive judge of the facts with respect to any matter before it."

162. *See* United States v. Dionisio, 410 U.S. 1, 17 (1973) ("The grand jury may not always serve its historical role as a protective bulwark standing solidly between the ordinary citizen and an overzealous prosecutor . . ."); *id.* at 23 (Douglas, J., dissenting) ("It is, indeed, common knowledge that the grand jury, having been conceived as a bulwark between the citizen and the Government, is now a tool of the Executive"). *See also* Frankel and Naftalis, THE GRAND JURY 21–22 (Hill & Wang 1977):

> The show is run by the prosecutors. . . . The prosecutors decide what is to be investigated, who will be brought before the grand jurors, and—practically and generally speaking—who should be indicted and for what. . . . Day in and day out, the grand jury affirms what the prosecutor calls upon it to affirm—investigating as it is led, ignoring what it is never advised to notice, failing to indict or indicting as the prosecutor "submits" that it should. Not surprisingly, the somewhat technical, somewhat complex, occasionally arcane language of indictments is drafted by the prosecutor and handed to the grand jury foreman or forelady for the signature which is almost invariably affixed. It could not more than rarely be otherwise.

163. N.C.G.S. § 15A–627.
164. N.C.G.S. § 15A–626.

> (a) Except as provided in this section, no person has a right to call a witness or appear as a witness in a grand jury proceeding. (b) In proceedings upon bills of indictment submitted by the prosecutor to the grand jury, the clerk must call as witnesses the persons whose names are listed on the bills by the prosecutor. If the grand jury desires to hear any witness not named on the bill under consideration, it must through its foreman request the prosecutor

to call the witness. The prosecutor in his discretion may call, or refuse to call, the witness.

165. N.C.G.S. § 15A–644(a)(4). The statute specifies that omission of the prosecutor's signature is not a fatal defect.

166. N.C.G.S. § 15A–644(a)(5).

167. *See* Silberman, CRIMINAL VIOLENCE, CRIMINAL JUSTICE 218 (Random House 1978); U.S. Department of Justice, Federal Bureau of Investigation, Uniform Crime Reports, CRIME IN THE UNITED STATES 1983 at 11, 159–160 (1984).

168. N.C.G.S. § 130A–383.

169. N.C.G.S. § 130A–385(a).

170. *Id.*

171. *Id.*

172. Because the purpose of the study was to examine the judicial process for potentially capital cases, no effort was made to review the medical examiner's certification process.

173. N.C.G.S. § 20–141.4 establishes the offenses of felony and misdemeanor death by vehicle. Both are defined as unintentionally causing the death of another person while engaged in the violation of a motor vehicle driving violation, if that violation is the proximate cause of death. The offense is a felony if the motor vehicle violation was driving under the influence of an impairing substance or with an alcohol concentration of 0.10 or more; otherwise, it is a misdemeanor.

174. N.C.G.S. § 7A–608 provides that persons over age 14 charged with a capital offense shall be tried as adults, and that persons under age 14 may be processed only in the juvenile courts.

175. Clark and Kurtz, "The Importance of Interim Decisions to Felony Trial Court Dispositions," 74 J. Crim. L. and Crim. 476 (1983), in an analysis of felony cases in North Carolina, found mixed results of the effects of retained versus appointed counsel on felony case dispositions. No effect was found for severity of sentence for violent felonies. *Id.* at 507.

176. N.C. Const., Art. I, § 22.

177. N.C.G.S. § 15–144.

178. *Id.*; State v. King, 311 N.C. 603, 608 and n.1, 320 S.E.2d 1, 5 and n.1 (1984).

179. *Id.*

180. *See* State v. Britt, 285 N.C. 256, 262–263, 204 S.E.2d 817, 822 (1974); *see generally* Geimer, "The Law of Homicide in North Carolina: Brand New Cart Before Tired Old Horse," 19 Wake Forest L. Rev. 331 (1983).

181. *See* State v. Goodman, 298 N.C. 1, 12–13, 257 S.E.2d 116 (1979).

182. State v. Norris, 303 N.C. 526, 529–530, 279 S.E.2d 570, 572–573 (1981).

183. N.C.G.S. § 15A–2000(a)(1).

184. N.C.G.S. § 15A–2000(a)(2).

185. N.C.G.S. § 15A–2000(b).

186. *Id.*

187. As discussed, the "recommendation" of the jury is decisive.

188. Subsection (e) provides:

Aggravating circumstances which may be considered shall be limited to the following:

(1) The capital felony was committed by a person lawfully incarcerated.

(2) The defendant had been previously convicted of another capital felony.

(3) The defendant had been previously convicted of a felony involving the use or threat of violence to the person.

(4) The capital felony was committed for the purpose of avoiding or preventing a lawful arrest or effecting an escape from custody.

(5) The capital felony was committed while the defendant was engaged, or was an aider or abettor, in the commission of, or an attempt to commit, or flight after committing or attempting to commit, any homicide, robbery, rape or a sex offense, arson, burglary, kidnapping, or aircraft piracy or the unlawful throwing, placing, or discharge of a destructive device or bomb.

(6) The capital felony was committed for pecuniary gain.

(7) The capital felony was committed to disrupt or hinder the lawful exercise of any governmental function or the enforcement of laws.

(8) The capital felony was committed against a law-enforcement officer, employee of the Department of Correction, jailer, fireman, judge or justice, former judge or justice, prosecutor or former prosecutor, juror or former juror, or witness or former witness against the defendant, while engaged in the performance of his official duties or because of the exercise of his official duty.

(9) The capital felony was especially heinous, atrocious, or cruel.

(10) The defendant knowingly created a great risk of death to more than one person by means of a weapon or device which would normally be hazardous to the lives of more than one person.

(11) The murder for which the defendant stands convicted was part of a course of conduct in which the defendant engaged and which included the commission by the defendant of other crimes of violence against another person or persons.

The only aggravating circumstances on which the state may rely are those enumerated in that statute. State v. Brown, 306 N.C. 151, 183, 293 S.E.2d 569, 589 (1982).

189. Subsection (f) provides:

Mitigating circumstances which may be considered shall include, but not be limited to, the following:

(1) The defendant has no significant history of prior criminal activity.

(2) The capital felony was committed while the defendant was under the influence of mental or emotional disturbance.

(3) The victim was a voluntary participant in the defendant's homicidal conduct or consented to the homicidal act.

(4) The defendant was an accomplice in or accessory to the capital felony committed by another person and his participation was relatively minor.

(5) The defendant acted under duress or under the domination of another person.

(6) The capacity of the defendant to appreciate the criminality of his

conduct or to conform his conduct to the requirements of law was impaired.

(7) The age of the defendant at the time of the crime.

(8) The defendant aided in the apprehension of another capital felon or testified truthfully on behalf of the prosecution in another prosecution of a felony.

(9) Any other circumstance arising from the evidence which the jury deems to have mitigating value.

190. N.C.G.S. § 15A–2000(b).

See Exum, *supra* note 156, at 7–8:

Certain patterns seem to be developing in the way juries are deciding whether to impose capital punishment. Of the aggravating factors specified in the death penalty statute, the most important ones seem to be: first, whether the murder "was especially heinous, atrocious, or cruel;" second, whether the murder was "committed for the purpose of avoiding or preventing a lawful arrest," i.e. the witness elimination kind of murder; third, whether the murder was "part of a course of conduct . . . which included the commission by the defendant of other crimes of violence against another person or persons;" and fourth, whether the defendant had been convicted of prior crimes of violence against persons. Of the death verdicts reviewed by the court, almost all involve one or more of these aggravating factors. . . .

Of the mitigating circumstances enumerated in the statute, the most important seem to be whether the murder "was committed while the defendant was under the influence of mental or emotional disturbance," and whether "[t]he capacity of the defendant to appreciate the criminality of his conduct or to conform his conduct to the requirements of law was impaired." Of the death verdicts reviewed by the court, rarely have juries recommended death where one or more of these mitigating factors were present, and in only one case has the jury recommended death where both were present.

191. *See* note 423 in Chapter II.

192. The coding was performed on the part of the data collection instrument reproduced in Appendix A. The instrument itself demonstrates the process and the strategy, so a review of it is recommended for an understanding of how the quantitative measure is obtained. The explanation in the text is designed to supplement that review.

193. The cases did not raise any causation issues. Insanity was not raised as a defense with sufficient frequency or seriousness to merit a separate classification.

194. The act element for homicide liability includes planning or facilitation of the commission of the crime by another as well as the direct infliction of the fatal injury. The study year produced no cases in which the defendant was accused of involvement only before the actual commission of the crime. In all cases, therefore, the prosecution theory placed the defendant at the scene of the crime. The defendants who denied any role in the crime, then, either denied that they were present, by contesting the prosecution's evidence or by presenting alibi

evidence, or claimed that they were innocently present. The study regarded evidence of the defendant's mere presence at the crime as neutral until it was accompanied by some incriminating aspect, such as where the location was an unlikely place for an innocent person, where the defendant was with the victim shortly before the victim's death or disappearance, or where the evidence contradicted the defendant's claim that he or she was not at the site or was elsewhere at the time. A defendant might be identified as the perpetrator by evidence linking the defendant to others whose involvement was independently established. This kind of evidence did not appear in the cases in the study.

The most frequent kinds of evidence on the issue of identity were eyewitness testimony of the killing or of the defendant's suspicious presence at the scene or with the victim, confessions, evidence of motive, preparations, prior similar crimes, and subsequent concealment. The study prepared an extensive classification of scientific evidence, including body traces (fingerprints, blood, hair), physical traces (footprints, possession of objects, receipt of injuries), and weapons and ballistic evidence, but did not have much chance to use it.

The impeachment categories for eyewitness identification included the following factors: the opportunity to view, and limits on the observation (for example, based on voice or walk only), the accuracy or inaccuracy of the description, the relationship of the witness to the defendant or the victim, the suggestiveness of the identification procedure, whether the witness identified somebody else or failed to identify the defendant in any identification procedure, or made any other statements inconsistent with the identification, and the use of alcohol or drugs by the witness.

195. Of course, cases involving claims of self-defense raised the question of "imperfect self-defense" if the defendant's belief of imminent danger was unreasonable, if the defendant was the aggressor, or if the defendant used excessive force. *See* State v. Norris, 303 N.C. 526, 530, 279 S.E.2d 570, 573 (1981).

196. A defendant's claim that he or she acted in self-defense or in defense of others raised the following questions: (*a*) whether the defendant was the aggressor at the time that the defendant used the deadly force; (*b*) whether the victim threatened the defendant; (*c*) whether the threat involved the danger of death or serious bodily injury; (*d*) whether the threat had been interrupted by an adequate "cooling-off period"; and (*e*) whether the use of deadly force was a necessary response, or whether the defendant had available a less violent means of protection. State v. Deck, 285 N.C. 209, 214, 203 S.E.2d 830, 834 (1974); State v. Jones, 56 N.C. App. 259, 289 S.E.2d 383, *appeal dism'd*, 305 N.C. 762, 292 S.E.2d 578 (1982). If there was in fact no threat of imminent death or serious bodily injury, or the use of deadly force was not in fact necessary, there were the further questions whether the defendant nevertheless reasonably believed that a serious threat existed or that deadly force was necessary, in which case the defense of self-defense was the same as if the circumstances were as the defendant reasonably believed them to be. *See* State v. Deck, *supra*. The study took each of these into account, but assigned them different weight in the quantitative coding as discussed below. Often, the facts regarding the self-defense issue were unclear, the testimony of the witnesses ambiguous. As a result, the decision whether to classify a witness in a case that did not go to trial as a prosecution or defense

witness was often difficult. This problem of witness alignment was resolved in the quantitative coding scheme by limiting the numerical consequences of the decision.

The relevant facts in a self-defense case include not only the events directly associated with the homicidal occurrence but also such circumstantial evidence as planning activity, motive, character, and previous threats or assaults. Some scientific evidence might support or rebut aspects of a self-defense claim, such as evidence of whether the victim had a weapon and the number or angle of the shots. All these items were accounted for in the study.

197. N.C.G.S. § 15A–2000(e); State v. Brown, 306 N.C. 151, 183, 293 S.E.2d 569, 589 (1982).

198. N.C.G.S. § 15A–2000(e)(10) and (11). *See* note 188, *supra*.

199. All analyses are performed using the PROC LOGIST program found in SAS Institute, Inc., SUGI SUPPLEMENTAL LIBRARY USER'S GUIDE (SAS 1983 ed.).

The use of multiple regression analysis in a legal context has been discussed in Fisher, "Multiple Regression in Legal Proceedings," 80 Col. L. Rev. 702 (1980); Baldus and Cole, STATISTICAL PROOF OF DISCRIMINATION (Shepard's 1980); Barnes, STATISTICS AS PROOF (Little, Brown 1983); Barnes and Conley, *supra* note 11; Channels, SOCIAL SCIENCE METHODS IN THE LEGAL PROCESS (Rowman & Allanheld 1985); Vinson and Anthony, SOCIAL SCIENCE RESEARCH METHODS FOR LITIGATION (Michie 1985).

200. *See* Cox, ANALYSIS OF BINARY DATA (Methuen 1970); Theil, "On the Estimation of Relationships Involving Qualitative Variables." 76 Am. J. of Sociology 103–154 (1970).

201. For statistical reasons, the total number of variables and interactions of variables in a logistic regression analysis should be considerably less than the number of cases. The more variables in relation to the data, the less stable is the estimation; hence, significance (.05 or better) can be less apparent.

Furthermore, the greater the number of questions asked in any statistical analysis, the greater the likelihood that one may yield results that appear significant, although actually due to chance. To say that a result is significant at the .05 level means that if enough questions are asked, the result will occur by chance 5% of the time. For this reason, the greater the number of variables, relative to the amount of data included in an analysis, the more cautious the interpretation must be.

202. In order to meet technical assumptions about the minimum number of cases in each variable category that is necessary to produce reasonable estimates of variable effects, the 30 districts were arranged into 10 categories as follows: (*a*) Each judicial district that had at least 10 defendant–victim units and took at least 3 of them to trial was considered as a separate district. There were 8 such districts, hence 8 categories. (*b*) The ninth category, called Judicial District Group A, consisted of a combination of 1 district that had only 8 cases but took 3 of them to trial and all districts that took 2 cases to trial regardless of the total number of cases in the district. (*c*) The tenth category, called Judicial District Group B, consisted of all districts that took 1 or zero cases to trial regardless of the total number of cases in the district.

For the trial stages, the total number of cases had been reduced so low that the study performed the supplemental analyses after eliminating the judicial district factor altogether.

203. This is recommended by the customary statistical principle of parsimony.

204. Excepting only multiple victims, which involved very few defendants.

205. Even more complicated interactions among these variables could plausibly be included in a model, but this was not possible because of the necessary limitations imposed by statistical assumptions on the number of variables that could be included.

206. The basic formula for predicting the odds of an outcome for a particular group from the estimated coefficients of a model is

$$\text{Predicted Odds} = e^{(b_0 + b_1 x_1 + b_2 x_2 + \ldots b_n x_n)}$$

where e is the base for the natural logarithm (2.718); the b_i's are the coefficient estimates; and the x_i's are the values of various variables for that group. Assuming that the prediction model is accurate for the data, the magnitude of the effect of any value of a variable or combination of values of several variables may be expressed as a multiplier of the odds of the event happening. The reason for this is that the prediction equation algebraically represents the addition of logarithms which is numerically equivalent to the multiplication of numbers. Therefore, the odds multiplier for the effect of one variable at a given value is simply the value 2.718 raised to the power of the product of its value and its coefficient estimate. The odds multiplier for the effect of a set of variables at given values is computed by adding the products of the variable values and their respective coefficients and then raising 2.718 to the power of that sum.

Chapter IV

1. District 16 had a rate of 87.5%, but the number of cases in that district was insufficient for its rate to be significant.

2. The study year included two other cases involving female defendants who were convicted of poisoning their husbands. Both of those defendants and their victims were also white. Neither of the defendants was shown to have poisoned more than one person.

In one case, the defendant was a devoutly religious church member. Her husband was a heavy drinker. The prosecution evidence showed that the defendant believed that her husband was cruel to the family. She denied responsibility for his death, but several witnesses testified that she confided to them her desire to kill her husband and asked them for help, including the purchase of ant poison. The evidence showed that the defendant administered the poison before the new death penalty statute, but that the arsenic took effect shortly after the new statute did and her husband then died.

At trial, the jury convicted the defendant. After a penalty hearing, the same jury found as an aggravating circumstance that the murder was especially heinous, atrocious, or cruel. It found only one mitigating circumstance, that the defendant had no prior criminal record. It recommended a sentence of death. On appeal, the North Carolina Supreme Court reversed the death penalty on the ground that, because the defendant committed all the murderous acts before the death penalty statute was in effect, she was not subject to sentencing under it. State v. Detter, 298 N.C. 604, 260 S.E.2d 567 (1979).

The defendant in the other case had apparently been involved in minor thefts that had caused her to lose one job as a store clerk and that had also led to a shoplifting charge. Several people described her as mean. Her husband, by contrast, was a city employee with a general good reputation. He had told several people that he was in the process of separating from the defendant.

The defendant gave the police a statement admitting that she put ant poison in her husband's coffee over several days. She said she was tired of his staying away from home and intended only to make him sick in order to keep him at home. She admitted that she had in the back of her mind that her husband had life insurance.

The prosecutor permitted the defendant to plead guilty to second degree murder, and she was sentenced to life imprisonment.

The jury in the case that resulted in an execution found that the poisoning was an especially heinous, atrocious, or cruel murder. The North Carolina Supreme Court later described this case as one in which the "defendant coldly calculated or planned the commission of this crime over a period of time." State v. Hill, 311 N.C. 465, 319 S.E.2d 163, 171 (1984). In another case, that court described the case as one in which "the motivation for the murder was to avoid detection or arrest for other crimes." State v. Maynard, 311 N.C. 1, 36 n.3, 316 S.E.2d 197, 216 n.3 (1984). Although that jury also based its decision for the death penalty on other aggravating circumstances, the jury in the second case recommended a death sentence solely on the basis that the defendant's poisoning of her husband was an especially heinous, atrocious, or cruel killing. Thus those two cases would seem to establish that juries find that prolonged poisoning satisfies the especially heinous, atrocious, or cruel aggravating circumstance.

The third case was identical with the first two in the method of the killing. Yet the prosecutor in that case allowed the defendant to plead guilty to second degree murder and thereby avoid even facing a jury and risking a death sentence. The difference in treatment between the second and third cases does not seem to have any meaningful basis. If the defendant in the second case was as deserving of the death penalty as the defendant who was executed, the defendant in the third case appears even less sympathetic. Despite the comparable quality of the killings, one prosecutor treated leniently a petty criminal who murdered an apparently solid citizen who was in the process of separating from her, while a different prosecutor and jury, by contrast, processed along the death penalty track a devoutly religious defendant who killed her alcoholic husband. *Cf.* Bentele, "The Death Penalty in Georgia: Still Arbitrary," 62 Wash. U.L.Q. 573, 585–586 (1985). This article compared two poisoning cases in Georgia, each involving a single victim. In one, a couple added arsenic to the beer of their employer. They were buying their house from him, were behind in their payments, and mistakenly believed his death would leave them clear title to it. The prosecutor sought the death penalty against the husband and not the wife, but the jury recommended a life sentence for him. In the other, a woman put rat poison in her husband's chili and beans. The prosecution presented evidence that the husband had a $15,000 life insurance policy. She denied knowledge of the policy and claimed that she acted to prevent her husband from hurting her child. The jury sentenced her to death.

Chapter V

1. The discretion that the prosecutor exercises in plea bargaining is largely a subcategory of charging discretion. Abrams, "Prosecutorial Discretion," 3 ENCY. OF CRIME AND JUSTICE 1272, 1272 (Free Press 1983).

2. "The prosecutor's decision whether and what to charge is the broadest discretionary power in criminal administration." Vorenberg, "Narrowing the Discretion of Criminal Justice Officials," 1976 Duke Law J. 651, 678; *see also* Jackson, "The Federal Prosecutor," 24 J. Am. Jud. Soc. 18, 18 (1940) ("The prosecutor has more control over life, liberty, and reputation than any other person in America. His discretion is tremendous"); Note, "Prosecutor's Discretion," 103 U. Pa. L. Rev. 1057, 1057 (1955) ("The discretionary power exercised by the prosecuting attorney in initiation, accusation, and discontinuance of prosecution gives him more control over an individual's liberty than any other public official"); Foley and Powell, "The Discretion of Prosecutors, Judges, and Juries in Capital Cases," 7 Crim. J. Rev. 16, 17 (1982); *see generally* Miller, PROSECUTION: THE DECISION TO CHARGE A SUSPECT WITH CRIME (Little, Brown 1969); Goldstein, THE PASSIVE JUDICIARY: PROSECUTORIAL DISCRETION AND THE GUILTY PLEA 3 (Louisiana State 1981); National Commission on Law Observance and Enforcement (Wickersham Commission), REPORT ON PROSECUTION 19 (1931); Newman, CONVICTION: THE DETERMINATION OF GUILT OR INNOCENCE WITHOUT TRIAL (Little, Brown 1966); President's Commission on Law Enforcement and Administration of Justice, TASK FORCE REPORT: THE COURTS 5–13, 72–78 (U.S. Gov't. Printing Office 1967); Alschuller, "The Prosecutor's Role in Plea Bargaining," 36 U. Chi. L. Rev. 50 (1968); Baker and DeLong, "The Prosecuting Attorney," 2 J. Crim. L. and Crim. 1025 (1934); Ferguson, "Formulation of Enforcement Policy: An Anatomy of the Prosecutor's Discretion Prior to Accusation," 11 Rutgers L. Rev. 507, 507 (1957); Heumann, "A Note on Plea Bargaining and Case Pressure," 9 Law and Soc. Rev. 515 (1976); LaFave, "The Prosecutor's Discretion in the United States," 18 Am. J. Comp. L. 532 (1970). Mills, "The Prosecutor: Charging and 'Bargaining,'" 1966 U. Ill. L. F. 511; Vorenberg, "Decent Restraint of Prosecutorial Power," 94 Harv. L. Rev. 1521, 1522 (1981).

3. N.C. Const., Art. IV, § 18; N.C.G.S. §§ 7A–60(a), 7A–61.

4. 408 U.S. at 309; *see also id.* at 310.

5. *Furman*, 408 U.S. at 255; *see also id.* at 253: "[W]e deal with a system of law and justice that leaves to the uncontrolled discretion of judges or juries the determination of whether defendants committing these crimes shall die or be imprisoned."

6. 408 U.S. at 311.

Chief Justice Burger recognized that "by the choice of juries—sometimes judges—the death penalty is imposed in far fewer than half the cases in which it is available," 408 U.S. at 386; *see also id.* at 388, 389, 398, but argued that "[t]he selectivity of juries in imposing the punishment of death is properly viewed as a refinement on, rather than a repudiation of, the statutory authorization for the penalty." 408 U.S. at 388. In *Gregg*, Justice Stewart agreed with this statement. 428 U.S. at 182. Justice Rehnquist, too, read the prevailing opinions to rely on "the reluctance of judges and juries actually to impose the death penalty in the majority of capital cases." 408 U.S. at 465–466.

Justice Brennan laid the blame on governors as well as juries. 408 U.S. at 299.

In Lockett v. Ohio, 438 U.S. 586 (1978), Chief Justice Burger, joined by Justices Stewart, Powell, and Stevens, explained that in *Furman* three Justices "concluded that discretionary sentencing, unguided by legislatively defined standards, violated the Eighth Amendment . . . ." 438 U.S. at 599, and that in *Gregg* the plurality "reasoned that to comply with *Furman*, sentencing procedures should not create 'a substantial risk that the death penalty [will] be inflicted in an arbitrary and capricious manner.'" 438 U.S. at 601.

7. "Under the procedures before the Court in that case [*Furman*], sentencing authorities were not directed to give attention to the nature or circumstances of the crime committed or to the character or record of the defendant. Left unguided, juries imposed the death sentence in a way that could only be called freakish." *Gregg*, 428 U.S. at 206.

In *Woodson v. North Carolina*, Justice Stewart was even more explicit: "Central to the limited holding in *Furman* was a conviction that the vesting of standardless sentencing discretion in the jury violated the Eighth and Fourteenth Amendments." *Woodson*, 428 U.S. at 302.

8. 428 U.S. at 199.

9. *Id.*

10. *Id.* at 199–200 n.50.

11. *Gregg*, 428 U.S. at 220 (White, J., concurring): "In *Furman*, this Court held that as a result of giving the sentencer unguided discretion to impose or not to impose the death penalty for murder . . ."; Roberts v. Louisiana, 428 U.S. at 346 (White, J., dissenting) (emphasis added): "It is undeniable that the unfettered discretion of the jury to save the defendant from death was *a major contributing factor* in the developments which led us to invalidate the death penalty in *Furman v. Georgia*"; *id.* at 345: In *Furman*, "the Court concluded that in practice criminal juries, exercising their lawful discretion, were imposing it so seldom and so freakishly and arbitrarily . . .;" *see also* Lockett v. Ohio, 438 U.S. 586, 622 (1978) (White, J., concurring and dissenting): "*Furman* held that as a result of permitting the sentencer to exercise unfettered discretion to impose or not to impose the death penalty for murder . . ."; Pulley v. Harris, 104 S.Ct. 871, 876 (1984) (White, J., for the Court): "In *Furman*, the Court concluded that capital punishment, as then administered under statutes resting unguided sentencing discretion in juries and trial judges, had become unconstitutionally cruel and unusual punishment."

12. 428 U.S. at 225. *See also Roberts*, 428 U.S. at 348–349; State v. Noland, 312 N.C. 1, 12–13, 320 S.E.2d 642, 649–650 (1984); State v. Jarrette, 284 N.C. 625, 202 S.E.2d 721, 741–742 (1974) ("The decision of the Solicitor as to the offense for which he will seek an indictment from the grand jury and his decision as to whether to accept . . . a plea to a lesser charge . . . are the results of an evaluation of the available evidence, including its credibility. . . . This is a human evaluation. There is often room for difference of opinion concerning it"); Kamisar, LaFave, and Israel, MODERN CRIMINAL PROCEDURE 924 (West 1980):

The prosecutor's decision not to prosecute in a given case notwithstanding adequate evidence for prosecution is often based upon his own assessment of the nature of the crime, the circumstances of its commission, and the characteristics of the offender. However, the prosecutor does not function in a vacuum, and thus a decision not to prosecute is often based upon the expectation that the judge or jury would refuse to convict notwithstanding proof of guilt beyond a reasonable doubt.

The jury in a criminal case has uncontrolled discretion to acquit the guilty. An empirical study has shown that juries acquit the guilty because: (a) they sympathize with the defendant as a person; (b) they apply personal attitudes as to when self-defense should be recognized; (c) they take into account the contributory fault of the victim; (d) they believe the offense is de minimus; (e) they take into account the fact that the statute violated is an unpopular law; (f) they feel the defendant has already been punished enough; (g) they feel the defendant was subjected to improper police or prosecution practices; (h) they refuse to apply strict liability statutes to inadvertent conduct; (i) they apply their own standards as to when mental illness or intoxication should be a defense; and (j) they believe the offense is accepted conduct in the subculture of the defendant and victim. See Kalven & Zeisel, THE AMERICAN JURY chs. 15–27 (1966).

By the same token, it should be noted, in *Woodson v. North Carolina*, Justice Stewart's plurality opinion condemned the North Carolina statute because it provided no accommodation for "relevant facets of the character and record of the individual offender or the circumstances of the particular offense," *Woodson*, 428 U.S. at 304, and did not consider whether prosecutorial discretion to screen cases from the death penalty track after consideration of such factors might save the otherwise mandatory statute. *Accord*, Roberts v. Louisiana, 428 U.S. at 334–335. Of course, the exercise of such discretion in the mandatory death penalty states had no sentencing standards to follow.

Cf. Heckler v. Chaney, 105 S.Ct. 1649, 1656 (1985):

[A]n agency decision not to enforce often involves a complicated balance of a number of factors which are peculiarly within its expertise. Thus, the agency must not only assess whether a violation had occurred, but whether agency resources are best spent on this violation or another, whether the agency is likely to succeed if it acts, whether the particular enforcement action requested best fits the agency's overall policies, and indeed whether the agency has enough resources to undertake the action at all.

13. *Roberts*, 428 U.S. at 349.

The North Carolina Supreme Court has upheld the practice of granting immunity to one defendant in exchange for his testimony against another in a capital case. State v. Maynard, 311 N.C. 1, 34, 316 S.E.2d 197, 215 (1984); State v. Williams II, 305 N.C. 656, 687, 292 S.E.2d 243, *cert. denied*, 459 U.S. 1056 (1982); State v. Irwin, 304 N.C. 93, 104, 282 S.E.2d 439, 446–447 (1981). In addition, that court has held that: "The fact that the defendant's accomplices received a lesser sentence is not an extenuating circumstance. It does not reduce the moral culpability of the killing nor make it less deserving of the penalty of death than other first-degree murders." State v. Williams II, 305 N.C. at 687, 292 S.E.2d at 261. In each case, that court pointed out that the evidence showed that the capital defendant was the more culpable participant in the killing. State v. Maynard, 311 N.C. at 6–7, 316 S.E.2d at 200–201; State v. Williams II, 305 N.C. at 661–662, 292 S.E.2d at 248; State v. Irwin, 304 N.C. at 104, 282 S.E.2d at 447; *cf.* State v. White, 68 N.C. App. 671, 675, 316 S.E.2d 112, 115 (1984) (upholding in a noncapital case disparate sentences against defendants who were tried separately in which the more culpable defendant received the shorter prison sentence [17 years versus 25 years]).

14. 459 U.S. 808 (1982).

15. *See* Williams v. State, 430 N.E.2d 759, 764 (Ind. 1982).

16. *Id.* at 764; *see also id.* at 765–766.

17. 428 U.S. at 225. Justice White also wrote: "As for executive clemency, I cannot assume that this power . . . will be used in a standardless and arbitrary manner." *Roberts,* 428 U.S. at 349.

18. 428 U.S. at 225.

19. In *Roberts,* Justice White characterized jury discretion as "a major contributing factor in the developments which led us to invalidate the death penalty in *Furman v. Georgia,*" 428 U.S. at 346, thereby recognizing a role for the other discretionary stages.

In a later opinion, Justice White wrote: "[I]t would be relevant if prosecutors rarely sought the death penalty for accomplice felony murder, for it would tend to indicate that prosecutors, who represent society's interest in punishing crime, consider the death penalty excessive for accomplice felony murder." Enmund v. Florida, 458 U.S. 782, 796 (1982). This language demonstrates that Justice White's concern extends to prosecutorial discretion. Its thesis, however, seems different from an arbitrariness or infrequency theory.

20. 428 U.S. at 199 n.50.

21. *Proffitt,* 428 U.S. at 258.

22. *Id.* at 251, 253.

23. *Id.* at 251.

24. *Jurek,* 428 U.S. at 273–276. Addressing the argument "that arbitrariness still pervades the entire criminal justice system of Texas—from the prosecutor's decision whether to charge a capital offense in the first place and then whether to engage in plea bargaining, through the jury's consideration of lesser included offenses, to the Governor's ultimate power to commute death sentences," 428 U.S. at 274, Justice Stevens simply cited the answer Justice Stewart wrote in *Gregg.* 428 U.S. at 274.

25. Wayte v. United States, 105 S.Ct. 1524, 1531 (1985); *see also* United States v. Goodwin, 457 U.S. 368, 382 (1982) ("A prosecutor should remain free before trial to exercise the broad discretion entrusted to him to determine the extent of the societal interest in prosecution"); Bordenkircher v. Hayes, 434 U.S. 357, 364 (1978) ("In our system, so long as the prosecutor has probable cause to believe that the accused committed an offense defined by statute, the decision whether or not to prosecute, and what charge to file or bring before a grand jury, generally rests entirely in his discretion"); United States v. Lovasco, 431 U.S. 783, 794 and n.15 (1977); State v. Jarrette, 284 N.C. 625, 202 S.E.2d 721, 741–743 (1974); *cf.* Cuyahoga Valley Ry. Co. v. United Transp. Union, 106 S.Ct. 286, 287–288

(1986) (holding that the Secretary of Labor has unreviewable discretion to withdraw a citation charging an employer with a safety or health violation and may do so to enter into settlement discussions); Heckler v. Chaney, 105 S.Ct. 1649, 1656 (1985): "Finally, we recognize that an agency's refusal to institute proceedings shares to some extent the characteristics of the decision of a prosecutor in the Executive Branch not to indict—a decision which has long been regarded as the special province of the Executive Branch, inasmuch as it is the executive who is charged by the Constitution to 'take care that the laws are faithfully executed.'" *But see* Batson v. Kentucky, 106 S.Ct. 1712 (1986).

Justice Marshall recently observed:

> Legal historians have suggested that the notion of prosecutorial discretion developed in England and America largely because private prosecutions were simultaneously available at the time. See Langbein, Controlling Prosecutorial Discretion in Germany, 41 U.Chi.L.Rev. 439, 443–446 (1974) . . . .
>
> In addition, scholars have noted that the tradition of unreviewability of prosecutor's decisions developed at a time when virtually all executive action was considered unreviewable. In asking what accounts for this "tradition," one scholar offered the following rhetorical questions:
>
> "Is it because the tradition became settled during the nineteenth century when courts were generally assuming that judicial intrusion into any administration would be unfortunate? Is it because the tradition became settled while the Supreme Court was actuated by its 1840 remark that 'The interference of the Courts with the performance of the ordinary duties of the executive departments of the government, would be productive of nothing but mischief.' [citing *Decatur v. Paulding*, 14 Pet. 497, 516, 10 L.Ed. 559 (1840)]. Is it because the tradition became settled before the courts made the twentieth-century discovery that the courts can interfere with executive action to protect against abuses but at the same time can avoid taking over the executive function? Is it because the tradition became settled before the successes of the modern system of *limited* judicial review became fully recognized?
>
> "On the basis of what the courts know today about leaving administration to administrators but at the same time providing an effective check to protect against abuses, should the courts not take a fresh look at the tradition that prevents them from reviewing the prosecuting function?" K. Davis, Discretionary Justice 211 (1969) (footnote omitted). Heckler v. Chaney, 105 S.Ct. 1649, 1665 n.6 (1985) (Marshall, J., dissenting).

26. Gerstein v. Pugh, 420 U.S. 103, 119 (1975).

27. *Id.* at 114, 120.

28. Wayte v. United States, 105 S.Ct. 1524, 1531 (1985).

29. Bordenkircher v. Hayes, 434 U.S. 357, 365 (1978); Blackledge v. Allison, 431 U.S. 63 (1977); Thigpen v. Roberts, 104 S.Ct. 2916 (1984); *cf.* Goodwin v. United States, 457 U.S. 368, 378–380 nn.10, 11 (1982).

30. Santobello v. New York, 404 U.S. 257, 262 (1971).

31. 106 S.Ct. 1712 (1986).

32. *Cf.* Weisberg, "Deregulating Death," 1983 Sup. Ct. Rev. 305, 305 (in 1982 the "Court essentially announced that it was going out of the business of

telling the states how to administer the death penalty phase of capital murder trials"); Geimer, "Death at Any Cost: A Critique of the Supreme Court's Recent Retreat from Its Death Penalty Standards," 12 Fla. St. U. L. Rev. 737, 760–778 (1985) (in 1983 the Supreme Court began to abandon its previous due process standards in death penalty cases); Marshall, "Remarks on the Death Penalty Made at the Judicial Conference of the Second Circuit," 86 Col. L. Rev. 1, 3 (1986) ("The Court purports to have created a host of rights that protect a capital defendant at the sentencing phase of a proceeding. But at the same time it has limited appellate and collateral review of those rights, and of the correctness of the sentencer's decision").

33. It has concentrated there on the sentencing jury or judge as the discretionary decision maker. *See* Pulley v. Harris, 104 S.Ct. 871, 876 (1984): "In *Furman*, the Court concluded that capital punishment, as then administered under statutes vesting unguided sentencing discretion in juries and trial judges, had become unconstitutionally cruel and unusual punishment"; *see also* Tichnell v. State, 297 Md. 1, 468 A.2d 1, 17 (1981). The Court has assumed that any safeguard for jury discretion would also safeguard judicial discretion in sentencing. Although it has not expressly held that a judge who makes the capital sentencing decision must be guided by the same safeguards as a jury, such a conclusion was implicit in *Proffitt*. *See* Richmond v. Arizona, 434 U.S. 1323, 1325 (1977) (Powell, Circuit Justice). The Court has given little discussion to the other discretionary officials in the process, including the prosecutor.

34. Beck v. Alabama, 447 U.S. 625 (1980); *cf.* Spaziano v. Florida, 104 S.Ct. 3154, 3160–3161 (1984).

35. Lockett v. Ohio, *supra* note 6.

36. Gardner v. Florida, 430 U.S. 349 (1977).

37. Godfrey v. Georgia, 446 U.S. 420 (1980).

38. Bullington v. Missouri, 451 U.S. 430 (1981).

39. Estelle v. Smith, 451 U.S. 454 (1981).

40. Coker v. Georgia, 433 U.S. 584 (1977).

41. Enmund v. Florida, 458 U.S. 782 (1976).

42. *Id.* at 794–795; *Coker*, 433 U.S. at 596–597.

43. *Cf.* Eddmonds v. Illinois, 105 S.Ct. 271 (1984) (denial of certiorari to review an Illinois statute providing for a penalty hearing only if the prosecutor requests one).

44. *Roberts*, 428 U.S. at 335.

45. Note, 87 *Harv. L. Rev.* 1690, 1713–1714 (1974).

46. *Cf.* Garcia v. San Antonio Metro. Transit Authority, 105 S.Ct. 1005, 1019 (1985): "[T]he fundamental limitation that the constitutional scheme imposes on the Commerce Clause to protect the 'States as States' is one of process rather than one of result."

47. *See* DeGarmo v. Texas, 106 S.Ct. 337, 338 (1985) (Brennan with Marshall, JJ., dissenting from denial of certiorari):

> When *Gregg* was decided several members of the Court expressed the belief that channeling juror discretion would minimize the risk that the death penalty "would be imposed on a capriciously selected group of offenders," thereby making it unnecessary to channel discretion at earlier

stages in the criminal justice system. . . . But discrimination and arbitrariness at an earlier point in the selection process nullify the value of later controls on the jury. The selection process for the imposition of the death penalty does not begin at trial; it begins in the prosecutor's office. His decision whether or not to seek capital punishment is no less important than the jury's. Just like the jury, then, where death is the consequence, the prosecutor's "discretion must be suitably directed and limited so as to minimize the risk of wholly arbitrary and capricious action."

See also Black, CAPITAL PUNISHMENT: THE INEVITABILITY OF CAPRICE AND MISTAKE 127 (2d ed. Norton 1981); Bentele, "The Death Penalty in Georgia: Still Arbitrary," 62 Wash. U. L. Q. 573, 611 (1985); Note, "Discretion and the Constitutionality of the New Death Penalty Statutes," 87 Harv. L. Rev. 1690, 1712–1719 (1974).

48. Batson v. Kentucky, 106 S.Ct. 1712, 1718 (1986).

49. Fowler v. North Carolina, 428 U.S. 904 (1976) (oral argument April 21, 1975).

50. In Baldwin v. Alabama, 105 S.Ct. 2727 (1985), the Court upheld a procedure formerly used in Alabama whereby a conviction of a number of specified crimes "with aggravation" automatically resulted in a formal death sentence, but the actual sentence was set by a judge after a penalty hearing. The Court found that the procedure, resulting in a formally but not actually mandatory death sentence, did not result in the kind of arbitrariness that was the concern of *Woodson* because "only 2 of the first 50 defendants tried for capital crimes during the time the 1975 Act was in effect were acquitted." 105 S.Ct. at 2737.

51. 408 U.S. at 281.

52. 408 U.S. at 389.

53. 428 U.S. at 203. Justice White wrote in *Gregg*:

Petitioner's argument that there is an unconstitutional amount of discretion in the system which separates those suspects who receive the death penalty from those who receive life imprisonment, a lesser penalty, or are acquitted or never charged, seems to be in final analysis an indictment of our entire system of justice. Petitioner has argued, in effect, that no matter how effective the death penalty may be as a punishment, government, created and run as it must be by humans, is inevitably incompetent to administer it. This cannot be accepted as a proposition of constitutional law. . . . Mistakes will be made and discriminations will occur which will be difficult to explain. 428 U.S. at 225–226.

54. 104 S.Ct. 871 (1984).

55. *Id.* at 881. It bears repeating that *Furman* did not identify any particular systemic defect or require any particular corrective procedure.

56. 428 U.S. at 189.

57. 428 U.S. at 258.

58. 456 U.S. 410 (1982).

59. *Id.* at 413 (emphasis added).

60. 408 U.S. at 398.

61. 428 U.S. at 199. *Cf.* Williams v. State, 430 N.E.2d 759, 765 (Ind. 1982), *dismissed for lack of a substantial federal question,* 459 U.S. 808 (1982) ("The fact

that defendant's two accomplices were given significantly less severe sentences as a result of plea bargains does not affect the reasonableness of defendant's own sentence. Defendant's sentence must be judged by the facts of his own case, not the facts accompanying his accomplices' cases)."

62. 428 U.S. at 222.

63. *Cf.* Ely, DEMOCRACY AND DISTRUST 177 (Harvard 1980): "[A] discretionary system of selection *always* carries the potential for invidious discrimination . . . . Such systems amount to failure of representation, in that those who make the laws (by refusing effectively to make the laws) have provided a buffer to ensure that they and theirs will not effectively be subjected to them"; Davis, DISCRETIONARY JUSTICE 170 (Louisiana State University Press 1969): "The discretionary power to be lenient is an impossibility without a concomitant discretionary power not to be lenient, and injustice from the discretionary power not to be lenient is especially frequent; the power to be lenient is the power to discriminate"; Michael and Wechsler, "A Rationale of the Law of Homicide II," 37 Colum. L. Rev. 1261, 1268 (1937): "Unbridled administrative discretion, particularly if vested in the shifting and relatively incompetent personnel of juries, thwarts the development and articulation of uniform policies, with consequent inequality of treatment"; Radin, "Proportionality, Subjectivity and Tragedy," 18 U.C. Davis L. Rev. 1165, 1170 (1985): "If the liberal rule of law cannot choose who dies with satisfactory (appearance of) equal treatment, then under the liberal rule of law no one chosen can deserve to die." *See also* Black, *supra* note 47, at 56, 104, 129; 2 LaFave and Israel, CRIMINAL PROCEDURE 167–168 (West 1984) ("The inevitable corollary of sparing some people through mere grace or favor is standardless condemnation of others. . . . Arbitrary lenience equals arbitrary harshness"); Bentele, *supra* note 47, at 611–612; Greenberg, "Against the American System of Capital Punishment," 99 Harv. L. Rev. 1670 (1986); Hubbard, "'Reasonable Levels of Arbitrariness' in Death Sentencing Patterns: A Tragic Perspective on Capital Punishment," 18 U.C. Davis L. Rev. 1113, 1127–1129 (1985); Kaplan, "Administering Capital Punishment," 36 U. Fla. L. Rev. 177, 188 (1984) ("In adjudicating who should receive the death penalty, both the procedures used and the results produced should advance our moral values. Even if capital punishment verdicts cannot be said to be wrong, they should not be arbitrary either"); Krivosha, Copple, and McDonough, "A Historical and Philosophical Look at the Death Penalty—Does It Serve Society's Needs?" 16 Creighton L. Rev. 1, 36, 40 (1982); Radin, "Cruel Punishment and Respect for Persons," 53 So. Cal. L. Rev. 1143, 1150, 1168 (1980). *Contra*, Heckler v. Chaney, 105 S.Ct. 1649, 1656 (1985): "[W]hen an agency refuses to act, it generally does not exercise its *coercive* power over an individual's liberty or property rights, and thus does not infringe upon areas that courts often are called upon to protect. Similarly, when an agency *does* act to enforce, that action itself provides a focus for judicial review . . . ."; Little, "Another View," 36 U. Fla. L. Rev. 200, 202, 204 (1984) ("If the death penalty is not immoral per se, it is not immoral to execute a man deserving of death merely because others deserving of death are not executed"); Van den Haag, "Comment on John Kaplan's 'Administering Capital Punishment,'" 36 U. Fla. L. Rev. 193, 194–195, 198–199 (1984) ("We succeed in punishing as deserved only some of the guilty. Is it an excuse in law, or morality, for the guilty who have been sentenced, to point out that others have escaped their deserved punishment, totally or in part? If we accepted such an excuse nobody ever could be punished."

"[T]he law can make it likely that mainly those convicted murderers who are regarded as among the worst by local courts will be executed. This satisfies me"); Van den Haag, "The Death Penalty Once More," 18 U.C. Davis L. Rev. 957, 962–964 (1985); Van den Haag, "The Death Penalty Vindicates the Law," 71 A.B.A.J. 38, 40 (April 1985); Van den Haag, "The Ultimate Punishment: A Defense," 99 Harv. L. Rev. 1662, 1662–1664 (1986); *see also* Davis, "Sentencing: Must Justice Be Even-Handed," 1 Law and Phil. 77 (1982) (discussing standardless prison sentences rather than death sentences based on statutory guidelines).

64. Pomerance, THE ELEPHANT MAN 27 (Grove Press 1979). Or *see* Mencken, PREJUDICES; THE THIRD SERIES 101 (Knopf 1922): "Injustice is relatively easy to bear; what stings is justice."

65. Ordinarily "a private citizen lacks a judicially cognizable interest in the prosecution or nonprosecution of another." Linda R.S. v. Richard D., 410 U.S. 614, 619 (1973). Even a person prosecuted for crime could not ordinarily complain because another person in the same position was not prosecuted. Oyler v. Boles, 368 U.S. 448, 456 (1962) ("[T]he conscious exercise of some selectivity in enforcement is not in itself a federal constitutional violation"); *see also* Standefer v. United States, 447 U.S. 10, 11, 25 (1980) (holding that "a defendant accused of aiding and abetting in the commission of a federal offense may be convicted after the named principal has been acquitted of that offense"). A systematic pattern of discrimination presents a cognizable problem, however. Oyler v. Boles, *supra* (allegations that "the selection was deliberately based upon an unjustifiable standard such as race, religion, or other arbitrary classification" might constitute grounds for a constitutional violation); O'Shea v. Littleton, 414 U.S. 488, 495–497 (1974) (although black defendants might have standing to complain about favorable treatment for white defendants in bail setting and sentencing decisions, black citizens who have not committed crimes or been arrested lack standing to raise those issues); Yick Wo v. Hopkins, 118 U.S. 356 (1886); *see also* McCleskey v. Zant, 580 F. Supp. 338, 346–349 (N.D. Ga. 1984), *aff'd. sub nom.*, McCleskey v. Kemp, 753 F.2d 877 (11th Cir. 1985), *cert. granted*, 106 S.Ct. 1331 (1986) (holding that a capital defendant has standing to claim that the state permits the imposition of the death penalty to be based on the race of the victim); *cf.* Britton v. Rogers, 631 F.2d 572, 577 n.3 (8th Cir. 1980), *cert. den.*, 451 U.S. 939 (1981) (holding in a noncapital context that a rape defendant had no standing to claim that the state punished rape more harshly when the victim was white than when the victim was black).

In Loving v. Virginia, 388 U.S. 1 (1967), and Mclaughin v. Florida, 379 U.S. 184 (1964), the U.S. Supreme Court held that a state statute that prohibited interracial marriages and another that prohibited interracial cohabitation violated the equal protection clause, even though the black and the white members of the offending couples were treated equally. 388 U.S. at 8. The presence in a statute of a racial classification subjects the statute to the most rigid constitutional scrutiny. 388 U.S. at 11; 379 U.S. at 191–193. A capital punishment statute that is neutral on its face but is applied disproportionately to cases with white victims presents a corollary proposition. The application of the statute is based largely on a racial classification and therefore should be constitutionally suspect. Of course, under current doctrine an equal protection argument faces the obstacle of proving that the discrimination on the basis of race in any case is intentional.

66. *See* Ballew v. Georgia, 435 U.S. 223, 239 (1978): "But the assembled data raise substantial doubt about the reliability and appropriate representation of panels smaller than six"; *see also id.* at 231–232: "These writings . . . raise significant questions about the wisdom and constitutionality of a reduction below six." *Cf. Gregg,* 428 U.S. at 195 n.47 ("*McGautha*'s assumption that it is not possible to devise standards to guide and regularize jury sentencing in capital cases has been undermined by subsequent experience").

Index